WITHDRAWN

The Construction of Minorities

THE COMPARATIVE STUDIES IN SOCIETY AND HISTORY BOOK SERIES

Raymond Grew, Series Editor

Comparing Muslim Societies:
Knowledge and the State in a World Civilization
    Juan R. I. Cole, editor

Colonialism and Culture
    Nicholas B. Dirks, editor

Constructing Culture and Power in Latin America
    Daniel H. Levine, editor

Time: Histories and Ethnologies
    Diane Owen Hughes and Thomas R. Trautmann, editors

Cultures of Scholarship
    S. C. Humphreys, editor

Comparing Jewish Societies
    Todd M. Endelman, editor

The Construction of Minorities: Cases for Comparison
Across Time and Around the World
    André Burguière and Raymond Grew, editors

The Construction of Minorities

Cases for Comparison Across
Time and Around the World

EDITED BY
ANDRÉ BURGUIÈRE AND RAYMOND GREW

Ann Arbor

THE UNIVERSITY OF MICHIGAN PRESS

Copyright © by the University of Michigan 2001
All rights reserved
Published in the United States of America by
The University of Michigan Press
Manufactured in the United States of America
⊚ Printed on acid-free paper

2004   2003   2002   2001   4   3   2   1

A CIP catalog record for this book is available from the British Library.

Library of Congress Cataloging-in-Publication Data

The construction of minorities : cases for comparison across time and
   around the world / edited by André Burguière and Raymond Grew.
       p.   cm. — (The comparative studies in society and history book
   series)
     Includes bibliographical references and index.
     ISBN 0-472-09737-7 (alk. paper) — ISBN 0-472-06737-0 (pbk. : alk.
   paper)
       1. Minorities.   2. Ethnicity.   3. Ethnic relations.
   4. Marginality, Social.   5. Refugees.   I. Burguière, André.
   II. Grew, Raymond.   III. Series.

   GN495.6 .C68   2000
   305.8—dc21   00-010460

Contents

Introduction

Raymond Grew

In its ambivalent contemporary usage, the concept of a minority designates a weakness and affirms a strength. Viewed from Europe, the idea
seems American, associated both with legislation in behalf of and movements in defense of certain minorities (blacks, homosexuals, women), even
when, as in the last instance, they constitute a numerical majority. Negative in the sense that it identifies a group in terms of its vulnerability to a
majority that threatens to oppress or reject it, the concept is positive in its
recognition of a group's cultural or moral value, which must be affirmed
or recognized or protected. This ambivalence rests on the ideological foundations of modern societies, and it is hardly surprising that it should be
especially marked in American society, built from the beginning on democratic beliefs.

In France, after 1968, the talk has been much less of minorities than of
marginaux, becoming over the years a fashionable theme in social history,
in place of the poor. The marginals are those who resist society's integrative pressures (which have recently come to be perceived as destructive or
impoverishing). This critique of modern society, nourished in particular
by the thought of Michel Foucault, conceives of modernization as a
process of classification, of separation and exclusion, that leads to a society divided between, in Norbert Elias's terms, insiders and outsiders.
Today, the preferred term in French discussions is the *excluded,* maintaining a reluctance to speak of minorities. Between marginality and exclusion, the idea remains of a society directed by the principle of unity (hence
integration) more than by democratic rule of the majority. These differences express national traditions and different conceptions among democratic societies. But carried across space and time to undemocratic societies,
the concept of minorities loses some of its ambiguity.

Of all the historical cases considered here, only three (those dealing with the United States, India, and Australia) clearly have to do with democracy. Although discussions of minorities are usually set within a national context, many of the polities treated in these essays (Renaissance Florence, Spain's American empire, and the Ottoman empire, for example) were hardly modern nations. These essays range across six or seven centuries and several continents. Most, but not all, treat issues of ethnic identity, religious community, and social position; they are nevertheless unanimous in seeing none of this as primordial, inevitable, or permanent.

This variety adds a general interest to the themes that emerge. All of these essays are about the ways that formal, public distinctions are constructed, all reveal the operation of an almost manic logic, whereby differences—once they have been socially or politically defined—take on a life of their own. Conflicting pressures obscure and erode some differences and reify others. Interestingly, in none of these cases does the state or state policy fully control or necessarily initiate these divisive distinctions; yet in all of them states were heavily engaged in their shifting meanings. Governments, while making universalistic claims in the name of the state, handed out privileges, defined groups and imposed restraints on them, and then feared that differences would become a source of revolt. All of this involved constant renegotiation, with distinctions made, obliterated, and resurrected in new forms. Boundaries defined by religious groups tended to be slightly clearer, although they, too, often proved flexible and contradictory.

If more than merely quantitative, *minority* is a loaded term; and its meaning is always culture-bound. When in 1992 the General Assembly of the United Nations issued a declaration on the rights of minorities belonging to "national, ethnic, religious, and linguistic communities," *community* appeared to be the decisive term. One accomplishment of the project that produced this book was the resolute refusal to define the word *minority,* despite the temptation to do so, especially in a symposium. That refusal makes a point about comparison. Definitions are crucial to some kinds of comparisons, especially when the goal is to establish general laws or test some formal theory. Then the definition determines what is comparable. Comparison is used differently here, and used on two levels.

It is meant, first, to stimulate specialists to think anew about a subject they already know well, by considering it in a new light and then posing fresh questions. For this purpose, it does not matter if the term *minority* is not commonly used in studies of the society in question—a disjunction many authors noted—provided the concept of a minority has sufficient resonance to invite some significant reconsideration of social relations. The disquieting effects of the connotations the term may currently carry (including its ideological implications or its association with American experience) can even be advantageous, for the initial aim lies in the challenge to think again about how a given society constructed distinctive social groups and sought to circumscribe them. Thus the authors began by asking whether, in the history of a given society, this term loosely conceived becomes an interesting addition to analytic vocabulary, or an abrasive intrusion, or both (more commonly the case). It is this inherently comparative assessment and not the term itself that matters.

In a second step, each author used this rethinking to establish what seemed to be the significant historical problematic for the chosen case and then posed the historical questions that followed in that context. Those questions, more than the different meanings of minority, became the principal subject of discussion. Differences were as important as similarities in the comparisons that resulted. And those differences among societies were found at many different levels: in conceptual frameworks, in the historical problem and the evidence associated with it, in specific historical policies and contingencies, in the characteristics of the groups that might be called minorities, and so forth. Analytically, these distinctions were critical, allowing comparison, without seeking to compare whole societies.

What leads societies to construct a special status that in effect defines some group as a minority? That often starts from some claim that the society as a whole shares values and loyalties that others, who are nevertheless part of the polity, do not. The way minorities come to be constructed reveals something important about networks of association and lines of division. Minorities in turn tend to assert some special needs, protections, or rights, claims that may be both acknowledged and violated as the existence of a minority becomes socially and institutionally embedded. To be considered a minority, a group must be both an integral element in the larger society and sufficiently outside its sociopolitical core to lack that access to status and power considered normal (even when in practice only dominant elites exercise that access). The significance of minority status thus differs from society to society, according to which characteristics come to be treated as critically distinctive (attributes of race, ethnicity, region, religion, or class are among the most common) and according to the disadvantages or advantages that accompanied that status.

Constraints on a minority's access to power may be a matter of social custom, economic condition, regional difference, or formal, legal restriction; but that differential access, more than its number relative to the population at large, marks a minority. As governing authorities hand out privileges, they may also be constructing minorities, among those who benefit as well as those who do not. Thus the construction of minorities is likely to be associated, often from the top down, with state building and, sometimes from the bottom up, with increased efforts at social mobilization. The processes creating minorities need not move in one direction only, and the recognition of minorities (whether through labels imposed or claims acknowledged) establishes fields of tension that can foster assimilation, persecution, or pluralism.

Not surprisingly, the essays that follow find minorities constructed in many different ways. In fact, nearly all the authors had some initial doubt as to whether *minority* was a term usefully applicable to the societies they knew best. Together, however, these essays, so attentive to cultural and historical context, give voice to a series of common themes; and they are arranged in an order intended to encourage the reader to join in exploring the topic, by observing its ramifications broaden with each new inquiry and by comparing each successive study with those that precede it. Despite their diversity, these essays have in common a recognition that minorities everywhere are socially constructed. No ineluctable difference necessitated the distinctions that became important (and divisive) in each society. Repetition and conflict rather than nature made difference seem natural.

Earl Lewis's essay on the United States makes a valuable beginning for reflecting on the construction of minorities, and not merely because American usage of the term is so prominent. Indeed, Lewis shows that Americans adapted it from Europe, and he finds its construction as a social category uneven and hesitant, its meanings shifting and multiple. The analogy with European issues of national minorities and claims to a right of self-determination after World War I had radical implications in the United States, ringing like a confession of failure in a society supposed to provide universal equality. Thus the political meaning of a minority status changed. Adopted by American communists as a justification for revolt and an assertion of black autonomy, it became something else with the civil rights movement after World War II. Gaining currency with programs of affirmative action, it was often used as a kind of euphemism, an antidiscriminatory description of discrimination, an acknowledgment that race and class, living conditions and education, opportunity and social attitudes are confusingly intertwined. Its ambiguities remain, for there is little consensus as to how many minorities there can be, the degree to which their status is meant to be impermanent, which special protections they merit, and how their recognition jibes with the U.S. Constitution and values publicly affirmed. In his comment, Jean Heffer largely agrees with Lewis. By exploring its demographic aspects, he pushes against any assumption that minority status is a quantitative term. He also reinforces our topic's comparative aspects when he uses a word like *apartheid,* when he notes the similarity between the dilemmas of American liberalism and European social democratic humanism, and when he concludes with a reference to contemporary France.

Applied to diverse societies, the concept of minority need not be limited to groups considered marginal or powerless, a point Christiane Klapisch-Zuber demonstrates in her discussion of the *magnati* of Renaissance Florence. Here is a social category invented from popular attitudes and made a legal device for circumscribing families (often noble) considered too arrogant and too inclined to abuse their wealth and power. If that seems to reverse the more common pattern, it also brings to light an element often important in labeling minorities. Inchoate or rather ambiguous communal values are identified more clearly by naming the qualities a minority is alleged to lack or violate. Florentine magnates, seen as threats to a developing sense of civic peace, were too powerful to expel or impoverish; but they could be constrained and even selectively rewarded for good behavior. A tumultuous, mercantile city-state had, in its own self-defense, cleverly created legal distinctions among the prominent; and magnates learned to speak the humbler language of civic responsibility. Later, in the more stable and hierarchical Grand Duchy of Tuscany, in which belonging to the aristocracy was desirable, prominent families would cite a former standing as magnates as proof both of their respect for the law and their claim to aristocratic lineage. Past acceptance of discrimination had become a claim to privilege—not the only instance in this volume in which the construction of minorities had unanticipated, long-term consequences.

These American and Florentine instances are clearly political, which helps the historian uncover the complex process of their construction. Religious minorities, the subject of the next four essays, are often treated as (and frequently present themselves as being) the necessary result of distinctive systems of belief and practice and of defining institutions; yet, as these essays show, religious minorities, too, are socially constructed. David Bien turns to one of the famous European examples of a religious minority. The Huguenots in France fit all standard conceptions of a minority and were the target of some of the most noted actions and edicts of the French crown. This was not, Bien shows, a simple or necessary response to social reality. French Protestants were identified as a single group on religious grounds alone, despite their ties to figures of prominence and despite the significant discordance between the Huguenots in cities and those in the countryside. The persecution that followed, Bien argues, resulted less from the religious fervor of Protestants—or that of their opponents—than from a secularizing inability to accept religious fervor as a matter of belief. Calvinist intransigence was assumed to have other, covert aims. Protestant reactions to repression then provided reasons, fed by fear, for restricting Huguenots and for identifying them as a distinctive subcommunity. Those reasons were ultimately political. By setting standards of conformity, the state in effect insisted on assimilation (a term that in itself invites further comparison, as Bien notes). These policies gained resonance in a culture that shared a widespread view of human nature that saw in *emulation* the key to education and an opportunity to become like others. Widening horizons for social mobility and civic utility more than bigotry made stubborn loyalty to religious principle suspect and potentially subversive.

Jacques Revel generally accepts Bien's assessment of the Huguenots' status within ancien régime society while giving it a historiographical context—Bien's own previous work. Revel also adds a crucial point: Huguenots were considered as a single bloc, despite their differences, whereas Jews, for example, although restricted and repressed, were viewed as multiple communities within a society that was comfortable with the existence of distinctive corps. In other societies, too, homogenizing perceptions contributed to the construction of minorities; and Revel concludes with a point applicable elsewhere, too. Hesitant to embrace Bien's interpretation of the long-term historical processes at work (despite the attractive ironies that follow from them), Revel turns to imagining a different sort of history, one focused on the practices and on the psychological life of the minority itself, a history from below and from inside, a history of the processes whereby a group contributes to its reconstruction as a minority. Revel has in mind patterns of marriage, especially; and that is taken up in the next chapter.

Less demanding of its subjects and less ambitious to mobilize them for public service, the Ottoman state was famously more tolerant of religious diversity. Penalties for apostasy from Islam were nevertheless severe, and Lucette Valensi investigates the surprising phenomena of religious conversions. This is a look at minorities from below, small groups with changing memberships, reconstituting themselves through individual choices. Stories of love and marriage refurbished diverse religious communities, confused categories, and obscured bureaucratic boundaries, challenging the state's ideas of efficiency and order. A place could be found for religious minorities; but shifting ones, difficult to define, threatened the systematizing instincts of the Ottoman state. While underscoring the small numbers involved, Juan Cole in his comment agrees that the phenomenon was significant (and finds important parallels in the twentieth century). He also speculates on the possible importance of factors beyond the social ones Valensi emphasizes in tracking intermarriage. Religious conversions, he suggests, were also spiritual. Choosing to belong to a minority invoked issues of identity, raising another important theme in the construction of minorities and one crucial to their communal life.

In Europe, too, toleration obscured lines of demarcation that had once been sharply drawn. Jews were Europe's classic example of a religious minority (a note in Klapisch-Zuber's essay finds a parallel with Florentine magnates). Their special status over the centuries had been maintained by an extraordinary range of legal restrictions, communal rights, and shifting relations with the Christian majority, ranging from friendship to persecution. Then the Enlightenment and the French Revolution brought welcome changes that largely eliminated the formal barriers isolating European Jews. That raised the possibility (both promise and specter) of conversion. Paradoxically, prospects of toleration, which had been confusing enough under Ottoman rule and in Old Regime France, now expanded into profoundly modern concerns: questions of policy—the place of religion in a secular society, what it meant for a state to be neutral toward religion, the kinds of difference liberalism could or should allow—and, more troubling still, issues of identity, national belonging, and ethical engagement with an ever-widening array of personal choices. Noting the play of all these issues, Todd Endelman highlights a critical reality that affects them all. Underneath the impact of policies imposed, a minority is also constructed from the web of its own social ties. That leads Sylvie-Anne Goldberg in her comment to tackle again the question of what makes Jews different. She resists an emphasis on changes since the French Revolution, noting Jews' distinctive beliefs and ancient responses to gentiles, and she lists dozens of other ways to categorize modern Jews. Goldberg in effect deconstructs the concept of Jews as a minority, either ancient or modern, while writing with passion of Jewish identity. Her doubts and paradoxes, like Endelman's emphasis on social relations, deepen the discussion of how minorities are constructed.

Writing about the spread of Islam into China and Southeast Asia, Denis Lombard draws attention to religious minorities that were numerically larger, ethnically more diverse, and regionally farther dispersed than any considered so far. His striking comparison with Chinese merchants, however, points to something other than religion. If the followers of Islam recognized each other, across this space and despite great cultural differences, the networks they created proved valuable for trade as well as religion. Both Muslims and Chinese may have been minorities, he notes, but they were hardly marginal. Their histories intertwined with Asian economic development; the alliances and enmities they formed intersected with a growing European presence. In her comment Ann Stoler welcomes an analysis that moves beyond conventional historiographic boundaries of state and region, which leads her to reflect on issues of method. She identifies a "technology of power" in the construction of minorities that operates in modern empires as well as the state of Louis XIV. Yet, she argues, that very unit of analysis—state or empire—like distinctions of race and nationality and gender (to which she would give more attention), is a social construction as well. When those constructions are themselves made the object of study, research on the shaping of minorities exposes often-overlooked historical forces that shaped the complex interactions among specific social groups.

In their essay Serge Gruzinski and Nathan Wachtel also consider an empire, revealing techniques, specific measures, and cultural encounters critical to the process of making a minority. Their analysis of the stark realities of Spanish rule in the New World begins with a striking paradox: The minority they consider constituted the vast majority of the population. That majority was treated as children (minors, if not a minority); and force, legislation, physical separation, an intrusive clergy, and administrative practice were essential to controlling it. Although newcomers and natives mingled in trade, festivals, and marriage, minority status was sharply marked by demands of language, Catholicism, costume, and hygiene. Indigenous peoples in turn responded to new circumstances by reinforcing social networks and reconstructing their identities. Division and syncretism, cultural destruction and preservation occurred simultaneously, as unpredictable and far-reaching as disease and avarice. That cultural process attracts the attention of Sabine MacCormack, who in her comment emphasizes that the strategies native peoples evolved were not just passive nor merely matters of resistance. She compares Peruvian and Mexican experience to illustrate that native peoples were active participants in a complex process, which interwove old and new, indigenous and alien, and used both current social practice and recaptured history to reconstruct communities that then sometimes chose to see themselves as a minority.

Surprisingly, all the familiar issues about minorities emerge in India's debates about affirmative action. The minorities in this case are the peoples at the bottom of India's hierarchy of castes, and the surprise is that a social system seemingly so ancient could give rise to debates so modern. In probing these arguments, Nicholas Dirks finds underlying myths, interests, and discourses peculiar to India yet relevant to the social construction of minorities more generally. The desire to lessen inequality is not disputed, at least openly; yet the policies proposed and the play of democratic politics open up confusing questions. Is caste the heritage from a mythic past, a timeless part of Indian identity, or are efforts to mobilize those at the bottom of society a continuation of divisive British imperial practice? Are matters of religious and national identity really at stake, or is this rather a problem of social class? Answers to such questions, crucial to the legitimacy of conflicting political positions, make use of anthropological theories and social science that, Dirks argues, has its own ideological and cultural underpinnings. What tribes or castes or classes belong to the minorities for which special opportunities should be reserved thus becomes a heated contemporary debate about how, through India's long history, minorities have been constructed.

Differences in the nature of empire were crucial to the different constructions of minorities in the Soviet Union (as they were in Spanish America, China and Southeast Asia, and India), and Ron Suny underscores the distinction between empire and nation. He sets his analysis in the context of the rising concern for national self-determination, especially important in Eastern Europe and after World War I (issues that influenced African Americans) and in the context of civil war in Russia and Soviet rule. In Eastern Europe the term *minority* has long been used with greater comfort than elsewhere, and Suny sets forth some striking contradictions. Recognition of supposedly ancient ethnic identities required defining new ones. Communists opposed to nationalism created nations. As these opponents of imperialism redrew maps, they reified, carved up, and repressed ethnic groups as ruthlessly and arbitrarily as imperialists in sub-

Saharan Africa. Communist theories that considered nationalism a false ideology inhibited Soviet demands for assimilation and assertions of its own overarching nationality; yet scores of diverse ethnicities were recognized out of political necessity and democratic aspiration. A government intent on ending class differences measured ethnicity by descent, and a highly centralized system pretending to be a federation found it necessary to define and label new administrative units underneath it. The history of the Soviet Union made the process of constructing and reconstructing minorities uniquely visible and the effects especially explosive. That was especially true during Gorbachev's perestroika, and Marc Ferro (who incidentally suggests an interesting contrast with French Algeria) pays particular attention to that critical period and the ironies apparent then. Changes that promised greater freedom troubled many of the regional and ethnic elites who had prospered from their connections in Moscow as well as their regional base. Demands for self-government did not necessarily imply separatism, and political interests often triumphed over ethnic ones. The nation-state, Ferro concludes in a remark important for any consideration of minorities, was not an inevitable goal.

In contrast to a Soviet state that inscribed national identities on various parts of its empire, the Australian state acted as if Aboriginals were invisible or, rather, as Aram Yengoyan explains, did so until Aboriginal Australians responded by creating their own foundational ideology. Controlling an alternative history proved crucial, an aspect that invites comparison with previous essays (especially those on American blacks, European Jews, and American Indians in the Spanish empire). Yet this is the only instance in which a minority consistently contested the very existence of a state, and Yengoyan devotes most of his discussion to explaining how that came about and to assessing responses to Aboriginal assertion. Like Dirks on India, he finds Western social science and anthropology implicated in policies of domination. The history of minorities provides an x-ray of power within discourse as well as politics. Extending Yengoyan's analysis, Alban Bensa underscores the remarkable development of what he calls a pan-Oceanic ideology developed in opposition to colonial, Western domination. Values like those espoused by Australia's Aboriginals spread through modern travel and education and find their foundation in reinvented traditions and the discovery of a common history in which life was peaceful and lived in harmony with nature. It makes a difference, Bensa shows, whether these minorities have any chance at political power; yet all engage in this construction of an identity that overcomes significant local difference and provides an alternative to white expectations. The reaction is a modern one, using as well as resisting Western influences, from acrylic paints to anthropology; it resonates with movements among the marginalized in developed countries and may, Bensa suggests, point to the future as well as the past.

The essays of this book have treated many different and diverse minorities and analyzed how they were constructed around ascribed differences defined by social practice and the state. At first, a very different set of questions seems to emerge from the AIDS epidemic, and Claudine Herzlich begins by asking what it takes to make a minority. Sick people may have much in common, but that is not enough to make them a group. Herzlich then considers historical responses to plague, to leprosy, and to tuberculosis, identifying factors important for the construction of minorities. Widespread fear of the minority is a powerful element in its identification as well as in responses to it. So is the sense that the members of a minority are somehow to blame for their condition (a perverse rejection of truth among religious minorities, laziness among the lower classes, defects of character among ethnic minorities, socially proscribed behavior among those infected by disease). While remaining doubtful that HIV-positive people constitute a minority, Herzlich notes how greatly responses to them (as with minorities) are affected by the degree to which they are associated with marginal groups and with more general social problems. Public responses range between the punitive or coercive and what she calls "liberal management," emphasizing individual choice and cooperation. A comparable range can be found among the victims of AIDS themselves, extending from silent denial to claims on society for sympathy and help and to accusations against those who wield medical and political power. Many of the psychological and social burdens borne by minorities are recapitulated here; but in this case public attitudes and policies, in France and developed countries generally, have been shaped by concern for civil rights, the dissemination of medical knowledge, and by mobilization within affected groups. Herzlich cautions against easy optimism, however. If this epidemic has not created a constricted minority, responses nevertheless remain tied to older patterns of discrimination (against certain classes, ethnic groups, and disapproved behavior). The arsenal of stigma remains accessible; and beyond individual tragedy, AIDS plumbs tragic social inequalities, within societies and between rich and poor nations, everywhere exposing the fractures as well as the sinews of the social fabric. This essay, then, raises an array of questions about the nature of minorities; and in her comment Kim Scheppele continues from there to offer a series of observations that help to sharpen comparison of the construction of minorities. She proposes five characteristics that mark minorities— insularity, narrativity, modality, inevitability, and juridicality—and her reflections on each of them stimulate analysis and open avenues of comparison.

The recognition that minorities are socially constructed is not a new finding, but there are reasons to emphasize its import. Established societies strengthen their legitimacy by representing social boundaries as having emerged spontaneously, independent of any particular interest or intention. Groups in conflict benefit by pretending that the boundaries between them are clear and fixed and that attempts to traverse those boundaries carry penalties. Assuming the differences that mark minorities to be primordial and beyond repair offers everyone some inoculation against critical thought—and guilt. For scholars, then, recognizing that minorities are socially constructed opens questions easily overlooked and often gladly avoided. It also gives some guidance as to how comparative analysis can be helpful. If minorities are differently constructed within each society and in each era, comparing minorities (as if that were a fixed and defined category of analysis) will not in itself be very fruitful.

The subject to compare is rather the process that constructs minorities (higher tests of belief and loyalty to church, king, or nation; state building; political mobilization; expanding systems of justice; theories of civil rights; increased communication; and structural changes that affect social links based on kinship or economic interest). Obviously, the analysis of process must be attentive to the subtleties of context, as all of these essays are. Comparison can usefully suggest factors to look for—such elements in these studies as the available ideologies, self-awareness within a minority, social networks, economic needs and pressures, state policies, and so forth—but does not determine which of them matters most in specific instances. Often, as these essays show, differences proved more telling than similarities, for the construction of minorities bears with special sensitivity the imprint of particular histories. Declaring minorities to be socially constructed is no mere relativism, nor does it mean that minorities are merely imagined.

Collectively, these essays do suggest some general comments about the historical processes that construct minorities. Once a group is defined as subordinate and subject to special provisions, the sense of difference tends to be reinforced by social discrimination, spatial separation, or legislation in a process that is reciprocal, involving responses within the minority as well as the larger society. Thus, society's categorizers—census-takers, linguists, and social scientists as well as religious leaders and politicians—play an important role even when more direct applications of power are limited or muffled. In this process the minority is likely to become more cohesive and to develop its own self-definition, which often increases the dissonance between internal and external perceptions of how the minority is constituted and what it stands for. Powerful myths and symbols are woven into competing histories, narratives that imply future directions using reconstructed pasts.

These tensions grow greater when demands increase. These may come from the larger society, especially through state making and democratization. Similarly, demands from the minority tend to become stronger as its ideology and interests become more explicit. In practice, all sides absorb each other's tactics and arguments. Because such conflicts are facilitated by claims to universal values (from citizenship to civil rights) and by broader and freer participation, the construction of minorities is sometimes seen as distinctly modern. Many of these essays challenge that impression, and all of them reject any assumption that conflicts involving minorities must evolve in a single direction. Violence is always more visible than mutual influence, and it contributes significantly to the stories told that justify further opposition. The same tensions and cultural ambitions that sustain difference, however, can also erode it; for the construction of minorities requires overcoming internal differences, leads to reciprocal change, and often makes apparent opponents in fact more similar. Minorities adopt much from the dominant society and often succeed in altering it. Concerns seen as particular or traditional can come to be considered universal, and vice versa. Hence, many of these essays explore how some distinctions lose their significance while others do not. In their attention to particular circumstances, these essays argue in effect that histories matter, and they demonstrate that the process by which minorities are produced reveals much both about how specific societies have functioned and about how selective memories of their past have helped to shape them.

All of these essays were initially written for a conference in Paris jointly sponsored by *Annales: Histoire, Sciences Sociales* and *Comparative Studies in Society and History*. Three of the essays written by American scholars were published in the May–June 1997 issue of *Annales* (52:3); and three of those by French scholars were published in the April 1997 issue of *CSSH* (39:2). The versions printed here have been revised in light of the lively discussions the conference produced. Readers can share something of that conversation in the formal comments included in this volume, but other participants also made valuable contributions. We wish in particular to thank Marc Augé, Maurice Aymard, the late François Furet, Jean-Claude Galey, Diane Owen Hughes, Emmanuel Le Roy Ladurie, and Natalie Zemon Davis, in addition to many members of the audience.

The conference was held at the Maison des Sciences de L'Homme and organized with the help in Paris of the Ecole des Hautes Etudes and its Centre de Recherches Historiques and at the University of Michigan by the Office of the Vice President for Research, the Rackham School of Graduate Studies, the International Institute, and the Department of History. We are grateful to them all, to Albert Feuerwerker and Victor Lieberman, who helped along the way, and to James Schaefer who coordinated a complicated project. French texts were translated by John Cornell, Esther Heitler, and Pamela Waxman, who also helped conform the translations to a common style.

Constructing African Americans as Minorities

Earl Lewis

> I have not written about being a Negro at such length because I expect that to be my only subject, but only because it was the gate that I had to unlock before I could hope to write about anything else. I don't think that the Negro problem in America can be even discussed coherently without bearing in mind its context; its context being the history, traditions, customs, the moral assumptions and preoccupations of the country.
>
> James Baldwin, *Notes of a Native Son*

Few African-American writers asked as much of their country as James Baldwin, who saw himself as a native son. Even as others spit upon his likeness, Baldwin asserted his American birthright: He criticized, cajoled, harangued, and bemoaned those who would deny him a voice in the land of his birth. Like many men and women of his race and background, Baldwin fashioned African Americans as the guardians of American democracy. On their bodies and through their actions America would one day realize its ambitions of becoming a shining city on a hill, a beacon of hope and democracy for the world.

Interestingly, at no time in *Notes of a Native Son* did Baldwin explicitly address his minority status. We are left to wonder why. The word *minority* was certainly in circulation by the mid-1950s, even if the concept lacked the kind of rhetorical depth it would acquire a decade later. Perhaps for Baldwin *minority* had little saliency because *Negro* had grown in saliency. Certainly 1955 was a critical year. The U.S. Supreme Court would rule in the second *Brown* decision that desegregation should come to American classrooms with "all deliberate speed."[1] That same year, men and women in Montgomery, Alabama, followed the enabling actions of blacks in other movement centers, organizing a pivotal bus boycott. More than in the other centers, however, residents of Montgomery registered their complaints before a national and international audience that came to enjoy the oratorical gifts of a young Martin Luther King.[2]

Among the events of that single year, few seared the consciousness of a nation and soldered the lines of affiliation among blacks as the discovery of the tortured and mutilated body of Emmett Till. Till was the fourteen-year-old Chicago teenager who went to Mississippi for summer vacation and paid the ultimate price for his actions. Emboldened by the bravado of youth, on a hot August day, he suspended caution and is said to have remarked "bye, baby" to the pretty white woman behind the counter at Bryant's Grocery and Meat Market in Money, Mississippi. Three days later Carolyn Bryant's husband and his half brother pulled the youth from a bed in the cabin of his granduncle Mose Wright. The duo maintained they simply wanted to extract an apology and plea of repentance; failing this, they beat, tortured, and then shot at point-blank range the now defenseless Till. They then weighted his body with a seventy-pound fan and tossed it into the Tallahatchie River.

Although the body was later recovered and displayed; although Bryant and Milam stood trial but were never convicted of a crime; and although Till joined a long list of black men and women who lost their lives in the Mississippi corridors of horror, the Till incident left a real imprint. As Ann Moody eloquently observed in her autobiography *Coming of Age in Mississippi,* "Before Emmett Till's murder, I had known the fear of hunger, hell and the Devil. But now there was a new fear known to me—the fear of being killed because I was black."[3]

Till's murder, the Montgomery boycott movement, and the Supreme Court decision became parts of the contents of black life that Baldwin insisted needed contextualizing. More important, these contexts became a part of the matrix of social relations that gave meaning to the lives of U.S. citizens. In a sense, the contexts spoke ever so quietly to the question of a subordinate status. That Baldwin did not explicitly address what it meant to be a minority does not mean he ignored it. In effect, the need to call attention to his place as a native son underscored his minority station.

In a way, then, Baldwin asks us to consider what it means to be a racial minority in a democratic land. Or stated more directly, he asks, What does it mean to be African American in the United States? Combined, the two questions force us to consider the processes by which African Americans were and are minorities. The questions oblige us to consider the multiple meanings of race and the language of subordination that both organize social relations and alter social meaning. This essay traces the power of language and meaning to cohere and diverge by looking at moments in the historical construction of African Americans as minorities. It argues that before African Americans could be defined as minorities with attendant rights, they had to be perceived as injured citizens with legitimate claims on the nation. And once defined as minorities, the term came to be used by state actors and policymakers more than by African Americans.

The History of a Concept

Insofar as it is possible to trace, the reference to African Americans as a minority is of fairly modern usage. Philip Gleason has fixed the lexical introduction with the appearance of Donald Young's 1932 work *American Minority Peoples: A Study in Racial and Cultural Conflicts in the United States.* Until that point *minorities* had been a word closely associated with the sociopolitical situations of populations within various European countries—for example, Jews throughout Europe. As a result, Gleason concludes that until the early 1930s, *minority* was a word most often associated with the problems of what many Americans considered a somewhat decadent Europe.[4]

Discussion of race, race relations, and minority status were rare but not unheard of in pre-1932 America. Prominent figures in the race relations historiography such as sociologist Robert Park made occasional references to blacks as minorities. So too did noted African-American philosophy professor Alain Locke. It was Young, however, who successfully integrated race relations and minority status. Worried that the dichotomous study of specific white-"other" pairings—that is, white-Asian, white-black, and so forth—shielded commonalities, he complained, "The problems and principles of race relations are remarkably similar, regardless of what group is involved." Young concluded therefore "that only by an integrated study of all minority peoples in the United States can a real understanding and sociological analysis of the involved social phenomena be achieved."[5]

Young, moreover, found a close connection between an individual's minority status and the social concern with race. To begin, Young distinguished between national minorities and racial minorities. Turks, Greeks, Poles, Armenians, and others belonged to the list of national minorities; blacks, Native Americans, Asians, and others belonged to groups of racial minorities. Prejudice potentially narrowed the social divide between the national and the racial. But in the United States, Young concluded, racial factors engendered certain groups (who otherwise may have been viewed as national groups) with minority status.

Still, there is a difference between the introduction and broad usage of the word *minority*. Before the late 1960s, *Negro, colored, sepia,* and even *Afro-American* were used to capture a certain social existence; *nigger, coon, rascal,* and a long list of other names spoke to an equally palpable essence. Yet, with the notable exception of the Communist Party, well into the 1960s, few uttered *minority* when speaking of African Americans. As important, *minority* was not a word used by African Americans to describe themselves or their situation. Prominent black writers never ignored their numerical or social subordination, they simply defined it in other terms.

From the colonial period through the 1960s, much of the debate turned on the question of what people of African descent would call themselves. At various times Anglo-African, Afro-American, Negro, colored, black American, and African American competed for prominence. Throughout the history of this naming controversy, *minority* as a synonym for blacks lacked specificity and depth.[6] It described African Americans certainly, but it also defined many others. In the lexicon of American social relations, where a name was a shorthand for decades of history, well into the 1960s, African Americans were yet to become fully minorities.

In part, it was the curious juxtaposition of *minority* and *problem* that struck some as an odd self-expression. As noted intellectual W. E. B. Du Bois elegantly intimated in 1903, no one wanted to be known as just a problem. Moreover, as Gunnar Myrdal observed in his exhaustive study of race relations and American democracy, *An American Dilemma,* the word *minority* did not share a universal etymology. "In the United States, the term 'minority people' has a connotation different from that in other parts of the world," he would write at the close of World War II. "The minority peoples in the United States are fighting for a status in the larger society; the minorities of Europe are mainly fighting for independence from it."[7] Theoretically at least, such inclusion compromised the meaning of minority since blacks and whites spoke of a time when race would not matter, when the minority would meld with the whole to form a new majority. When this occurred *minority* would cease to be the twin of *problem*.

To the degree that Myrdal was correct, he missed one important point: through slavery, emancipation, and the codification of Jim Crow, blacks represented a threat or social danger that belied their minority status.

Some saw them as a contaminant so powerful that only their complete removal or containment would suffice. Thus, before they could become minorities in the eyes of the majority, let alone in their own eyes, they had to be redeemed socially. First, they had to be made socially innocent. If they were to become a minority with attendant rights and privileges, they had to become injured citizens. Until the 1950s or civil rights era few non-black scholars, politicians, or citizens manufactured such images. In an odd twist in American history, a recognition of injury enabled African Americans to become minority citizens. Why one followed (rather than caused) the other is key to understanding the construction of blacks as racial minorities.

The Early Demography of Minority Status

The processes by which African Americans became a minority is at once complicated and revealing. After all, contemporary figures showing black Americans comprising 10 to 14 percent of the nation's population this century produced a compelling logic: blacks were numerical minorities. Buried in the contemporary figures is a long history of a demonstrable African presence, one that belies the aggregate statistics. Certainly, from colonial times through the present some blacks lived and died as members of a majority. They live or lived in settings so removed from whites and other nonblacks that minority status was not only a fiction, but the first chapter in a national myth.

The myth of the numerical minority, in fact, proved critical to the social construction of blacks as minorities. In 1660 African Americans accounted for a measly 1.7 percent of the population of New England, a more generous 11.5 percent of the Middle Colonies, and an anemic 3.6 and 2.0 percent of the Upper (Maryland and Virginia) and Lower (South Carolina) South, respectively. Comparatively, in the West Indies, where the word *minority* does not have the same historical resonance, blacks were 42.0 percent of the total population.

By the American Revolution (circa 1780) a demographic revolution had occurred. African peoples remained a significant proportion of the overall population, but their numbers were not evenly distributed. Whereas 1 in every 50 residents of New England was viewed as black, 38.6 percent and 41.2 percent of the populations of the Upper and Lower South, respectively, were now of African descent. Compared to the West

Indies, where 91.1 percent claimed African ancestry, African peoples in the United States still had a minority presence; nonetheless, they had become a significant rather than insignificant subset of the population.[8]

The dictates of slavery encouraged such shifts. Sugar, rice, and to a lesser degree tobacco responded to economies of scale. As multi-day crops, sugar and rice particularly, and tobacco less so, demanded sizable, stable labor forces. As the relative price of African slaves decreased and the value of American staples increased, the costs of an African labor force stabilized and in some cases declined. Concomitantly, the relative costs of European coerced labor climbed, producing in part the conditions for the noted demographic shift and a change from servants to slaves.[9]

This shift had profound cultural ramifications. In South Carolina, for example, the black population grew at such a staggering rate between 1660 and 1740 that by 1710 the once obvious minority came to constitute a discernible majority. Observers found the face of the colony so altered that one likened it to "a Negro Country." South Carolina became "a Negro Country" because to the degree possible, African peoples rebuilt the world in their own images. These forced migrants from West Africa and their descendants introduced their own methods of rice cultivation, used pastoralist skills learned in Africa, developed a complex religious system, and created a creole language called *gullah* to broker the differences among them. With few whites in their midst, and those around indifferent to some of their wants, blacks lived in a world where *minority* had little meaning.[10] They were slaves and in the majority.

As important, sequestered in the mental chambers of daily interaction resided what has been called the "unthinking decision." Winthrop Jordan used the phrase more than two decades ago when he tendered his answer to the question, What came first, racial prejudice or slavery? Jordan succeeded in showcasing the ways in which blackness gained meaning as Europeans, especially the English, increased their interactions with African peoples. Through travel accounts, Shakespearean dramas, and daily language, Europeans began the practice of defining the dangerous; in the context of Elizabethan England and colonial America this twining of race and language signaled the start of the awkward dance toward social meaning. The Oxford English Dictionary, for example, equated blackness with dirt, filth, evil, death, and danger. With time, congregations of blacks became the ultimate sites of danger, filth, and disease. This sense of danger grew in relation to the appearance of black majorities and with examples of black armed resistance to slavery.[11]

The Politics of Being a Danger

Periods of civil war and reconstruction ultimately did little to obliterate images of a black danger. For a moment Southern Negrophobes boasted that without the guiding hands of paternalistic masters, blacks would soon disappear. Writers in journals such as the *Southern Review* gleefully pronounced that "the lithe African race would go on to extinction."[12]

In a few short years the fear that blacks would feebly degenerate into a state of squalor and vanish was replaced with the fear that blacks might be outproducing whites. The first word of alarm was signaled by Dr. Edward Gilliam in an 1883 edition of *Popular Science Monthly*. The popular press had long debated the place of blacks in a competitive world. If Gilliam's calculations were correct and blacks had a reproduction rate of 30 percent in a ten-year period, black fecundity suggested a decent ability to compete. In Gilliam's view, such competition only hastened the demand for social equality. He would write, "This dark, swelling mass . . . gathering strength with education, and ambitious to rise, will grow increasingly restless and sullen under repression, until . . . conscious through numbers of superior power, it will assert that power destructively, and, bursting forth like [an] angry furious crowd, avenge in tumult and disorder, the social law broken against them."[13] Once again the danger of a black majority struck chords of fear.

Inasmuch as blacks entered the Reconstruction period determined to exercise their full rights as free citizens, all that had happened previously was called into question. So at a certain level a black presence surely signaled a danger to the pre–Civil War status quo. At the national level, for example, twenty blacks served in the U.S. Congress between 1869 and 1901, with the majority from the states of South Carolina, North Carolina, and Alabama. Hiram Revels and Blanche Bruce, both from Mississippi, even took the oath of office as U.S. Senators.[14] Even at state and city levels, African Americans made political headway. Two hundred and fifty-five blacks served in the South Carolina legislature between 1868 and 1876, while nearly three dozen African Americans served on the Richmond, Virginia, city council between 1871 and 1898.

Nor was this the extent of political activity. Black men and women in Richmond asserted their rights to instruct the convention writing the postwar Virginia constitution. They came in large numbers and, although not official delegates, joined in discussions from the galleries. They lived in a community where the political grew out of the communal: all could participate because all in essence belonged.[15]

The growth of the black population and parallel increase in political activity produced a powerful reaction, one central to the history of the social construction of blacks as minorities. In the meeting halls and offices, and porches and kitchens of white Southerners a consensus emerged by the 1890s: blacks had to be dealt with. Some reached this conclusion later than others, and some certainly harbored other beliefs, but on the whole this perspective won favor. Across the South, therefore, on the heels of Democratic Party ascendancy in the 1890s, state constitutions were again rewritten. Most participants aspired to eliminate black voters altogether. Few spoke as forthrightly as Carter Glass. The future U.S. Senator from Virginia served as a Lynchburg delegate to the Virginia Constitutional Convention. He announced:

> Discrimination! Why, that is exactly what we propose; that exactly is why this convention was elected to discriminate to the very extremity of permissible action under the limitations of the Federal Constitution with the view to the elimination of every Negro who can be gotten rid of, legally, without materially impairing the strength of the white electorate.[16]

From Virginia to Texas the regionwide results of disfranchisement were staggering. In Louisiana alone the number of registered black voters dropped from 130,344 in 1896 to 5,320 in 1900.[17]

The enfranchisement and disfranchisement of blacks did have a profound effect on social relations and the ways in which black Americans became minorities. First, the statutes of liberty—the Thirteenth, Fourteenth, and Fifteenth Amendments to the Constitution—had been written to guarantee an unimpeachable place for African Americans. The amendments in effect abolished slavery, established African Americans as citizens of the United States, and extended the vote to black males. As important, once assured of constitutional citizenship rights, blacks actively participated in all facets of American life, determined to be "slaves no more."[18]

Second, subsequent actions helped to establish African Americans as injured citizens, once established as citizens. Of course, this was not immediately obvious at the end of the nineteenth century. Rather, after the compromised election of Rutherford B. Hayes as president in 1876, which resulted in federal withdrawal from occupied regions in the South, it became clear that the federal government was prepared to turn its back on black Southerners. Furthermore, the U.S. Supreme Court in two land-mark cases—Civil Rights (1883) and the *Plessy* decision (1896)—signaled that it too was willing to circumscribe blacks' social and political rights. In the 1883 decision it ruled that the Fourteenth Amendment flatly prohib-ited state discrimination but not individual discrimination.[19] Through the ruling the Court created the legal and social space for the imposition of racial segregation. In effect it also aided in further naturalizing race by legitimating the right of one group of citizens to injure another (by treat-ing them differently) solely based on the color of their skin.

The 1896 *Plessy* decision proved the capstone. Homer Adolph Plessy was a New Orleans creole who, on appearance, was indistinguishable from any "white" Louisianan. But in Gilded Age America race was not just written on the body, it was established in the blood. By the mathematics of Louisiana law, Plessy, who was seven-eighths white and one-eight black, was "black." Although different states had different quotients, in essence one drop was all it took. As a "black" man Plessy felt himself and others to be disadvantaged by the new law proscribing seating on intrastate rail-roads. Louisiana had followed other states in attempting to separate the races, further removing blacks from the core of American life, and expanding the notion that their presence was a contaminant, a danger. The Supreme Court upheld the right of Louisiana and other states to seg-regate racially as long as the facilities remained "separate but equal." Thus the state played an active role in constructing African Americans as dan-gerous and as the antithesis of whites.[20]

Danger in the late nineteenth century was racial and sexual. Against the backdrop of momentary examples of interracial cooperation within the Knights of Labor, along the docks of New Orleans, and within the Farm-ers Alliances and Populist Party, a more compellingly sinister portrait appeared.[21] The end of slavery threatened the social hierarchy that had long governed interracial relations. Much of the action taken in the late nineteenth and early twentieth centuries sought its reestablishment. Joel Williamson has called the countervailing and dominant picture a "rage for order." At its core rested the image of the fiendish black purveyor.

Popular culture played a central role in concretizing this new narrative. Instead of black citizens, or injured citizens (after the *Plessy* decision), authors such as Thomas Dixon immortalized the image of the lustful black rapist or beast—see, for instance, *The Leopard's Spots* (1902) and *The Clansman* (1905). The themes in the two works were similar: the retrogres-sive, devilish black (often written as a black male) and the helpless, virtuous, and defenseless white woman. In a South truly uncomfortable with black citizens, and in a nation prepared to accept the Southern version of blacks, many concocted a story of black transgressors, rapists, and fiends. Given by then more than two hundred years of a historical relationship and its associated imagery, scores could see blacks as the supreme embodiment of danger.[22]

The portrayal of the black rapist appeared a new creation to many African Americans. Both Ida B. Wells-Barnett and Frederick Douglass tied its creation to a country unaccustomed and unwilling to view blacks as coequal citizens. Complained Douglass: "It has only been since the Negro has become a citizen and a voter that this charge has been made." At the same time Wells-Barnett argued: "During all the years of slavery, no such charge was ever made, not even during the dark days of the rebellion. . . . While the master was away fighting to forge the fetters upon the slave he left his wife and children with no protectors save the Negroes themselves."[23] Wells-Barnett, Douglass, and countless others wanted to know if the crimes had so increased, or if this was a way to police black male–white female relations. Thus, despite eloquent pleas for reason, black men and women found themselves represented as the locus of danger: black men since they committed the rapes; black women because they birthed black men, because their highly sexualized natures "inflamed" men, especially black men, and because they then failed to rein in the "lustful" tendencies of their menfolks.[24]

Once constructed as victimizers it proved difficult to view blacks as injured citizens. Lynching, rioting, and wanton violence became the prescription; whites, North and South, became willing and sometimes eager patients. Consider, for example, Rebecca Latimer Felton, a woman of superb accomplishment and somewhat progressive views. Born into a slaveholding family, she came of age in the post-Reconstruction era in time to have careers as a feminist, prohibitionist, politician, and journalist. Following the death of Tom Watson of Georgia, she became the first woman appointed to the U.S. Senate. At one point in 1897 she ascribed the increase in rapes to black political ascendancy: "I told them that the crimes had grown and increased by reason of the corruption and debasement of the right of suffrage; that it would grow and increase with every election where white men equalized themselves at the polls with an inferior race." She even advised, "if it takes lynchings to protect woman's dearest possession from drunken, ravening beasts, then I say lynch a thousand a week."[25] Felton was no lunatic. In her view, and in the view of thousands, blacks had been reborn in the postwar era as dangerous victimizers.

Constructing a Social Democracy

African Americans abided neither disfranchisement nor second-class citizenship well. Into the breach of a Jim Crow world, characterized by the solidification and rationalization of segregation, they mounted a strenuous assault and defense. Francis Grimke, a prominent Washington, D.C., minister, spoke for many African Americans when he proclaimed in an 1898 sermon, "We are not going to secure our rights in this land without a struggle. We have got to contend, and contend earnestly, for what belongs to us. Victory isn't coming in any other way."[26] Thousands of others, in both hush tones and loud protests, uttered similar statements. They encompassed the millions who gathered themselves and left the rural South between 1900 and 1920—1.5 million between the two dates, the vast majority leaving between 1916 and 1918. They included the generation of men and women who built the African-American social infrastructure of schools, colleges, fraternal orders, churches, and protest organizations. A commitment to change even surfaced in blues lyrics and jazz tunes, novels, essays, and academic tracts.

While each new institution made a contribution, a few proved pivotal additions. Collectively and individually, these institutions competed to establish blacks as injured citizens rather than dangerous victimizers. Two organizations warrant mention here. The first was the National Association for the Advancement of Colored People, created as an immediate response to the riotous onslaught that took the lives of several longtime residents of Springfield, Illinois, in 1908. Shocked by the riot, an interracial group of men and women met to discuss the dismal conditions for blacks in the United States. Ironically, in an organization ostensibly identified with justice for blacks, most attending the first National Negro Congress or NNC (1909) came from the country's white communities. In that sense the birth of the NAACP started differently than the birth of the Niagara Movement, which was organized by and for African Americans to protest their subordinate position in American society.[27]

The NAACP, founded in 1910 to help ameliorate the nation's worsening race relations, became America's preeminent civil rights organization. Adopting what can best be called an aggressive civil libertarian approach, the association and its group of attorneys initiated a careful, direct attack on all vestiges of segregation. Over the course of three decades a team of lawyers that included William Hastie, Thurgood Marshall, Jack Greenberg, Leon Ransom, and others eliminated segregation in housing and on public conveyances, desegregated graduate and professional schools, ended the practice of the white primary, and litigated on behalf of equal pay for equal work for black teachers.[28]

The fight for equal justice also spurred membership. Chicago opened the first branch after passage of the organization's 1911 constitution; by 1921 the NAACP reported more than 400 branches nationwide. The number grew to 481 branches, 77 youth councils, and 22 college chapters, with approximately 85,000 members by 1940.[29]

Meanwhile, in other sectors of America thousands came to join the Universal Negro Improvement Association (UNIA) with Jamaican-born Marcus Garvey at its helm. Garvey came to the United States in 1915 with hopes of meeting Booker T. Washington. Washington died before a meeting could occur. Garvey's trip to the United States, plus similar trips throughout Latin America and Great Britain, revealed that African peoples shared a remarkably similar subordinate status. Garvey resolved to change this and used the UNIA as a powerful vehicle to supplement his own rhetorical skills.

Among Garvey's greatest contributions was his ability to articulate a message of hope and deliverance to a people who believed in their own redemption. Scholars have called Garvey's efforts a revitalization. That characterization captured a part of his reach. When he thundered "Up, You Mighty Race" and preached that blacks build grand armies, kingdoms, and visions, he put into play an alternative to the victimizer/victim dichotomy. Garvey introduced a language of belief that made Garveyism a kind of civil religion. Even by conservative estimates Garvey built one of the largest social movements in the twentieth century. Chapters appeared across the United States and the globe. Through an elaborate mixture of salesmanship and ritual (e.g., large parades and weekly churchlike services), scores inverted the social paradigm predicated on black inferiority. Two generations before the saying "Black is Beautiful" grew in popularity, Garvey's followers made such claims.[30]

It is important to remember, consequently, that African Americans took full stock of the myriad implications of American prejudice and racism long before the nation would do so. In the process they constructed a place for themselves in America by constructing a shared belief in the meanings of American democracy. Central was their ability to see themselves as the last best chance for America. In effect they created an image of themselves as the chosen within the chosen.[31]

As the chosen within the chosen, African Americans essentially turned victimization on its side. In letters to newspapers and journals, public statements, even verbal games, they reminded America during this period of its failure to extend the full benefit of citizenship. As NAACP official William Pickens stated in 1917 and writer and NAACP official James Weldon Johnson echoed in 1919 and 1923, a democracy predicated on individual rights and freedoms that excluded the Negro was a bogus democracy.[32]

Nor were blacks merely clay puppets molded by white actions. They were citizens with unquestioned rights who were capable of plotting actions, expressing thoughts, issuing demands, and envisioning their place at the national table. Failure to acknowledge their rights injured the nation and falsified bold claims about democracy and liberty, they asserted. After all, they too sang "America," to paraphrase Langston Hughes.[33]

Toward a Minority Status

Matters of race did not go completely unnoticed by the larger society through the 1930s, nor were blacks completely unheard. Federal officials had taken careful note of the activities of a broad cross section of black Americans during World War I and the postwar years. After the war, and especially after the Bolshevik Revolution in Russia, many feared a double contaminant: the "dangerous" and "slackminded" black would fall prey to conniving communists. In the minds of J. Edgar Hoover's FBI, black and red went together.

Hoover may have been paranoid, but a historical relationship between blacks and communists did evolve. This relationship also had a bearing on the construction of blacks as minorities. In response to Marcus Garvey's unmitigated success in mobilizing and organizing members of the African diaspora, V. I. Lenin in particular forced a new look at the place of race in international communism. Early in the 1920s race was presented as yet another bourgeois corruption, yet another way to sidetrack the revolutionary potential of workers. But as Robin Kelley has indicated, "A major turning point . . . occurred in 1928." At the Sixth World Congress of the Comintern, delegates passed a resolution that characterized the Black Belt counties of the South as an oppressed nation with the right to self-determination. For the first time an international movement of nonblacks recognized the plight of American blacks.

In doing so, the Communist Party brought the "Negro Question" into the orbit of minority affairs. Prior to the 1928 meeting Lenin and other theoreticians discussed and debated the place of minority populations within European national settings. The idea of a nation within a nation had taken form in that context. Thus, in recognizing Southern blacks as an oppressed nation within the United States, the Communist Party helped internationalize the plight of African Americans as minorities, by blurring the lines between national and racial minorities.[34]

Still, well into the 1940s, American use of the term was limited and conceptually circumscribed. Americans seduced themselves in the reality of the melting pot. Unlike European communities with their unmeltable nationals, the argument went that the United States consisted of millions from diverse backgrounds who would ultimately become Americans, shedding ethnic particularities. The national motto, after all, made it clear: out of many, one. Further, the horrors of Nazi Germany confirmed the dangers of a minority problem. Nazism worked, some decried, because societies made a point of excluding, of rendering some minorities and thus marginal and open to attack.

The European Holocaust opened a new social space in post–World War II America for the creation of blacks as injured minority citizens. Even as the nation quickly became consumed with the dangers of Soviet aggression and the communist "menace," it was also sensitized to the depths of human hatred. Hatred created the context for the mass slaughter of thousands because they were Jews, Gypsies, North Africans, or anything other than White and Aryan. Nationally produced and reproduced hatreds helped naturalize categories others knew as mere social constructions. After all, in Nazi Germany one needed just one Jewish grandparent to be sufficiently Jewish and hence expendable. In the United States one needed just one drop of African blood to be sufficiently black and thus subjected to the extremes of law and practice.

The vulgarities of war forced many scholars to weigh into subsequent social debates. "Postwar America was," Elaine Tyler May has written, "the era of the expert." Americans turned to Benjamin Spock for advice on child rearing and Norman Vincent Peale for spiritual guidance. Americans also turned to social psychologists such as Gordon Allport for assistance in grappling with prejudice and discrimination. Allport and others did not disappoint. In *The Nature of Prejudice* readers found intolerance a socially ameliorable condition.[35] Individuals were instructed on how to take control of their own lives, noting that racism, discrimination, and prejudice could be eliminated.

Elsewhere, away from the front pages of newspapers and the best-seller list, Kenneth and Mamie Clark labored to understand the effects of prejudice on black children. Although later researchers criticized their methods, the pair found convincing evidence that young black children internalized their subordinate positions. When asked to identify the colored and white dolls on a table three-fourths of the children did so easily. When asked to identify the "nice" doll, the doll they most wished to play with, the doll with "nice" color, the youngsters overwhelming chose the "white" dolls and rejected the colored or Negro dolls. After surveying and studying children in Philadelphia, Boston, and across Arkansas, the Clarks concluded that segregation, discrimination, and racism taught black kids to hate themselves. This was the legacy of separate but equal.[36]

The U.S. Supreme Court came to share the assessment that legislated segregation was harmful. In the early 1950s, NAACP attorneys added the Clarks' findings to the arsenal of social science data presented to challenge the efficacy of continued segregation in public schools. When the Court issued its first ruling in the *Brown* case (1954) the legal question was: "Does segregation of children in public schools solely on basis of race . . . deprive the children of the minority group of equal educational opportunities?" The Court answered its own question with the response: "We believe that it does." Chief Justice Earl Warren, speaking for a unanimous Court, went on to say, "We conclude that in the field of public education the doctrine of 'separate but equal' has no place. Separate educational facilities are inherently unequal."

On that May 17, the Court wrote blacks into the nation's legal history as minorities deserving of redress. By overturning the doctrine of separate but equal, the Court reinvigorated a commitment and obligation to equal protection under the law. More important, in a country trying to balance between conservative tendencies and the maturation of a liberal welfare state, the *Brown* decision permanently opened the door for African Americans.[37]

Brown represented a chapter rather than the entire story, however. As a number of writers have noted in different ways, it took concerted and sustained protest for the nation to truly abolish most vestiges of segregation. In large measure, this break with the past came between 1954 and 1968.

For purposes of this essay, a detailed accounting of what became known as the civil rights era is not required. Instead, it is important to understand how the battle waged over civil rights resulted in the continued social construction of blacks as minorities.

All in the Family

As assistant secretary of labor, Daniel Patrick Moynihan created a social tempest when he zeroed in on the increasing prevalence of female-headed households among black Americans. Even though in time Moynihan would be proved correct—more and more children entered the world as the sole responsibility of one parent—few found comfort in his findings in 1965. Nor were they pleased that he blamed contemporary problems on slavery and a "tangled web of pathology." Although he simply resurrected some points made by the eminent black sociologist E. Franklin Frazier, Moynihan was wrong, according to his critics, and they were prepared to show how.[38]

The debate over the black family returned the focus to slavery and reestablished the social scientist's importance in the social construction of blacks as minorities. Slavery remained the central paradox in American history. In a nation so deeply attached to the prospects of freedom, slavery not only had existed, it had thrived. More important, excluding the vigorous efforts of African Americans, the majority of historians accepted the portrait of paternal masters, mostly benign slavery, and the arrested development of blacks that made slavery necessary and a positive good.[39]

By the 1950s, a new generation of historians altered this view. Most were influenced by the advent of liberal democracy and the conviction that African Americans, to paraphrase Kenneth Stampp, were simply white men with black faces. Stampp and his generation accepted the call issued by an earlier generation of black historians, such as Carter G. Woodson, Luther Porter Jackson, and Benjamin Brawley, to display the range of human potential that was black life and history. Endowing blacks with the same human qualities as whites became a necessary first step.

The second step followed soon thereafter in what would become the highly influential work of Stanley Elkins. The young Elkins studied psychology, particularly the work of Bruno Bettelheim, who examined what happened to those interned in German concentration camps. Elkins, who studied with Richard Hofstadter while at Columbia University, found Bettelheim's work on personality development persuasive and illuminating and thought it applicable to slavery. Accordingly, Elkins went on to argue that slavery was a total institution, similar to a concentration camp. As a total institution, slaves lacked social and psychic freedom, masters had absolute control, and under this system slaves came to internalize their inferiority. Complete infantilism was the result of this process of exploitation or what Elkins called the making of Sambo—docile, infantile, cultureless, and malleable.[40]

Initially ignored, Elkins had a tremendous impact on slavery historiography for nearly thirty years. Even as more complete and refined research upended his findings and conclusions, few could ignore the power of the Elkins thesis. Coming as it did in 1959, it fueled the debate over black injury (which quickly shifted to a discussion of victimization). Elkins placed responsibility for black Americans squarely in the hands of white America. White power had injured black Americans. This theme reemerged over and over again in works by (among others) Kenneth Clark, Charles Silberman, and Moynihan. At the same time, images of badly beaten Freedom riders, mutilated bodies unearthed in Mississippi, firebombed churches, slain teenagers, and rabidly racist white crowds fed public perceptions. By 1963, in fact, polls revealed that a majority of Americans agreed the nation should extend civil rights protection to African Americans.

For a time, however, most commentators lost sight of "injury" and instead emphasized "victimization." The conflation produced a fair share of confusion. Historians and sociologists demanded to know how a people so thoroughly victimized had managed to resist the institution of slavery and the assaults of Jim Crow. They pointed to open acts of resistance and rebellion, the creation of new cultural forms, and the survival of a people. Thus there was a somewhat unarticulated effort to distinguish between injury and victimization.

Nonacademics acknowledged the passage of important civil rights legislation at the same time that cities burned and urban rebellions pockmarked the nation. With Black Power and both its positive and negative connotations crowding out Martin Luther King's image of a beloved community, many whites began to ask, "What more does the Negro want?" A poll of Americans taken in 1971 revealed that a majority of whites believed civil rights for blacks no longer a national priority; it ranked fifth in a list of needs, lower than it had in 1962. By the middle 1970s, what had started as the perspective of a few had gained adherents: voters across the political spectrum feared that black power meant black liberation at the expense of white. As one Detroit resident put it, the shift in emphasis signaled "black takeover."[41]

Hence blacks ironically became minorities at the same moment others trumpeted as loudly as possible that they were dangerous. The image of the dangerous black person was of course an old trope in American social discourse. The only difference, from the late 1960s through the early 1980s, was that "black as dangerous" did not completely subordinate the countervailing narrative of blacks as injured citizens with legitimate rights as minorities. In this context Richard Nixon, who remained ambivalent about civil rights, expanded some aspects of affirmative action during his presidency. The cynical view is that, by recognizing blacks as injured minority citizens, politicians hoped the majority of blacks would seek redress through socially sanctioned channels rather than radical groups or urban rebellions.[42] To make them minorities was to reracialize both blacks and nonblacks.

Later Demography of Minority Status

Even as the government took great pains to define who was a minority it remained a word seldom uttered by blacks to describe themselves, other than in formal or official contexts. In part the hesitancy stemmed from the heated debate that evolved over minority status. Few African Americans found comfort in *minority*'s root meaning; they were not minor in any sense. In addition who was a minority was unclear. Did the phrase apply to racial groups only? Were women, ostensibly the majority, socially a minority as well? On this point, noted public intellectual Harold Cruse complained in 1987 that *minority* came to include white women at the expense of blacks, who shouldered the brunt of criticism and attacks from opponents of affirmative action.[43]

For other African Americans, the word *minority* had many levels of social meaning, at least some of which contradicted features of their daily experiences. Just as in generations before them, many blacks now lived as members of a majority. Coincident with the mass influx of an estimated 5.3 million blacks into the urban environment between 1940 and 1960 came a persistent pattern of residential segregation. A study of thirty large American cities revealed that no 1940 city had a residential segregation index (an areal measure of how many people would have to move so that the proportion of a population is distributed evenly across the city) of less than 77. Most indexes were in the upper 80s and even 90s, suggesting that blacks and whites lived in largely different spaces in the urban environment. Little had changed by 1970. Aside from San Francisco, with an index of 55.5, block-level residential segregation was pronounced. Over time there was also a tendency for blacks and whites to become more isolated: that is, less common for the two to share a neighborhood. Residential patterns created social spaces in which African Americans lived as members of the majority, becoming minorities only in relation to whites or social service workers.[44]

In that sense the construction of African Americans as minorities in the last quarter of the twentieth century has served the added purpose of talking about race. In many works, *minority* became a shorthand for *black*. Once used in that fashion the history of the word *black* connected to the word *minority* to put their many possible meanings into motion. Thus *black, minority, dangerous,* and *injured citizen* combined in socially structured ways. This explains in part the competing and contradictory portraits of Black America and its minority constituency. The collage included the model-minority-citizen Colin Powell, the dangerous outlaw hipster Tupac Shakur, the once-model-turned-danger O. J. Simpson, and the generic black woman on welfare. Each image underscores the depths of the social construction of African Americans as minorities, and the attendant positive and negative purposes and consequences.

In sum, this essay has sought to broadly outline the construction of African Americans as a minority in the United States. It is a history deeply rooted in the story of American freedom and American slavery. Ultimately, it is the story of how black Americans used the language of equality and justice to secure safe haven in the body politic. Toward that end, minority status pivoted on questions of race and democracy.

The question becomes, therefore, not only when did blacks become a minority but how. Clearly, early usage of the phrase *racial minority* in reference to blacks dates from the 1930s. More common usage awaited the arrival of the civil rights struggles and the associated governmental responses of the 1960s. Before then, a vast majority of Americans (meaning here the various European groups that came to think of themselves as and to be perceived as white Americans) saw blacks as outside the national framework. Blacks were the sites of danger and undeserving of federal protections, civil rights, or equal opportunity. This changed once blacks were socially constructed as injured citizens. As citizens they had certain rights, and as injured citizens they deserved certain protections. That this construction paralleled the birth of the civil rights era reinforced the demands for effective action. It also created the space for *blacks* to become *minority*.

But as this essay also notes, *minority* soon became another code word for *black*. In the context of post-1970 America, *minority* became another way of denoting danger. This central trope in American letters has enabled the nation to write about race even when no blacks exist. Similarly, invocation of the word *minority* has enabled a generation of politicians and their aides to talk about and inflate the importance of race, under a range of circumstances. Nor have blacks avoided the troubling effects of the term. To the generation of African Americans who benefited most handsomely from being a minority has come the realization that the tag victimizes them and re-creates in them the embodiment of the dangerously incompetent, underachieving, overly sensitive race-focused being.[45] They may be native sons and daughters, but they feel their alienation as strongly and painfully as Baldwin did four decades earlier. More than anything, they are reminded of Baldwin's words: "I have not written about being a Negro at such length because I expect that to be my only subject, but only because it was the gate that I had to unlock before I could hope to write about anything else. I don't think that the Negro problem in America can be even discussed coherently without bearing in mind its context; its context being the history, traditions, customs, the moral assumptions and preoccupations of the country." The ways in which blacks became minorities is certainly part of Baldwin's call for understanding the relationship between history and context.

NOTES

1. *Brown v. Board of Education of Topeka*, 347 U.S. 483; 74 S. Ct. 686; 98 L.Ed. 873 (1954); 349 U.S. 294; 75 S. Ct. 753; 99 L. Ed. 1083 (1955).

2. Richard H. King, "Citizenship and Self-Respect: The Experience of Politics in the Civil Rights Movement," *Journal of American Studies* 22 (1988): 7; Robert Korstad and Nelson Lichtenstein, "Opportunities Found and Lost: Labor, Radicals, and the Early Civil Rights Movement," *Journal of American History* 75 (December 1988): 786–811; Earl Lewis, *In Their Own Interests* (Berkeley: University of California Press, 1991), 173–78; Robin D. G. Kelley, "'We Are Not What We Seem': Rethinking Black Working Class Opposition in the Jim Crow South," *Journal of American History* 80 (June 1993): 75–112; Aldon Morris, *Origins of the Civil Rights Movement* (New York: Free Press, 1984), chap. 2.

3. Charles M. Payne, *I've Got the Light of Freedom* (Berkeley: University of

California Press, 1995), 53–55; John Dittmer, *Local People: The Struggle for Civil Rights in Mississippi* (Urbana: University of Illinois Press, 1995), 55–58; Juan Williams, *Eyes on The Prize: America's Civil Rights Years, 1954–1965* (New York: Viking Penguin, 1987), 39–45; and Anne Moody, *Coming of Age in Mississippi* (New York: Dell Publishing, 1976; originally published 1968), 125.

4. Philip Gleason, "Minorities (Almost) All: The Minority Concept in American Social Thought," *American Quarterly* 43 (September 1991): 392–424, especially 393–94. Donald Ramsey Young, *American Minority Peoples: A Study in Racial and Cultural Conflicts in the United States* (New York: Harper & Brothers, 1932).

5. For a full detailing of early usage see Gleason, "Minorities (Almost) All." Also see Robert E. Park, *Race and Culture* (Glencoe, Ill.: Free Press, 1950), 233, 249, 368–69; Young, *American Minority Peoples,* xiii.

6. Sterling Stuckey, *Slave Culture: Nationalist Theory and the Foundation of Black America* (New York: Oxford University Press, 1987), chap. 4.

7. W. E. B. Du Bois, *The Souls of Black Folk,* in *Three Negro Classics* (New York: Avon Books, 1965; originally 1903), 213–14. Gunnar Myrdal, *An American Dilemma* (New York: Pantheon, 1944, rpt. 1972), 50.

8. John J. McCusker and Russell R. Menard, *The Economy of British America* (Chapel Hill: University of North Carolina Press, 1985), 222.

9. McCusker and Menard, *The Economy of British America,* 18–32, and chaps. 1–13; Russell R. Menard, "From Servants to Slaves," *Southern Studies* 16 (1977): 355–90; David Galenson, *White Servitude in Colonial America* (Cambridge, 1981); A. Leon Higginbotham Jr., *In the Matter of Color: Race and the American Legal Process: The Colonial Period* (New York: Oxford University Press, 1978).

10. Peter Wood, *Black Majority: Negroes in Colonial South Carolina from 1670 through the Stono Rebellion* (New York: Alfred A. Knopf, 1974), chap. 5.

11. Winthrop Jordan, *White Over Black: American Attitudes Toward the Negro, 1550–1812* (Chapel Hill: University of North Carolina Press, 1968), chap. 2, discusses slavery as an "unthinking decision"; chapter 1 outlines the vernacular usage of *black.* Wood, *Black Majority,* 285–326; Eugene D. Genovese, *From Rebellion to Revolution* (New York: Vintage Books, 1981), 21, 42–43. Fear of slave uprisings and rebellions was not limited to this one example, however, as works by Herbert Aptheker, Genovese, John Blassingame, and Vincent Harding among others suggest.

12. George Frederickson, *The Black Image in the White Mind* (New York: Harper, 1971), 238–40; Margo J. Anderson, *A Social History of the American Census* (New Haven: Yale University Press, 1988), 89–90, on undercounting blacks.

13. Frederickson, *Black Image in the White Mind,* 228–55; quote, at 239.

14. John Hope Franklin and Alfred Moss, *From Slavery to Freedom* (New York: McGraw Hill, 1988), 21–23. P. B. S. Pinchback, Louisiana, was elected but never served in the Senate.

15. Franklin and Moss, *From Slavery to Freedom*, 218–20; Michael B. Chesson, "Richmond's Black Councilmen, 1871–1896," in Howard Rabinowitz, ed., *Southern Black Leaders of the Reconstruction Era*, 191–222 (Urbana: University of Illinois Press, 1982). Elsa Barkley Brown, "'Negotiating and Transforming the Public Sphere: African American Political Life in the Transition from Slavery to Freedom," *Public Culture* 7 (fall 1994), 107–46.

16. *Report of the Proceedings and Debates of the Constitutional Convention, State of Virginia, 1901–1902* (Richmond, 1906), 2958–93; quote in *The Negro in Virginia* (New York: Hastings House, 1940), 239.

17. Franklin and Moss, *From Slavery to Freedom*, 237.

18. Ira Berlin et al., *Slaves No More: Three Essays on Emancipation and the Civil War* (Cambridge: Cambridge University Press, 1992). Eric Foner, *Reconstruction, America's Unfinished Revolution, 1863–1877* (New York: Harper and Row, 1988), especially chaps. 6–8.

19. Hayes won, promising to end military occupation of the South by federal troops and agreeing to ease federal oversight, more generally. *The Civil Rights Cases*, 109 U.S. 3; 3 S Ct. 18; 27 L. Ed. 835 (1883).

20. The *Plessy* decision is discussed in a number of places. Among them see Charles Lofgren, *The Plessy Case* (New York: Oxford University Press, 1987); Eric J. Sundquist, *To Wake The Nations: Race in the Making of American Literature* (Cambridge: Harvard University Press, 1993), chap. 3.

21. See, for example, Peter Rachleff, *Black Labor in the South* (Philadelphia: Temple University Press, 1984); Eric Foner, *Nothing But Freedom: Emancipation and Its Legacy* (Baton Rouge: Louisiana State University Press, 1983); Joe William Trotter Jr., *Coal, Class, and Color: Blacks in Southern West Virginia* (Urbana: University of Illinois Press, 1990); Eric Arnesen, *Waterfront Workers of New Orleans* (New York: Oxford University Press, 1991).

22. Joel Williamson, *A Rage for Order* (New York: Oxford University Press, 1986), 98–116; Frederickson, *The Black Image in the White Mind*, chap. 9, especially 280–82.

23. Douglass as quoted in Martha Hodes, "The Sexualization of Reconstruction Politics: White Women and Black Men in the South after the Civil War," in John C. Fout and Muara Shaw Tantillo, eds., *American Sexual Politics* (Chicago: University of Chicago Press, 1993), 73; Ida B. Wells-Barnett, "A Red Record" in Gerda Lerner, ed., *Black Women in White America: A Documentary History* (New York: Vintage, 1973), 203.

24. Peter L. Berger and Thomas Luckmann, *The Social Construction of Reality* (Garden City: Anchor Books, 1966).

25. Williamson, *A Rage for Order*, 90–95; quote, at 95. The durability of the "black fiend" incited mob action well into the late 1950s. See, for instance, Howard Smead, *Blood Justice: The Lynching of Mack Charles Parker* (New York: Oxford University Press, 1986).

26. As quoted in Philip S. Foner, ed., *The Voice of Black America* (New York: Capricorn Books, 1972), 55.

27. See among other studies, Gunnar Myrdal, *An American Dilemma* (1944; reissued, New York: Pantheon Books, 1972), vol.II: 819–36. Richard Kluger, *Simple Justice* (New York: Vintage Books, 1977); and David Levering Lewis, *W.E.B. Du Bois: Biography of a Race* (New York: Henry Holt and Company, 1993), chaps. 12 and 14.

28. Charles Kellogg, *NAACP* (Baltimore: Johns Hopkins University Press, 1967), and Robert Zangrando, *The NAACP Campaign Against Lynching, 1909–1950* (Philadelphia: Temple University Press, 1980); Myrdal, *An American Dilemma*, vol.II: 819–36; Kluger, *Simple Justice*, 95–104.

29. Myrdal, *An American Dilemma*, vol. II: 820–26, 1402.

30. For a sample of the literature on Garvey, see E. David Cronon, *Black Moses: The Story of Marcus Garvey and the Universal Negro Improvement Association* (Madison: University of Wisconsin Press, 1955); Tony Martin, *Race First: The Ideological and Organizational Struggles of Marcus Garvey and the Universal Negro Improvement Association* (Westport, Conn.: Greenwood Press, 1976); Lawrence Levine, "Marcus Garvey and the Politics of Revitalization," in *Black Leaders in the Twentieth Century,* John Hope Franklin and August Meier, eds. (Urbana: University of Illinois Press, 1982), 104–38; Robert A. Hill, ed., *The Marcus Garvey and Universal Negro Improvement Association Papers,* 8 vols. to date (Berkeley: University of California Press, 1983–); and Judith Stein, *The World of Marcus Garvey* (Baton Rouge: Louisiana State University Press, 1986).

31. David Howard-Pitney, *The Afro-American Jeremiad: Appeals for Justice in America* (Philadelphia: Temple University Press, 1990), 15.

32. Perry Miller, *Errand in the Wilderness* (New York: Harper, 1964; Sacvan Berkovitch, *The American Jeremiad* (Madison: University of Wisconsin Press, 1978). Also see William Pickens, "The Kind of Democracy the Negro Race Expects," and James Weldon Johnson, "Our Democracy and the Ballot," in Foner, ed., *The Voice of Black America,* vol. 2: 99–103, 141–47.

33. Quoted in Arnold Rampersad, *The Life of Langston Hughes,* vol. I: *1902–1941, I, Too, Sing America* (New York: Oxford University Press, 1986); poem quoted on 95.

34. See Robin Kelley, *Race Rebels* (New York: Free Press, 1994), 103–9; Kelley, "Hammer n' Hoe: Black Radicalism and the Communist Party in Alabama, 1929–1941" (UCLA, Ph.D. diss., 1987), 25–42.

35. Elaine Tyler May, "Cold War—Warm Hearth: Politics and the Family in Postwar America," in Steven Fraser and Gary Gerstle, eds., *The Rise and Fall of the New Deal Order, 1930–1980* (Princeton: Princeton University Press, 1989), 164. Gordon Allport, *The Nature of Prejudice* (New York: Doubleday-Anchor, 1958).

36. Kluger, *Simple Justice,* 324–30.

37. Kluger, *Simple Justice,* 779–87; Ira Katznelson, "Was the Great Society a

Lost Opportunity," and Jonathan Rieder, "The Rise of the 'Silent Majority,'" in Fraser and Gerstle, *The Rise and Fall of the New Deal Order,* chaps. 7 and 9, respectively. Legal scholars, however, also point to footnote 4 in the *United States versus Carolene Products Co.,* 304 U.S. 144 (1938), which introduced the idea of the insular minority. For an elaboration on the connection to blacks see John David Skrentny, *The Ironies of Affirmative Action* (Chicago: University of Chicago Press, 1996), 171–76.

38. For a very good review of the Moynihan report and its relations to the slavery historiography, read August Meier and Elliott Rudwick, *Black History and the Historical Profession* (Urbana: University of Illinois Press, 1986), 239–76.

39. See Earl Lewis, "'To Turn As On a Pivot: History, Race, and African Americans in a World of Overlapping Diasporas," *American Historical Review* 100 (June 1995): 7, for a detailed discussion of the emergent consensus.

40. Meier and Rudwick, *Black History and the Historical Profession,* 241–47; Peter Novick, *That Noble Dream,* 480–86. Ironically, Phillips had reached similar conclusions, stressing of course the congenital childishness of blacks and the paternalistic oversight of whites. Elkins attributed the end result to the victimizing nature of slavery. Stanley Elkins, *Slavery: A Problem in American Institutional and Intellectual Life* (New York: Grosset and Dunlap, 1963), part III.

41. For a fuller discussion see Earl Lewis, "Race, Equity, and Democracy: African Americans and the Struggle for Civil Rights," in Herrick Chapman and Reid Andrews, eds., *The Social Construction of Democracy* (New York: New York University Press, 1995), 193–217.

42. Hugh Davis Graham, *The Civil Rights Era: Origins and Development of National Policy* (New York: Oxford University Press, 1990), 33–36, 50–112; Nicholas Lemann, *The Promised Land* (New York: Alfred A. Knopf, 1991), 148–221.

43. Harold Cruse, *Plural But Equal* (New York: William Morrow, 1987), 362. Gleason, "Minorities (Almost) All," 405–6.

44. The average level of isolation in Northern cities in 1930 was 31.7; by 1970, the average stood at 73.5. Douglass Massey and Nancy Denton, *American Apartheid* (Cambridge: Harvard University Press, 1993), 60–123.

45. Shelby Steele, *Content of the Character* (New York: St. Martin's Press, 1990); Stephen L. Carter, *Reflections of an Affirmative Action Baby* (New York: Basic Books, 1991); Ellis Close, *The Rage of a Privileged Class* (New York: Harpercollins, 1993).

Comment

Jean Heffer

Earl Lewis's subject is important not only for a colloquium on "the construction of minorities" but also for contemporary America, where we see Republicans, most recently in California and elsewhere, contesting affirmative action that favors minorities. The very fact that we speak of affirmative action, and not of reverse discrimination, clearly indicates that in the United States the term *minority* has taken on a positive connotation, but that was not always the case.

In contrast to Europe, where ethnic and religious minorities have long held specific status, the concept of minority was not used in America in social affairs until relatively recently. In the country that was the first liberal democracy, the word was originally confined to the field of politics. Until the 1820s American society preferred the term *opposition,* as in England, rather than *minority* (a term that evoked treason in the organic conception of the city carried along by the republican tradition). This was no longer the case under the second system of parties, created in the Jacksonian era: The minority became institutionalized as part of political life, and alternating parties became a normal event. From this moment on, a party was destined to be the minority at some given moment. Lincoln drew the consequences in his first inaugural address, March 4, 1861: with regard to political issues, "we divide upon them into majorities and minorities. If the minority will not acquiesce, the majority must, or the Government must cease. . . . Unanimity is impossible. The rule of a minority, as a permanent arrangement, is wholly inadmissible; so that, rejecting the majority principle, anarchy or despotism in some form is all that is left." But the minority must be respected. "If by the mere force of numbers," Lincoln adds, "a majority should deprive a minority of any clearly written constitutional right, it might in a moral point of view justify revolution; certainly would if such right were a vital one."[1]

39

The notion of a minority thus had neither positive nor negative implications, nor did it entail special rights; whether they liked it or not, the minority had to acquiesce in the laws voted for by the majority. Underneath this lay an egalitarian conception where one citizen equals another; the law is a product of the decisions of a plurality of individuals, usually through the mediation of their representatives, rather than of communities.

In contrast to that situation, which aptly describes the nineteenth century and the beginning of the twentieth, we have, since the 1960s, seen the concept of the minority being extended beyond the field of politics (in the strict sense) toward the social arena. That results from a rebellion against the domination of the so-called male WASP (White Anglo-Saxon Protestant) "majority." The "minorities" actually constitute the majority, in particular women (51.2 percent of the American population in 1992). This notion of minority harks back not to numbers, in contrast to the field of politics, but to power.

In his article, Lewis excellently demonstrates that, for blacks, who have always been perceived as the first minority, this idea is recent and a question of a historical process, a social construction. Broadly, despite a few earlier indications, the concept appeared in the 1930s, even though, ever since the legalization of segregation at the end of the nineteenth century, African Americans living in the South were put in a state of subordination worse than that of the European minorities of the same epoch (with the possible exception of those in the Ottoman Empire before 1918). These people shared all the characteristics of an oppressed minority as understood in Europe. Why were they not perceived as a minority in the United States? Undoubtedly because of the fiction of the always powerful egalitarian myth, the ideology of the melting pot; perhaps their situation was seen as only a temporary failure, a brief aberration in the course of American history. As Lewis indicates, the blacks themselves did not define themselves as a minority because their ultimate goal remained integration. They thus refused to be classified in a separate category.

They are, nevertheless, a minority—and that interpretation rests on demography—even though they are not randomly dispersed throughout the American landscape but, rather, concentrated in limited areas: In the South around 1860, they were the majority in South Carolina and Mississippi, remaining so in numerous counties until the twentieth century; in the North, they lived in ghettos and inner cities after the exodus, which became sizable beginning with World War I and reached its peak in the 1960s. Locally a majority, blacks in these areas were perceived by whites as a threat; consequently, segregation was imposed in order to contain them. This sort of demographic argument sparks two comments: (1) In the North before the Civil War, blacks constituted a small minority in large cities and yet fell victim to discriminatory actions independent of their demographic weight; (2) since 1880, the black portion of the population has regularly declined in the South (see table 1), a trend particularly clear in the first half of the twentieth century. They thus more and more became a minority, although the same period corresponds to the apogee of apartheid. One would have expected a diminution of white fear if it were a function of the relative weight of each community. That did not occur. Is this an effect of behavioral inertia, reinforced by the loss of the right to vote among all blacks and numerous poor whites, as J. Morgan Kousser has argued?

The change in perception during the 1960s could have emerged from the fact that blacks were finally recognized as minorities everywhere, including the South, where their proportion became smaller and smaller (the city of Washington was the only exception), as well as in the North, where they lived in ghettos occupying a small part of the total space. One also sees in this the role of a new definition of equality, of educational progress, and of the success of American "liberalism," similar in some ways to northwestern Europe's social-democratic humanism. Blacks were henceforth viewed as innocents and no longer threatening; as victims, no longer potential aggressors. Add to this the legal arguments of the NAACP and even the contributions of historians.

Consequently, the minority is seen as something weak whose rights must be protected in the face of the possible tyranny of the majority. This leads to an ambivalent situation, which in a democracy based on meritocracy can only be temporary. At first, it is a question of procuring advantages for the minority in order to make up for its lag. But with what time limit? Obviously, the protected status cannot be extended indefinitely, otherwise there is a risk of confining the beneficiaries to a second-class citizenship. The ultimate goal can be neither cultural separatism, which leads to an impasse, nor a system of quotas, intolerable in the long run to a society composed of individuals and not of communities. Rejoining the mainstream is the objective to aim for, and that goes not only for the United States but also for France. And for that, we have no magic recipe.

TABLE 1. Proportion of Afro-Americans in the Population of Eleven States in the Confederacy and the Federal Capital, 1860–1990

	AL	AR	DC	FL	GA	LA	MS	NC	SC	TN	TX	VA	South
1860	45.4	25.5	18.7	45.0	44.1	49.4	55.2	36.5	58.5	25.5	30.3	43.5	36.8
1870	47.1	75.2	32.6	48.9	46.0	50.1	53.6	36.6	58.9	25.6	30.9	41.9	36.0
1880	47.5	26.3	33.7	47.2	47.0	51.5	57.4	37.9	60.6	26.1	24.7	41.8	36.0
1890	44.8	97.4	33.0	42.5	46.8	50.0	57.6	34.7	59.9	24.4	21.8	38.3	33.8
1900	45.2	28.0	31.0	43.7	46.7	47.1	58.5	32.9	58.4	23.8	20.4	35.7	32.3
1910	42.5	28.1	28.4	41.0	45.1	43.1	56.1	31.6	55.2	21.6	17.7	32.5	29.8
1920	38.4	26.9	25.1	34.0	41.6	38.9	52.2	29.8	51.4	19.3	15.9	29.9	26.9
1930	35.7	25.8	27.1	29.4	36.8	36.9	50.2	29.0	45.7	18.3	14.7	26.8	24.7
1940	34.7	24.8	28.2	27.1	34.7	35.9	49.2	27.5	42.8	17.5	14.4	24.7	23.8
1950	32.0	22.4	35.0	21.8	30.9	32.9	45.3	25.8	38.8	16.1	12.7	22.1	21.7
1960	30.0	21.8	53.9	17.8	28.5	31.9	42.1	24.5	34.8	16.5	12.4	20.1	20.6
1970	26.2	18.3	71.1	15.3	25.9	29.9	36.8	22.2	30.5	15.8	12.5	18.5	19.1
1980	25.6	16.4	70.4	13.8	26.8	29.4	35.2	22.4	30.4	15.8	12.0	18.9	18.6
1990	25.3	15.9	65.9	13.6	27.0	30.8	35.6	22.0	29.8	16.0	11.9	18.8	18.5

Source: Historical Statistics of the United States, 1975J, series A: 195, 200; *Statistical Abstract,* 1985: 31; 1993: 30.

AL: Alabama; AR: Arkansas; DC: District of Columbia; FL: Florida; GA: Georgia; LA: Louisiana; MS: Mississippi; NC: North Carolina; SC: South Carolina; TN: Tennessee; TX: Texas; VA: Virginia. "South" adds Delaware, Maryland, West Virginia, Kentucky, and Oklahoma to the other eleven states.

NOTE

1. Henry S. Commager, ed., *Documents of American History,* 7th ed., (New York: Appleton-Century-Crofts, 1963), vol. 1, 387.

Nobles or Pariahs? The Exclusion of Florentine Magnates from the Thirteenth to the Fifteenth Centuries

Christiane Klapisch-Zuber

"It is one thing to be one of the Great; it is another to be noble." The first are perhaps nobles as defined by locality, but they are not loved nor recognized by the People or by the Prince; the others are "well regarded and appreciated," their nobility being linked not only to their birth but also to the recognition of their titles and merits. According to Bartolo, the Florentine jurist Lapo da Castiglionchio attempted, around 1370, the difficult exercise of combining the rival definitions of nobility that circulated in the Italy of his times, and the justification of his own nobility.[1] He wanted very much to be noble, but not "great." Who then are these great people from whom these nobles mean to distinguish themselves?

In the political and social vocabulary of the Italian communes of the thirteenth and fourteenth centuries, the term *great* has a very specific significance. The most apparent is that from the thirteenth century on, in Florence and other communes, the term carries a musty odor of haughtiness and arrogant disdain (*grandigia, prepotenza*) quickly detected by the common people. *Great* in the fourteenth century signifies first of all the wealth and political power of the most prominent families of the city; but it is not neutral, it retains the unfavorable connotation inherited from the thirteenth century, and from ordinary citizens it calls forth a negative judgment: its use, by an artisan or by a man of the people, remains most often pejorative. It is ambiguous, however, in keeping not only its social or moral but also its political meaning. When Lapo da Castiglionchio invokes the term *great,* he specifically alludes to the second of these levels by using another word, *magnate,* that has come to have a special meaning.

In the rather confused mass of powerful and rich lineages, one might in effect distinguish after the end of the thirteenth century a group far better defined as *magnats,* a word that takes on a precise technical meaning. Used throughout Europe to describe the highest strata of feudal aristocracy (it kept more or less the same meaning in England until late into the early modern period),[2] *magnas,* which is the Latin equivalent of *grande,* is, in Tuscany, frequently associated with *nobiles* or *potentes.* In thirteenth-century usage, *grande* and *magnas* refer to the same notions of social ascent and supremacy. Nevertheless, after the 1280s, the second usage, *magnas,* is isolated within this group of terms and comes to refer exclusively to the part of the aristocracy, urban or rural, marked and set apart by the Ordonnances of 1293–95. The standard literature has shown the stages of the process by which, inside a larger social stratum—that of the *nobiles et potentes*—and in comparison to all the citizens of Florence, those described as *popolani,* regardless of their social standing, formed a particular group that came to be distinguished and to take on a frankly discriminatory value.[3]

In effect, the majority of nobiles et potentes remained members of the body of fully active citizens, belonged to the polity of the people, and were fit to occupy the highest municipal positions. In referring to them, one spoke of *grandi popolani* or *nobiles populares* or *grandi nobili popolani.* On the other hand, the two terms *magnas* (Ital.: *magnate*) and *popularis* (Ital.: *popolano*) became and remain incompatible. One always excludes the other. In the time in which Lapo da Castiglionchio wrote, the double sense of *grande* was still retained; one could therefore be a magnate without being noble or noble without being a magnate. Neither term excluded the other; the first is the result of an administrative act, while the other reflects a judgment of style and bearing.

Salvemini saw a vicious circle in the mutual exclusion of definitions of magnates and popularis that was emphasized as much by contemporaries as by the historians of his own time: The issue of whether and to what degree one is shaped by the exclusion of the other has become, to most authors, no more than a battle of words, "because, given the one, it becomes necessary to grant the other."[4] One can escape this vicious circle, however, by noting that it is always the popularis who define the magnates by taking the initiative in providing definitions throughout the turbulent political history of Florence from the thirteenth to the fifteenth centuries. This is precisely what makes it impossible for us to dismiss the definitions of *magnates* and *popularis.* In fact, these words are not pure substances: They take their meaning in a dialectical relationship of forces, just as

Salvemini himself first pointed out. Because it is built around not only the idea of exclusion but also ideas of distance and difference, the meaning of magnate could be constantly revised because that meaning followed from the idea that the people had of itself.

The term *magnate* refers, therefore, to an undesirable judicial and political status that was progressively constructed in the last decades of the thirteenth century and finalized in *les Ordonnances de Justice* of 1293–95.[5] Its limits are drawn and fixed by a theoretically irrevocable list: We will find it in fact copied from one revision to another up to the statutes of the fifteenth century. By the end of the thirteenth century the names of about seventy lineages in the city of Florence and those of an equivalent number in the contado are listed in the statutes of the *podestà;* when necessary, the family name of a member of the local aristocracy could be verified in order to apply the appropriate measures and sanctions anticipated in the Ordonnances. The term *magnate* stigmatized some of the best families in the city for more than two centuries. What were the criteria for applying such a negative distinction?

Entering and Leaving a Minority

Born of the need to isolate and thereby to identify a group whose behavior made it an enemy of the regime of the Arte, the families of Florentine "magnates" were also defined by the *popolo* of those times as being particularly inclined toward violence. The best indication of this violence and arrogance is the bearing and use of arms.[6] Those who bore arms were first of all members of the knightly class, which is why the only truly clear criterion for defining the magnates is to discern the presence of a knight in a lineage. Indeed, this criterion marked the initial formation of the group but disappeared rather quickly at the beginning of the fourteenth century, when the Commune and the people themselves created knights.

Although the term *nobiles* lost, in thirteenth-century Florence, the meaning it had in feudal society, becoming diluted and colorless to the point of seeming useless when it was necessary to define the terms of exclusion, the popolo constantly characterized the magnates in terms of violence, regarding that to be the prerogative of the ancient nobility, and linked violence to the condition of the *milites,* the warriors on horseback, who were ill constrained by the ideals of ancient chivalry. The situation is paradoxical, for the group of "magnates" defined by the list of Statutes of the pedestal had long been shown to be a heterogenous group containing

a mishmash of authentic feudal lineages, families of ancient consular aristocracy, and lines enriched by commerce and banking in the thirteenth
century.[7] In short, it contained a social spectrum that seemed absolutely
comparable to that of the families of the popolo grasso, which monopo-
lized the power in the government of the Arte from the end of the thirteenth century. In other words, the people cut the *membra domorum magnatum* from its own body.

The part was not completely severed, however. First of all, being named
a magnate did not amount to a proscription and did not eliminate from
the commune people designated on the basis of their family (or rather their
lineage). The magnates were not rebels, exiles, or utter outlaws. They
remained citizens, could still appear before the tribunals to defend their
rights, and retained the same civil rights as other citizens; but for them the
penal procedures were quicker, and the sanctions harsher. Their political
capacity was diminished, for they could neither rise to the leadership of the
Arte—a loss because of their group's singular desire to be elected to the
highest governmental positions—nor to positions within the People's
Council because of their exclusion by definition; magnates could, however, participate in political life at many different levels. They could sit on
one of the principal city councils, the Communal Council. Also, separately
from the popolani, they were in charge of the Parte Guelfa, the aristocratic
association that defended the Guelf ideals as well as the class interests of
all the Grandi. They remained military leaders, directed communal mili-
tias, or fought with them on horseback in battle. The Commune sent those
reputed to be sufficiently loyal to command important strategic posts of
the contado or to administer justice in its name in the localities of its territory.[8] It counted as well upon their imposing bearing when sending them
abroad on diplomatic missions or assigning them to prestigious appointments in foreign cities. The magnates were, therefore, belittled as citizens,
but they were not entirely excluded from political life. They were a constrained minority, but an active one.

They were all the more difficult to disregard in the life of the Commune,
since many bonds between grandi popolani and the magnates were formed
in the thirteenth century and continued to be formed in the centuries that
followed. Grandi formed bonds of an economic nature that were so strong
that it is difficult to agree with Salvemini that it was above all their status
as grain producers that brought about the ire of other popolani in the thirteenth century and caused their segregation. The majority of the urban
magnates' lineages were profoundly implicated in the banking and in the

commercial life of the city before and after 1300; they were doubtless landowners and, especially in cities, landlords and proprietors who even owned entire neighborhoods. Some of them were moreover associated with the popolani through mutual commercial contacts, a characteristic that persisted into the middle of the fifteenth century. Although these business contacts were solidified through numerous marriage alliances, this was not a situation of group endogamy but a unique phenomenon because it involved members of a single group.

In the everyday life of the neighborhood, these mutual connections translated into multiple interdependencies. There were cases of many popularis who vouched for the magnates in legal acts which concerned them. A frequent example was the appearance of *afidejussores* of the populani at the posting of bail and at the ceremony of oath required of the magnates annually. Donato Velluti and his cousins, for example, intervened in this capacity many times, and not solely because their allies, the Frescobaldi, occupied such a prominent place in the *Cronica domestica.*

The Good Use of a Minority

To repeat an expression of Maurice Kriegel,[9] the magnates were negatively privileged, in the sense that their status, defined by restrictions and by negative dispensations under common law, benefited them in a certain way. The magnates formed neither a caste nor a minority confined to activities that are looked down upon. On the contrary: They were given honorary functions and were what we would call representatives of the community. In fact, the complicity between the popolani grassi and the magnates was often denounced by the members of the minor Arte, or the *minuti.* They knew well that within the *popolano grasso* unknowingly slept a magnate (and as we will see, within more than one magnate was a populano who was not always grasso, but who would like to be!). The constraints that bound magnates and against which they often rebelled can neither offset nor efface all the signs of their position of dominance—the bearing of arms, solidarity and vendetta, positions of leadership—no more than the essence of their prestige: the antiquity of their stock, the wealth that allowed their generosity. The communal power made use of them only to better control them.

The magnates of the fourteenth century were not subject to exclusion but to exception. Maintained because of pressure from the popular classes, the magnate status was often put under scrutiny, becoming definitive only in those moments when social and political struggle intensified; and its forms never ceased undergoing revision. Florentine leaders close enough to the magnates to be able to understand their reactions and to exercise pressure upon them were without a doubt convinced that the magnates, being in a position of relative exteriority, could be useful in serving the community. One might add that the success of the status of a magnate consisted of bringing together political limitations and judicial constraints. In this way magnates were rendered socially very vulnerable. Their interests depended strongly on the protection of their counterparts among the popolani who were in power and, in the end, of the state that was produced little by little out of partisan struggles. The magnates' negative privileges rendered them harmless and allowed them to exercise honorary and representative functions in the community and in the popolo to which they did not belong, functions that were given to them if they were sufficiently loyal. Assignments to these functions were not simply tossed to them as a bone to soften their resentment for being excluded from the real positions of power in the city. Instead, duties in these functions had to appeal not only to the magnates' vanity and vainglory. In order to grant honor, to honor a partner, one must take the notion of honor seriously. The citizens selected the diplomatic magnates to be assigned with the defense of the People's honor because the magnates were in the best position to know what honor meant. I can only refer to the superb analysis of Trexler.[10]

How Does One Leave a Minority?

Placed partially on the margins of political life, Florentine magnates saw themselves as being restricted to the fringes primarily when they were implicated in a violent affair involving the popolani. The Ordonnances were intended above all to protect the popolani from the oppression of the powerful designated as magnates. This protection, as I have said, is based on the principle of exceptional measures. In fulfilling their duties, the magnates established a distance between themselves and the popolani. This allowed either the mitigation of the punishment inflicted upon the popolani offender facing a magnate or on the contrary increased the punishment facing a magnate who victimized a popolano. During the fourteenth century many deviations from this rule can be observed. Little by little a custom developed that created ad hominem just such a difference between the two parties. Depending on the case, for example, a popolano might be at least temporarily declared a magnate for the purpose of a harsher punishment or a magnate might become temporarily a popolano when facing another magnate as an adversary.[11]

Before they even considered using the royal route of *popularitas,* that is, asking for the transfer of an individual or a family into the ranks of the popolani, magnates made use of the exception, which for a long time seemed to be the best—or the only—way of escaping the constraints of their position. Many, especially after 1340, asked to be granted a measure that either disregarded or transgressed deliberately the indelible mark of their birth for a particular matter. As a minority within their own minority they did not enjoy to the same extent the advantages of the status of popolani. Not surprisingly, under these circumstances many of those who first seized on the possibilities offered by the Ordonnances and used the discriminatory measures for their benefit took the next step and asked to become popolani. In the 1340s, the *popularitates* realized that the number of families of magnates who had become inoffensive had declined and that a great number of those, often reputed to be of Ghibeline tradition, had been admitted into the ranks of the people, sometimes in exchange for considerable cash. In the following decade governmental authorities granted the change of status bit by bit to the magnates who distinguished themselves by serving the community. Only after 1360 did the privileges of popularitas multiply and begin to reduce the size of the magnates as a group. The erosion of this group, which took on the aspect of an epidemic, was strong enough to make the total drop by 1,200, from some 1,400 men taking the annual oath at the beginning of 1340 to 200 between 1382 and 1384, a time when we can still count them in this way. Cosimo the Elder granted almost all of the last magnates—231 of them—the status they sought.[12]

The status itself was still used, to my knowledge, until the end of the fifteenth century as a weapon against political enemies, but this practice was not new, as additions to the number of magistrates began in the 1310s with the Bordonis and accompanied proscriptions throughout the last decades of the fourteenth century. What remains is that the designation of magnate, tarnished by the extensions given to it since the fourteenth century (it allowed one to force the parents of a convict to bear witness against him or to bring sanctions against recalcitrant taxpayers), was above all blurred by the evolution of mentalities. Among the magnates, this was because they sought to align themselves with the behavior of their fellow citizens during the entire second half of the fourteenth century; among the popolani grassi, this was because what separated them from the older group of magnates became less important than what was keeping them together, insofar as the ensemble of ruling classes had supplanted the middle classes or kept them on the margins of real power. The two factions of the dominant class found it in their interests to cooperate openly after 1390 rather than to maintain an artificial division.

In this strategy of assimilation, the magnates evidently strove to put themselves in the shoes of the people. They mimicked the characteristics that seemed to contradict what was strongest in their own "nature" as magnates, using for their own advantage arguments on which the difference in status had been substantially founded in order to persuade their partners that they were no different. Their speech made it clear how the designations of the thirteenth century were internalized by those who had borne them in the fourteenth and fifteenth centuries and, finally, how these changed in meaning.

Being Part of a Minority

If it is rather simple to grasp the significance given to the term *magnate* by the popolani, the perception of the quality and "nature" attributed to it remains rather obscure. Let us take them at their own word from the discourse in which this term was given different levels of meaning.

In the first, and most basic, kind of discourse, the words of convicted magnates, repeated by defendants and plaintiffs, have their roots in popular speech. It was a voice that therefore, was polemical or aggressive. Whether insults, threats, or boasts, the words put in the mouth of the denounced or accused magnate are part of the argument of an adversary and quoted accordingly. They paint the portrait of the magnate as one might expect to confront him on the streets or the fields of Tuscany: violent, destructive, a thief, rapist, weapon in hand, insult on the tongue. Let us take a closer look at some of these insults.[13] The most frequent is that of "traitor," an accusation thrown back at them naturally enough by the popolani: The difference is that incriminated magnates are traitors to the community or to the people, whereas the insulted (popolani) are simply "traitors," in other words treacherous to their natural superiors.[14] Their threats menace not only life ("I'm going to massacre those peasants," boasts an Ubaldini in 1366)[15] but also the property of their victims, as do the Gherardini in 1377, crying, at the expense of their host and in spite of him: "Let us eat, drink and ruin him, for he well deserves it."[16] They all

seem to be certain of their impunity and of silence, the silence that resonates through the Florentine judicial archives that show us frightened
witnesses who exhibit little enthusiasm for corroborating such accusations. Frescobaldi knew this well, summing it up with great ease in 1405: "I
am more powerful [*maggiore*] than you, and nobody will say a word
against me if I kill you."[17] The threats of the magnates that were repeated
in denunciations to the Executor of the Ordonnances concern, thus, the
popolo in its entirety and the honor of the Florentine Commune to which
the "little ones," the "powerless," appeal as the only real means of eliciting
an official reaction, the only hope that justice will be done and that the
affair will not be buried. "In Ferrara, there are no people, filthy dog,"
cried a Donati to his victim, finding refuge in that city in 1344;[18] and the
Bardi repeat it after him, boasting once in 1349 before the peasants whom
they ransack that "we have ruined more than once the popolo of Florence,
we can very well do it again to those of St. Cristofano of Perticaia."[19]

The oppositions little–grand and weak–strong form the rhetoric of
these complaints, almost all of them protected by the anonymity accorded
by law to those who denounce the magnates. It is significant, however,
that the magnates, in their excessive and foolish pride, took up this language and accord themselves, like the Frescobaldi above, a quasi-physical
"superiority" in relation to the popolani. Taller, stronger, bigger, more
powerful than the popolani—this language of dimensions, of size, is as
pregnant with meaning as that founded upon the opposition of "rich" and
"humble," which relates to the relationship between people in power and
subordinates or proletariat.

Believing That One Is of the People

The second kind of language, which is no longer one of aggression and
demands of revenge made with hostile intent, is instead that of a discourse
of presentation and persuasion. I have already referred to the privileges of
popularitas, partial or complete, that communal power granted to the
magnates. In fact, the introduction of the policy of the restitution of civil
rights to the magnates is perceptible from the middle of the century; from
1349, those who could not tolerate being part of that lineage were offered
the possibility of separating themselves from it. These "divisions," like the
privileges of popularitas, have given us a large number of speeches concerning them that were presented before the communal government and
were given in a manner aimed to convince.

The majority of applicants saw themselves, therefore, as driven to flaunt their conformity to behaviors that the popolani valued. The language of greatness is of no use here. Nevertheless, many of them do not shy away from it completely but present it in a Guelf manner intended to be convincing to their partners in the popolo grasso: As Guelf, their ancestors fought against the enemies of the Commune and of the Parte; Guelf they will remain, but in the service of the people. If not *greatness,* than at least *honor* is the key word. The honor of the magnates who aspire to being popolano is not incompatible with that of the people.

The introduction of the *arma populi* under their own shield is a very clear sign of the proposal to integrate the people into their military tradition. In fact, since they are obliged by the law of 1361 to change their coat of arms, once they are admitted in the ranks of the popolani, a measure obviously vexing to them, they appropriate for themselves the "coat of arms of the people" (a cross of yules on a silver background) as if they deserved the right to bear it in compensation for services rendered. Indeed, it was customary to confer these on foreign magistrates to thank them according to their mandate or as if they were given to them in a ceremony that confers the knighthood in the name of the Florentine people. In a desperate effort to reconcile their knightly tradition and their peaceful mercantile occupations, many of them wanted to become *milites populi.*

This aspiration, however, is better seen in the language of signs—heraldic, anthroponomic—than in the speeches themselves. The majority of magnates who wished to normalize their situation as citizens after 1350 kept a low profile. Their speech presented them as nothing more than popolani, men with nothing exceptional about them, who dreamed of nothing more than being able to disappear into the masses. How do they perceive these masses? Their basic vocabulary rests upon the notion of peace: They talk about peaceful personal occupations and quiet relationships with others; their vision of the social world in which they evolve is consensual. These would be the foundations of their reformed behavior, close to the way of living of the popolani, thus worthy of the popularitas. These people do not want to be members of a feared minority; they aspire to become part of the peace-loving majority. In sum, they want to be good merchants, citizens with no past(s), men who wear the people's coat of arms, not only on their shields (as do the proudest of them), but also in their hearts.

Let us listen to some of them. Geri, son of Arriguccio degli Agli, set the tone in 1355: "He lives and intends always to live in a peaceful manner, tranquil and of the people; and it is well known that he exercised his profession in a way common to all the other artisans of the city."[20] Others added an important reason: to become popolani when one is already so in heart and in manners, to renounce explicitly the *mores magnatum*,[21] allows for a better defense of one's heritage. Few expressed this hope as bluntly as, in 1372, the tutors of Giovanni di Francesco "Cipolla" Adimari, a little boy of seven who finds himself alone in the world. When these tutors asked that he be granted the status of a popolano, it is "because the affairs of those who are known as magnates are not treated as favorably as the affairs of the popolani, which are handled, thanks to the Ordonnances of the Commune, in a more favorable atmosphere."[22]

Another group distinguished itself by the humility with which they asked to become popolani. Their voices were hushed, sometimes plaintive, a sharp contrast to the arrogant tone or the conformity of the majority of demands. In the most neutral form, at least in appearance, the discourse of this group put forward as a pretext the decline of a lineage once strong in numbers. From 1325 on, the decadence or the ruin of ten magnate lineages in the city and twenty-five others in the contado justified, according to Vallani, their massive admission to the popolo. This argument was taken up by the Visdomini, for example, who together presented a nearly unanimous demand to receive their status of popolano in 1372 and then received it on the basis of the argument that they constituted a danger "neither in number nor in wealth."[23] In 1369, the Gianfigliazzi also claimed they were in a state of "exhaustion of wealth and of people, due to their bad fortune as much as to the very favors granted to them by the people and the commune of Florence, an exhaustion so complete that it might qualify them to join the ranks of the powerless or weak popolani."[24] Five members of the Mannelli, another magnate lineage, watched all their cousins acquire the status of popolano but were passed over by this measure because they were regarded "as powerless people not even worth mentioning [to receive this privilege] by reason of their debasement."[25]

Individually, the magnates marginal in their own families also petitioned to join the popolani into which they are assimilated by their weakness. The most frequent case of marginality is the isolation within the very status of being a magnate. Many of them found themselves the only representatives of their lineage or their branch in the ranks of the magnates and used this argument to rejoin their cousins in the popolani.[26] Weakness due to age sometimes adds to the isolation of being without kin. Such were the arguments for orphaned children such as Gherardo di Guccio Nerli, a *puer* whose father had shown that he had a peace-loving spirit,[27] or Niccolo di Francesco della Foresta, another little boy of seven, who, "almost all the nearest of his lineage and his house" having already acquired the status of popolano, promised to behave like a good popolano upon reaching adulthood.[28] If marginality often resulted when relatives were already among the ranks of the popolani, it could also be the result of disagreement with cousins or of poverty and the weakness that are its consequences. Rinieri di Donato Tedaldini saw himself "in a way completely helpless and completely lacking in the favor of his kin or consorts."[29] A bastard of the Cerchi who worked in the humble profession of clog maker claimed his undesirable condition and his poverty as reasons to join the popolo,[30] just as did a lanifex, who, despite the name Frescobaldi, "was weak and helpless due to his maternal line."[31] The Bostichi consider themselves "people long without power and not really magnates, let us say even more so than all the little people by their intentions and their power; for they earn their living by the sweat of their brow as honestly as possible, being licensed as wine merchants."[32]

Whether they put forward their intentions to behave well or to have particular vulnerability or whether they considered themselves merchants, poor artisans, or deposed nobles, all these people presented a negative image of what the word *magnate* meant to their contemporaries in order to obtain the desired privilege: an excessive sense of honor, a belligerent spirit, a propensity to quarrel with their neighbors, the refusal to submit their economic activities to the restrictions of the Arte, solidarity with groups having too many relatives, excessive urgency, turbulence, and disorder in the management of their estate and their life. Conversely, the proclaimed intention was to "live like a [popolano], a peaceful man, a merchant."[33] What better recognition of civic and mercantile ideals, even in the old families of magnates, than the retainer voted in favor of a certain Tornaquinci! In changing his status, the priors maintained that they were rewarding "the purity of his loyalty, the seriousness of his morals, and the prudence he shows in everything."[34] It is true that, according to the chronicler (and magnate) Giovanni Cavalcanti, the Tornaquinci, "the most noble" of Florentine families, were "in their morals more soft than robust, men a little sleepy and timid."[35]

Let us note that few statements remain that refer to explicitly hostile reactions, within the group of magnates, to the movement that brought many of them to adopt a language contrary to their traditions. Even if they did so, was it not without hidden intentions? In 1430 the sons of Andrea di

Rinaldo da Ricasoli were granted the status of popolani. They emphasized the spirit of enterprise they acquired in childhood and their devotion to the Florentine populus. Their father is not involved in their petition. Luigi Passerini, author of the nineteenth-century history of this family, interpreted the father's abstention as an explicit refusal to accept the advantages of popolo status and as loyalty to a noble ideal, "the quiet awareness of not debasing oneself by refuting the noble blood that runs in his veins."[36] But this late judgment, felt through centuries of the building-up and collapsing of the Tuscan nobility, was not perhaps that of Andrea da Ricasoli. For who, if not he, could have prepared the supplication of his sons, all minors at this time?[37] Although Andrea, like many other magnates, had to count upon a division of personal positions to secure the future of his sons in the ranks of the popolani while retaining his own status, this did not bar him from occupying important functions of regional command and from keeping up his connections of *consorteria.*

From Magnates to Nobles, an Inversion of the Medieval Scheme

The third kind of discourse on the magnates is the historical and genealogical account or juridical rationalization that some of them used concerning themselves. They devoted themselves to it, especially after they were rehabilitated as popolani, a status acquired, for the great majority of them, with the return of Cosimo the Elder in 1434. Later, once the court of the Grand Duke aspired to surround itself with a nobility similar to that of other countries, the magnates continued these accounts in order to justify their entry into the ranks of the new nobility. From the end of the fourteenth century and into the beginning of the fifteenth, we see, therefore, that many Florentines worked with the idea that the reputation of nobility rested upon the antiquity and continuity of lineage that linked ancestors without dubious gaps—an idea, J. Boutier justly reminds us,[38] that will remain valid in the modern reexamination of the criteria for nobility in Florence.

Let us return to master Lapo da Castiglionchio, from whence we started. In his "Epistola" to his son, written in the 1370s, this important member of the very conservative and aristocratic Parte Guelfa wished to justify the nobility of his family in a city where there was no univocal definition of nobility and where the *plebei* ran the state. His position was even more delicate, as his family, of authentic feudal origins, was related to

Ghibelines declared to be magnates. Descendants of the ancient lords of Cuona, the Castiglionchio attained their autonomy and later adopted this name to distinguish themselves from the branch that became Ghibelines under the name of da Volognano. The first remain popolani after 1293; the Volognano were labeled as magnates until 1434. Lord Lapo could not challenge the nobility of people like the Volognano, the consorts of whom bear common ancestry with him, without challenging his own. How did he manage to set apart the two branches, the Guelf and the Ghibeline, the popolani and the magnates? His son worried about the near extinction of his own family. "Our race," responds the father, "has aged and lost its strength well before those who are noble today even came into being."[39] From number, which makes strength, is born presumptuousness, which predisposed one to become Ghibeline and, later, to become a magnate. He proceeds to explain that the Florentines destroyed the castle of Cuona "because the Cuona, on account of their riches, possessions, villages and vassals were made great and powerful; and the branch today called da Volognano were more powerful than the branch today called da Castiglionchio because they were more numerous and had more possessions, and were more wicked and harmful. Their power and arrogance pushed them into turpitude and homicides to impose their tyranny upon the countryside."[40] Those destined to remain popolani, the da Castiglionchio, far from giving themselves over to the misdeeds of their consorts, "were modest and mild people." Lapo looked, therefore, at the old magnate consorts of his own family through the perspective commonly used to define them in the thirteenth century. At the time when the Parte Guelfa, of which he was one of the active captains, devoted itself to hunting down Ghibelines, it was not detrimental to him if he shook off his burdensome relatives, exaggerating their traits as needed.

An anonymous chronicler of the Tornaquinci family, writing about the same time, did not have the same problem. He put together a few family traditions and dissected various documents concerning its lineage, which was never tainted by Ghibelinism and which indeed did not fail to be of the good party of black Guelf.[41] Many of its numerous branches did choose to join the people (under various names), but only while maintaining a certain complicity with the old Tornaquinci and their other separated cousins. This anonymous person, who wrote at a time when the first magnate in this family stepped forward and crossed the threshold to join the people, did not report the divisions and clashes in this wide group of relatives. His entire work consisted, on the contrary, of putting forward an image of unity that was not erased by the dispersion of branches and of rights. And no more than Lapo da Castiglionchio did he boast of their incredible antiquity, a nation which will nourish, from the end of the fifteenth century, the imagined idea of the old families, the *famiglie,* as they began to be known, to designating the lineages of very old stock. With the Tornaquinci, we observe, rather, a progressive absorption into a political community, a gentle integration that allowed every chance for their beneficiaries in the era of the Grand Duke to take their place in the new Florentine nobility. Without either effacing or renouncing their membership in the community but instead taking advantage of it (for the Tornaquinci were already in the priorate from 1282 to 1292), they could have argued that if they could not occupy those high offices, which was the decisive criterion determining nobility, it was their status as magnates that made it impossible after the Ordonnances. Unlike Lapo da Castiglionchio, who as a popolano could count all his ancestors and relatives, who were priors or judiciary gonfaloniers since the end of the thirteenth century, the Tornaquinci became like other ancient magnates, obliged in the sixteenth to eighteenth centuries to put forward their nobility, which became an impediment because they were then obligated to prove, in a somewhat absurd fashion, that their nobility was often more ancient than that of the "powerful popolani who had held the reins" of power in the city during the fourteenth century.

Later, as a pretext, some will cite magnate ascendancy, although none existed, in order to explain not having attained higher offices in the communal government. In this way the da Filicaia vindicated an honorable antiquity of 600 years for their family while recognizing that they could not count priors among them because they were descended from magnates.[42] Sometimes, on the contrary, they were explicitly exempted from having this label attached to their consorts who became magnates, as the (Tedaldi) delta Vitella, whom the most ancient rolls recognized was independent, *"popolani et chase per se"*! With a certain artfulness they doubtless hid the fact that if they did not attain the priorate from its beginnings in the fourteenth century, it was because that office interested them less than commerce or the lucrative positions in higher administration.[43] In their own manner they prolonged the ambiguous process of Andrea de Ricasoli, mentioned above, who played all the angles. Henceforth, they would completely reverse the stigma of the condition of magnate.

In the process of recuperating the rights of the active citizen or the entry into the nobility of the grand duchy, the use of the position of magnate allowed, therefore, a complete reversal of argumentation. For a long time, magnates who wished to collaborate with the popular regime fought to refute the image that people had of them, arguing their conformity to the reigning model in the mercantile society. In the princely and courtly context of the early modern period, the "negative privileges" of the old magnates changed in meaning. Becoming positive, they helped to constitute a new group enclosed within its specific characteristics, a minority to be sure, but not an imposed one: a consensual minority.

NOTES

1. *Epistola a sia ragionamento di Messer Lapo da Castiglionchio,* L. Mehus, ed. (Bologna, 1753), 25–26. C. Donati, *L'idea di nobilità in Italia, Secoli XIV–XVIII* (Bari, 1988).

2. N. Rubinstein, "Le origini della legge sul sodamento," *Archivio storico italiano* 96 (1939): 5–57, in particular 7–8, in which French expressions of the end of the twelfth century are quoted, such as "*regni proceres aliosque magnates,*" and German and Catalan texts ("*magnatibus seu militibus*").

3. G. Salvemini, *Magnati e popolani in Firenze dal 1280 al 1295* (Florence, 1899; rev.: Milan, 1966). N. Ottokar, *Comune di Firenze alla fine del Dugento* (Florence, 1926; rev.: Turin, 1962). N. Rubinstein, "La lotta contra i magnati a Firenze. I: La prima legge sul 'sodamento' e la pace del cardinale Latino," *Archivio storico italiano* 93 (1935): 161–72, and "Le origini della legge sul 'sodamento.'"

4. To repeat Donato Giannotti, cited by Salvemini, *Magnati e popolani* (1966 ed.), 21. The text of Giannotti is published by Giovanni Silvano, *Repubblica fiorentina: A Critical Edition and Introduction* (Geneva: Bibliothèque d'humanisme et Renaissance, 1990, 237), 94.

5. C. Lansing, *The Florentine Magnates: Lineage and Faction in a Medieval Commune* (Princeton, 1991).

6. Rubinstein, "Le origini."

7. Salvemini, *Magnati e popolani;* S. Raveggi, M. Tarasi, D. Medici, and R. Parenti, *Ghibellini, Guelfi e Popolo grasso. I detentori del potere politico a Firenze nella seconda meta del Dugento* (Florence, 1978).

8. Cf. M. Becker, *Florence in Transition,* 2 vols. (Baltimore, 1967–68).

9. M. Kriegel locates, in the central Middle Ages, the logic of a politics of states placing the Jewish communities at their service and wonders: "The conjuncture of a social insertion *negatively privileged* and of the exercise of defined economic functions justifies referring to the notion of a caste" or, rather, "of a group forming a caste in the interior of society organized according to principles of stratification different from those which govern the societies of caste."

10. R. C. Trexler, *Public Life in Renaissance Florence* (New York, 1980).

11. C. Klapisch-Zuber, "Vrais et faux magnats. L'application des Ordonnances de justice au XIVe siècle," *Atti del XV Convegno internazionale di studi Magnati e popolani nell'Italia comunale* (Pistoia, 15–18 mad) (1995).

12. I will refer on this point to the "Dossier florentin du XIVe siècle" which Michel Pastoureau and I have commented on in *Annales, E.S.C.* 5, no. 2a (1988): 1205–56.

13. Cf. also the analysis of complaints against the rural magnates in C. Carduff, "Magnati e popolani net contado fiorentino: dinamiche sociali e rapporti di potere net Trecento," *Rivista di storia dell'agricoltura*, a. 33, no. 2 (1993): 15–63.

14. "Riconosci la vita per noi zozzo ladro traditore che tu sei," from the Bardi to the Rignano (Archivo di Stato, Florence (NB: all archival documents), *Esecutore degli ordinamenti di giustizia* (henceforth abbreviated as *EOJ*), 119 bis, Feb. 6, 1349); "sieno morti questi traditori," from the Rossi to the Castelfiorentino (*EOJ* 119 bis, f. 24, Jan. 24, 1349); "Traditore, e' chonvene ch'io t'uccida," from Conti Guidi, to Pieve a Cascia (*EOJ* 1566, f. 4, June 20, 1405); "Traditore, ladro che tu sia," from Frescobaldi (*EOJ* 1566 f. 15, Sept. 26, 1405).

15. "Io farò pure stratio di lore contadinni," from Luco Badia (*EOJ* 500, f. 5, Dec. 10, 1366). Threats of delta Tosa, Dec. 29, 1344, against a curate: "Se tu entrarai e qua noti passarò dall'atro lato con questa lancia" (*EOJ* 21, f69).

16. A Petriolo, "Manichiamo e beviamo e ghiastemiamo chi il'a guadagniato" (*EOJ* 802 bis, f. 213v, Dec. 5, 1377).

17. "Traditore, ladro che tu sia, Io son magiore de te e non c'è persona che contra à mi dicesse nulla io t'ociderò" (*EOJ* 1566 f. 15v, Sept. 26, 1405).

18. "A Ferrara non a popolo, sozo cane" (*EOJ* 21, f. 65, Nov. 25, 1344).

19. "Noi abbiamo già piu volte rotto il popolo di Firenze, bene possiamo rompere sicuramente quello de Santo Cristofano in Perticaia" (*EOJ,* 119 bis, Feb. 6, 1349).

20. "Semper tamen vixit et vivere intendit pacifice populariter et quiete, et prout omnibus est notorium a pueritia sue exercuit et exercet artem more aliorum artificum popularium de civitate predicta" (*Provvisioni, Registri* [Hereafter, *Prov.*] 42, f Feb. 26, 1355).

21. *Prov.* 70, f 62v, June 7, 1381, petition of money changers Francesco and Matteo di Agnolo Cavalcanti.

22. "Quia negotia eorum qui dicuntur magnates non eo favore tractantur sicut sunt negotia populairum qui per ordinamenta Communis favorabilius prosequuntur" (*Prov.* 60, f. 25v–26r, June 8, 1372). What one reads in the petition of ser Giovanni di ser Domenico Foraboschi may also be read in watermark: "ut dictam suam artem liberius exercere possit" (*Prov.* 72, f. 158v, Oct. 21, 1383).

23. ". . . divitiis et personis" (Prov 60, f. 128r-v). They take as their name *Cortigiani* on Feb. 5, 1373 (*Capitol*), Registri 22, f. 1v.

24. "Sunt tum ob varios fortune casus tum etiam ob gratias a populo et com-

muni florentinis factas olim quibusdam de domo predicta ita extrenuati [*sic*] viribus et personis quod merito possum in numero impotentum et debilium popularium aggregari" (*Prov.* 57, f. 12v, June 7, 1369).

25. "Veluti homines impotentes et de quibus propter eorum vilitate nulla mentio facta fait" (*Prov.* 54, f. 101v–102r, Dec. 29, 1366).

26. Tomaquinci, Dec. 9, 1385 (*Prov.* 74, f. 203r), della Tosa, Jan. 24, 1365 (*Prov.* 52, f. 110r–v; *Prov.* 58, f. 10v, Oct. 24, 1370). G. Brucker, *Florentine Politics and Society, 1343–1378* (Princeton, 1962), 156, wrongly asserts that all the Tosinghi were made populani in 1370. Instead, the applicant of the document of 1370, Simone di Baldo, alleges simply that "omnes ipsius Simonis consortes fuerint et sint populares . . . et solum dictus S. et duo eius nepotes . . . hodie sint et reperiantur descripti pro magnatibus" (*Prov.* 59, f. 261 rev, March 23, 1372).

27. "Stare intendit ad artem et in mercantiarum exercitio vivere et mori intendit ut quicumque pacificus artifex et mercator, similiterque eius peter quiete vixit" (*Prov.* 70, f. 56v, June 7, 1381).

28. "Quasi omnes de sue progenie et domo sunt populares" (*Prov.* 74, f. 203v, Dec. 9, 1385).

29. "Et sit quodammodo omnino impotens et omni favore consanquineorum et seu consortium totaliter destitutus" (*Prov.* 70, f. 71r, June 21, 1381).

30. *Prov.* 39, f. 177r–v, July 27, 1352: a petition of Agnolo, voc. bastardo, di Gianni Cerchi, "artificis pauperis in arte et ministerio chalzolarie seu zoccholarie."

31. *Prov.* 60, f. 129 rev, Dec. 21, 1372: a petition of Ippolito di m. Guglielmino. C76 Brucker, *Florentine Politics,* 155.

32. "Persone diutius impotentes et nedum actualiter magnates, quin ymo animo et potentia plus quam parvuli et de sudore vultus eorum in hiis que honeste possum et presertim circa artem vinacteriorum in qua matriculati sunt" (*Prov.* 59, f. 235v, Feb. 23, 1372).

33. "Populariter et pacifice et mercantiliter vixerunt," *Prov.* 59, f. 250v, March 10, 1372, petition of Ghirigoro et Niccolo di Pagnozzo Tornaquinci.

34. "Quantaque puritate fidei morum gravitate et ex omni parse prudentia . . . cognoscentes . . . et ob id eius vitam laudabilem re munerare volentes et eius consorti o populum agumentare" (*Prov.* 51, f. 147v, May 29, 1364, concerns one Niccolo di Ghino, who took the name Popoleschi).

35. ". . . costumi mansueti più che robusti; . . . huomini sopnolenti et timidi." M. Grendler, ed., *The "Trattato politico-morale" of Giovanni Cavalcanti (1381–c. 1451). A Critical Edition and Interpretation* (Geneva: Droz, 1974); *Travaux d'humanisme et Renaissance* 135:104.

36. *Prov.* 120, f 472v–473v, Feb. 4, 1430: "Tranquillo nella conscienza di non essersi avvilito a mentire l'illustre sangue che scorreva nelle sue vene" (L. Passerini, *Genealogia e storia della famiglia da Ricasoli* [Florence, 1861]).

37. The oldest, Rinieri, was thirteen; the youngest, four.

38. J. Boutier, *Anatomie d'une noblesse urbaine. Florence, 16e–18e siècles* (Paris, 1995).

39. "Ancora, come appresso leggerai, questa tua origine se nobile fu, è si invecchiata, che quasi è venuta in oblivione; e quasi la nostra progenie prima invecchiata et estenuata fu, che molti che oggi sono nobili, avessero principio: e per tanto conviene a te fare pensiero e proposito per tua virtù ritrovarla" (*Epistola,* 9 and 51).

40. "Perciocchè i detti da Cuona per le dette loro castella, tenute, e ville, e fedeli erano fatti grandi et potenti: e il detto lato che oggi si chiama da Volognano, era assai più possente che l'altro lato, che oggi si chiama da Castiglionchio: perocchè erano più delle persone, et aveano più tenute, ed erano più maligni et malferati. E per loro potenza e superbia cominciarono a fare delle cose sconcie, omicidj, forze et tirannie per lo paese" (Ibid., 33–34).

41. Florence, Biblioteca Riccardiana, ms. 1885. G. Pampaloni, "I Tornaquinci poi Tornabuoni fino al primi del Cinquccento," *ASI,* 126 (1968), 331–62. P. Simons, "Portraiture and Patronage in Quattrocento Florence with Specific Reference to the Tornaquinci and Their Chapel in S. Maria Novella" (Ph.D. diss., Melbourne, 1985).

42. Boutier, *Anatomic d'une noblesse,* chap. 1.

43. L. Martines, *The Social World of the Florentine Humanists, 1390–1460* (Princeton, 1963), 217–18 (with minor errors); Brucker, *Florentine Politics,* 383n.

Imagining the Huguenot Minority in Old Regime France

David D. Bien

This is, in one sense, an essay on a nontopic. Officially there was no Calvinist minority in eighteenth-century France. By relentless action from the 1670s to the 1720s the state could declare that it had eradicated the practice of Calvinism from the country. That practice, tolerated since the Edict of Nantes (1598) in regions where the Huguenots lived, was ended by the Revocation of that edict in 1685. Tough penal laws made it a capital crime to be a pastor in France or to attend a forbidden Calvinist assembly bearing arms. Merely being at such an assembly could bring life on the galleys. Calvinist writings were proscribed, and henceforth to enter an office or any of a number of occupations (law, medicine, and midwifery among them) required a certificate proving one's Catholicism. An ambiguity in the Revocation—whose last article seemed to provide for freedom of conscience if nothing else—was removed in 1715 by another edict stating flatly that all French subjects were Catholics. In the administrative records the Protestants were now, and until 1789, called "New Converts." Simply living in France was evidence of Catholicism, and the failure to perform as a Catholic reflected not conscience but backsliding and rebellion. Anyone who refused the last sacrament of the Church died a relapsed heretic whose body was subject to desecration and property to seizure. The only recognized marriage being Catholic, couples married surreptitiously by a pastor rather than a priest were not legally married at all; they lived in concubinage, their children bastards and as such ineligible to inherit their parents' estates. Married or not, New Converts had to have their newborn baptized by the parish priest within a day of their birth, and to raise their children as Catholics under pain of having them taken away at age seven. Calvinists, then, unlike the Jews or the Lutherans in Alsace, were not a defined minority; they were only Catholics whose behavior demanded especially careful surveillance by the state and clergy.[1]

For all that, there were Calvinists in France, and everyone knew it. Their number is difficult to count. Estimates place them at 15 percent of the total population early, less than 10 percent at the time of the Revocation, 5 percent in 1700, and perhaps 2 to 3 percent in 1789. Probably the pressures of law and actual violence against the Protestants in some regions thinned their ranks, and 200,000 or so emigrated between 1685 and 1715.[2] The solid base of the organized Calvinism that survived the persecution was rural and peasant, and its outline is fairly clear. Those Calvinists were concentrated mainly in the south, in a large semicircle starting in Dauphiné and the Vivarais to the east, extending through Languedoc almost to the Mediterranean, and from there west and north into Aquitaine and Poitou. These were *religionnaires* who violated the laws by consorting with pastors and attending the assemblies in remote places (in the "desert," it was said). They stood in sharp contrast to the urban Calvinists who engaged in what the English called "occasional conformity." More visible to the authorities as individuals, they often did the minimum that the law required, marrying as Catholics (even if sometimes secretly as Calvinists as well) and having their children baptized by a priest. Some became *avocats* and *procureurs* by presenting certificates of Catholicism acquired from a friendly cleric or one who took money under the table. These Calvinists avoided most contact with pastors and stayed away from the assemblies. Their worship was inconspicuous—they met quietly with one another in small, informal groups in their homes where they read the psalms and scripture behind closed shutters. This worship, of course, left no records, and it was far from easy to distinguish such Calvinists from the Jansenists who took communion only rarely, and from the religiously indifferent who did not appear regularly in the churches either. The number of Calvinists, then, is uncertain, and they could have been somewhat more numerous than is commonly thought. Many, perhaps most, Catholics in the south had a good chance of knowing one or more of them.

It was fortunate for the Protestants that Catholics did not usually impute to them as individuals all the antisocial traits that the sect more generally evoked. The image of Calvinism in the minds of administrators, magistrates, and the overwhelming Catholic majority was always negative and at times frightening. The words and terms that the Protestant sect evoked were resistance to authority, rebellion, anarchy, "republicanism," "democracy," state within the state, sedition, treason. To those, add especially "fanaticism," a word that took on its modern meaning only in the later seventeenth century. The picture was rooted most obviously in a selective reading of history. Catholic observers disregarded the pastors' and synods' repeated professions of fidelity to king and state, and seemed not to notice that the Calvinists generally did not participate in the provincial rebellions of the early seventeenth century. What Catholics saw in Calvinism instead was its unalterably seditious essence that, they thought, caused the long religious wars of the sixteenth century. The period from the 1560s to 1598 was marked by the horrors—the terror, arson, pillage, and murderous depredations of foreign armies intervening freely—that civil wars always produce (Vietnam, Lebanon, and Bosnia come readily to mind). That period (together with the feudal "anarchy" of the ninth and tenth centuries, and perhaps parts of the Hundred Years War) was thought the worst in French history. Popular histories in eighteenth-century almanacs (read by "the least learned and most credulous of men," according to Malesherbes) told how the spread of Protestantism, "lit by a false principle of religion," brought nothing but "massacre, burnings, sacrileges."[3] Catholics would remember how Protestants advanced high-sounding constitutionalist ideas to cover their dark intentions after Saint Bartholomew's Day in 1572: Calvinists talked then of contract, the king under law, a kind of popular sovereignty implying a right to resistance, and tyrannicide, but what they really meant was faction, destruction, and regicide. Looking back from the later seventeenth century and after, Catholics noted that Protestants, holed up in La Rochelle and in league with the British, had still been making trouble as late as 1628. No wonder that the Calvinists were like that, of course, considering that their discipline and organization were built on consistories and synods operating by elections, taking votes, majority rule, laymen involved in making decisions, all the trappings of a republic. For confirmation of its necessary outcome one had only to look at England in the mid–seventeenth century to see how Calvinism led to civil war and also beheaded a king before establishing a republic called the Commonwealth.

From those dangers, then, what evidently saved France was a series of strong kings and the absolute state. The heroic and charismatic Henri IV came first, though unfortunately he had to compromise. By the Edict of Nantes he permitted establishment of Europe's only religiously pluralist regime in the seventeenth century. That regime, however, reflected circumstances, not the principle of toleration. The state on its own was still too weak to keep order and to enforce peace everywhere, and so it had to entrust arms and power to Calvinists in cities where Protestants predominated. But that arrangement was only temporary. With Louis XIV, the state was at last strong enough to achieve what was needed. Catholics, with lingering fears over real and recent threats to the still fragile state, applauded when Louis XIV launched the plan to eliminate French Calvinism. Toleration was no sign of progress. With victory the state could end faction and declare the minority nonexistent.

The initiative for the persecution of the Huguenots in the later seventeenth century and after came from above. It seems not to have emerged from popular hatreds. At the level of actual interactions, face to face, between Protestants and Catholics in regions where Calvinists lived, the relations in fact seem to have been rather good, at least until the 1670s. Gregory Hanlon has studied in detail communities west of Montauban where the two confessions coexisted. There were quarrels, but also cross-confessional marriages and godparenting, inheritance, shared wedding feasts, patterns of lending irrespective of religion, joint participation in gambling or dancing or carnival. Later, when royal policy excluded Protestants from judgeships and access to nobility, the two elites were increasingly differentiated, with the better-off Calvinists being deflected into trade. But in daily life, an atmosphere of de facto tolerance was at first normal.[4] It was in the state and within the elite more broadly that the idea of the Calvinist menace sharpened and spread. At the center of the perceived threat were unknown people in unregulated and proscribed corps, distant, evoking fears of hidden conspiracies in a largely opaque peasant society. Perhaps the conspiracies were inspired by the state's foreign enemies. The other Calvinists, in cities, conformed to the law at least outwardly and did not comprise collectivities. They were individuals with names and faces. The two parts of Calvinism seemed to call for separate treatment: the one, organized, was thought nonassimilable and could require the use of military force; the other was subject to legal and administrative pressures to assimilate individuals.

At this point one might say that, if the images were accurate, the Catholic elite's mind-set needs no further analysis. Catholics simply saw the minority clearly. That is not altogether wrong, but it does omit an important if disturbing fact, namely, that persecution can impart to its victims the very qualities that its architects supposed those victims to possess all along. Voltaire understood the mechanism. He favored a policy of toleration because sects, left alone, would forget their differences based on revealed, and therefore unverifiable, truths. Louis XIV and his state, however, made a fateful error with the Calvinists: by persecuting, they returned prideful Huguenots to old beliefs and restored the seditious essence that they had been close to outgrowing.[5] Voltaire's point can perhaps be extended sociologically. The penal laws against organized Calvinism fragmented the Huguenot community along the lines suggested above. The result was to eliminate from leadership in that community the security-conscious urban members who were wealthier and educated, and who might have played a moderating role. In addition, when the state started to hang some of the pastors, it drove the rest, the older and stable spiritual leaders, out of France. Even in the countryside the better-off Protestants—the notables and all with something to lose—mimicked their urban brethren by avoiding regular contact with what was left of organized Calvinism. This left a large stratum of the poorest Huguenots, downwardly mobile artisans and peasants become farm laborers, on their own. They were illiterate and trapped in place—Protestant employers in the two cities where the Calvinists were important, Montauban and Nîmes, did not often hire their co-religionists lest they draw attention to their own religion. In the War of the Spanish Succession, a time of economic misery for most of the population, the Protestant poor were especially miserable. They were harassed by the clergy and the object of renewed military repression, the famous *dragonnades,* that was no less brutal for being episodic. Into this explosive social and religious mix came *prédicants* to fill the leadership vacuum in part. They were enthusiasts, sometimes teenagers, drawn from the same social milieu as their followers. When these local "prophets," unkempt and equally illiterate, began to have eschatological visions and to walk through flames as proof they possessed the Holy Spirit, the Huguenot lower class responded in a holy war against the whole oppressive order of religion, politics, and economy. This was the Camisard rebellion in which a ragged army of rebels numbering sometimes up to three or four thousand roamed the Cévennes region, the rough and hilly country north of Nîmes. Supported by foreign money, the Camisards tied up royal armed forces from 1702 to 1704, and with guerrilla operations even to 1710.

And so, the "Protestants" acted just like many Catholics expected and feared. Lacking "respectable" leadership, they looked filthy, murderous, fanatical, frightening. Predictably they rebelled and linked up with the English and Dutch enemy at a time when terrible weather, disease, economic crisis, and invasion from outside appeared close to destroying France. Memories of what the Camisard rebels did and the treason they represented revived old Catholic fears and froze an image that lasted through the eighteenth century. Calvinism meant subversion. It is worth emphasizing, however, that the survival of that image was owing to the symbiosis between Catholic expectations of Calvinism that led to its repression, on the one hand, and the wild and violent reaction to that repression by one section of the Calvinists, on the other. In short, the image held by Catholics came first and was self-validating; it generated the conditions for the behavior on which it fed.

This takes us back to the Catholic authorities and the elite that were ready to believe the worst of the Protestants. Many of the Catholics who were receptive to such beliefs were cultivated, rational, even "secularist," and they would have been shocked at being thought bigots. How, then, to explain the resonance of anti-Protestantism among them and their direct or tacit approval of various degrees of persecution? Here the traditions already discussed, from the sixteenth-century religious wars to the eighteenth-century Camisards, are less the explanation than what needs to be explained. It may help now to turn to three long-term processes that broadly conditioned the minds of elites, from the middle of the seventeenth century through the eighteenth. These processes—they had nothing to do with the Protestants explicitly—gave rise to new ways of seeing, thinking, and defining the "normal." The new ways were "modern," though it will become clear that modernity of that kind was not always favorable to the Calvinists.

The first process, the growth in "scientific" understanding and the secularization that was its by-product, is well known in its broad outlines. Through the sixteenth century the old Aristotelian vision of nature disappeared only very slowly. That vision was of a full world where objects and inert bodies had souls, sorcerers used rituals and potions to ward off threats, talismans blocked the effects of curses, and so on. Nature and supernature ran together in a universe run by beings and things rather than laws. The great mental change came in the course of the seventeenth century when a nature full of good and evil wills and exceptions gave way to Cartesian nature that worked by invariable, mathematical laws. Motion, for example, once supposed circular in the heavens (symbolizing perfection) but linear on earth (reflecting "contraries"), was henceforth the same everywhere in the universe. The regular and unvarying operation of laws in the material world became an accepted idea among the educated, an assumption no longer requiring discussion or debate.[6]

But what did the change mean for religion? The orderliness and uniformity of nature, its design, could be taken as assurance that God as creator exists. Christianity, however, was something else. The mere existence of a creator did not easily establish truths about the suspensions of nature or miracles essential to the Christian story. Thus, in a Cartesian universe believers would necessarily find Christianity more mysterious, inscrutable, ineffable than before. For most, Christianity was not less true, but the operations of its God in saving human beings were distant and unverifiable; more and more, Christianity required a leap of faith by its adherents. It was a leap that nearly all Christians made with rather less effort than skeptics might suppose. But what is important for our story in this development is that the new ideas supposed a nature from which it would be difficult to extract the details about how God acted to save human beings. Did he do it the way the Catholics said? or Calvinists? or Anabaptists? or still others? Who could tell? In the end the old and burning question of grace lost meaning when the evidence to treat it evaporated. It was better to accept truths in that sphere by faith or tradition without puzzling too much over what could not be proved, and to think that a good and honest life would somehow have a happy ending. With such simple assumptions it was not hard to be a Catholic if French (or an Anglican, if English; a Lutheran, if German; and so on). Old differences in doctrine mattered less among the vast majority of persons who nonetheless remained Christian.

And yet, there were the French Calvinists apparently making a fuss over those small differences, insisting on unknowable truths about how God works and assembling illegally to attest them. Why could they not be like the rest of their countrymen? The answer, within the mental framework of evolving Catholic attitudes, was that the Calvinists were not thinking about religion at all. Having compartmentalized revealed religion in their own increasingly scientific understanding, eighteenth-century Catholics, when they noticed the Calvinists at all, would suppose that their illegal actions were inspired by political, social, or economic motives. In that respect the motives imputed to Protestants were exactly those imputed to fellow Catholics, except that in the Protestants they were inverted. Secularized Catholics wanted peace, order, prosperity; secularized Calvinists, by refusing so simple a thing as accepting what the law prescribed, showed that they were merely using religion to hide their real interest in disorder, subversion, rebellion. The prosecutor at the Parlement of Toulouse stated this durable idea directly when, in 1745, he asked the court to condemn a Protestant writing. Referring to "unknown people" raising their "rebellious heads" while the king's troops were away, he stated the need to stop the "seditious undertakings of those who seek to sow trouble and division in the state under the pretext of religion."[7] Religion was pretext, and subversion the real motive. The situation for the Protestant minority, therefore, remained precarious even in the age of *lumières,* science, and secularism.

The other two processes were parts of the vast early modern European effort to control and reorder society through pedagogy. Codes were proposed to teach civility to nobles or more elegant behavior to bourgeois, the army established small training units (companies, platoons) to condition soldiers to respond automatically to orders, and so on. The processes important here, however, were the educating of the upper and middle classes in the new *collèges* and the reform of Catholicism and the clergy. In both several tendencies that might loosely be called Cartesian converged: one was toward uniformity, homogenization, interchangeability; another involved individualizing, breaking down old unregulated groupings, decomposing and then recomposing, reconstituting hierarchies on objective criteria. The tendencies, if never fully realized, nonetheless supplied new models and unconscious ways of perceiving that accentuated distrust of certain kinds of corps and favored a view of individuals as assimilable. The significance for the images of Huguenots was considerable.

In the sixteenth century and after, the collèges spread through France, educating ever-larger parts of the old and new elites. The influence of the collèges was of course visible at one level in language and styles of expression tied to the immersion of the young in Latin and the classics. But the more important effect for our purpose came from the discipline that the collèges applied to boys starting from age ten or so. That discipline, set out before 1600 by the Jesuits, eventually infused schools of all kinds and, I think, profoundly shaped a persisting French sense of self and community. The essence of the discipline lay in *émulation,* which means competition between equals to attain some position in a rank order based on achievement or merit. Competition was thought crucial for embedding work habits and ambition in students. To energize the system, rankings had to be public and regular, making known the degrees of pride and humiliation individual students should feel. In a class of nineteen, for example, all should know where each stood; to be tenth meant looking up with respect to nine, and down with a certain contempt on the other nine. This would inculcate in students a healthy striving to rise above others in the scale. The system's conscious aim was to isolate individuals and to break down informal community, an effect reinforced in the collèges by the use of monitors and student spies to report signs of cabal. Students in unsupervised groups were always objects of suspicion. One might suggest that the habits deriving from years of experience in the schools, when carried into the larger society, contributed to forming subjects who could live easily under the new absolute state. Perhaps the elites' internalization of individualism and the undivided community implicit in émulation contributed as much to ending rebellions and disorders in the seventeenth century as did the growth in state power that is more commonly invoked. Such speculation aside, the formation in schools was consistent with fear of informal and unregulated corps like organized Calvinism, and with the evaluation of peaceable Calvinist individuals on their personal merits, as if Catholics.[8]

The third process involved the simultaneous growth in state power and Catholic reform. The two were intimately connected. That connection posed few problems in a society understood to be Christian, and in which church and state were merely two cooperating and overlapping jurisdictions. As the state's power grew, the king of course ruled by divine right, and it was his role to give unity and purpose to the society. He should inspire the social harmony in which all superiors—social, familial, ecclesiastical, and those of the state—were aligned. It followed naturally that the religion of the prince should be that of the people, and the harmony left no room for nonconformity in religion. Nonconformity took on the aura of civil disobedience; it was insubordination, at once a political act and a sin. All well and good, but to achieve that unity through social control, the state had only a limited machinery of its own. It is true that in the seventeenth century the king finally achieved a monopoly of military force and could put down armed rebellion. But civil administration remained thin and inadequate until at least the mid–eighteenth century. Thus, the vast pedagogic structure that emerged to unify the society around principles of political subordination and purified Christianity could only have been built on the clergy. Here was a dense network of 40,000 or more agents of the state and church who could implement the vision. The Erastian state preceded the administrative state.

The first step was to remake the clergy. By the end of the seventeenth century most *curés* had studied in one of the proliferating seminaries, absenteeism from parishes was no longer common, and clerical concubinage was rare. The status of priests rose as they were separated from the laity more clearly, even visibly, since by 1700 most wore the cassock. The reformed priesthood was not unaffected by the new scientific culture whose leaders the Church often condemned. Priests, no longer magicians, abandoned "superstition." To purify and spiritualize Christianity, they distinguished the sacred from the profane more sharply; they heightened the sacred by extracting it from a material world drained at last of spirit. In their hands revealed truths and miracles were objects of pure faith when, as noted above, nature by itself established only the need for a creator. The reformed God, both creator and father, moved to the spiritual center: the curé Dusol in the town of Layrac in Aquitaine, writing out extracts of sermons in 1653, mentioned God the Father, usually as prime mover of the universe, eighty-three times, Jesus Christ sixteen times, Satan on four occasions, and the Virgin Mary but once.[9] God, both powerful and distant, was henceforth in a more unmediated relationship with individual Christians.

That relationship and the fears it engendered, very clear in Jansenism, were evident everywhere. Catholic reform in the seventeenth century was a massive pedagogical effort intended to train, to develop conscience, to interiorize the sense of divine majesty, and to prepare the individual to communicate with God. It was an intense indoctrination inculcating terror of sin, an awareness of sin's enormity and God's rigorous justice. The catechism, knowledge of the sacraments, the critical importance of penitential practices, prayers of propitiation, all had to be learned by heart so that correct observances were habitual. To achieve it, waves of six- to eight-week missions conducted by Eudistes and others swept over whole regions, covering villages in sequence before beginning again. Each village could expect the onslaught every four to eight years. The effort to remake the Christian was astonishingly methodical and a testimony to the stamina of Eudistes scheduled to hear confessions nine hours a day. The technique of the mission was to impose a kind of grid over the body of the faithful, thereby isolating and displaying the faith and behavior of individuals. Confession, absolution, and communion, which were the goal, ended the operation. After a mission it was the task of the parish clergy to keep the process alive; the curé was to see that the reformed practices entered into everyday life. To assure that all conformed, priests used some of the same methods that appeared in school classrooms. Persons who failed to take communion got their names onto lists that were posted on the church door. For the bishop, the curé kept lists that included, in addition to the noncommunicants, persons who failed to send their children for catechism instruction, or who hobnobbed with heretics, or who lived scandalously. The results were extraordinary: 99 percent took communion at Easter at La Rochelle in 1648, 99.8 percent in the rural archidiaconé of Paris in 1672.[10]

The consequences of the preceding for a way of seeing and treating Protestants were major. Revoking the Edict of Nantes and putting into place the body of anti-Protestant laws were in a direct line of development coming out of the Counter Reformation. It was time to complete the work by reabsorbing the Calvinists into the national political and religious consensus, by persuasion if possible and by force if needed. The extension to Protestants of reform applied first to Catholics was a national operation. That operation was the more feasible because Calvinists were increasingly defined as schismatic Christians rather than as heretics. They were "frères séparés" or "frères errans." To bring them back, writers downplayed their differences from Catholics, implying that Gallicanism united the confessions. The notion of schism made Calvinist doctrines even more inexplicable, and the Calvinists' holding onto them a matter of pure stubborn rebellion. If schism was just a misunderstanding, as Bossuet said, then why did not the Calvinists yield? Protestants, after all, had been baptized, and Catholics recognized those baptisms as valid. Resistance, then, was not innocent.[11]

By the later eighteenth century, attitudes and behavior had changed, and actual violence against the Protestants was neither practiced nor thinkable. It is nonetheless striking how the old ideas were attenuated without being transformed. The story from the death of Louis XIV divides itself naturally into three periods: 1715–39, 1740–62, and 1763–89. This is not the place for detailed narrative, but it is possible to sketch briefly changes and continuity in the perceptions (and misperceptions) of the Protestants by the principal actors—the royal administration and law courts, clergy, and Catholic public.[12]

From 1715 to 1740 was a time of national recovery and almost unbroken peace—the war of the Polish Succession (1733–34) was short and relatively undemanding. The duc d'Orléans, regent through 1723, was a religious skeptic, tolerant, and perfectly willing to look the other way if the Protestants were quiet. He encouraged a pastor to write a work telling Calvinists that worship in public was, after all, not spiritually essential.

Antoine Court, the Protestant leader, was not persuaded, and together with other pastors and a dedicated laity he began to rebuild the shattered Calvinist church. From 1726 a seminary at Lausanne trained new pastors who infiltrated southern France. By the 1730s they were conducting services at more-or-less secret assemblies in full violation of the anti-Protestant laws, no matter that the government had codified and reissued those laws in 1724. For the time being, however, the authorities were not preoccupied with their enforcement. In that setting the revived Calvinist church, while insisting on its loyalty to the monarchy, renewed also its moral obligation to oversee the spiritual well-being of its adherents, as well as to baptize and marry them.

Under the surface calm, a collision between the Catholic clergy and the Calvinists was certain to occur. The issue was marriage. Protestants knew well that the only legal and recognized marriage was the one conducted by a Catholic priest. Many, even most, Calvinists were willing to go through the Catholic ceremony for the sake of the families they wanted to establish, provided that the demands were not too great. Some hoped that the priest, being a state official—it was he who registered all births, deaths, and marriages and kept the official records—might offer for Protestants a nuptial blessing couched in general terms that would be a kind of civil marriage. It was a marriage that Calvinists should not find offensive. The hope was misplaced. The reformed Catholic clergy, now trained to watch closely the thoughts and practice of individual Catholics in confession and penance, saw no reason why the beliefs of "New Catholics" should not be similarly examined. Anything less could profane the marriage sacrament. Many priests began to test the beliefs of known or suspected Calvinists, and even to require public and written abjurations of heresy from them. To the Protestants this was an intolerable spiritual intrusion, as if preparing them for Catholic communion. Two kinds of conscience, then, were in irrevocable conflict. The result, especially in the villages, was that each party began to go its own way, the Protestants to the pastors and the Catholics to their priests. Less literal-minded persons on either side might compromise, but many could not. Finally, in 1739, the royal court (*présidial*) at Nîmes took action to suppress the supposed disorder. That court declared null a number of Protestant marriages and ordered the couples to separate. Soon the parlements at Bordeaux, Grenoble, and Toulouse did the same. By 1740 it appeared that the courts intended to assimilate Calvinist individuals to the law whether they liked it or not.

In the second period the conditioning fact was the wars that opened again in 1740 and, interrupted only by an uneasy truce, lasted twenty-three years. It was a time of severe troubles—the wars going badly, threats of foreign invasion, navy and merchant shipping destroyed, colonies lost and trade drying up, heavy taxes and mountainous state debt, periodic bad harvests bringing latent social fears into sharp focus. The situation favored the search for simplistic explanations, and as before "seditious" Calvinism was one. For Catholics, the Protestants who had ignited the dangerous social and political conflagration in Louis XIV's last years could be expected to try it again. And now the existence of the restored Calvinist church reinforced the fears. In war, with the troops drawn away to fight the foreign enemy, that church became more visible. Pastors showed themselves openly, they began to hold assemblies in daylight and closer to cities, and in 1744 they even convoked a national synod. Why? Catholics knew that it could only have been to plan rebellion, to fan the fanaticism of the lower orders, and to receive foreign money. With the wars, Catholic paranoia and Calvinist activity seemed to set the stage for renewed violence and persecution.

In this atmosphere the royal authorities were alternately tough and repressive when they could be, but restrained through fear. The repression was real. Officials watched for signs of the Reformed Church's activities and did not hesitate to send troops to attack and disperse assemblies, to take prisoners, and to seize pastors whom they called "enemy agents." Between 1745 and 1762 another six pastors were caught and hanged. Off and on, the intendants levied fines on the communities where assemblies occurred or priests were attacked, and they used the proceeds to pay spies whose reports, as usual in such cases, were a mirror to their employers' fears. For all that, repression was less continuous than might have been expected. Authorities at all levels intermittently advised prudence. Without the regular troops, a mounted constabulary (*maréchaussée*) of no more than 2,000 or so men policed the whole of rural France, and in any given locality the force it represented was much too small to deal with collective action involving groups of villages. If the state failed to press on with the persecution, it was owing to the authorities' fear of the Protestant revolt that they were powerless to control if it should occur. It is for this reason that the more systematic repression came not during the actual wars (1740–48, 1756–63), but in the armed peace in between. From 1750 to 1756 military action against peasant Protestantism became more intense. The government sent troops to sweep the Cévennes in order to shut down the assemblies and to drive the pastors from France once and for all.

Although the practical result was only to renew the cycles of murders and reprisals on both sides after the troops left, the government was determined to make it clear that the lenience it allowed during the war did not imply a policy of toleration.

With war again in 1756 the pressures had to be eased and fears of the Protestants revived. When in 1758 the maréchal de Thomond took up his duties as military governor in Languedoc, the minister, Saint-Florentin, sent him the mémoire he had drawn up and that the royal council had just approved.[13] The document is a set of instructions that reveals nicely the accumulated wisdom of the preceding eighteen years and the delicate nature of the operation an administrator had to conduct. With the troops away, Saint-Florentin wrote, there would be more pastors about and frequent assemblies. But for now the harshest treatment—raids, arrests, fines—should be avoided if at all possible, because it could set off the Protestant revolt. Thomond should not even try to disarm communities, because the effort would alarm Catholics and show Protestants that the authorities feared them. On the other hand, too much leniency was equally a mistake. Never negotiate with the pastors—it acknowledged their existence and only made them bolder. The best policy was to leave the Protestants alone when they got together in their homes for worship, but to be on guard against the big assemblies, that is, gatherings so obvious that the Protestants had to know that the authorities saw them. That could call for action, but in all other cases Thomond should not compromise royal authority by noticing too much. This was how, Saint-Florentin concluded, the Protestants were contained in the last war and so far in this. The instructions were not easy to implement—was an assembly in a barn, for example, like one in a house or in public? When to react, and when not to? The situation called for calm and measured judgment by officials at all levels. But the nervousness that infused the mémoire to Thomond, and that appears in all the administrative correspondence of the period, led to fitful actions by the authorities. Anxious officials, looking for signs in always ambiguous Protestant behavior, often supposed intent where there was none, and gave in to inaction and overreaction alternately.

In this atmosphere tensions within and between organizations came into the open. In the southwest, some Calvinists started to build temples and excluded from the faith any member who went to a Catholic priest for baptism or marriage. In the north, others, more security-conscious, opposed any effort to organize Calvinist worship in public. The mainstream position of Antoine Court and Paul Rabaut retained full loyalty to the monarchy and its laws except the one forbidding the public exercise of their cult. The Catholic clergy was apparently more solid, at least at first. It expected the government to enforce its own laws fully, that is, to drive out pastors, prevent assemblies, and support priests when they examined the beliefs and practices of the "New Converts" individually. With its periodic assemblies run by the bishops who negotiated the "free gifts" and loans that the hard-pressed king had to have, the clergy possessed the means to press its views on the government. That government, however, did not share all the clergy's ideas. Its approach was political and tactical. The secular authorities agreed that it would be good to crack down hard on organized Calvinism and, as noted, wished that they could have been tougher still in dealing with the "fanatics." Where they differed with the clergy, especially the rural clergy through the south, was on the proper approach to take to those who contracted "clandestine" (Calvinist) marriages. When couples lived quietly, working and paying taxes, government officials preferred a policy of tacit toleration toward them. They did not want to break up such marriages over a "technicality," and above all they feared increasing the power of sedition by driving law-abiding Protestants into the arms of the fanatics. On this issue, therefore, the government thought the clergy should be more moderate. Priests should receive the "New Converts" without making a fuss over details. This was the key to reducing the danger: most Calvinists would not need pastors if the Catholic priests were more accessible. Some bishops cooperated, though others and the lower clergy often did not. In the mid-1750s Saint-Florentin, a hard-liner against organized Protestantism when circumstances permitted, nonetheless threatened to use no troops at all against Calvinist assemblies in dioceses where the Catholic clergy would not accommodate peaceable New Converts.

Later in each war the fear of Protestantism spread equally through the larger society. In Dauphiné, after Austrian and Piedmontese troops entered Provence in 1745, popular rumor had it that twenty-five Protestant noblemen planned to lead 25,000 Camisards to join the enemy. That same year in Toulouse, where no more than 200 of over 50,000 inhabitants were Calvinists, the subdelegate reported that many believed the rifle or pistol shots heard from rooftops at night were the signal for Huguenots to gather. People imagined that strangers they saw were a minister and other Protestants sneaking into the city in small groups to avoid recognition. What they might have intended was unclear but ominous, and so the subdelegate stationed troops in the parts of the city where Calvinists were known to live. Nothing happened. The same cycle of fear and rumor rose again in 1761 and 1762, and it provides the backdrop for two striking episodes—the pastor Rochette and Calas affairs—that climaxed the heroic period of Protestant suffering.

Both episodes led to the execution of one or more Calvinists at Toulouse. The first originated in a mass hysteria among the inhabitants of Caussade, a small town north of Montauban, after Rochette's chance arrest nearby on a Sunday night in September 1761.[14] A fair scheduled in the town the next day brought a crowd of visitors from outside where at least half the peasant population was Protestant. At the town hall on that Monday several Calvinists apparently tried to get their minister out, and the incident set off portentous rumors. The townspeople, fearing both peasants and Protestantism, quickly supposed that Calvinist mobs of up to 600 persons were roaming the countryside. They were said to be fanatics chanting "Kill! Kill!" and were evidently on the way to release the pastor and to cut the throats and burn the property of Caussade's Catholic inhabitants. The town officials promptly postponed the fair and hastily organized the defense. They closed shops and taverns, distributed available firearms, and directed men to break up chairs to make clubs. The authorities also required that all houses keep lights burning through the night, and they posted a sentinel to the bell tower to watch for the attack. Reinforced patrols by a makeshift militia circled the town. On one foray they arrested three "gentlemen glassmakers," the Grenier brothers, calling them the ringleaders of an armed and dangerous force said at first to number 200—later, at the trial, witnesses would reduce that number to nine. Nothing else occurred during two frenzied days at Caussade, no attacks on the town, no hard evidence of large-scale, organized Protestant activity. In its panic the town had prepared for an imaginary attack. But at the time, and later, inhabitants believed that the threat was real, and that they were saved only by the extraordinary precautions they took.

That view was shared elsewhere. The threat imagined at Caussade differed only in degree from the one felt widely and in all circles, including government. It was the kind of sedition expected of Calvinists, and the fear spread to Toulouse. When the prisoners were transferred there from Montauban in October, a heavy military escort went with them. In the city, when stories circulated that Huguenots were infiltrating, ten or twelve at a time, the authorities reinforced the normal police guard and placed extra sentries near the courthouse. When the executions of Rochette and the Greniers were carried out in February 1762, they took place not in the large Place Saint-Georges, as was usual, but in the small and easily defended Place du Salin near the court and prison. At 2 P.M., when the executions began, the parts of two royal regiments garrisoned in the city were stationed in the square and adjoining streets. The city, like Caussade earlier, was ready for the Protestant attack that of course never came.

The second episode took place simultaneously.[15] It was different in that it involved not the putative representatives of organized Protestantism, but a peaceable Calvinist individual. As told by the defense lawyers and especially by Voltaire, the story was about a judicial murder by almost medieval Catholic magistrates—"barbarous Druids," Voltaire called them—and for France, and Europe generally, the case dramatized the effects of religious intolerance. The victim was Jean Calas, a small-scale merchant of cloth goods who had lived in Toulouse with his growing family for twenty-seven years. On an evening in October 1761 Calas, his wife, two of their sons, and a young Protestant friend just passing through the city took dinner together in the family's lodgings above the shop. After dinner Marc-Antoine, the eldest son (then twenty-nine years old), went downstairs, apparently on his way out to play billiards. Later, as the guest was leaving, he and the younger son noticed the shop door ajar and, entering, saw Marc-Antoine's dead body. Rope marks at the neck showed that the death was not a natural one. The facts that emerged in successive trials by the city officials and the parlement are ambiguous. Repeated examinations of the scene apparently convinced the magistrates that suicide was unlikely. But the murder they imagined came to seem far more unlikely: The accused having spent the evening together, if one was guilty, all must have been. The officials nonetheless rejected the hypothesis of suicide and charged the whole family and the visitor with premeditated murder. The assumed motive for it was religious. Rumors quickly surfaced to the effect that Marc-Antoine had been preparing his conversion to Catholicism, and that the accused decided collectively to kill him to prevent his deserting the Calvinist faith. No evidence for the supposed conversion ever appeared despite the prosecutors' determined efforts to find it.

At the trial no less than 193 witnesses gave depositions, most of them reporting the hearsay and rumor that French courts not only accepted but actively sought through issuance of a general subpoena, called *Monitoire*. That Monitoire, both posted and read aloud in churches through the city, called for information about the crime, the family's collective involvement, its religious cause, and even the possibility that there was a conspiracy among Calvinists more generally. The Monitoire itself seemed to encourage the rumors that twenty-three witnesses, mainly living at some distance from the accused and unable to identify any of them by sight, felt they had to report. Their testimony suggested that "Protestant justice" required the "execution" of deserters, and retailed stories about the "assembly" where the murder was probably decided and an executioner named. A larger number of witnesses simply supposed that the whole family was guilty, and that hatred of Catholicism was the reason, but without involving all Protestants and Protestantism on a national scale. Many witnesses merely reported seeing Marc-Antoine in church, or hearing that he had been there, though the occasions were almost always concerts or lectures he attended with Catholic friends. No one saw him at Mass or confession. In the end the thirteen magistrates in the criminal section of the parlement were divided, but they agreed by the necessary majority of two to condemn Jean Calas to questioning under torture to discover his accomplices, and then to be broken on the wheel in the Place Saint-Georges. They delayed judging the others to await news of what Calas might reveal. After learning he had said nothing, the judges, again divided, decided to release the others. To Toulousains, who had been led to expect four more executions, this turn of events was astonishing—either all were guilty, or none. And releasing the others was effectively to deny the original proposition that the tie of religious fanaticism linked all the accused. It was this inconsistency that was to reinforce the case made by Voltaire as he pursued his press campaign leading to the rehabilitation of Calas's memory by the Royal Council in 1765.

What is unusual about the Calas case is that the charge of fanaticism normally reserved for a distant peasant Calvinism was this time brought into the city and applied to peaceful urban Huguenots. The accused were the respectable friends and neighbors of Catholics, but now charged with having conspired to murder a family member for a purely ideological reason. With this, the line distinguishing between two kinds of Huguenots, the one assimilated and the other nonassimilable, was momentarily obliterated at Toulouse. That obliteration, however, was local, and it did not last long even at Toulouse where the Rochette and Grenier trials taking place simultaneously may have contributed to it. As the story spread, soon almost no one believed the accusation against the Calas family, and in turn it produced the countercharge of bigotry or worse against the magistrates. With relief, the enlightened, including most Catholics, returned to the view that only some Protestants, the ones they did not know, were fanatics.

The wider view is encapsulated in the responses of Voltaire and

Rousseau to the two episodes. When the Protestant Ribotte at Montauban wrote to the two philosophes to ask them to intervene in behalf of Rochette and the Greniers, both refused. Rousseau replied somewhat pompously that seizing anyone, even if held unjustly, from the hands of justice is a rebellion that the authorities are always right to punish. Voltaire, with the lighter touch, answered that while "Jesus Christ said He was to be found where two or three were gathered in His name . . . , when there are three or four thousand, it's the devil who is found there." The point is simply that both Rousseau and Voltaire assumed without question that there *had* been a Protestant revolt involving peasants, and that the fact was not surprising. It required no further investigation. A close reader of Voltaire's *Siècle de Louis XIV* (1744) could have guessed his position earlier. Calvinism, he had written, "from its very nature necessarily produced civil wars and shook the foundations of states."[16] With Calas, of course, it was quite different. Voltaire turned the case into a cause célèbre as important in its own day as those of Dreyfus or Sacco and Vanzetti in theirs. But what is crucial to see is that, as Voltaire described him, Jean Calas was scarcely a Calvinist at all. A kindly and moral *père de famille,* he thought virtuously like any ordinary deist; he cared so little about the details of his own religion that he actually approved the earlier conversion of another son, Louis, to Catholicism (an approval, incidentally, that the records do not confirm). This was the idealized Protestant, fully assimilated but horribly and gratuitously persecuted. The name of Calas, soon known everywhere, evoked hatred for injustice and intolerance. By contrast, few ever spoke of Rochette and the equally innocent Grenier brothers. They had no defenders. Their execution, marked only by the boycott of a concert on that day by a few Calvinist bourgeois in Montauban, faded quickly from memory.

After 1763 Calvinism quickly lost its power to arouse French secular anxieties, and a movement for a kind of toleration was launched. The centerpiece of that toleration was the guarantee of security to Calvinist couples in their legal status and family affairs, especially regarding inheritance. Malesherbes, Gilbert de Voisins, and many lawyers and magistrates advanced arguments that built on the mid-century ideas that the parlements had used to defend Jansenists. The courts invoked rights that they found inscribed in an increasingly generous natural law. For the Protestants the parlements would decide that the natural right to form a civil contract of marriage took precedence over any positive law that denied it.

In a series of decisions from 1767 to 1783 the magistrates, step by step and using subterfuges at first, found pretexts for recognizing Protestant marriages and for excluding the claims of Catholic collateral relatives to the inheritances. The most common basis for that decision was public recognition of a couple as husband and wife, which recognition could stand in place of documentary proof of the marriage. When in one case in 1783 a pastor's certificate did establish the fact of the Calvinist marriage, the parlement of Toulouse simply threw out the evidence—the word of a pastor, a proscribed man, could have no value in law and could not be used against the couple. In the same case the lawyer for the Calvinists referred to the "tacit agreement" on the part of society to respect any honest conjugal union. At last, in November 1787, the Crown completed the work by issuing what is often called the "Edict of Toleration." That act gave a positive, statutory basis for the Huguenots' civil status and marriage rights. Henceforth non-Catholics would be free to ask a royal judge to marry them by non-Catholic forms. Civil marriage was at last a reality.[17]

That was the essence of what most urban Calvinists wanted. But it did nothing for the others scattered through the countryside who desired the free and public exercise of their cult. For that the law did not change at all. In the same year, 1765, when Louis XV awarded 36,000 livres to the Calas family in partial compensation for its suffering, he insisted again that the Calvinist pastors should be arrested and that no "false ideas of tolerance" were allowable. By the late 1760s, however, the problem of organized Calvinism was clearly less urgent. When in 1768 pastors began to publicize the assemblies they convoked near Nîmes, the official order came down to seize not the minister but the animals and means of transport that people used to get there. In the same year near Limoges, when a parish priest complained about an assembly of Calvinists held in a "temple," really a barn, the only legal action was against the persons who rented out the barn, not against the Protestants. By the 1770s administrative documents referring to the Calvinists grew scarce, and in 1785 the intendant of Languedoc could use the term "tacit toleration" to describe state policy. By then, when it was known that the courts would no longer enforce the old laws, many more Protestants went to a pastor to be married. For all that, none of the laws criminalizing Calvinist practice had been rescinded.[18]

Nor did the distrust of organized Protestantism go away. The so-called Edict of Toleration did nothing for the Calvinists collectively. Its correct title was "Edict concerning those who do not profess the Catholic religion," and its purpose was specific and narrow. Louis XVI explained it: "The edict concerning my non-Catholic subjects is limited to giving a civil standing to those who do not profess the true religion. . . . Before the revocation of the Edict of Nantes, the Protestants had a religious existence; my edict does not give them one, the Protestants are not even named in it."[19] When the parlement of Paris objected that the edict was not sufficiently explicit in stating the exclusion of Calvinists from magistracies and teaching, the Crown responded only that the new law changed nothing in the old ones that demanded proofs of Catholicism for those sensitive functions. In the wave of pamphlets that flooded France before the Revolution, only a dozen or so treated the Protestant question. Some of the authors were warmly disposed toward the Protestants, others hostile in the old style, but what is striking is that none proposed granting the Calvinists a corporate existence. And when, in August 1789, the National Assembly debated the articles to go into the Declaration of the Rights of Man and of the Citizen, the one having to do with freedom of religion was at the least prudent. Article 10 stated: "No one must be disturbed because of his opinions, even in religious matters, provided their expression does not trouble the public order established by law."[20] When France finally renewed the religiously pluralist regime that preceded 1685, it would be done slowly and tentatively.

To conclude, then, the treatment of the Calvinists under the Old Regime reveals a political system and culture that simultaneously favored assimilation and rejected pluralism. Calvinists individually were absorbable, Calvinism as a corps was not. The fact is curious because France, more than other countries, was full of corps before 1789. But those corps—guilds, law courts at all levels, municipalities, provincial estates, clergy, and many others—were created or authorized by the state. They survived because they sustained a debt for kings whose personal credit was bad. Calvinist bankers too lent money to French kings, and a recognized Calvinist church might have been one more instrument of royal credit. But this was almost the only such opportunity (the lawyers were another) that the Crown failed to seize. Why? Was it the exclusionist nature of Catholicism? Special characteristics of Louis XIV? Widespread fear of faction rooted in the common perception of the past? At another level, did the habits deriving from the educational discipline (see above) play a role? Or, to add one more possibility and to be even more speculative, did the practices of self-governance in the ubiquitous French corps also contribute?

Those practices, in the style of Rousseau, were simultaneously democratic and nonpluralist.[21] No doubt there is much to discuss.

Whatever may explain their existence, both the nonpluralist and assimilationist ideas have had a long life. Anti-Protestantism was a staple in the thinking of the Right from 1793 to the twentieth century. Charles Maurras wrote that the French Protestants chose to be foreigners, by emigrating or living in self-contained communities, with the result that "the Protestant spirit is our enemy." In *La France juive* Louis Drumont stated that "every Protestant is a half-Jew."[22] The mainstream position, however, was not that, and when the practicing Calvinists (who were not numerous) built their temples here and there, Catholics did not much notice. In religion a pluralism by indifference grew at last. But in the areas that came to matter most, principally ethnicity, the dominating theme continued to be assimilationism. Even in the era of the *Front National,* it remains true that, almost unnoticed, one of every four grandparents of the French who are alive today was an immigrant to France, all quickly made French in language and culture. And unlike Americans, the assimilated in France do not insist strongly on their ethnicity and foreign roots. Every Saint Patrick's Day, March 17, Irish-Americans in New York celebrate their ancestry and culture by painting a green line down Fifth Avenue, by a massive parade, and by a conviviality with peers that lasts well into the night. By contrast, it is difficult to imagine anyone in Paris painting a stripe down the Champs Elysées for a similar purpose. The balance in France from the Old Regime until today has favored assimilationism over pluralism, and minorities are commonly absorbed and cease to exist as minorities. With the severe problems that exist today, will that continue? One can hope.

NOTES

1. The anti-Protestant laws are described in Burdette C. Poland, *French Protestantism and the French Revolution* (Princeton, 1957), 20–26, and the texts are in François-André Isambert et al., ed., *Recueil général des anciennes lois françaises . . .*, 29 vols. (Paris, 1822–33).

2. Warren C. Scoville, *The Persecution of Huguenots and French Economic Development, 1680–1720* (Berkeley, 1960), 7–13, 118–30; Poland, *French Protestantism,* 8.

3. *Almanach historique et chronologique de Languedoc, et des provinces du ressort du Parlement de Toulouse* (Toulouse, 1752), 14.

4. *Confession and Community in Seventeenth-Century France: Catholic and Protestant Coexistence in Aquitaine* (Philadelphia, 1993).

5. References and comment in D. Bien, "Religious Persecution in the French Enlightenment," *Church History* 30, no. 3 (1961): 3–11.

6. Of many works that treat the theme, Basil Willey's *The Seventeenth-Century Background* (New York, 1953; 1st ed., 1934) remains especially imaginative and analytical; see also Jean Delumeau, *Le Catholicisme entre Luther et Voltaire* (Paris, 1971), 3d part, chaps. 3–5.

7. Archives départementales de la Haute Garonne, B 1544, October 29, 1745, quoted by David D. Bien, *The Calas Affair: Persecution, Toleration, and Heresy in Eighteenth-Century Toulouse* (Princeton, N.J., 1960), 57.

8. Philippe Ariès, *Centuries of Childhood: A Social History of Family Life,* Robert Baldick, trans. (New York, 1962), 252–68; Emile Durkheim, *L'évolution pédagogique en France,* vol. 2 (Paris, 1938), 109–18. Neither work, however, entirely develops the significance of émulation for French society. The meaning emerges when one reads in the vast literature generated by institutions and the interminable debates over education. Parties in conflict over other matters invariably converged on the value and importance of émulation.

9. Hanlon, *Confession and Community,* 181–82.

10. Delumeau, *Catholicisme,* 293, and chap. 4 more generally for the themes of the Counter Reformation.

11. Elisabeth Labrousse, *La révocation de l'Edit de Nantes. Une foi, une loi, un roi?* (Paris, 1985, 1990), 85–90, and passim for all the broader issues of Catholic and Protestant perceptions of one another.

12. In addition to Bien, *Calas Affair,* chap. 3, sources include the rich work of the abbé Joseph Dedieu, *Histoire politique des protestants français, 1715–1794,* 2 vols. (Paris, 1925), based on archival records of the royal administration, and an important article by John Pappas, "La répression contre les protestants dans la seconde moitié du siècle, d'après les registres de l'ancien régime," *Dix-huitième siècle* 17 (1985): 111–28. A good summary treatment of the Protestants interacting with the state is D. Ligou and Ph. Joutard, "Les déserts (1685–1800)," in *Histoire des protestants en France* (Toulouse, 1977), 189–262. For the evolution of eighteenth-century Protestantism there are various works by Emile Léonard, including *Le protestant français* (Paris, 1955), and Poland, *French Protestantism,* chap. 2.

13. "Les protestants sous Louis XV. Mémoire lu et approuvé au Conseil, pour servir d'instruction à M. le maréchal de Thomond, dans la conduite qu'il doit tenir à l'égard des protestants du Languedoc (7 janvier 1758)," *Bulletin de la Société de l'histoire du Protestantisme français* (hereafter *BPF*) 18 (1869), 429–35.

14. For the Rochette episode, see Bien, *Calas Affair,* chap. 4.

15. The following abridges Bien, *Calas Affair,* chaps. 1, 5, 6.

16. The two letters to Ribotte are in "Réponse de J.-J. Rousseau à Paul Rabaut au sujet de François Rochette et des trois gentilshommes verriers, 1761," *BPF* 2

(1854), 364; and "La tolérance au XVIIIe siècle. Lettres inédites de Voltaire à M. Ribotte de Montauban (1761–1769)," *BPF* 31 (1882), 167; Voltaire's remark about Calvinism can be found in *Oeuvres complètes de Voltaire*, Louis Moland, ed. (52 vols. 1877–85), XV, 39.

17. For the court decisions and the ideas that the magistrates and lawyers built on, see D. Bien, "Catholic Magistrates and Protestant Marriage in the French Enlightenment," *French Historical Studies* 11, no. 4 (1962): 3–23; and for the broad movement of ideas among intellectuals and administrators, see Raymond Birn, "Religious Toleration and Freedom of Expression," in Dale Van Kley, ed., *The French Idea of Freedom: The Old Regime and the Declaration of Rights of 1789* (Stanford, 1994), 265–99, and Geoffrey Adams, *The Huguenots and French Opinion, 1685–1787*, Toronto, 1991.

18. For the weakening enforcement of the laws, see Pappas, "La répression," 123–28.

19. *Remontrances du Parlement de Paris au XVIIIe siècle*, Jules Flammermont, ed. (Paris, 1898), III, 701.

20. For the Declaration and generally the nature of the idea of toleration before the Revolution, see Birn, "Religious Toleration."

21. For the corps, their ubiquity, their practices, the habits they engendered, see D. Bien, "Old Regime Origins of Democratic Liberty," in Van Kley, ed., *The French Idea of Freedom*, 23–71. Democracy necessarily, of course, involves the right for individuals to participate in the polity and to make decisions, either directly or through representatives, but it does not require the guarantee of rights of individuals independent of the polity. That is, of course, why in the great revolutions of the eighteenth century the questions about bills of rights and their forms were taken up only after the new polities had been formed. The "democracy" of the French corps, from the guilds through many hundreds of judicial and administrative bodies, favored self-governance without any concept of independent rights or pluralism. In this way the habits of democracy were congruent with those of emulation and absolutism, and did not automatically favor freedom for diverse religious cults.

22. Citations in Steven C. Hause, "Anti-Protestant Rhetoric in the Early Third Republic," *French Historical Studies* 16, no. 1 (1989): 186, 200.

Comment

Jacques Revel

No one will dispute the power of the synthesis or the consistency of interpretation in David Bien's penetrating essay. It intersects with some of the concerns that ran through his first book in which, forty years ago now, he wondered about the "extraordinary conditions" that might explain the Calas affair,[1] and with the concerns that more recently shaped his reflection on the characterization of French society at the end of the ancien régime. Starting from that double foundation, Bien does not just content himself with setting forth the representation (or representations) of the Huguenot minority between the Edict of Nantes and the Revolution, as his title too restrictively implies. He reflects on the experience of a religious minority and about its status in eighteenth-century France, and he proposes a doubly paradoxical interpretation. *The first paradox:* In this society described, not without reason, as in the grip of an accelerated process of secularization (if not *laïcisation*), the religious aspect of Protestantism constituted an obstacle to assimilation up to the Revolution and again in its early years. *The second paradox:* In a society that David Bien himself has shown us (and with what force of logic) must be understood as a society of *corps,*[2] what seemed to create an obstacle to the integration of Protestants was precisely that they constituted an irreducible corps. We should examine these paradoxes.

But to begin we should follow Bien as he sets about distinguishing the problem of a Huguenot minority in French society from the way it was posed in philosophical polemic during the eighteenth century. The question of religious tolerance and respect for conscience was not central and is, in large part, anachronistic. Bien usefully recalls, as have others, that the Edict of Nantes responded to a real situation, an exhausted monarchy, and that it invented an empirical solution designed to pacify the kingdom much more than to implement a program of "tolerance." That Louis XIV, more confident of his power, should decide in 1685 to suppress this arrangement dictated by circumstance only confirms an evolution that was not unique to France, although the absolute monarchy effected it with a particularly vigorous force of conviction. Not only should the religion of the prince impose itself on his subjects according to the old principle, *"cujus regio, ejus religio"* but the movement for Catholic reconquest launched by the Counter Reformation was by and large taken in hand by the state to serve its own ends. Religion was henceforth enrolled in the service of the monarchy and should serve "to provide the state with its tranquillity and . . . the authority of its laws" as Louis XIV himself said.[3]

In this return to order, the Protestants had no place and found themselves recognized in neither religious nor civil statutes. This double denial certainly did not make them "a nontopic" as Bien mischievously suggests at the beginning of his essay. There was indeed a Protestant minority during the last century of the ancien régime, but in fact this minority was not the object of any recognition and was in principle doomed to disappear. To persuade oneself of the uniqueness of this situation, one need only compare it with that of the Jews at the same time. They were the object of still much stronger rejection and stigma, stigmatized in the name of the traditional accusation of deicide and for the most part repressed into a despised social fringe. That did not keep the different Jewish communities from being recognized as having a contractual right to exist which was defined by texts, statutes, privileges, and constraints that varied very much from one community to another according to the logic of a society of corps. That the overall tone was hostile and repressive changes nothing: They had a place in the social body, even if on the margins and in precarious and often humiliating circumstances. On the other hand, there was not a unified Jewish community. The participation of different Jewish "nations" in the debate about access to citizenship during the disorder of the first days of the Revolution would make that apparent.

The Huguenots, however, were considered as a bloc (if one leaves aside, as Bien quite rightly does, the special case of Alsatian Protestants who escaped the provisions of the Edict of Fontainebleau). They were perceived as an entity but also seen as one denied all right to exist. The only way out offered Protestants was acceptance of the Catholic order, individual adherence given civic recognition. It is here that the question of marriage became crucial and explosive; for it tied to the administration of a sacrament the juridical right to exist and legally to establish a marital union, descendance and the transmission of goods through inheritance.

The hardening of policies in the years 1730 to 1740, those of the Catholic clergy as well as those of the judicial courts, showed that the spirit of the Revocation of 1685 was not forgotten, not at all, even though by then the most violent repressive phase had long been over. Nor had it been abandoned at midcentury, even if royal policy grew more prudent. Yet in 1752 a *secrétaire d'Etat* reminded the military commander in the Cévennes that "His Majesty's intention is always to listen to any idea of tolerance."[4] The question, of course, is the reason for this persistence.

David Bien suggests two levels of explanation. The first is classic and not the less convincing of the two. It relates back to the negative image of Calvinism in the kingdom, which links the existence of the Protestant sect to a threat of permanent subversion. In that regard, the wars of religion doubtless counted for less than the much more recent Camisard episode, a true challenge to the restored monarchical state.[5] Protestants found in the persecution against them reasons for a new mobilization that constrained them to keep a greater distance from society and at the same time implanted a militant memory, as the work of Philippe Joutard, *La légende des Camisards* (1978), has clearly shown. Unequal repression against different segments of Huguenot society undoubtedly contributed, as Bien suggests, to strengthening identity among the less integrated elements rather than the better assimilated urban elites. The result was that the condemned and partially marginalized Protestant minority was more and more perceived as foreign and threatening for social order in general but also for the security of the kingdom. As historians of the eighteenth century know well, there was no war or fairly strong internal tension that did not occasion a readiness to invoke the combined activity of the Calvinists, English, and Dutch, "natural" allies in the monarchical imagination.

The second level of explanation Bien employs has an entirely different nature. It relates to three great, fundamental movements, "three long-term processes," which he says shaped the social and political representations of French elites. The first he mentions is the progressive "secularization" of the world—its disenchantment, to use Max Weber's term—in which questions of faith and grace change status. They are henceforth confined to private experience while two trends occur, disassociating religion and morality and enrolling ecclesiastical institutions in the service of the monarchical state. M. de Certeau has powerfully summarized this major transformation: "The system that made *beliefs* the frame of reference for practice is replaced by a social *ethic* formulating an order of social practices and relativizing religious belief as an 'object' to be used."[6] It is not at all surprising that such a conception of religion—which one finds among believers in *raison d'État* but also at the heart of the *parti philosophique*—collided head on with a doctrine that placed faith and grace alone at its center. The partly parallel history of Jansenism in the eighteenth century provides another example, still more convincing if need be, of such a tension in confronting a more and more instrumental conception of religion.[7] The fact remains that if the Jansenist rupture was from the first unacceptable, because it took place within the Catholic church itself, the reformed religion had shown before 1685—and actually, in more than one case, after the Revocation—that it was in practice capable of compromising with the state provided it retained the freedom to exercise its religion. Without rejecting the interpretation of David Bien, don't we have to conclude that the mechanisms of repression played a decisive role in the marginalization of a Calvinism driven into hiding, into informal and seditious organization, and to prophecy and the mobilization of memory?

The second long-term process has a Tocquevillean flavor, which will not surprise those familiar with Bien's thought. He sees in the homogenization and codification of behavior, as shaped in particular by schools in the modern period, a pattern of singling out individuals that contradicted the collective logic of corps well in advance of the Revolution and facilitated the tactics by which the monarchical state imposed itself. However incomplete, this transformation was sufficient to make the existence of "informal communities" unacceptable in society as a whole. The hypothesis is, to be sure, suggestive. But, aside from the fact that it rests on a process that, we are reminded, is not unique to ancien régime France, it appears in a way too broad to explain the rejection of Calvinism as such. Besides, was Protestantism less prepared than the Catholic tradition to adapt to such an individualization of conduct? Nothing is less certain. Many examples show, however, that after the Revocation as earlier in the seventeenth century Protestants were ready to demonstrate their attachment and personal loyalty to the monarchical state. Indeed, repression and more generally the effort to exclude Protestants from regular social roles conferred on the Protestant presence a menacing density and reinforced the image of their unity. But in whose eyes? Some Catholic elites whose members despite everything happened to sit next to some Protestant classmates at school? The popular masses? Probably, but they had undoubtedly been less deeply affected by the process of individualization than Bien suggests.

While awaiting the possibility of refining the analysis, everything leads toward the third hypothesis, the most classic but also the most convincing and one already invoked in passing; it is a question not only of "the simultaneous growth in state power and Catholic reform," but of the state's taking in hand the ends and means of the Counter Reformation. From now on, it is the monarchy that labels heterodoxy and more generally every uncivil split in the coherent order it claims to maintain as heresy. The Church and its agents enrolled in the service of the state for purposes that continued to be formulated in the language of religion but the stakes in this conquest of society had already been profoundly secularized. At least it was that way on the part of the monarchy. One could be tempted, on the other hand, to understand Calvinist resistance—and still much more so the interminable and multiform Jansenist resistance through the eighteenth century—as an effort to remove the domain of faith and revealed truth from that process of secularization that tended to make them marginal and more generally to reduce religion to its social function. Hence the central place in this affair of the law and courts of justice, especially the *parlements*. It is they that, at bottom, had to examine and cut through the issues of religious practice that contravened the law of the kingdom and appeared capable of challenging the social and political order (they would behave similarly, we know, with regard to Company of Jesus in the middle of the eighteenth century). That anti-Protestant repression had a missionary dimension and that it expressed a wish to reintegrate "separated brethren" or "errant brothers" into the Church, as David Bien reminds us, one does not doubt. This is no longer that opposition between orthodoxy and heresy that had been so central two centuries before; but for the Catholic majority in particular, the theological and doctrinal stakes gave way to preoccupation with civil order. Similarly, legal questions were the points at which efforts to arrange some solution to this conflict were persistently blocked, especially, we are correctly reminded, the legal recognition of marriage.

It was also on this issue that the beginning of a minimal solution began to emerge during the last twenty years of the ancien régime. That probably had less to do with the progress of the Enlightenment and *l'esprit philosophique* than with the more and more explicit concern to guarantee civil order, ultimately formalized by the Edict of Tolerance of 1787. It was not a question here of any legal recognition of reformed religion but of settling problems about the civil status of the, well-named, Protestants: allowing unions celebrated outside the Catholic church to be recognized in French law (with the consequences for matters of succession such recognition carried). Increasingly everything tended to be dealt with more in terms of morality than religion, of natural law that should prevail over all other legislation and inform it.[8] But such an evolution was only possible because the problem of religious pluralism as a matter of principle was set aside in favor of a judicial arrangement that made it possible to settle questions of fact from a secular point of view or, if one wants to use a term then still anachronistic, a "laicized" one. It needs to be remembered that this conception still prevailed in August 1789, during the drafting of the Declaration of the Rights of Man, with its moderate and restrictive formulation of Article X, which has often been emphasized: "No one may be harassed for his opinions, even religious ones, provided that their expression does not disturb the public order established by law." Today, thanks to the work of Marcel Gauchet, we are aware of the extraordinary fierceness of the arguments that accompanied the difficult genesis of this text. There is a better understanding, too, of what was finally decreed, which was less a positive affirmation of liberty of conscience than the preeminence of public order expressed in law.[9] The juridico-political fiction to which that order refers recognizes only the individual citizen. In addition, the position taken with regard to Protestants is roughly the same as that which would soon be taken with regard to Jews, while the conditions of their possible access to French citizenship were being examined. And the famous statement of Count Clermont-Tonnere with regard to them ("Jews must be refused everything as a nation and granted everything as individuals; they must be neither a political body nor an order in the state; they must, individually, be citizens."[10]) in a way retrospectively hands us the key to what had taken place since the end of the 1760s: It was within the framework of the state that the religious problem tended to be treated in terms of law, and it was in that framework that civil "tolerance" was conceivable. There was no question whatsoever of recognizing the status of a religious minority but of rendering the civil existence of those who identified themselves as a minority compatible with legislation. With the Revolution, minorities are called upon to dissolve themselves into citizenship. If one wants to uncover a basic continuity between the ancien régime that was ending and the new order, this is where it is likely to be found. That underscores this paradox: The same reasons that for long rendered the presence of a Protestant corps unacceptable within monarchical society are the reasons that ultimately made a place for its individual members at the end of the day.

It remains to be determined to what extent it is legitimate to speak of a

Protestant minority in the seventeenth century. The question might seem rhetorical. Did the century that followed the Revocation of 1685 not illustrate in exemplary fashion the capacity of a persecuted group to endure and to defend its collective identity? That group was for long denied not only the right to practice its religion but any civil existence. It declined in numbers and was constrained to take refuge in secrecy for the most important of its collective activities and to live in every respect within the interstices of ancien régime society. Now, through adversity and coercion this group appears to have found some specific resources of identity, and what collective memory has preserved of persecution remains even today the core of Protestant identity in France. The case thus appears closed: It was indeed then that the Protestant minority became conscious of itself and of the place it was coming to claim in the nation.

Is this standard schema adequate to take into account the complexity of this experience and the questions it poses? One is not entirely reassured. David Bien does not forget to mention the very great diversity among the concrete forms of French Protestantism, from strongly organized rural communities, which are thus the favored targets of royal repression, to an urban Calvinism at the other extreme, which was much more discreet and hence better tolerated (even if there, too, a combination of exceptional circumstances was capable, as in the Calas affair, of provoking a flare-up of persecution). The organized forms of repression were not all that varied according to the situation. The same was true for religious practice and for relations between Catholics and Protestants. Protestant memory had, as is normal, preserved in a special way the most spectacular and the most heroic aspects of resistance, the Camisard war, the assemblies in the desert, prophecies, and clandestine militancy. But there is agreement that the most common situation was one of passive resistance, which often implied that one conformed to the law of the kingdom in the matter of sacraments—one married and had one's children baptized in the Catholic Church—reserving for one's interior life the practice of the "true" confession. That by the eighteenth century this double track was accused of being "pharisaism" (nicodémisme) changes nothing, nor does the fact that Protestants were able to benefit, to a degree difficult for us to appreciate, by the at least passive support of the Catholic environment. The fact remains that there was no single way to be a Calvinist after the Revocation, far from it, and that in the absence of inclusive institutional structures, the factors of diversification could work that much more strongly.

Where, then, did so strong a minority assertion come from? There are some classic answers to this question: Persecution could only reinforce Protestant solidarity as in their tenacious efforts at organizing themselves; the effect of memory, immediately and following through three or four generations, doubtless played a decisive role; more discreetly but not less powerfully, a marked endogamy protected and reinforced the unity of the group. These explanations are certainly persuasive but leave a feeling that they are too sweeping. One could imagine a history still to be written of the construction of a minority, a history closer to the people it is about and that above all avoids forms of theological reasoning, does not assume that a unified minority existed by right, whether because it was a group placed in a subordinate position and under duress or because it identified itself principally in terms of its religious character. One would hope to understand better how and why, according to what process, members of society are recognized within that which becomes what we call a minority. One would like to know more about the variety of local experiences, individual trajectories, interactions between Catholics and Protestants but also, and first of all, among the Protestants themselves. They had to deal with legal coercion and public violence that weighed on their everyday life. But they also had to find local solutions, compromise with rules and constraints, arrange some space for individual and collective survival in which they could develop not only their religious activity but also their occupations, their social relations, and so forth. This was a question of realities less spectacular than those ordinarily fixed in Protestant memory and historiography but that undoubtedly played a major role in strengthening a community identity. But this other history has scarcely been attempted and first of all because the sources are both scarce and scattered. That is to be regretted because they would doubtless provide us with a richer and more complex picture of a minority in ancien régime society—much more so, in any case, than results from confronting collective representations.

NOTES

1. D. Bien, *The Calas Affair* (Princeton: Princeton University Press, 1960).

2. D. Bien, "Offices, Corps, and a System of State Credit: The Uses of Privilege under the Ancien Regime," in *The French Revolution and the Creation of Modern Political Culture,* I, *The Political Culture of the Old Regime,* Keith, Baker, ed. (Oxford: Pergamon Press, 1987), 89–114.

3. This point is effectively underscored in the remarkable study by J. Orcibal, *Louis XIV et les protestants* (Paris: Vrin, 1951), and has been developed at length

by M. de Certeau, "La formalité des pratiques. Du système religieux à l'éthique des lumières (xviie–xviiie siècles)" in *L'Écriture et l'histoire* (Paris: Gallimard, 1975), 153–212.

4. Cited by Ph. Joutard in J. Le Goff and R. Rémond, eds., *Histoire de la France religieuse*, vol. 3, *XVIIe–XIXe siècles* (Paris: Seuil, 1991), 51.

5. Even if, as Bien reminds us with regard to Toulouse, the almanac still kept in the eighteenth century preserved the memory of the clashes of the sixteenth century and if the civic ritual celebrated each year with some effectiveness the expulsion from the city of the Protestants while recalling the atrocities attributed to them. Cf., *The Calas Affair*, Chap. 7.

6. Certeau, "La formalité des pratiques," 154.

7. With regard to these issues I refer to the thoroughly convincing reinterpretation of Jansenism in the eighteenth century set forth by Catherine Maire, *Les convulsionnaires de Saint-Médard. Miracles, convulsions et prophéties à Paris au XVIIIe siècle* (Paris: Gallimard, 1985); and especially, *De la cause de Dieu à la cause the la nation. Le jansenisme au XVIIIe siècle* (Paris: Gallimard, 1998).

8. David Bien has elegantly analyzed the logic and mechanisms of this evolution for the Toulousan case, *Calas Affair*, Chap. 7.

9. M. Gauchet, *La Révolution des droits de l'homme* (Paris: Gallimard, 1989), 167–74.

10. *Archives Parlementaires*, X, 754–56 (December 23, 1789). We should remember that the debate concerned not just the Jews but also Protestants (and certain occupations traditionally considered dishonorable).

Intercommunal Relations and Changes in Religious Affiliation in the Middle East, Seventeenth to Nineteenth Centuries

Lucette Valensi

Religion . . . appears in all different sorts in Syria: Turks, Jews, Heretics, Schismatics, Naturalists, Idolaters; or to be more exact these are genera that have their species in great number, for in Aleppo alone we counted sixteen types of religions of which four were Turks different from each other; of Idolaters, there remains only one sort which worships the sun; of Naturalists, those who maintain the natural essence of God with some superstition concerning cows and who come from this side of the borders of Mogor; and the others without superstitions named Druze, living in Anti-Lebanon under a prince called the Emir. They pay a tribute to the Great Lord, and live in their own manner, naturally. From this one can see how necessary it is to have good missionaries, and virtuous ones, for all the scandals that go on in this Babylon, and learned men to refute so many errors.[1]

There are fourteen Sects or Nations differing from each other completely in Religion, in rite, in language, and in their manner of dressing: seven of these are Infidels, and seven Christians. The Infidels are Turks or Ottomans, Arabs, Kurds, Turcomans, Jezides, Druze and Jews. Among the Turks there are, moreover, several sects and cabals affecting Religious sentiments just as there are among the Jews. The other nations, that is the Arabs, Kurds, etc. are in such a profound state of ignorance that they do not know what they believe. The seven Christianities are the Greeks, the Armenians, the Surians, the Maronites, the Nestorians, the Copts and the Solaires called Chamsis.

One must remark that most of these sects are mixed and confused one among the other, not only in the same country, and in the same Town; but often enough in the same lodgings: those in which Turks, Greeks, Armenians, whose Idioms and Religions are all different, such that one cannot understand another's speech: From this it follows that Turkey is a true Babylon of confusion.[2]

These two texts, which provide an epigraph, describe with eloquence but without sympathy the extreme diversity of Middle Eastern society in the seventeenth century. The multilingualism, the plurality and resilience of religious confessions have not ceased to be emphasized down to our own time. If the authors of the seventeenth century quoted above associated this diversity with the curse of Babel, more neutral notions are used to describe it today: it is the metaphor of carpet motifs for Jacques Berque, of mosaic pieces assembled for Carlton Coon, or of a kaleidoscope for Pierre Bourdieu.[3]

The accelerated and cumulative changes that have taken place since the nineteenth century have not dissolved diverse communities. Neither the emergence of new nation-states nor the diverse utopias that have had their course in the region—Arab nationalism, pan-Islamicism, communism to a weak degree—have reduced religious and linguistic diversity. Certain communities became minorities, then disappeared by expulsion (Jews from Iraq and Egypt), by destruction (Armenians in Turkey), or by emigration (Jews, Greeks, Armenians from Turkey as from the Arab provinces turned states). But, inversely, a large number of minorities have become more visible, politicized, even militarized. Far from subsiding, diversity remains the order of the day and what is called *ethnopolitics* is at the center of public life in most of the region's states.[4]

It is not at all a matter of calling into question these ancient communal divisions that have marked and continue to mark the societies of the Middle East.[5] But until now, studies have more often accentuated national constructions, unitary by nature, or conflicts between minorities and their states (the "minorities question," after the "question of Christians in the Orient"). Hence the teleological character of such studies, where the end (alas, often tragic) of the story as it is told determines the selection of facts coming before it. It was appropriate, in order to refine the social history of these regions and to better capture the secular modus vivendi of various religious communities, to orient research in other directions. One such effort has led to the analysis of the social formulas that flourished, however briefly: in other words, the transcommunal experiences that found fertile ground between the nineteenth and twentieth centuries, particularly in towns. Such was the case of cosmopolitanism studied notably by Robert Ilbert for Egypt or by Alcalay for Levantine culture in general.[6] If we admit that social identity is formed in relation to others,[7] we can shift attention to focus on the social practices shared by all the groups as well as the places and forms of interaction among groups or among individuals belonging to different communities. There is, finally, the need to consider the experiences of rupture, transgression, and particularly the cases of movements of religious conversion. Little studied until now, such changes in religious affiliation occurred in various forms between the sixteenth and nineteenth centuries: forced conversion, in the case of the Armenian Khamshin of the Trebizond region; voluntary conversion, where Jews are concerned, who, having followed the false messiah Shabbatai Sevi, convert like him to Islam in the seventeenth century and are known from then on by the name *Donmeh;* massive adherence to the Shi'ism of the Iraqi nomads in the nineteenth century; and the individual conversion in the sixteenth and seventeenth centuries of the innumerable "Christians of Allah," splendidly described by J. and B. Bennassar.[8] The scope of this topic, subjected to documentary restrictions often impossible to overcome, does not permit us to encompass all of these movements. Conversions to Islam in particular seem to have left little trace in the Ottoman archives. The communal archives are meager. The collections of the churches of the Orient (and those of the missionary orders in the Orient) remain inaccessible. We do not pretend, therefore, to make more than a limited contribution to the study of social relations among the followers of distinct groups and to that of the changes in religious affiliation, in particular by observing conversions to the Roman Catholic Church.[9]

The Work of Conversion: Global Reflection

The principal post of observation was that occupied by the Franciscans in the Holy Land. Established in the Middle East since the thirteenth century to guard the Holy Places, they also performed missionary work. Franciscans were present in Egypt (Cairo, Damietta, and Alexandria), Cyprus (Arnice and Nicosia), Syria-Palestine (Jerusalem, St. John of the Mountain, Bethlehem, Nazareth, Arissa, Damascus, Aleppo), and finally in the capital of the empire, Constantinople. All the information concerning their houses was gathered in Jerusalem, and because the friars of the Holy

Land took care to record conversions one by one and then periodically recapitulate these records, the effects of the missionary efforts must be measured over the long term and over a considerable territory.

As a result of the gaps that they contain, we will not grant rigorous statistical importance to these compilations (in which serial and quantitative history would once have delighted).[10] The aim here will be only to locate in them a few large trends, the clearest being the insignificance of the annual number of conversions in the seventeenth century. One notices only a certain agitation in Aleppo in 1630–31, then in Palestine in the 1670s. Yet between 1627 and 1697 the annual number of conversions did not exceed 8, if the reversions of repentant renegades to Catholicism and of Protestants making the pilgrimage to the Holy Land are excluded. More elevated in the very last years of the seventeenth century and during the first third of the eighteenth century, the annual numbers reached or exceeded 80 in 1715 and 1727, then fell back to modest levels. With about 1,286 conversions for the years 1698 through 1767, the average number of yearly conversions was 18. For the following period, 1768 through 1856, according to calculations done by the friars, the conversions exceeded 3,297 individuals, renegades and Protestants included, an average of 37 per year. The statistics change dramatically (see table 1).[11]

These numbers do not fail to surprise, as much by the high number of Muslims converted to Christianity as by the presence of those called gentiles. The latter were in fact black slaves who came from Africa. The former included the black slaves brought from Africa and counted as Muslims and renegades of Christian birth: If these two categories are excluded, the conversion of indigenous Muslims remains thus in all likelihood exceptional.

These limited quantitative data, approximate for that concerning the Franciscans, did not assess the results obtained by other missionary orders present in the region, such as the Carmelites, Jesuits, Capuchins, or Anglicans. The Carmelites, for example, received 48 converts in Aleppo between 1669 and 1681 (that is 3 a year on average); their results were not therefore more spectacular than those of the guardians of the Holy Land.[12] It was doubtless the same with other orders. Together these data furnish at least a clear indication of three kinds of facts: First, conversions were rare; second, the identities acquired at birth were strong; and, third, changes in religious identity either were not sought after or were difficult. Whether these facts resulted from the efficiency of Ottoman interdictions, the solidity of communal organization, or the timidity of the offer of conversion is what must be determined (see table 1).

The limited statistical pertinence of available data rapidly leads one to abandon the macroscopic perspective. Can the microscopic one nevertheless be used? The information that comes to us was distilled. The scribe who compiled the data gathered in Jerusalem retained a date, the place, the proper name sometimes followed by patronymic, the nature of the operation carried out, and finally the nation or site of origin for each individual in only one line or little more. The circumstances of the conversion are not reported. When these brief announcements are read through the magnifying glass, indications of minor shifts affecting local society can sometimes be discovered. Moreover, the fathers of the Holy Land maintained a regular correspondence with Rome, a part of which has been published. And finally, the guardians of the Holy Land and the monks of other missionary orders periodically wrote reports that, intended for the Roman authorities, provide a summary of the situation. One of the regular rubrics of these accounts of activities concerns the salvation of souls, in other words, conversions, a synthesized rubric that does not revel in narrative or circumstantial detail. Nevertheless, it did furnish the elements of a puzzle for us to assemble.

Observing the Infinitesimal:[13] Interconfessional Relations

On the Complexity of Relations
between Christians in the Orient

Let us observe first of all the relations between contiguous areas. Several towns and villages jointly sheltered distinct religious communities of unequal numerical strength that benefited from a more or less solid insti-

TABLE 1.   Conversions and Reconciliations, 1768–1856

Nationality	Number	Religion	Number
Greeks	1,555	Protestants	149
Armenians	1,040	Jews	17
Copts	189	Muslims	220
Nestorians, etc.	110	Gentiles	17
Total	2,894		403

tutional anchorage. Other than the Turks (the term used to designate Muslims at that time), there was the pairing of Greeks and Armenians in Cyprus and, during the nineteenth century, at Latakia. In the majority of Christians in Egypt, the Copts found themselves a minority in Nazareth among Greeks and Armenians and, in Jerusalem, among the representatives from all the churches of the other religions. Four large cities offered a greater degree of diversity: Aleppo and Damascus, with its followers of the Greek, Armenian, Maronite, Nestorian, and Jacobite churches; Cairo, where Copts, Greeks, Armenians, Abyssinians, Maronites, and Jacobites lived together; and finally Jerusalem, where the faithful of all the churches and religions lived and converged.

This proximity facilitated the reciprocal borrowing of social practices and the sharing of customs and values among Muslims and non-Muslims. In this domain the data are remarkably abundant, if not always coherent, in particular with regard to public practices directly open to the gaze of observing foreigners. Travelers and missionaries in the Orient, in effect, never failed to be surprised by the cultural distance that separated them from the indigenous Christians and, correspondingly, by the homology between their practices and those of the Muslims. On their side, the Turkish authorities bound themselves to maintaining the manifest differences between Muslims and non-Muslims, reiterating prohibitions and regulations, while underlining the degree of osmosis that existed between the sociocultural practices of the diverse groups. In this manner the non-Muslims spoke the vernacular languages of the empire: Arab, Turkish, or Greek. Christians and Jews, men or women, frequented the public baths. The men, Christian or Jewish, wore turbans. What then made it possible to distinguish them from the Muslims was the presence of colored threads in the fabric used for these turbans.[14] But how did one distinguish Jews from Christians when their headdresses were alike? By their shoes, for those of the former were black or violet and those of the Christians, red or yellow.[15] In their religious practices, the Christians of Syria-Palestine and the pilgrims frequented the same holy places. In certain locations, the Christians of the Orient had to share the same churches, for there was not one to each sect. At the same time, like the Muslims in their mosques, Christians did not tolerate the presence of women in the churches. Again, like the Muslims and contrary to Occidental Christians, the Armenians practiced the sacrifice of sheep. The Copts, whose practice of circumcision and excision linked them to the Muslims, deviated from Catholic norms in many of their social relations: the laws of marriage, the practice of repudiation and divorce, and the marriage of priests. The reports note that the Christians are divided into the same system of factions as the society at large and that, like it, they practice vengeance for honor.[16]

This proximity similarly facilitated relations that ignored confessional frontiers. In 1617, an infant of Catholic Nestorian parents was baptized: The godfather was a Catholic from Marseilles; the godmother, a Maronite. Thus, for the five individuals concerned, there were three languages, three rites, and two political statutes. Two years later, the child of a Nestorian mother had Maronites for a godfather and godmother. Proximity brought promiscuity: marriage in effect clearly appears as the motive for attending two churches or switching to another. These practices sometimes expressed the ratios of comparative strength, the faithful of one minority church being forced to find a spouse among those of the relatively more numerous members of another church.[17] Such practices were favored by geographic mobility, a point that Bernard Heyberger is right to underline: Assigned in principle to a group from birth—a fact that had implications for the payment of taxes—the Christians in towns, like the Jews, moreover, stood out because of their constant movement among the diverse provinces of the Ottoman Empire.[18] Once estranged from his or her place of birth, a person could more easily seek out (or agree to) exogamy. The passage from one church to another could also result from the microstrategies of social advancement: The Greeks and Syrians marrying Latins serving the function of intermediaries were not choosing entry into a larger community but, rather, a change in status which allowed them to escape from the Ottoman system. Many such cases can be observed in the seventeenth century.

Changes in affiliation were frowned upon by the communities of origin, which sought to defend themselves by every available means, including the presentation of a denunciation before the Ottoman authorities. It was often displacement that, loosening communal ties, allowed the individual to take such a step. Conversion was much more possible when the religious community was distant: It was in the Holy Land that Copts of Egypt became Latins, and in Cairo; in contrast, the Armenians of Syria-Palestine converted to the Latin rite. The Jews from the Holy Land, from Livorno or from Ancona, came to Cairo or Alexandria to embrace Christianity. A Jewish rabbi from Safi converted and received, with baptism, the name Jean-Baptiste. But the "persecutions" to which the Jews subjected him were such that he returned to Judaism. In 1631, weary of war, he took himself to Cairo with his wife and children to enter again into the bosom of the Church. All seven persons of his family were finally brought to Christianity through the care of the Franciscans.[19]

The practices of interconfessional matrimony did not fail to raise disturbing questions for the Roman clergy. To what church did the children of mixed couples revert? Was it permissible for a faithful member of the Catholic Church to take communion in a schismatic church? What sanctions should one inflict upon ambivalent Catholics? In 1712 a Catholic of Bethlehem found himself in debt to a Turk. An Armenian agreed to pay his debt in return for compensation; he obtained in exchange the hand of the daughter of a Catholic without having to provide the dowry (for in the Orient, men brought the dowry). The Armenian promised to become a Catholic and to marry in the Latin Church. In fact he did neither. The marriage was celebrated in the Armenian church in the presence of the bride's father. The Custodian of the Holy Places, violently opposed to such deviations, deprived the Catholic of the sacraments. The latter pleaded, and the Custodian therefore imposed on him the punishment that he must hold the candle at the door of the church during a particularly busy day, Christmas in this case. In Rome, the prefect of Propaganda fide found the punishment normally inflicted on the excommunicated and on public blasphemers too severe and dangerous, as it might attract the attention of the Turks and provoke troubles. The affair ended without result[20] but reveals, however, the diversity of relations and interests that linked the members of different religious confessions with each other.

This contiguity and familiarity among individuals of varied confessions also led to syncretic practices that troubled the Franciscan friars. In Jaffa, in 1766, there was only one Catholic (Franciscan) church. The number of its faithful rose to 134, all Oriental. It was a small and homogenous congregation as a result, without the intrusion of Frankish merchants and other European Christians as is frequently the case in the ports. The situation was not so simple as it seemed, however; for these Catholics were Latin (45), Maronite (32), and Greek (57). Thus, the Catholics who followed the Eastern rite did not wish to follow their parish priest in the Latin rite for the practices of Lent, and they continued to eat fish and drink wine. Worse, they came to take sides with the local schismatics: "An insolent and seditious people, they freely permitted themselves to become incited by the schismatics into pillaging the almshouse and doing violence to the friars."[21]

The city of Acre provided an additional case illustrative of another form of confusion. The Franciscans of the Holy Land, according to a report by one of their number, had two parish churches for the 168 faithful there, one for the Orientals of the Latin rite, the other for French and other European merchants. Yet there were still two other Catholic churches, each with its own clergy and neither dependent on the Franciscans: one for the Greek Catholics, the other for the Maronites. The first had 1,000 parishioners; the second, 200. There were, finally, the schismatic churches. The Greek Catholics freely consented to being godparents to the children of schismatics or to offering their children and their vows to the schismatic churches. Taking a spouse from among the schismatics, they then consented to allowing their children to be educated in the schism. Greeks as well as Maronites did not rigorously respect the fasts of their (Latin) rite and, when required to observe them, retorted that they benefited from an exemption from the Holy See. The friar who reported all this complained that for several years a Syrian monk (we may surmise a Jacobite) named Fargialla heard the confessions of Christians from all the nations, assisted at marriages in private homes against the will of the curates of the diverse parishes, celebrated mass at the Maronite church with Latin pomp, and to top it all brought about confusion because the unfortunate Franciscans were powerless in the face of this mixture of forms, whereas the faithful seemed to find surer paths to salvation in the melange. What is revealed by the indictments of this type sent to Rome year after year is the strong religiosity of this group of Christians despite differences of dogma along with the similarity of the social practices among the faithful.[22]

Let us move on to Nazareth, where the rivalries between Catholics made the situation more confused. Trouble was not expected in a city that in 1766 had only one Catholic church, that of the Franciscans. The parish was served by three Arab missionaries and numbered about 870 faithful, the majority among them of the Latin rite (but also included Syrian, Copt, Maronite, and Greek Eastern Catholics who received the Roman sacrament but who were no less subjected to a particular regimen by virtue of the encyclical of Benedict XIV). The danger came, this time, from the Catholic priests of the neighboring towns. Thus, when the Greek Catholic bishop from Cana paid a visit in August, his arrival was well noted; for he was accompanied by a deacon and a subdeacon. In the church filled with followers, he ordered the Greek Catholics, in the presence of their two curates, not to take communion *in azimo* (the unleavened bread of the Roman mass; in the Greek rite the bread is leavened), for the sacraments of the Latins were worthless. He excommunicated the two curates and insulted the head Franciscan who had, nonetheless, just offered him hospitality.[23] This case was not an isolated one. In truth, the conflicts between friars had less to do with reasons of dogma than with their dual competition for followers, on the one hand, and for the access to the material resources that came from the faithful in the fees paid to Eastern priests for confessions and the absolution of sins, on the other.

Concurrent Clergies

Since the fall of Byzantium, the churches of the Orient have been maintained—without a state—the same rite supporting them from the outside. This is a paradox that has often been emphasized. In their situation they must find outside support sufficient to assure their permanence but not such that it will lead to their dissolution. The presence of Latin clergy was a menace in this regard (since its ultimate vocation was to reconcile the Eastern church with Rome and to bring an end to the schism), all the more so in that it supplied no institutional support to the Eastern clergy, although each tightened its alliances.

It is not our place here to follow the detail of events in the multiple quarrels that divided the Christians. It is sufficient to note the regularities to observe the major tendencies. The Franciscans of the Guardian of the Holy Places were dependent upon Rome from a religious and institutional point of view but not from a diplomatic and political point of view. In order to defend themselves before the Sublime Porte, they appealed for mediation by the ambassadors of France and Venice and, since the Serenissina remained a power in the region, by France alone thereafter. On a local scale, the consul of the French nation in this or that port might also defend the Franciscans before the agents of Turkish authority.

The Greek church, for its part, enjoyed a numerical and institutional superiority in the capital of the empire and in Asia Minor, as it did in the Holy Land and in Syria-Palestine. Thus, it found itself the most threatened when its followers defected in favor of the Latins; it also contended with the Franciscans over the guardianship of the Holy Places. Being in no position to seek an exterior source of political support until the nineteenth century (until the entry of Russia in the affairs of the Middle East), the Greek church could, on the other hand, flatter the Turkish authorities and denounce, in the case of the Latins' missionary work, a truly subversive policy. In general, the Ottomans insisted on seeing their subjects registered in their ta'ifa, translated by the Latins as sect and nation and called *millet* in the nineteenth century.

This communal organization assured both the collection of taxes and the judicial, philanthropic, and educational circumscription of non-Muslims. Although they did not maintain close surveillance of their subjects, the agents of the Ottoman authority did penalize, when they learned of such occurrences, those who changed churches. In particular, the transfer to Latin Catholicism (or to Anglicanism, moreover) adds another disorder and another threat, for the Greeks asserted to the Ottoman authorities that this meant becoming Frankish and thus escaping Turkish authority by entering under the protection of a foreign state, France in this case. To this denunciation, according to the Franciscans, the Greeks added arguments that managed to gain the sympathies of the Ottoman authorities. They urged the Turks to pass sanctions and to have the Porte renew the prohibition against changing churches. The question of guarding the Holy Places remained in other respects the apple of discord between the Franciscans and the Greek church, with episodes of overt crisis which we shall not report here except to note that there were many of them. This is not to say, however, that there were no periods of truce between Latins and Greeks.

Less powerful than the Greek church, the Armenian, Jacobite, and Nestorian churches generally maintained less contentious relations with the Latins. Yet when the need arose, these other churches used the same weapons to defend themselves, while the Latins, acculturated by their stay in the Orient, had no other weapons to counter with. The history that follows illustrates the mechanism of this daily strife. In 1631, an Armenian friar from Bethlehem wished to switch to the Roman Church. To avoid alerting his nation, he was rushed to Nazareth. But the news of his apostasy spread. Forming an alliance against the Latins, the Greeks and Armenians presented a plea to the pasha, asserting that the Franks, in converting the Greeks of Bethlehem en masse, were preparing a veritable reconquest of the Holy Land. The Greek *drogman* insisted that the pasha should force the renegades to return to their original religion and make them pay tribute. The Armenians, in their turn, accused the Latins of blaspheming against Islam and of bribing followers in order to obtain their conversion. Following these denunciations, the pasha ordered the imprisonment of all the Catholic friars of Jerusalem. In order to reestablish order, the monks' superior had to buy the favor of the pasha.[24]

When in turn they saw themselves threatened by the invasion of Carmelite, Jesuit, and Capuchin missionaries, the Franciscans put into action a strategy borrowed from the Christians of the Orient: They mobilized the faithful (in 1710, they encouraged the drawing-up of a petition signed in Aleppo by the representatives of the Chaldeans, the Armenians, the Maronites, and the Greeks to send to the consul of the French nation and the Roman authorities) to protest against the Turkish threat (of pressure and forced conversions) in order to keep the Franciscans' monopoly of missionary activity in the region.[25]

The Offer of Conversion and Its Social Effects

Conversion is not a univocal operation by which an individual X passes from religion A to religion B. First, the conditions that motivate X are varied. Second, the procedures of conversion are similarly varied. Third, the conversion is not always irreversible.

The Conversion as Seduction: "Caresses and Kindnesses"

We have already seen some of the social conditions that assisted passage from one church to another: marriage, proximity, entry into a more numerous community or alliance with the powerful, and so forth. Some of these movements mentioned here appear to be spontaneous and do not result therefore from a sustained action on the part of the clergy.

It was quite the reverse with the monks who came from Europe to do missionary work. They did offer conversion, although this offer, could not be made openly. Their action had to remain not only discreet but take forms that reflected varying degrees of subtlety. Less subtle was the conversion administered without the knowledge of the interested parties, as reflected in the words of Father Alexander of Rhodes, who came to Persia in 1659: "The first and principal fruit that our missionaries have begun to pick from this excellent field are the baptisms of a great quantity of little children, when they are near death; they can do this easily, all the more so in that the parents themselves bring them to our missionaries in hope that they might procure a remedy for the life of the body. . . . The harvest of these innocent souls is all the richer as the number of small children who die is great. It was recorded that in one single year some forty thousand children died in Aspahan; and besides, a single priest for his part baptized five or six in one day."[26]

Cases such as this were frequent throughout the region with which we are concerned here. The epidemics of smallpox and of the plague, which remained murderous and recurrent, were particularly favorable to gestures of despair, by which even the Muslim parents still hoped to save their children by entrusting them to the Christians.[27] The plague also incited renegades to seek reconciliation in order to find salvation and to die in peace.

The friars however generally used less direct means. They applied themselves to attracting the faithful of other churches or of other religions by gaining their confidence. One method was to use their technical or scientific knowledge. Medicine was one such knowledge that allowed them to attract the favor of the Turkish authorities when these benefited from efficacious treatments; at the same time it also furnished a pretext for entering the homes of Christian families and putting in a good word while providing remedies.[28] One such priest at Aleppo prepared a simple trilingual book in French, Latin, and Arabic in order to officiate among Arabic speakers and treat sick Christians for free, offering them medicine instead of the "supernatural" remedies such as water said to be St. Ignatius's, for "unnatural" illnesses due to Turkish or Christian sorcerers.[29] He attracted young Jews "by means of a few glasses and mathematical favors, designed to tame them into listening to us speak of our mysteries." His efforts were in vain, since the parents would irrevocably break off these suspicious relations. He had better success with young Greeks, who wanted him to exhibit his mathematical instruments, "globes, spheres, cards, triangular glasses" and who came voluntarily on Sundays and feast days to share his company.[30]

More subtle and more systematic was the exhortation of high-ranking clerics, for their "reconciliation" could sway all of their followers. The chase after influential people was constant, especially within those churches weakest from an institutional point of view and least endowed with material resources. There exists a rich record, which cannot be opened here. It will suffice to observe, as does Bernard Heyberger, that the heads of the Eastern churches, profoundly immersed in their society, were often the descendants of families of notables and participants in factional rivalries. Being swayed toward Catholicism could be useful as a strategy to reinforce their local power. To promise conversion could mobilize resources with which to prevail over another competitor for an important position.[31] Transferring to the Roman Church could thus be for superficial reasons and have no effect on the mass of followers. The fact remains that certain prelates paid with their lives for their shift in churches.

Of greater social significance, the work of teaching in schools won young souls to the Latin church or gave them the means to remain attached to it. All of the Franciscan houses maintained a school to teach Catholic children between the ages of six and eleven. The Franciscan house in Constantinople received children from Jerusalem and Bethlehem who, once tutored in Turkish, could then serve as intermediaries in the Holy Land. The missionaries had to overcome the difficulties of the Arabic language because they could not preach without mastering it. One complained about the "scabrousness" of this language and the ridicule they received from the Copts for pronouncing it badly or for not knowing the correct theological terms and concepts necessary for the work of conversion.[32] But they made sure that the teaching was done in Arabic.

Such pedagogical effort was extended by the manufacture and the distribution of books of piety, at first as manuscripts, for printing had not yet penetrated into the Ottoman Empire. At Aleppo in the seventeenth century, Father Chezaud prepared "devotional books which he had composed in Arabesque or Armenian languages in number. . . . He had to write them all by hand, there being no presses in Syria."[33] Subsequently, books printed in Arabic were imported from Europe by the case, an activity that became all the more pressing as the challenge made by the reformers, English most notably, was taken up after the end of the seventeenth century.[34] In 1731, these reformers began to distribute books printed in Arabic, including the Bible, in Jerusalem. The Guardian of the Holy Places purchased copies in order to burn them, except for two copies which he sent to Rome; even he emphasized the urgency of schooling children so that they might resist temptation.[35]

An even more ambitious activity of the reformers was sending young Eastern Christians to Europe, to such institutions as the College of the Maronites, the Urbain college in Rome, or even to France where the king decided to open a seminary at Marseilles, which accepted three pupils from each Christian Levantine nation. In the end it was found preferable to take them at the Jesuit college in Paris. When Coptic children could not be recruited, Ethiopian ones were sought.[36] Here again competition was fierce from the Anglicans, who had created an Eastern college at Oxford to educate young Greeks recruited from Smyrna. By this multiform strategy, the Roman clergy sought to reduce the cultural distance separating them from the Christians of the Orient and to have religious conversion accompanied by material and symbolic responses that could consolidate it.

The Procedures

The greatest number of individuals received into the bosom of the Roman church was formed from adults who belonged to an Eastern church. The Franciscans, as well as the members of other missionary orders, considered most of the new converts to be schismatics whom it was necessary not to convert but to reconcile. Reconciliation presupposed, according to the terms used by the scribes, that the interested parties "abjure their errors" or "detest their errors" before "entering into the bosom of the church" or to "embrace the Catholic faith." It is not known whether, for ordinary believers, these formulas resulted in a particular ceremony and to what degree the new converts were supposed to know the nature of the errors, which they were to "detest." The fathers knew what they were condemning in the dogma of the Eastern churches. But did the neophytes? One might suppose that questions of dogma were not what moved them the most. Be that as it may, the same procedure was not imposed on children, who merely received an affiliation upon birth: Their entry into the Roman church consisted, thus, of baptism and the attribution of a proper name.

However, not all neophytes were from the Eastern churches. In exceptional cases, some Muslims did embrace the Catholic faith. They were indiscriminately labeled Turks, whether they were Arabophones or Turkophones or even Ethiopian or Abyssinian blacks. Turks coming from the provinces of the Ottoman Empire had to undergo a three-stage conversion: catechization, baptism, and the attribution of a proper name. For security reasons they were then immediately sent to Christendom. The same procedures were used for blacks, except they were not transported to Christendom.

The questions of how catechization was conducted and what it consisted of remain to be explained. When a renegade who had begun a family in Islamic lands wanted to return to Christendom, that person had to give instruction to his wife before requesting baptism. The Pater noster, the Ave Maria, the Credo, and the Ten Commandments then formed the doctrinal stock of knowledge of the neophyte.[37]

The Social Effects of the Offer of Conversion:
"They Limp with Both Feet"

According to the report on the state of the Guardianship established in 1715 (after an outbreak of the plague which had decimated the population), the number of Eastern Catholics (excluding the Franks residing temporarily in the region) was less than 2,000 (see table 2). These figures rose strongly thereafter, passing 10,000 in 1760 (if one eliminates the overvalued figure for Aleppo) and continued to rise in 1765,[38] certainly a remarkable progression. But the figures remained modest in strength, compared with those of the Christian population of the East or, a fortiori, with those of the regional populations as a whole.

It remains difficult to evaluate the cumulative social effects of these conversions, for the friars themselves emphasized their fragility—fragility when these converts were at the point of death, notably in times of plague,[39] fragile also for indigents attracted by the assistance the Latins offered them but for whom reconciliation did not include their co-religionists. Conversion is a nearly impossible task when converts must be furnished with letters of recommendation, provisions of food and money, and the payment of their immediate passage to Christendom to remove them from the threats of reprisal.[40] Conversion was not only impossible but also a loss when the fathers succeeded in reconciling a prelate only to

TABLE 2. The Effects of the Offer of Conversion

City	1715	1727	1760	1765
Jerusalem	285	295	632	961
Bethlehem	438	592	1,000	1,030
St. Jean	46	49	95	90
Rama	30	46	78	95
Acre	21	130	25	168
Jaffa	40	134		
Nazareth	85	82	652	870
Damascus	181[a]		4,615	
Aleppo	75		[30,000][b]	
Alexandretta	10		12	
Tripoli			207	
Latakia			100	
Sayda			1,200	
Larnaca	107		194	
Licosia	13		10	
Alexandria	44		4	
Rosetta	28		27	
Cairo	298		1,500	
Fayoum	30	6		
Total	1,731	1,334	10,351	3,214

[a]Does not include reconciled Greeks.
[b]This overvalued number is not used.

have him lose his flock because his followers were protesting that they did not wish to change rites or when a rival gained the favor of the Turks and dismissed the neophyte.[41] At any rate, it is certain that the conversion to Latin doctrine, which promoted reconciliation and sought the unity of Christian believers, in fact created heterogeneity and accentuated religious diversity. In Jerusalem in 1761, out of 632 Catholics of diverse nations, 144 were Maronites and followed their own rite, although this was true in principle only, for certain Maronite families respected neither their own rite nor that of Rome and made a "*mescaglio* of one and the other," above all concerning Lent. Other Catholics had descended from the "reconciled" of a more or less recent date, Greeks being the greatest number of them and Syrians, Armenians, Copts, and Chaldeans comprising the others. Conversion, by all evidence, did not transform any of them into a docile troop united in the one faith. Each conserved his or her original religious affiliation, doubled by a new Latin identity.

The religious and social framework that the Latins provided was not sufficient to create communities capable of enduring and reproducing, nor did it anchor their catechism in the minds of their followers. Alongside the conversions that they succeeded in obtaining and the repentance of renegades which they were pleased to report, the friars never ceased to note the setbacks that they suffered. In 1639, in Jerusalem, a Syrian from Aleppo who had been forced to take the turban in Cairo had lived as a Muslim for fourteen months. He wished to be reconciled and was. At his request, he was sent to Venice in order to remain faithful to the Church. But when he returned to Aleppo, he fell back into abjectness, "ritorno al vomito di nuovo."[42] In 1702, in Old Cairo, Maria Omm Rohhme, "Goffita" (presumably a Copt), a Catholic, fell back into the Goffite errors.[43] The fruit of the labors of all the missionary orders together was weak, remarked the Guardian in 1711. There were few perfect reconciliations but many imperfect ones continued to frequent the church of their nation.[44]

Barriers to Conversion

It is true that the switch to Catholicism presented risks that discouraged candidates from converting. Sometimes, pursued by the members of their original church, candidates had to flee to another town or to Christendom, and clerics had to be hidden in a Latin monastery or with the Maronites of Lebanon.[45] At other times, denounced to the Turks, clerics found themselves offered the choice between death and conversion to Islam, as happened to the Armenians in the early years of the seventeenth century. "Faith appears to be truly unsteady in that nation," commented the Ambassador of France, "since of ten Armenians, nine have become Turks, and one only suffered death."[46] At least, they wavered.

The Guardian of the Holy Places had recourse in 1727 to a similar metaphor, "claudicant in duas parses"; they needed a custom-made rite, part Latin, part Greek. In truth, he continued, the reconciled seek less the purity of faith than the protection of the Franks. The friar concluded that what the reconciled say cannot be credited; these people "are neither cold nor hot." He denounced their comings and goings between religious practices that satisfied the principles of no single orthodoxy.[47]

The French Revolution and the imperial period caused the loss of territory to Catholic friars historically associated with French power. This troubled many, and the reconciled Greeks of Jerusalem and of the rest of the Holy Land went back, in great numbers, it seems, to the schismatic church, even if this meant returning later again to be reconciled with Rome. The nineteenth century inaugurated a new competition between the diverse indigenous religious groups who attempted to reform their methods and to improve the training of their clergy to better resist the pressures of missionaries from all orders.[48] When the Anglicans arrived on the Oriental scene in the 1840s, followed by other reformed missionaries, the offer of conversion produced a variety of effects and increased the unrest of the faithful. The Jews, Greeks, and Latins of Jerusalem, Damascus, Aleppo, or Acre, who had temporarily been tempted by Protestantism, came to embrace the Catholic faith between 1849 and 1862.[49] These back-and-forth movements expressed a powerful religious agitation[50] and a fierce competition between indigenous churches to rejuvenate their practices but doubtless was also the attraction that the Occidental powers exercised from that time on.

Despite all this, diversity resulting from conversion was not reduced. When the Sultan in 1831 recognized the legal existence of the Greek, Armenian, Chaldean, Syrian, and Coptic Uniate churches (notably to contain Russian influence), he consecrated this heterogeneity and finally domesticated the groups reunited with Rome by making a place for them within the traditional plan of the religious communities of the Empire.

NOTES

1. "Relation des missions de la Compagnie de Jésus en Syrie en l'année 1652, par le Père Nicolas Poirression," in Antoine Rabbathe, *Documents inédits pour sevir à l'histoire du christianisme en Orient (XVI–XIX siècle)*, 2 vols. (Paris, 1905–10), I:46.

2. Michel Febre, *Théâtre de la Turquie*, translated from Italian into French by the author (Paris, 1682). The author is a belated partisan of the anti-Turkish crusade.

3. Jacques Berque, in *De l'Euphrate à l'Atlas* (Paris: Sindbad, 1978); Carlton Coon, *The Story of the Middle East* (2d ed., 1958). Pierre Bourdieu, *Sociologie de l'Algerie* (5th ed., 1975).

4. Milton J. Esman and Itamar Rabinovich, eds., *Ethnicity, Pluralism, and the State in the Middle East* (Ithaca: Cornell University Press, 1988). The idea of ethnopolitics is borrowed from Joseph Rotschild, *Ethnopolitics: A Conceptual Framework* (New York: Columbia University Press, 1981).

5. For the current state of this issue (minus the state of Israel), see Lucette Valensi, "La Tour de Babel: groupes et relations ethniques au Moyen-Orient et en Afrique du Nord," *Annales, ESC* no. 4 (July–August 1986), 817–18.

6. Robert Ilbert, *Alexandrie 1860–1960. Un modèle éphémère de convivialité: communautés et identités cosmopolites* (Paris: Autrement, 1992). Ammiel Alcalay, *After Jews and Arabs: Remaking Levantine Culture* (Minneapolis: University of Minnesota Press, 1993). See also Gilles Veinstein, ed., *Salonique 1850–1918. La "ville des Juifs" et le réveil des Balkans* (Paris: Autrement, 1992). Stephane Yerasimos, ed., *Istanbul, 1914–1923. Capitale d'un monde illusoire ou l'agonie des vieux empires* (Paris: Autrement, 1992).

7. Frederik Barth, ed., *Ethnic Groups and Boundaries: The Social Organization of Cultural Difference* (Boston, 1969). Jean Loup Amselle and Elikia M'Bokolo, eds., *Au coeur de l'ethnie. Ethnies, tribalisme et Etat en Afrique* (Paris: La Découverte, 1985).

8. For the Khemchins, work in progress by Claire Mouradian. For the Dönmeh, there is an old bibliography and a study in progress on their descendants in the Society of Istanbul. For Iraq, Yitzhaq Nakash, *The Shi'is of Iraq* (Princeton: Princeton University Press, 1994) and idem, "The Conversion of Iraq's Tribes to Shi'ism," *International Journal of Middle East Studies* 26, no. 3 (August 1994): 443–53. Bartholome and Lucile Bennassar, *Les Chrétiens d'Allah* (Paris: Perrin, 1989).

9. The following pages being the result of research in progress, I underline their preliminary character. For an amply documented study treated from the perspective of social history, see Bernard Heyberger, *Les Chrétiens du Proche-Orient au temps de la Reforme catholique* (Rome: Ecole française de Rome, 1994), in which emphasis is placed upon the region of Alep but that extends well beyond this

frame. See also the same author, "Les Chrétiens d'Alep (Syrie) à travers les récits des conversions des missionnaires carmes déchaux (1657–1681)," *Mélanges de l'Ecole Française de Rome* 100 (1988–91): 461–69.

10. Franciscan archives, Jerusalem: Book of baptisms, marriages and recantations, 1555–1668. Reconciliations and converts, 1707 (this register contains also datum subsequent to 1707). Register of conversions to Catholicism: listed in 1853 by father Giuseppe del Tellaro, but continued until 1990. This register takes up data since the sixteenth century. It is published in part in *Saggio di quel che hanno fatto e fanno i missionari francescani in Terra Santa. Abjure e riconciliazioni ottenuti e battesimi conferiti ad adulti dall'anno 1768 a tutto it 1855* (Memorie estratte degli archivi di quella missione dal R Marcellino da Civezza. Florence, 1891). Besides these manuscript registers, I have relied upon published archives: Rabbath, previously cited (see note 1), and edited by Girolamo Golubovich, *Biblioteca bio-bibliografica delta Terra Sancta e dell'Oriente franciscano* (second set, 14 vols., Florence, 1921–23). We reserve the study of cases of mass conversions for another occasion.

11. Leonhard Lemmens, *Collectanea Terrae Sanctae ex archive hierosolymitano deprompta,* 300, in Golubovich, *Biblioteca,* 2d series, vol. 14 (Florence, 1933).

12. Rabbath, *Documents,* II, 86–87.

13. I borrow here an expression from Leon Werth, *33 jours* (Paris, 1992).

14. And still this was not always followed. Heyberger, *Les Chrétiens,* 53, relates that the Christian peasants of Nazareth wore white turbans in 1638.

15. Febvre, *Théâtre,* 376. See also Heyberger, *Les Chrétiens,* passim, on the adoption of Muslim dress by the Christians in order to avoid maltreatment and on the reminders reiterated by the Turkish authorities of prohibitions concerning vestimantary materials.

16. Rabbath, *Documents,* II, 71, on the vengeance of honor. There are innumerable notes on the practice of circumcision and excision among the Copts, polygamy, repudiation, and other practices judged aberrant by the Latin monks, in their reports sent to Rome. See Rabbath, *Documents,* I, 13, 54, 55, and so forth.

17. Because of the lack of Catholics in Bethlehem, the intermediaries of the Latin service were married to Greek schismatics. Some of these were reconciled, while others remained faithful to their own church; see Golubovich, *Croniche o vero annali,* vol. 6, 133.

18. Heyberger, *Les Chrétiens,* 26.

19. Franciscan Archives from Jerusalem, book of baptisms, marriages, abjurations and reconciliations, fol. 69. Similarly in 1716, a Jewish convert, returned "to his sect" because of violent acts committed by the Jews, rejoins the Church in Alexandria (Franciscan Archives of Jerusalem, Reconcilliations . . . Ist part. Alexandria). Golubovich, *Biblioteca,* 2d series, vol. 4, 365–66, contains vexations undergone by the reconciled Greeks from the Greek schismatics and requests for help from the Frankish consuls and merchants.

20. Golubovich, *Biblioteca,* 2d series, vol. 4, 225, 249.

21. Ibid., 2d series, vol. 2, 46.

22. Ibid., 2d series, vol. I, 89, 103, and so forth, on the marriages between schismatics and Catholics or on the frequenting of schismatic churches by Catholics, in the 1630s. See also vols. 11–12, p. 19, for the same years.

23. Ibid., 2d series, vol. 2, 2d part, 47.

24. Giovanni di Calaorra, *Historia chronologica della provincia di Svria, et Terra Santa di Gierusalemme,* translated from Spanish (Venice, 1684).

25. Golubovich, *Biblioteca,* 2d series, vol. 4, 49–50, 376.

26. Rabbath, *Documents,* II, 310. For the version in its entirety, see *Relation de la mission des Pères de la Compagnie de Jésus établie dans le Royaume de Perse par le R. P Alexandre de Rhodes: dressée et mise au jour par un Père de la même Compagnie* (Paris: Henault, 1659). The same friar, in a letter to a priest of the same company, at Lyon, in 1658: "Ordinarily I frequent the villages to seek out the little sick children, and to give them Holy Baptism when there is no remedy. We send these little angels into Heaven" (Rabbath, *Documents,* II, 85). See also Febvre, *Théâtre,* 516, in the archives of the Franciscans of Jerusalem, Registro delle conversione al cattolicismo, 1853, the year 1626 in Cairo.

27. See Heyberger, *Les Chrétiens;* Rabbath, *Documents,* II, 86–87: in 1669, 1674, 1675, for the baptisms administered by the Carmelites at Aleppo. Franciscan Archives of Jerusalem, Registre Tellaro, years 1626, etc., where the renegade, Turkish, Coptic parents entrust their children who are at the point of death.

28. Febvre, *Théâtre,* 516, on the relations between the exercise of medicine and missionary work.

29. Rabbath, *Documents,* I, 53, excerpt.

30. Ibid., 62.

31. Heyberger, *Les Chrétiens,* 119–27, and in particular 129. For three cases of the conversion of prelates richly documented, see Golubovich, *Biblioteca,* 2d series, vol. V. See also Robert M. Haddad, "On Melkite Passage to the Unia: The Case of Patriarch Cyril al-a'im (1672–1720)," in Benjamin Braude and Bernard Lewis, eds., *Christians and Jews in the Ottoman Empire,* vol. 2 of *The Arabic-Speaking Lands* (New York: Holmes and Meier, 1982), 67–70.

32. Golubovich, *Biblioteca,* series 2, vol. 7, 213 and 216 (date, 1631). Another testimony on the difficulties of interpreting a language wholly wild and barbaric in its pronunciation and its letters, whatever grace it may have in its manner of expression" (Rabbath, *Documents,* 11, 59).

33. Ibid., I, 52–53, Poirresson (1652).

34. Ibid., I, 519, for Syria in 1698. Heyberger, *Les Chrétiens,* 404, on shipping books.

35. Golubovich, *Biblioteca,* 2d series, vol. 2, 18.

36. Rabbath, *Documents,* I, 517–44. For Rome, Heyberger, *Les Chrétiens,* 423. The following are opened in succession: a Greek college in Rome, 1576; an Armen-

ian and Maronite college, in 1584; a college for Orientals attached to the Congregation de la Propaganda Fide in 1622. See G. C. Anawati, "The Roman Catholic Church and Churches in Communion with Rome," 389, in A. J. Arberry, *Religion in the Middle East*, vol. I of *Judaism and Christianity* (Cambridge, 1969), 347–422.

37. Calaorra, *Historian*, 759. The same catechization in 1627, in Arabic, for a "mora" who had married a renegade Sicilian, in Golubovich, *Biblioteca*, 2d series, vol. 7, 129.

38. Golubovich, *Biblioteca*, 2d series, vol. 4, 410–18. Missing are the "souls" of which the Capuchins from several parishes assure us. In 1731, the author of another report on the state of the custodianship counts 3,353 souls, including the Franks (I, vol. 2, 19). For 1727, 1760, and 1764, see 138–41 and 178–227.

39. Golubovich, *Biblioteca*, vol. VIII, 309, for the year 1636.

40. Golubovich, *Biblioteca*, vol. VII, "Chroniche," 22, 73. See also 129–34 for the year 1627; 181ff for the year 1630; 216ff for 1631.

41. Ibid., vol. VII, "Croniche" 22, vol. 11–2, 71–2 for the case of Cyprus, in 1639.

42. Ibid., 2d series, vol. 11–2, 80.

43. Franciscan Archives in Jerusalem. Reconciliations, 1st part, Old Cairo.

44. Golubovich, *Biblioteca*, 2d series, vol. 4, 157.

45. Rabbath, *Documents*, I, 55, concerning an Armenian bishop retired to Cappadoce (95 concerns a Jacobite bishop of Aleppo).

46. Ibid., 1, 126, Letters from the Ambassador of France at Constantinople to the Minister of Louis XIV, 1706–7. Golubovich, *Biblioteca*, 2d series, vol. 1, 1634, on the incarceration of reconciled members who are denounced to the Turks by the Greeks.

47. Golubovich, *Biblioteca*, 2d series, vol. 14, 141.

48. C. H. Malik, "The Orthodox Church," in A. J. Arberry, *Religion in the Middle East*, I: 297–346, and notably 317.

49. Franciscan Archives of Jerusalem, register of Tellaro.

50. On that which affects the Jews, see Arie Morgenstern, "Messianic Concepts and Settlement in the Land of Israel," in Richard E. Cohen, ed., *Vision and Conflict in the Holy Land* (Jerusalem: Yad Izhak Ben-vi, 1985), 141–42, and the debate that follows, 163–69. Sherman Lieber, *Mystics and Missionaries: The Jews in Palestine, 1799–1840* (Salt Lake City: University of Utah Press, 1992).

Comment

Juan R. I. Cole

Ethnic and religious identities are not only constructed, but are continually reconstructed on the contested field of culture. One virtue of Lucette Valensi's thought-provoking and original chapter is to question the tendency among observers of Middle Eastern religion to reify categories that are in fact much more fluid than they appear on the surface. Media observers often use words such as *traditional, rigid,* and *static* for Islam in particular. But if we look at developments over a century instead of over a decade, Middle Eastern religion has been extremely volatile and subject to change. As she notes, the Shi'ite majority in Iraq is probably only a century and a half old; and the large Shi'ite community of Pakistan is probably largely of a similar age. The Salafiyyah movement, or Muslim Puritanism, never took separate sectarian form, but it is only a century old and its beliefs are as different from the nineteenth-century Muslim mainstream as Calvinism is from Catholicism. Entire religions have grown up in the past century and a half, such as the Baha'i faith and the Ahmadiyyah.

Valensi wishes to recover the project of writing religion in the Middle East from the various state and nationalist imperatives that she rightly says have driven research in this field. Such motives have tended to reinforce assumptions about the necessity of ethnic struggles occurring along religious lines and turning out the way they have. She suggests that looking at a group of converts to a specific religion from disparate origins, who of necessity bring to their community great diversity of backgrounds, is one way to reconceptualize the religious experience of the early modern Middle East. In particular, she looks at conversions to Latin-rite Roman Catholicism. This choice certainly divorces the subject from any national project, since in the Middle East only Lebanese nationalism is intertwined with Catholicism in any substantial way, and there it is the Uniate Maronite rite that is involved rather than the Latin rite. Although she only

121

treats a few thousand converts to Roman Catholicism among some five million inhabitants of Egypt and Greater Syria during the eighteenth century, the phenomenon she is investigating therefore represents less than a thousandth of a percent or so of the population of the region in question. This study, however, does not rise or fall on the largeness of its numbers or the statistical significance of its correlations. It is about identity, and her essay certainly contains important findings that can legitimately be generalized. Religion in the Middle East was to some large extent a disciplining agent, intimately implicated in the power relations of kinship, community, the state, and the international order.

Most classical Muslim jurisprudence forbade polytheism; advocated war against non-Muslim states save those in treaty alliance with Muslims; made apostasy from Islam a capital offense; gave a sort of second-class citizenship to Jews and Christians; and advocated the persecution of Muslims viewed as heretical in that school of jurisprudence. During the eighteenth century, non-Muslims in the empire lived under a mixture of clerical jurisprudence, customary law, and royal decrees, not yet benefiting from Enlightenment freedoms. The major change in their status came about because the Sultan granted Capitulations to European Christian merchants living in the empire, exempting them from the authority of the qadi and placing them under the recognizance of their own consulate. These Capitulations gradually became more extensive, and they also eventuated in an exemption from local taxes. This situation impelled many members of religious minorities to seek foreign patrons and passports. European powers, making rapid economic and organizational advances that left the Ottomans behind and dimly signaled the beginnings of the age of imperialism, were often eager to cultivate local clients. This shift in global power relations and change in law provides a powerful context for the thousands of instances where Catholicism was embraced in the eighteenth century.

If we turn now from the classical statements of norms to Valensi's findings in the archives, we discover some surprises. That of some 3,000 converts to Roman Catholicism from the mid–eighteenth to the mid–nineteenth century in Jerusalem recorded by Franciscans, about 6 percent were Muslim is remarkable. Of course, some of these were former Christians now reentering their faith after having adopted Islam for whatever reason. Still, given that apostasy from Islam could often be harshly punished, in some instances by death, even this small number is surprising. But punishment required that the individual come to the attention of the state, and many converts seem have gained the sort of anonymity that accrues to those who travel far from their place of birth. The author, or the sources she quotes, suggests that its social context lay in cross-confessional love affairs or in the quest for the protection offered via the Capitulations by a French passport or even just a French connection. I will make some suggestions of other possible motives below. In any case, this phenomenon should not have existed, according to the Muslim jurists. The essay also suggests a fair amount of new church building, which most ulama or Muslim clerics would have forbidden, but which appears to have gone on just the same. The strong eighteenth-century restatement of the strict position on such matters by the rector of al-Azhar university in Cairo, Shaykh Ahmad ad-Damanhuri, becomes more understandable in the light of such vitality among Christian missionaries. The mechanisms whereby Ottoman officials were convinced to allow church building and active missionary work would be interesting to pursue and might appear in Ottoman records.

The author rightly reminds us of the ambiguity of identity. The early modern Vatican practice of recognizing as "Uniates" Eastern-rite groups who were willing to acknowledge the Pope, and of allowing them to retain their distinctive liturgical languages and rites, created such groups as Greek Catholics and Maronite Catholics, united in their ultimate subservience to Rome, but differing in most other regards. As she suggests, the very definition of a Catholic was full of uncertainties and boundary problems. When we find congregants from Uniate churches in a Latin-rite congregation, can they be thought of as converts? In one instance, they did not much care for the way the Latins commemorated Lent. On the other hand, it is worth remembering that the Uniate strategy with regard to the language of the rite was ultimately universalized, so that when American Catholics suddenly attended Mass in English, we do not usually think of them as having converted to anything. The interesting point is made that the Franciscans considered Eastern Orthodox Armenians and other Christian groups not converts but schismatics now being reconciled with the Church. Only the Jews and Muslims would then be converts in the parlance of the principals themselves.

Athough the author reviews the conditions for conversion, the procedures, the fluidity of it, and conversion as seduction, I think the meaning of conversion in this setting remains ambiguous. Given that literacy levels may have been as low as 1 or 2 percent in the Nile to Euphrates region during the eighteenth century, were doctrinal differences between Catholicism, Eastern Orthodoxy, and the Armenian and Coptic churches so well known and understood that for most believers changing churches involved any extensive subjective conversion? Did Arabic-speaking members of Eastern Orthodoxy have reason to care very much whether the liturgy was in Greek or in Latin, neither of which most of them were likely to know? Did the outstanding differences between Catholicism and Eastern Orthodoxy, such as the debate on the filioque or the question of primacy among the bishops, resonate very deeply with most churchgoers in Ramallah or Aleppo?

One finds relatively little mention anywhere in the essay of the possible spiritual or subjective reasons for conversions. The "social conditions" that formed the context for changing churches are given, quite plausibly, as marriage, neighborhood influences, the choice of a larger community over a smaller one, siding with the powerful, and so forth. Surely such considerations played a large part. And one is sympathetic about the paucity of accounts regarding subjective motivation, deriving from the converts themselves. Still, in everyday life in the late twentieth century, one knows converts from one religion to another: from Catholicism to Hinduism, from Judaism to Buddhism, from African-American Protestantism to Islam. Leaving aside the rice Christians and the Muslims by marriage, the stories of these conversions most often involve a spiritual awakening of some sort. There are peak experiences, revelations while listening to a sermon, visions, inner convincements. Surely eighteenth-century Middle Easterners also had such experiences, which could be important in their decision to change churches or even religions. For some Muslims the Franciscans would look an awfully lot like a Sufi order, replete with a healthy respect for poverty and extensive *dhikr* and *awrad* or mystical chants. That this subjective, spiritual dimension of conversion might not be documented is understandable. But surely some estimation of its likelihood can be made, so that these religious phenomena are not simply reduced to the operation of social conditions. Reference is, of course, made to the faith Muslims often had in Christian medicine or baptismal rites, and to the Iranian practice of baptizing doomed children (some few of whom survived). But this gesture of despair, wrought up with superstition, is not the sort of positive spiritual experience that I have in mind.

Aside from peak experiences and sudden insight, there are other subjective reasons to change religion besides the search for individual self-interest. Most of the motivations so far discussed have been what immigration specialists would call "pull" factors, reasons for embarking on a journey to another spiritual geography that derive from the attractions of the new religious world—its power, its numbers, the comeliness of its congregants, its wealth, even the beauty of its liturgy or values. But there are also "push" factors that might lead someone actively to seek an exit from an inherited faith. In my own research on conversions out of Islam in Iran, I have found what appears to me to be good evidence for such push factors. Within any religious community and within any social grouping or class in that religious community, there are fissures and conflicts. There are wife-beaters who die young and leave embittered widows, authoritarian fathers who expel their sons from their houses, siblings who engage in fierce rivalries, hidebound clergymen who alienate the spiritually or intellectually adventurous. For individuals scarred by such experiences, converting to another religion, despite all its severe disadvantages in a Middle Eastern context, does have the virtue of making public one's complete break with one's tormentor. In any one congregation, such restless individuals would constitute a small number, but if we are speaking of five million persons, then they are clearly among the few thousands primed for conversion to another religion.

Continuities and Discontinuities in Constructions of Jewishness in Europe, 1789–1945

Todd M. Endelman

In medieval and early modern Europe, Jews constituted a well-defined social and political unit, marked off from their neighbors by virtue of their religion, national background, legal status, and, in most cases, their language, costume, occupations, and social habits as well. For Jews living in these circumstances, in quasi-autonomous corporations (*kehillot*) with limited, mostly instrumental contact with Christians, the question of group definition—who are we and what is our place here?—did not arise. Religious tradition and political realities defined the borders of the Jewish world. Within this world, to be sure, sharp disagreements about the nature of Judaism erupted—between Maimonideans and anti-Maimonideans, between enthusiasts for and critics of *kabbalah,* between *hasidim* and *mitnagdim*—but these centered on internal issues of correct belief, authority, and observance, not external relations with the gentile world. In these controversies, the boundaries between Jews and non-Jews, Jewish society and Christendom, were not at stake.

The one exception to this generalization—the case of former New Christians, or *conversos*—is the proverbial exception that proves the proverbial rule. Having lived as nominal Christians in Spain, Portugal, France, and the Spanish Netherlands before rejoining tolerated Jewish communities elsewhere, ex-conversos were, in Yosef Yerushalmi's words, "the first considerable group of European Jews to have had their most extensive and direct personal experiences completely outside the organic Jewish community and the spiritual universe of normative Jewish tradition." Both before and after their return to Judaism, they experienced the tensions that later became characteristic of Jews who lived in two (or more) worlds at the same time. "Among these Jews," Miriam Bodian writes, "collective and individual self-perception entailed the balancing of two separate clusters of ideas, one associated with Jewish religion and peoplehood, the other with 'the Nation' [their Catholic, Iberian inheritance]." Whatever their beliefs and practices, all ex-conversos experienced "enmeshment in, and rejection by, Iberian society" and thus, once abroad, needed to fashion identities that acknowledged that experience, be it in positive or negative terms.[1]

Ex-conversos, however, were unrepresentative of the bulk of the European Jewish population, with its roots in northern and central Europe (Ashkenaz). The Jewishness of the Ashkenazim, their group identity, remained undisturbed until the Enlightenment, or even later.[2] It became problematic only when the corporate structure of state and society dissolved in the eighteenth and nineteenth centuries. As Jews were incorporated as individual citizens into the states of the West, the defining of Jewishness and the forging of new identities became a preoccupation for them and for their detractors as well. Even in the tsarist empire, where Jews remained unemancipated until 1917, social and economic modernization and exposure to Western intellectual currents problematized Jewishness for members of acculturated, secular-minded circles.

The movement "out of the ghetto" was a complex, multifaceted process, its pace and force varying from region to region and state to state. For most Jews in western and central Europe, it entailed the acquisition of full citizenship, the modernization of Jewish practice and belief, the adoption of new social and cultural values and new modes of deportment, dress, and speech, and the struggle for social acceptance in non-Jewish circles.[3] As Jews moved from exclusion to inclusion, from periphery to center, they found themselves reconsidering and redefining who they were. In earlier centuries, they had viewed themselves and were viewed by others as a separate people, for whom nation and religion (in the modern sense of these terms) were one and the same and whose links to the peoples in whose midst they lived were largely instrumental. But the emergence of liberal states based on individual rather than corporate rights made the survival of an undifferentiated sense of Jewishness difficult, if not impossible. Even if Jews had wanted to remain a people apart, occupying their own distinctive legal niche, their hosts would have been unwilling to tolerate this degree of separatism. In Salo Baron's now classic formulation, "emancipation was an even greater necessity for the modern state than it was for the Jews." Once corporate distinctions were abolished, it would have been "an outright anachronism" to allow the Jews to remain a separate body, with their own privileges and obligations.[4]

Jewish and Christian spokesmen for integration were in agreement: the Jewish component in Jews' identity was to shrink and become compartmentalized. They reasoned that if Jews continued to consider themselves a separate nation, with their own distinct allegiances and hopes, they could not be incorporated into the states in which they lived. In their view, inclusion demanded both compliance with the obligations of citizenship and cultural and social identificatian with their fellow citizens. Jewish peoplehood was to be abandoned, Jewish particularism to be muted. Judaism was to become a religion, like other religions, adherence to which was to be one element among several in the identity of emancipated, modern Jews. Inclusion in state and society could rest on no other basis. In the oft-cited declaration of the count of Clermont Tonnere in the debate on Jewish emancipation in December 1789: "Il faut refuser tout aux Juifs comme nation et accorder tout aux Juifs comme individus . . . ; il faut qu'ils ne fassent dans l'Etat ni un corps politique, ni un Ordre; il faut qu'ils soient individuellement citoyens." Jews who refused emancipation on these terms were to be expelled.[5]

From the perspective of the late twentieth century, with its notions of cultural pluralism, these terms seem harsh, even unreasonable. However, in the context of the period, they represent an advance, a sharp break with the past, when baptism was the sole avenue to acceptance and the sole cure for the curse of Jewishness. Moreover, while those who championed emancipation conceded that Jewish morals and customs were in a sorry state and needed to be reformed, they did not attribute this to the fundamentals of the Jews' religion or to their spiritual or corporeal essence. Rather, good children of the Enlightenment that they were, they believed that if Jews were unsocial, unproductive, and immoral, it was because Christian governments, Christian prejudices, and Christian ill-treatment had made them that way. The liberal historian Thomas Babington Macaulay was explicit about this in calling for the removal of Jewish disabilities in Britain. If English Jews lacked "patriotic feeling" and viewed Dutch Jews rather than English Christians as their compatriots, this was because an oppressive state had failed to protect them. "If the Jews have not felt towards England like children," he wrote in the *Edinburgh Review* in 1831, "it is because she has treated them like a step-mother." Once treated as equals, they would "know that they owe all their comforts and pleasures to the bond which united them in one community" and would be overcome with feelings of patriotism. In short, English Jews were "precisely what our government has made them."[6] Central to this and similar arguments was the liberal conviction that human character was not forever fixed but plastic and subject to environmental influence. Liberal supporters of emancipation were buoyant optimists, believers in human perfectibility, confident that toleration and equality would cleanse Jews of traits that they saw as objectionable.

While there was a consensus that political emancipation and social integration required the overhaul of Jewish behavior and identity, there was no agreement—nor even much discussion—about the parameters of this transformation. Indeed, in retrospect, one is struck by the vagueness of the demands that were made of Jews. What did proponents of their transformation mean when they called for their *régénération,*[7] their *Verbesserung, Veredelung, Reformezirung,*[8] or their "complete fusion . . . with their fellow subjects of every other denomination"?[9] At a minimum, they meant that Jews should speak and dress like other citizens, that they should embrace secular education and culture, that they should identify with their country of residence, becoming lawabiding, patriotic, productive citizens. About these matters, there was little confusion. But more than this was expected. The "clannishness" of the Jews, their concentration in commerce and finance and their adherence to "backward" religious customs, including dietary laws that were believed to hinder social intercourse—these too were considered ripe for reform. But, again, those who demanded the reformation of the Jews failed to specify what constituted sufficient change or to establish criteria to measure it. Did the metamorphosis of street traders into shopkeepers, wholesale merchants, and department-store magnates meet their expectations? Or did it demonstrate emancipation's failure, that is, the Jews' inability to escape trade (with its allegedly deleterious impact on character and morals) even when given the freedom to do so?[10]

More striking was the failure of both Jewish and non-Jewish reformers to envision the desired end of Jewish acculturation and integration, to describe in even broad strokes the hoped-for outcome of their legal, social, and cultural emancipation. Was their occupational distribution to resemble that of the population at large? Were they to be scattered hither and yon, throughout the land, sinking roots in every town and hamlet? Were they to find intimate companionship as much among Christians as among their co-religionists? Were they to seek husbands and wives outside the ethnic fold? Were they to so identify with the dominant culture that they embraced its religion as well? Were they, in time, to lose all internal and external marks of Jewishness and become invisible, that is, disappear via radical assimilation?

Although reformers tended to be vague about the future of the Jews, some, it is clear, envisioned their complete absorption or disappearance. In Britain, Christian defenders of the Jew Bill of 1753 argued that awarding rights to Jews would encourage their conformity to English customs and allow their integration into the English thus preparing the way for their conversion.[11] In France even before the revolution, the Abbé Grégoire, inspired by neo-Jansenist millenarianism, urged improvements in the socioeconomic status of the Ashkenazim of Alsace-Lorraine for the same reason. The state, he believed, should scatter Jews throughout rural France, thus undermining the control of their rabbis, and should also compel their children to attend state schools, thus exposing them to French culture. This would lead to more contact between Jews and Christians and in time bring the Jews to Christianity.[12] In the 1820s, the evangelical millenarian Philo-Judaean Society in London viewed improvements in Jewish status as promoting the same goal.[13] In tsarist Russia, minister of national enlightenment S. S. Uvarov expected his network of modern Jewish schools, launched in the 1840s, to weaken the hold of Talmudic traditions, dissolve separatism, and promote universal civility and true culture, the inevitable result of which would be recognition of the truth of Christianity.[14]

Some Jews also believed in a radical assimilationist vision of the Jewish future, in which Jews qua Jews would disappear, absorbed into some larger unit of humankind. Baptized Jews held such views—to the extent they thought about the future of the Jews at all, as distinct from their own personal fortunes. More unusual were radical assimilationists who dreamed of a future that was neither Jewish nor Christian, who envisioned a world in which divisions among religions, nations, and, in some versions, ranks and classes as well were effaced. David Friedländer's well-known "dry baptism" letter on behalf of Berlin Jews to Dean Teller in 1799, in which he proposed that Jews who had abandoned their ancestral rituals be admitted to the Protestant church without having to accept its nonrational dogmas, rested on the premise that there was one rational, natural religion that was the essence of both enlightened Christianity and enlightened Judaism.[15] A generation later, Jewish Saint-Simonians—Gustave d'Eichthal, Léon Halévy, the Rodrigues and Pereire brothers—spun dreams of a new universal order of one religion, one dogma, one cult, in which Judaism and Jews were to be absorbed. In their utopian gospel, nations disappeared, religion and politics merged, and universal harmony reigned.[16] Their contemporary Joseph Salvador, although never a Saint-Simonian, worked out a similar scheme of religious development, culminating in an imminent messianic era in which Mosaism (in effect, ethical monotheism), preserved by the Jews for centuries, provided a foundation for universal organization.[17]

In central and eastern Europe, Karl Marx and his Jewish disciples,[18] Ludwig Zamenhof, architect of the universal language Esperanto and its parallel universal religion Humanismo,[19] and Jacob Gordin, creator of the Spiritual Bible Brotherhood in southern Russia before his migration to the United States,[20] all looked forward to a future in which the categories of "Jew" and "Christian" disappeared. On the other hand, in imperial Germany polemicists for the dissolution of Jewry more frequently saw the future in terms of absorption into the German fold rather than a universalist utopia that transcended all particularisms. Writing in Maximilian Harden's journal *Die Zukunft* in 1904, Elias Jakob advised Germany's Jews,

> Dive under, disappear! Disappear with your oriental physiognomy, with your ways that contrast with your surroundings, with your mission, and, above all, with your exclusively ethical world view. Take the customs, the values, and the religion of your host people, seek to mix in with them and see to it that you are consumed in them without a trace.[21]

Views such as these, however, were exceptional. It is doubtful that most Jews imagined a future in which they would renounce or transcend their Jewishness. While willing, even eager, to redefine what it meant to be Jewish and to tailor their behavior and views accordingly, there is no evidence that they viewed their disappearance as desirable, necessary, or inevitable, as the final outcome of the assimilation process. If the behavior of most European Jews is indicative—as distinct from the programmatic utterances of their spokesmen—their understanding of assimilation demanded a much less radical and ruthless break with the past than their Christian supporters imagined. Moreover, while the Jewish communities of western and central Europe underwent far-reaching changes between the French Revolution and World War II, the scope and intensity of the changes were not uniform in all spheres of life or even within the same sphere. For example, while observance of most religious traditions declined, the practice of male circumcision remained almost universal, even in families otherwise alienated from traditional practice. In a similar vein, while most Jewish families in the West experienced *embourgeoisement* over two or three generations and ceased to be identified with disreputable street trades and petty commerce, the overall communal occupational profile remained skewed: most heads of families worked in commerce rather than in manufacturing, agriculture, or the liberal professions. The transformation of the Jews, then, was partial, uneven, and irregular.

This unevenness was most pronounced at the level of social relations between Jews and their fellow citizens. In one sense, middle-class Jews in Berlin, Paris, London, Amsterdam, Vienna, and Budapest were indistinguishable from non-Jews of similar rank. They wore the same clothes, spoke the same language, visited the same cafés, museums, and theaters, professed the same patriotic sentiments, educated their children at the same schools, enjoyed the same leisure-time activities. To be sure, there were subtle differences between the "intimate culture" of the Jews and that of their neighbors. While historians have just started to explore these differences and thus the evidence is not yet abundant, it appears, for example, that urban, middle-class German Jews read different books and newspapers, voted for different parties, responded to "Jewish" jokes in a different manner, and raised their children according to different norms.[22] But, on the surface, to the casual observer, little distinguished Jews from non-Jews in the broad externals of life.

However, if acculturation was well advanced by the turn of the century, integration, that is, acceptance into non-Jewish social and associational life, was not. During the nineteenth century, Jews gained access to institutions and organizations that had excluded them in the past: legislatures, municipal councils, the military, the liberal professions, fraternal groups, elite secondary schools, universities, clubs and casinos, charities, athletic and recreational associations. As a rule, English, French, Italian, and Dutch Jews were more successful in doing so than German, Austrian, Hungarian, and Czech Jews, let alone Russian and Polish Jews. Yet, despite these advances in institutional integration, Jews remained a people apart in terms of their most fundamental social ties. Most married Jews, formed their closest friendships with other Jews, relaxed and felt most comfortable in the homes of Jewish relatives and friends. In their descriptions of Jewish life before World War I, memoirists noted repeatedly the absence of true social integration, even in the most acculturated families. In recalling his youth in late imperial Berlin, Gershom Scholem told an interviewer that despite his father's firm commitment to liberal assimilationism "no Christian ever set foot in our home," not even Christians who were members of organizations in which his father was active (with the one exception of a formal fiftieth-birthday visit). The autobiographies of famous Jews (musicians, writers, scientists, intellectuals, bohemians), Scholem commented in another context, present a misleading picture. In "an ordinary, middle-class bourgeois home, neither rich nor poor" like his, there was no social mixing between Jews and Christians.[23] In recalling his childhood in Berlin of the 1890s, Richard Lichtheim also underlined the absence of social contact between Jews and Christians in upper-middle- and upper-class circles. When he visited the home of a non-Jewish school friend, who lived with his uncle, a general, or when his friend visited him, each was aware of entering "enemy territory." No Jew had ever before appeared in the general's house, nor Christian in the Lichtheim house, although, it should be added, the Lichtheims were unobservant and uneducated in matters Jewish and most of their relatives on his father's side were converts to Christianity.[24] Scholem's and Lichtheim's observations find confirmation in recent work of Werner Mosse, a historian who does not share their ideological commitment to view assimilation as a failure. In his exhaustive examination of the German-Jewish economic elite in imperial Germany, Mosse concluded that from the late-1870s "unselfconscious and more or less spontaneous social relations between Jew and Gentile virtually ceased." For the majority of German Jews, social relations were confined to the Jewish ambit.[25] From the 1870s on, even baptized Jews remained immersed in Jewish kinship and friendship networks, in which Jews, converted Jews, intermarried Jews, and Jews without religion (that is, who had withdrawn formally from the *Gemeinde* without converting to another faith) mixed. As social discrimination mounted, converts and those without religion were often forced to choose former Jews like themselves as their marriage partners. In Weimar Germany, Hannah Arendt recalled, the convert "only rarely left his family and even more rarely left his Jewish surroundings altogether."[26]

In more liberal states, France and Britain, in particular, there was greater social intimacy between Jews and non-Jews, just as there was greater integration at an institutional level.[27] But even in these states, Jewish social solidarity remained more or less firm. French and English Jews, like their German counterparts, kept Jewish company more often than not. The novelist Julia Frankau, a radical assimilationist who raised her children as Christians, noted the same absence of mixing as Scholem. In her novel *Dr. Phillips* (1887), middle-class London Jews live in social isolation, cut off from intimate contact with Christians. In "the heart of a great and cosmopolitan city," she wrote, they constitute "a whole nation dwelling apart in an inviolable seclusion." "There are houses upon houses in the West Central districts, in Maida Vale, in the City, which are barred to Christians, to which the very name of Jew is an open sesame." To their most common form of social intercourse—card games at each other's houses—"it was decidedly unusual to invite any but Jews."[28] In seeking to explain the prevalence of marriages between first cousins in late-Victorian Anglo-Jewry, the race scientist Joseph Jacobs cited, inter alia, what he termed "shoolism"—Jews' inclination to limit their circle of friends and acquaintances to the members of their own synagogue (*shul* in Yiddish).[29] In France, even those high-ranking judicial and administrative officials whom Pierre Birnbaum dubbed "les Juifs d'état," graduates of the universities and the *grandes écoles* who zealously served the Third Republic as prefects and subprefects and as members of the Conseil d'Etat, the Cour de cessation, and the cours d'appel, tended to marry within the fold, retain membership in Jewish organizations, and establish close social ties with other Jewish state functionaries and politicians. If they had become servants of the universal, laicized state in the public arena, they remained Jews in their private lives.[30]

Of course, it would be wrong to suggest that Jewish social cohesion in the nineteenth century remained rock-solid, unshaken by drift and defection. The stigmatization of Jewishness in cultural and social life and the persistence of legal and social barriers to integration took their toll, leading tens of thousands of Jews to cut their ties to Judaism, through baptism, intermarriage, and other forms of radical assimilation. In Vienna alone nine thousand Jews formally severed their ties to Judaism (withdrew from the Gemeinde) between 1868 and 1903—a figure that does not include an unknown but considerable number of children who were baptized by their parents, either at birth or later.[31] The German census of 1939 and the Hungarian census of 1941, both of which defined Jews in racial terms, provide evidence about the cumulative effect of communal secessions in Central Europe over several generations. In Berlin, 8.5 percent of the Jews were not members of the Gemeinde; in Vienna, 12 percent; in Budapest, 17 percent.[32] Of course, secession figures alone do not express the magnitude of the drift from Jewish distinctiveness. Among Jews who rejected conversion or secession, for reasons of conscience or otherwise, efforts to mute markers of Jewish difference became increasingly common from the 1870s. The Viennese novelist and satirist Robert Neumann recalled in his memoirs an incident about his mother that encapsulates these efforts. "To be a Jew [in pre–World War I Vienna] was one thing," he wrote, "but to discuss it was as much bad form as it was to swear, and almost as bad as mentioning anything connected with the functioning of the digestive or sexual organs." Once when his mother had to introduce to her guests a visitor "with the un-gentile name of Cohen . . . she pronounced his name again and again so unrecognizably and so much as if it were some painful infirmity from which he suffered that in the end he withdrew, red-faced."[33] To escape the stigma attached to Jewish names, central European Jews changed—or tried to change—their names, an assimilatory move that German officialdom fought tooth and nail.[34] Some changed even their noses, following the development of cosmetic rhinoplasty (nose job) by the Berlin Jewish orthopedic surgeon Jacques Joseph in 1898.[35]

The increase in intermarriage from the 1870s through the 1930s, though not a demographic threat to Jewish continuity, indicates that Jews were not confined entirely to their own social ghetto (intermarriage, then and now, presupposes sustained and more-or-less intimate social contact). In the Netherlands, the percentage of Jews marrying who took non-Jewish spouses rose from 6.02 percent in the period 1901 to 1905 to 16.86 percent in the period 1931 to 1934. In central European cities, intermarriage was even more common. In Berlin, in the period 1905 to 1906, there were 43.8 mixed marriages per one hundred pure Jewish marriages; in Hamburg, in the period 1903 to 1905, 49.5; in Frankfurt, in the period 1905 to 1909, 24.7. In Prussia, the rate of intermarriage almost doubled in the last quarter of the nineteenth century, rising from 9.8 intermarriages per one hundred Jewish marriages in the years 1875 to 1879 to 18.6 in the years 1900 to 1903.[36] On the eve of World War I, there were perhaps as many as ten thousand intermarried couples in Prussia.[37] Defection from Judaism in imperial Germany, whether through intermarriage, conversion, or formal withdrawal from the Gemeinde without baptism, was common enough to lead some observers to prophesy that German Jewry was fated to disappear of its own accord. Felix Theilhaber's *Der Untergang der deutschen Juden,* which appeared in 1911, was the best known exposition of this theme.[38]

Yet, if Jews were more integrated into state and society than earlier in the century, they still remained a recognizable social collectivity wherever they lived, defined less by their religious rites than their social patterns, historical memories, and communal ties. Indeed, what struck gentile contemporaries was the persistence of Jewish social separatism, not its breakdown and decay. Despite their seemingly rapid progress in becoming Germans, Englishmen, Frenchmen, and so on, Jews still seemed unable or unwilling to leave behind their Jewishness once and for all. Heinrich Treitschke complained that despite their emancipation German Jews rejected "the blood mixing [intermarriage]" that had been "the most effective way to equalize tribal differences."[39] To critics like Treitschke and even to some liberals and socialists, this was scandalous: was not the purpose of emancipation to eradicate Jewish tribalism? To dissolve social and cultural barriers? The success of Jews in using emancipation to achieve economic and cultural prominence—while at the same time declining to intermarry or abandon their social cohesion—as well as the contrast between their achievements and their marginal demographic status, compounded the scandal, fueling fears of Jewish domination of cultural and economic life. In rebutting Treitschke's antisemitic articles in the *Preussische Jahrbucher* in the winter of 1879–80, the liberal historian Theodor Mommsen also scolded Jews for failing to be completely absorbed into German society. Just as they had served as a universal element in the Roman Empire, "a force for cohesion, shattering particularistic tribal elements, so now they must serve as 'ein Element der Decomposition der Stamme.'" To enable them to carry out their historical task of aiding in German unification, Mommsen instructed them to dissolve their own associations that had the same goals as nondenominational integrated ones. In his view, the preservation of Jewish identity for secular reasons was an affront to the Christian character of modern civilization. In the following decade, the Verein zur Abwehr des Antisemitismus, which Christian liberals and progressives established in 1891 to combat the new racial antisemitism, denounced the formation of Jewish fraternities and sports clubs because they encouraged Jewish continuity and survival.[40] While the German case represents an extreme manifestation of liberal intolerance for Jewish survival, it embodies nonetheless a broader split in Jewish and non-Jewish understandings of what the transformation of the Jews meant.

Gentile opposition to the persistence of Jewish social isolation created a dilemma for communal spokesmen. Clearly, having accepted emancipation and its premises, Jews were no longer able to define themselves as members of a group except on religious grounds, that is, as citizens of their respective states whose religion alone distinguished them from other citizens. This was problematic in two ways. First, Judaism, even after emancipation, included within its orbit activities that Christian societies increasingly considered outside clerical control, such as marriage, divorce, burial, diet, dress, and work. Jewish claims to difference on the basis of religion in the nineteenth century thus extended into realms that went beyond conventional Christian understandings of religion. For example, in Victorian England, the fact that university entrance and scholarship examinations were administered on Saturdays, when Jews are forbidden to travel and write, led the Board of Deputies of British Jews to intervene repeatedly to make alternative arrangements for Jewish candidates.[41] These met with success in most cases, but elsewhere Jewish communal bodies did not seek similar exemptions, knowing full well that state officials neither understood nor felt sympathetic toward Jewish religious concerns. In the words of David Landes: "If you want a lively debate, try to explain to a group of French people, Jewish or non-Jewish, that the institution of Saturday classes is objectively anti-Jewish. Most Frenchmen cannot even understand the issue."[42]

Even more problematical: the ideological construction of the Jews as a religious minority did not fit the social facts. When Jews made religion the hallmark of their difference, they did so because there was no other reasonable alternative, not because they were blind to the social dimensions of their group life. They knew full well that emancipation had not dissolved their social bonds. From their perspective, what was awkward, even dangerous, was that the states that emancipated them tended to conflate citizenship and nationality. Loyal, law-abiding, productive citizens were expected to embrace the cultural habits and national characteristics of the majority; even more, they were to undergo an inner transformation that produced a total reorientation in thought, behavior, sentiments, and affections. Obedience to the law of the land was insufficient. Of course, states and societies varied in the degree to which cultural heterogeneity preoccupied them; German civil servants and statesmen were more concerned about Jewish particularism than their British, French, Italian, and Dutch counterparts, for example. But, in general, notions of multiculturalism, ethnic diversity, cultural pluralism, and the like were in the future. Political leaders, social theorists, and cultural spokesmen dreamed of national homogeneity, unity, solidarity, assimilation, integration, and so on. Given this, the sole basis for defining Jewish difference was religion, the West having renounced religious conformity as a requirement for active citizenship. As a result, in the face of cries to revoke emancipation and circumscribe their freedoms, cries that became increasingly common from the 1870s on, Jews declared themselves to be Germans (or whatever), reducing their Jewishness to a mere matter of religious difference. What they could not do was acknowledge their social cohesion and ethnic distinctiveness.

To have done so would have seemed to them dangerous, even suicidal, an invitation to disaster—aside from the issue of whether they possessed the conceptual tools to do so. And, when spokesmen for the nascent Zionist movement began to do just that, to define Jews in national terms, communal leaders throughout western and central Europe reacted with alarm, fearing that this characterization endangered their hard-won legal and social achievements.[43]

However, it would be wrong to infer that Jews were blind to the tension between their professed status as a religious minority and the social realities of their lives, which, after all, showed them to be something else. The gap between theory and practice, coupled with mounting attacks from antisemites who claimed that Jews were aliens and outsiders, led them to seek new terms to express more accurately the nature of their Jewishness—without, however, putting their legal status in danger. In fin de siècle France, for example, Jewish intellectuals referred to *la race juive,* a phrase with distinct biological overtones. By using the word *race,* they wanted to suggest a feeling of community with other Jews, a sense of common historical fate, and a deep emotional bond that did not fit conventional forms of group attachment in French society. But they also repeatedly invoked other terms as well to describe their sense of attachment—vague, unrigorous terms like *nos frères, solidarité, nation, peuple, famille.*[44]

In the Weimar period, leaders of the Centralverein Deutscher Staatsbürger jüdischen Glaubens, a liberal, assimilation-oriented self-defense organization dating from 1893, used various neologisms that departed from the strictly religious definition of Jewishness that an earlier generation had invoked in the struggle for emancipation. Recognizing that this definition did not encompass the tens of thousands of nonobservant Jews who still felt attached to other Jews, Ludwig Holländer, who headed the Centralverein from 1921 to 1933, spoke increasingly of the Jews' *Schicksalsgemeinschaft.* Words like *Stamm* and *Abstammung* were invoked in sermons, apologia, and Centralverein publications. In seeking to define what was uniquely Jewish, Rabbi Cesar Seligmann told his Frankfurt congregants: "It is not Jewish conviction, not Jewish doctrine, not the Jewish creed that is the leading, the primary, the inspirational; rather, it is Jewish sentiment, the instinctive, call it what you will, call it the community of blood, call it tribal consciousness [*Stammesgefühl*], call it the ethnic soul [*Volksseele*], but best of all call it: the Jewish heart."[45]

In Britain, the notables who established the Anglo-Jewish Association in 1871, in setting out their motives for creating an organization to aid unemancipated Jews in other lands, stressed the international, cosmopolitan character of Jewishness, invoking the omnipresent language of race. Their aim, they wrote, was "to knit more closely together the bond of brotherhood which united Jew with Jew throughout the world, and which should make its members and fellow-workers sensible of the grand fact that the race of Israel belongs not to England or France alone, but to all the countries of the globe." Even opponents of political Zionism in Britain admitted that Jews were not simply a religious minority. In a letter to Israel Zangwill in 1903, the journalist and historian Lucien Wolf, a fierce critic of Herzlian Zionism, admitted there was "a Jewish race" as well as "a Jewish religion"—though he denied there had been "a Jewish nationality" since the destruction of the Second Temple. For Wolf, to define Jews as a racial, but not national, minority was acceptable, even if viewing Jews as a race highlighted their difference from other citizens. The conceptual confusion that resulted from this straining to simultaneously minimize and acknowledge the ethnic basis of Jewish difference is evident in Charles Kensington Salaman's apologetic volume *Jews As They Are* (1882). In its opening pages, Salaman, a well-known pianist and composer, repeated the old assimilationist chestnut that Jews differed from country to country since they took on the coloration of their surroundings, even quoting Isaac D'Israeli's words to this effect in his *Genius of Judaism:* "After a few generations the Hebrews assimilate with the character, and are actuated by the feelings of the nation of which they become part." But two pages later Salaman asked his readers to reflect on the near-miraculous postbiblical history of the Jewish "nation" and, in particular, how modern Jews triumphed over "so terrible a state of racial adversity and degradation." He concluded: "None but a divinely-protected people could have done so."[46] Thus, in a mere few lines, Salaman managed to describe Jews as a race, a nation, and a people.

The internal tensions in Salaman's treatment of Jewishness reflect, in part, the nature of the Jewish Question in Britain. In contrast to Germany, it was not a burning issue, a matter of ferocious public debate, as a result of which there was less pressure on British Jews to make unambiguous declarations of their deracination. They enjoyed the luxury of being less than rigorous in their thinking about the character of their minority status. But, in another sense, Salaman's conceptual confusion was symptomatic of a broader, European-wide problem: Jews did not fit into the slot that classical liberalism created for them. Their social and emotional attachments overflowed the bounds of religion. Their Jewishness was not reducible to theology, worship, and ritual. While they and their Christian allies had agreed during the course of emancipation that their integration into state and society required their modernization, they had been remarkably vague about what this entailed. Still, it is clear that their gentile supporters had expected a more radical transformation than in fact occurred. In hindsight, it is now clear that the friends of the Jews had a naive faith in human perfectibility, in the power of laws and institutions to uproot and replace well-entrenched social and cultural traits. Their understanding of the visceral ties—memories, fears, affections, loathings—that bind historical minorities together was equally shallow. The persistence of Jewish ethnicity frustrated, irritated, and, in some cases, even enraged them. For their part, Jewish leaders had little ideological space in which to respond to this frustration and anger. When, in the face of mounting hostility, they were pressured to declare in public the character of their Jewishness, they invoked the notion of being a religious minority—what other choice was available? But at the same time, as we have seen, they also demonstrated how unsatisfactory this definition was. Their struggle to find new terms and expressions to describe their Jewish bonds—as well as their loose use of terms like *race, people,* and *nation*—reveals how inadequate it was in their eyes. Whatever they called themselves, we can be sure that the construction "German [French, English, Hungarian, etc.] citizens of the Mosaic faith" did not exhaust their self-understanding.

NOTES

I am grateful to my colleagues Miriam Bodian and Zvi Gitelman for their helpful comments on earlier drafts of this essay.

1. Yosef Hayim Yerushalmi, *From Spanish Court to Italian Ghetto—Isaac Cardoso: A Study in Seventeenth-Century Marranism and Jewish Apologetics* (New York, 1971), 44; Miriam Bodian, "'Men of the Nation': The Shaping of *Converso* Identity in Early Modern Europe," *Past and Present* 143 (May 1994): 48–49.

2. I use the term *Jewishness* in the context of modern Jewish history as a shorthand device to refer to that amorphous mix of sentiments, bonds, ideas, and associations that European Jews experienced as the basis of their Jewish identity. In other words, *Jewishness* refers to those properties and qualities that Jews (or Gentiles, for that matter) thought made them Jewish—their subjective sense of affiliation and collective uniqueness. Let me also add that the term has no relevance to the medieval and early modern periods, when the boundaries between Jews and their neighbors were more or less firm. Because Jewish identity was debated and

redefined in the modern period, it does not follow that this occurred earlier as well. I am aware that this is an unfashionable position, out of step with the trend to view "identity" at all times and in all places as "contested," "negotiable," "problematized," etc., but so be it. There is no evidence that medieval Jews were confused about or endlessly debated what made them Jewish.

3. On Jewish acculturation and integration, see Jacob Katz, *Out of the Ghetto: The Social Background of Jewish Emancipation, 1770–1870* (Cambridge, Mass., 1973); Todd M. Endelman, *The Jews of Georgian England, 1714–1830: Tradition and Change in a Liberal Society* (Philadelphia, 1979); Jacob Katz, ed., *Toward Modernity: The European Jewish Model* (New Brunswick, N.J., 1987); Paula E. Hyman, *The Emancipation of the Jews of Alsace: Acculturation and Tradition in the Nineteenth Century* (New Haven, 1991); Steven M. Lowenstein, *The Berlin Jewish Community: Enlightenment, Family and Crisis, 1770–1830* (New York, 1994); Pierre Birnbaum and Ira Katznelson, eds., *Paths of Emancipation: Jews, States, and Citizenship* (Princeton, 1995).

4. Salo W. Baron, "The Modern Age," in *Great Ages and Ideas of the Jewish People,* Leo W. Schwarz, ed. (New York, 1956), 317. Baron first advanced this view in the interwar period. See his "Ghetto and Emancipation: Shall We Revise the Traditional View?," *Menorah Journal* 14 (1928): 515–26; and his *Social and Religious History of the Jews,* 1st ed. (New York, 1937), vol. 2, chap. 11 ("Emancipation").

5. *Opinion de M. le comte Stanislas de Clermont-Tonnerre, député de Paris, le 23 décembre 1789* (Paris, 1789), 13, quoted in Patrick Girard, *Les Juifs de France de 1789 à 1860: de l'émancipation à l'égalité* (Paris, 1976).

6. Thomas Babington Macaulay, *Critical and Historical Essays,* 2 vols. (London, 1854), 1:142–44.

7. French schemes to transform the Jews are treated in Jay R. Berkovitz, *The Shaping of Jewish Identity in Nineteenth-Century France* (Detroit, 1989).

8. On the various German terms used to describe the transformation of the Jews and their political status see Jacob Toury, "Emantsipatsiyah ve-asimilatsiyah: musagim ve-tenaim" [Emancipation and Assimilation: Concepts and Terms] *Yalkut moreshet* 2 (1964): 167–82; and Jacob Katz, "The Term 'Jewish Emancipation': Its Origin and Historical *Emancipation and Assimilation: Studies in Modern History* (Westmead: Hants, 1972), 21–45.

9. *The Voice of Jacob,* 31 January 1845.

10. Arthur Hertzberg remarks that while those who championed Jewish emancipation in France demanded that Jews become "new men," they failed to specify what kind of new men. While agreeing that Jews make changes in their religion, they never indicated what changes were necessary. "Did the Jews need to prove to the most left-wing of revolutionaries that were the quickest to abandon all their ancient traditions and adopt the cult of civic virtue? Was it enough to be decently

inconspicuous in public by removing all marks of Jewish ritual distinctiveness outside the home? Who, for that matter, was to be the judge as to whether the Jews had, indeed, made adequate changes in their religion, economic conduct, and communal cohesion?" *The French Enlightenment and the Jews* (New York, 1968), 365.

11. Endelman, *The Jews of Georgian England*, 59–64.

12. Ruth F. Necheles, *The Abbé Grégoire, 1787–1831 Odyssey of an Egalitarian* (Westport, Conn., 1971).

13. Endelman, *The Jews of Georgian England*, 78–85.

14. Michael Stanislawski, *Tsar Nicholas I and the Transformation of Jewish Society in Russia, 1825–1855* (Philadelphia, 1983), 59–69.

15. Ellen Littmann, "David Friedländers Sendschreiben an Probst Teller und sein Echo," *Zeitschrift für die der Juden in Deutschland*, 6 (1935), 92–112. See also the useful introduction of Richard Cohen to the 1975 reprint of the original German text, along with a Hebrew translation that the Zalman Shazar Center and the Hebrew University published in their *Kuntrasim* series, no. 44.

16. Barrie M. Ratcliffe, "Some Jewish Problems in the Early Careers of Emile and Isaac Pereire," *Jewish Social Studies* 34 (1972): 189–206; Michael Graetz, "Une Initiative saint-simonienne pour l' émancipation des Juifs," *Revue des études juives* 129 (1970): 67–84; idem, *Ha-peiriferyah haytah la-merkaz: perakim be-toldot yahadut tsarfat ba-meah ha-shmonah esreh mi-Saint Simon ad li-yessud "kol yisrael haverim"* [The Periphery Became the Center: Chapters in the History of French Jewry in the Nineteenth Century from Saint Simon to the Founding of the Alliance Israelite Universelle] (Jerusalem, 1982), chap. 4.

17. Graetz, *Ha-peiriferyah haytah la-merkaz*, chap. 6.

18. The literature on this is voluminous. See, in particular, Edmund Silberner, *Sozialisten zur Judenfrage* (Berlin, 1962); Robert S. Wistrich, *Socialism and the Jews: The Dilemmas of Assimilation in Germany and Austria-Hungary* (Rutherford, N.J., 1982); Isaiah Berlin, "Benjamin Disraeli, Karl Marx and the Search for Identity," in *Against the Current: Essays in the History of Ideas* (Oxford 1991).

19. *London Jewish Chronicle*, 6 September 1907; Joseph Klausner, *Be-darkhei tsiyyon ve-tehiyyat ha-dibbur ha-ivri* [In the Paths of Zionism: Chapters in the History of Zionism and the Revival of Spoken Hebrew] (Jerusalem, 1978), 152–67: Edmond Privat, *The Life of Zamenhof,* trans. Ralph Eliot (London, 1931); Marjorie Boulton, *Zamenhof* (London, 1960).

20. Simon M. Dubnow, *History of the Jews in Russia and Poland from the Earliest Times to the Present Day,* Israel Friedlander, trans., 3 vols. (Philadelphia, 1916–20), 2:333–34: *Encyclopaedia Judaica,* s.v. "Gordin, Jacob."

21. Elias Jakob, "Das Wesen des Judentums," quoted in Alan Levenson, "Jewish Reactions to Intermarriage in Nineteenth Century Germany" (Ph.D. diss.,

Ohio State University, 1990), 36. Levenson discusses a number of advocates of Jewish dissolution in chap. 4 and in "The Conversionary Impulse in Fin de Siècle Germany," *Leo Baeck Institute Year Book* 40 (1995): 107–22.

22. Henry Wassermann, "Tarbutam ha-intimit shel yehudei germanyah" [The Intimate Culture of German Jewry], in *Crises of German National Consciousness in the 19th and 20th Centuries,* Moshe Zimmermann, ed. (Jerusalem, 1983), 187–98; Shulamit Volkov, "Yihud u-temiyah: paradaks ha-zehut ha-yehudit hatslahah ha-sheni" [Unity and Assimilation: The Paradox of Jewish Identity in the Second Empire], in *Crises of German National Consciousness,* 169–85; idem, "Yehudei germanyah be-meah ha-tesha-esreih: sheaftanut, hatalahah, temiyah" [The Jews of Germany in the Nineteenth Century: Ambition, Success, Assimilation], in *Hitbollelut u-temiyah: hemshekhiyyut u-temurah be-tarbut ha-amim u-ve-yisrael* [Acculturation and Assimilation: Continuity and Change in Jewish and Non-Jewish Culture], Yosef Kaplan and Menahem Stern, eds. (Jerusalem, 1989), 173–88; Jacob Katz, "German Culture and the Jews," in *The Jewish Response to German Culture: From the Enlightenment to the Second World War,* Jehuda Reinharz and Walter Schatzberg, eds. (Hanover, N.H., 1985), 58–99.

23. Gershom Scholem, "With Gershom Scholem: An Interview," in *On Jews and Judaism in Crisis: Selected Essays,* Werner J. Dannhauser, ed. (New York, 1976), 5–6; idem, "On the Social Psychology of the Jews in Germany, 1900–1933," in David Bronsen, ed., *Jews and Germans from 1860 to 1933: The Problematic Symbiosis* (Heidelberg, 1979), 18–19.

24. Richard Lichtheim, *Shear yashuv: zikhronot tsiyoni mi-germanyah* [A Remnant Shall Return: Memoirs of a Zionist from Germany] (Jerusalem, 1953), 37.

25. Werner E. Mosse, *The German-Jewish Economic Elite, 1820–1935* (Oxford, 1989), 93, 95.

26. Mosse, *The German-Jewish Economic Elite,* 116, 121, 127, 130, 133; Gustav Levinstein, *Zur Ehre des Judentums: Gesammelte Schriften* (Berlin, 1911), 80; Hannah Arendt, *The Origins of Totalitarianism* (new ed., New York, 1966), 64.

27. Todd M. Endelman, *Radical Assimilation in English Jewish History, 1656–1945* (Bloomington, Ind., 1990), chaps. 3–4. There is no parallel work on the social history of the Jews in other liberal, western states in the nineteenth century.

28. Julia Frankau [Frank Danby], *Dr. Phillips: A Maida Vale Idyll* (London, 1887), 55, 168. See also Todd M. Endelman, "The Frankaus of London: A Study in Radical Assimilation, 1837–1867," *Jewish History* 8, no. 1–2 (1994): 117–54.

29. Joseph Jacobs, *Jewish Statistics: Social, Vital and Anthropometric* (London, 1891), 6.

30. Pierre Birnbaum, *Les Fous de la République: Histoire politique des Juifs d'État de Gambetta à Vichy* (Paris, 1992).

31. Jakob Thon, *Die Juden in Österreich* (Berlin, 1908), 69–70.

32. Peter Honigmann, "Jewish Conversions—A Measure of Assimilation? A Discussion of the Berlin Secession Statistics of 1770–1941," *Leo Baeck Institute*

Year Book 34 (1989): 5. Honigmann acknowledges that these figures are not precise and "at best give no more than the order of magnitude" of formal defection. This is because the considerable emigration that occurred after 1933 might have changed the balance between the two groups (Jews by virtue of their formal communal membership and Jews by virtue of their racial background).

33. Robert Neumann, *The Plague House Papers* (London, 1959), 85–86.

34. Dietz Bering, *The Stigma of Names: Antisemitism in German Daily Life, 1812–1933,* trans. Neville Plaice (Ann Arbor, 1992).

35. Sander Gilman, *The Jew's Body* (London, 1991), 181–88.

36. E. Boekman, *Demografie van de Joden in Nederland* (Amsterdam, 1936), 59; Arthur Ruppin, *The Jews of To-Day,* Margery Bentwich, trans. (London, 1913), 163; Yaakov Lestschinsky, "Ha-shemad be-aratsot shonot" [Apostasy in Different Lands], *Ha-olam,* 5, no. 9 (1911): 4.

37. Levenson, "Jewish Reactions to Intermarriage," 24.

38. John M. Efron, *Defenders of the Race: Jewish Doctors and Race Science in Fin-de-Siecle Europe* (New Haven, Conn., 1994), 143–51; Levenson, "Jewish Reactions to Intermarriage," chap. 7.

39. Quoted in Walter Boehlich, ed., *Der Berliner Antisemitismusstreit* (Frankfurt a.M., 1965), 79.

40. Uriel Tal, *Yahadut ve-natsrut ba"reikh ha-sheni," 1870–1914* [Jews and Christians in the "Second Reich"] (Jerusalem, 1969), 26–27; Ismar Schorsch, *Jewish Reactions to German Anti-Semitism, 1870–1914* (New York, 1972), 63, 95–97.

41. Charles H. L. Emanuel, *A Century and a Half of Jewish History Extracted from the Minute Books of the London Committee of Deputies of the British Jews* (London, 1910), passim; David C. Itzkowitz, "Cultural Pluralism and the Board of Deputies of British Jews," in *Religion and Irreligion in Victorian Society: Essays in Honor of R. K. Webb,* R. W. Davis and R. J. Helmstadter, eds. (London, 1992), 85–101.

42. David S. Landes, "Two Cheers for Emancipation," in *The Jews in Modern France,* Frances Malino and Bernard Wasserstein, eds. (Hanover, N.H., 1985), 291n. 4.

43. Stuart A. Cohen, *English Zionists and British Jews: The Communal Politics of Anglo-Jewry, 1895–1920* (Princeton, 1982), chaps. 5–8; Jehuda Reinharz, *Fatherland or Promised Land: The Dilemma of the German Jew, 1893–1914* (Ann Arbor, 1975), chap. 5; Paula Hyman, *From Dreyfus to Vichy: The Remaking of French Jewry, 1906–1939* (New York, 1979), 155–69.

44. Michael R. Marrus, *The Politics of Assimilation: A Study of the French Jewish Community at the Time of the Dreyfus Affair* (Oxford, 1971), chap. 2; Phyllis Cohen Albert, "Ethnicity and Jewish Solidarity in Nineteenth-Century France," in *Mystics, Philosophers, and Politicians: Essays in Jewish Intellectual History in Honor of Alexander Altmann,* Jehuda Reinharz et al., eds. (Durham, N.C., 1982), 257–60.

45. Donald L. Niewyk, *The Jews in Weimar Germany* (Baton Rouge, La., 1980), 103–6; Ruth Louise Pierson, "German Jewish Identity in the Weimar Republic" (Ph.D. diss., Yale University, 1970), chap. 1.

46. *Report of* the *Anglo-Jewish Association, 1871–1872* (London, 1872), 8; Cohen, *English Zionists and British Jews,* 173; Charles Kensington Salaman, *Jews As They Are* (London, 1882), 7, 9. For an example of the indiscriminate mixing of racial, national, and religious terms in the American context, see the collection of public lectures of Israel Friedlaender, professor of Bible studies at the Jewish Theological Seminary from 1904 to 1920, *Past and Present: Selected Essays* (New York, 1961).

Comment

Sylvie-Anne Goldberg

To Be Finished with the Jewish Question
(Continuity, Discontinuity, Always There?)

In order to comment on the discourse of Todd Endelman, who describes the "Continuities and Discontinuities in Constructions of Jewishness in Europe" which he dates between 1789 and 1945, I will engage myself in questioning rather than in annotating. Since earliest ancient times, it seems that we have never tired of questioning the Jews on their "singularity," their essential "difference" which has made them wander endlessly among the multiple categories of barbarians, sects, or pariahs (even in the social sciences) to the point where, after having endured such epithets as assassin, unbeliever, infidel, antisocial, and obscurantist, their "Jewishness" emerges as the case of a species, an irreducible phenomenon—a phenomenon that recently Derrida vehemently pointed to when he said: "For Yerushalmi, there surely is a determining and irreducible essence of Jewishness . . . it is not to be confused with Judaism nor with religion, nor even with a belief in God."[1]

This irreducibility of Jewishness irresistibly reminds me of what in earlier times was sought under headings of the "genius," even "essence," not to say "prodigiousness" of Judaism, when historians and theologians asked themselves about the perpetuation of this people across the centuries in spite of all the humiliations they were made the victims of and the base acts that befell them. Christians of the eighteenth century (historians) saw this as evidence of the mark of divine punishment brought down on the Jews and preserved their existence so that they could serve as living witnesses: "We have already seen the passing of seventeen hundred years of Misery . . . without seeing any appearance of relief. This is an event without equal";[2] the Jews, for their part, see in this a sign of their election.

147

"He who does not believe in miracles should recognize that there is in the history of the Jewish people something which is close to the miraculous."[3]

Thus weary of comprehending this occurrence without example or prodigy, we are here led back to a Jewishness that nothing, not even emancipation, baptism, or assimilation, has been able to pass by. In order to play a contradictory role or that of devil's advocate, since it is good to brighten things a bit, I propose, for what is after all a comparative conference, to compare the Jews not with other "minorities" recognized as such—as represented by women (even though they are, it is well known, half of the population), Native Americans, or blacks, or schizophrenics, or those infected with AIDS, or hemophiliacs—but rather among themselves and to research that which could well, in the process of producing minorities, bring together the Jews of the Persian, medieval or Hellenic period in this very improbable quest for Jewishness. Why, in effect, not take as a point of departure the customs tried out by the Israelites in Babylon to call attention to themselves while a part of their number returned to Palestine? Or further, why not compare the practices of the Middle Ages and Antiquity, or indeed between the communities of Alsace and of the Contat Venaisson? And, again, the customs that differentiate the Sephardic and Ashkenazy without forgetting those practiced by "East Jews" and "West Jews" (German and Polish/Russian Jews) who quite recently found a culminating point in the distinction between "Israelites" (French) and "foreign" Jews (immigrants from central Europe and from Germany)?

Pushing the art of classifying random categories as cultural minorities, why not class together those that one would define by multilingualism or according to their tastes in food (sweet, salty, for example), cinema (fans of cloak and dagger or thriller movies!), literature, music, or politics, which would allow for the redefinition of Jewishness to a more or less refined degree: to speak several languages, to savor more sweetened foods, to vote more to the left, and to have a penchant for poetry could become useful indicators, like customs of dress that, far from servile variations of fashion, similarly serve to describe these groups. I must confess that outside of voluntary practices of differentiation by some, I hesitate to define all Jews as a minority in the Western society of 1945. Let us try therefore to understand.

As far as we know, the injunction to be distinctive is tied to the prohibition against exogamy: It is only after the return from Babylon, after having endured a first exile, a first experience of life as minority guests, that it becomes essential to put into practice the rites and customs of differentiation. For Flavius Joseph "even our enemies admit that our institutions are divine."[4] This is a certainty shared by Philon when he affirmed that a state founded on institutions of the Mosaic Law would be bound to be perfect:[5] The great difference of the Jews of Antiquity would be their theocratic claim that would have followed the victory of Pharisaism or, in other words, the triumph of the Law.[6]

With regard to the religious domain, it goes without saying that everyone agrees in recognizing that it is particularist: Since their formation as a people, it is especially by their rites that Hebrews, Israelites, and Jews distinguish themselves from others but, from the moment when they are no longer master of their choices and submit to their "condition" (as Jews), things change somewhat. It is no longer the choices of the Jews themselves that prevail in these matters of establishing distinction, but those put in place by societies to separate them. Therefore, these processes of producing more differentiation by means of segregation (social and religious) are extremely ambiguous because, at first warmly welcomed by the Jews who felt themselves thus preserved, they will end up by becoming the paradigm—embraced by some and refused by others—of a secular Judaism, always presented in contemporary times as a tug this way between exclusion and integration, separation and assimilation.

It would be tedious to linger over the legislation of exclusion put into place in medieval Christian society or in Islamic society with regard to the Jews, as it would be superfluous to evoke the interdictions against Jews with regard to the sociability and conviviality with their environment. But this archetype, so accepted, of Jewish singularity, goes how far? In effect, from the twelfth and thirteenth centuries, the Sèfer Hasidim predicts that, in spite of everything: "The people who travel through a country to find a place to live will examine the way the region is populated, the mentality of the Christians, their reserve in matters of sexual behavior. It is necessary to know that, if Jews live in this town, their sons and their daughters will act like these Christians. Because everywhere, the habits of Jews resemble, in the majority of cases, those of the Christian."[7]

Let us admit therefore, with common sense and Todd Endelman, that problems of identity among Jews do not begin to establish themselves until their gradual emancipation from Jewish law and their entrance into civil society. The reading of F. Barth[8] convinces us that identity is not a condition immanent in the individual, a given defining him in a consistent and invariable manner, but rather a posture adopted through interaction, one possibility among others, an occurrence that is produced in a particular situation. The individual is no longer in the grip of his own group membership, because it is he who gives it meaning. It would thus be necessary to envisage the many facets of "Jewish identity" and the diverse transformations it could adopt over the period that extends nearly two centuries between the French Revolution and 1945 as having only been various changes of dress over a Jewishness constant and transcendent, whatever the intentions of the individuals who carried it. Hence, why indeed not declare with Todd Endelman the "failure of emancipation"? In any case, in the various ways individuals are connected to their family origins, history, and memory, the elements due to loyalty, denial, and affirmation, to forgetting and to memory, act in different and variable degrees. All these individual variations ground through the mill of categorization could give uncertain results: one could expose different categorical examples: to put a beret or a scarf on the leader, to like cakes more than pickles (or the reverse), to begin reading the daily paper at the obituaries, and to be French (or English, Hungarian, or German) would return one to a sort of Jewish faith, stylistic, culinary, journalistic, national, whereas not to speak any foreign language, read any detective stories, detest Woody Allen and the Opera would be negative criteria of identity that certain cantors of immanent Jewishness could even, why not, qualify as "self-hatred." When Todd Endelman observes, for the first period of emancipation, that Jews and non-Jews were in agreement about the necessity to "shrink and compartmentalize" the "content" of "Jewish identity," that does not prevent him from stating later, with regard to German Jews at the beginning of the twentieth century, that "if Jews were more integrated into state and society than earlier in the century, they still remained a recognizable social collectivity wherever they lived, defined less by their religious rites than their social patterns, historical memories, and communal ties," which had earlier led Joseph Jacobs to characterize as "shoolist" (from the Yiddish word for synagogue) the attitude of preferential conviviality of English Jews at the end of the nineteenth century. Thus, despite the progressive abandonment of religious practices "their Jewishness was not reducible to theology, worship, and ritual"; there remains "something" ethnically Jewish that transcends history, culture, but above all sociability at the same time and that leads Jews to form, all the same, a separate entity, despite everything, confined this time to an invisible and impalpable ghetto, which World War II had only to gather up. This periodization seems to me infinitely problematic. Almost from ethnic concerns, I would prefer to see the idea challenged that the decimation of the Jews of Europe had come to destroy a Jewish population marked out by its singularity. This recourse to identity seems to me suspect if not dangerous in its method of reading a posteriori as well as unsatisfactory in terms of understanding. Why, surprisingly, this complete avoidance of an overview of the rise of Jewish nationalist movements, which indeed played the minority card on the political chessboard? In his essay, Ron Suny declared that the "minorities" policy of the former Union of Soviet Socialist Republics was directed toward the non-Russian nations, which were, in fact, "peoples," an assertion that brings us back to the heart of the eternal question of the approach to the Jews. The problem inherent in categorizing the Jewish population after its emancipation is that of its definition: for as much as it designates a people, a religious affiliation, or a social stigma, the category obliges us to think of these "niches" differently . . . but this would be another discussion.

To conclude, I will limit myself to returning once more to the heady dialogue that Derrida pursues with Yerushalmi—and that seems to me to illustrate in exemplary fashion the ambiguity of the idea of "Jewishness" used here by Endelman as a sign of "minority": While Derrida disputes the usage made by Yerushalmi of the confrontation with ghosts, he is unable to prevent himself, to read what he wrote, from being assailed by his own phantoms (his grandfathers, in this case),[9] thus confessing that he chooses or holds on to his personal Jewishness as an impression of memory and of loyalty. Hence, to return to the point of departure, according to what criteria are we to place the Jews in a minority?

NOTES

1. Jacques Derrida, *Mal d'Archive* (Paris: Galilée, 1995), 115.

2. Jacques Basnage, *L'Histoire et la religion des Juifs, depuis J.C. jusqu'à présent* (Rotterdam, 1706–7).

3. Henrich Graetz, *L'Histoire des Juifs* (Paris, 1882), I:1, p. 10.

4. From the last paragram of *Les Antiquités juives,* Book III, 322, text, translation, and notes by Étienne Nodet (Paris: Cerf, 1992).

5. See Harry Austryn Wolfson, *Philo, Foundations of Religious Philosophy in Judaism Christianity and Islam* (Cambridge: Harvard University Press, 1947, 1968), especially the introductory chapter to the first volume on Hellenistic Judaism but also the chapter dedicated to the Messianic era.

6. On this subject, see Sylvia Berti and Arnoldo Momigliano, eds., *Essays on Ancient and Modern Judaism* (Chicago: University of Chicago Press, 1994); Ger-

shon Weiler, *La Tentation théocratique. Israel, la loi et le politique* (Paris: Calmann-Lévy, 1991).

7. From Edouard Gourévitch, *Le Guide des hassidim* (Paris: Cerf, 1988), 315, from the Parma Edition §1301.

8. Frederick Barth, *Ethnic Groups and Boundaries* (Bergen: Universitets Forlaget, 1969).

9. Derrida, *Mal d'Archive,* 140.

Muslim Minorities in China, Chinese Minorities in Islamic Southeast Asia

(from the fifteenth to the twentieth century)

Denis Lombard

In abundant discussions largely inspired by anthropology that in recent years have raised questions related to ethnicity, identity, and minorities, we too often note the absence or at least the insufficiency of any truly diachronic perspective. Although the geographic dimension is generally taken into account quite correctly, and the modalities of otherness well analyzed, authors are too likely in contrast to adhere to synchrony and to deplore that situation implicitly, without taking advantage of the benefit that comes from study of the formative process.

The present essay, which attempts to encompass in a single glance two among the most important "minorities" in East Asia and over a long period of time, has as its essential purpose the demonstration that these questions cannot and should not be disconnected from a perspective that is fundamentally historical. It is not without interest, as we shall try to show, to compare the case of the Hui "minority" of China on one hand to the Chinese "minorities" of Insulinde (essentially Malaysia and Indonesia) where, as we know, today the "majorities" are Chinese.

Islam seems to have arrived in China very early, as much by sea as by land. Tradition even has it that the first Muslims arrived in China shortly after the Hegira (622); and thus one can still visit, in what was once a suburb of Canton but now is found nearly at the center of that enormous conurbation, the tomb of one Abu Wakas, considered a close relative of the prophet and who would have died before the end of the seventh century of the Christian era. What is certain is that there was a significant Muslim community of several thousand people from the eighth century and that this community (which had a mosque, the minaret of which can still be seen) was in part destroyed during the revolt of Huang Chao (879).[1] There were also Muslims who had arrived via Central Asia at Changan, the capital of the Tang empire (the modern city of Xi'an, in Northern China), and during the famous battle of Talas (south of Lake Balkach) where in 751 troops of the caliphate opposed those of the Tang, a certain number of Chinese artisans were made prisoners and taken off to Baghdad. The event is important because it was these artisans who transmitted to the Muslims of the Middle East the technique of making paper (well documented in China from the end of the first century of our era and probably in use even earlier), a technique transmitted to the West much later by way of the Spanish.

For China, however, the main epoch of Islamification occurred some six centuries later, following the great Mongol effort at the unification of Eurasia.[2] On installing themselves in Beijing and founding the Yuan dynasty, the Mongols did not themselves convert but relied on their Muslim allies (notably the Uygurs) and on new communities established in China, which would last into our time, in Yunnan for example.[3] From the Ming era on, one can more easily follow, at least in some regions, the history of particular communities and families. The Hui were often small businessmen and artisans but also soldiers.

Today, the People's Republic of China contains a significant Muslim community whose numbers vary, according to estimates, from 12 to 20 million people (or even more). The Muslim minorities who still speak their language of origin (for example, the Uygurs, who live mostly in Xinjiang and speak a language close to Turkish) are sharply distinguished from the Hui minority,[4] which is distinctive in that they are as "Chinese" as others and speak the Han dialect of their region; they in fact differ from the non-Muslims only in certain cultural traits that could appear to be residual.

As "minorities" (*shaoshu minzu*), they benefit legally from certain much-appreciated advantages, such as being authorized to have more than one child or benefiting from specific quotas in the universities, while on a purely ritualistic level, they appear to be entirely disconnected from Muslim law[5] and in a more general way from all the major political preoccupations of international Islam.[6] They distinguish themselves essentially, in daily life, by refusing to eat pork and by overseeing their own canteens as well as their own restaurants, which in addition to this taboo take into account some other traditions of eating, such as, for example, a taste for dairy products, a practice undoubtedly brought from Central Asia and one that in the eyes of other Chinese adds a certain exoticism. Some Hui, but only some of them, also maintain a certain relationship with the mosques (in Chinese: *gingzhens,* literally, "temples of pureness and truth"), which have been, as we will see in a moment, one of the issues at stake in the fight that the community has waged in the course of recent years in order to maintain its identity.[7]

Thus defined, the specificity of the Hui may appear, to a Western eye in any case, rather thin. The fact remains, however, that for a century and a half this "minority" has repeatedly found itself in the reordering optic of official central policy. In the years from 1860 to 1880, several large revolts inspired by Muslim communities shook the power of the Qing, as much in Xinjiang as in Yunnan,[8] and unleashed a terrible repression in return.[9] The Kuomintang inaugurated a policy deliberately favorable to minorities, especially the Muslims, in the 1930s.[10] The Communist regime followed approximately the same line at the beginning. Starting in 1965, however, the Cultural Revolution, wishing to fit everyone in the same mold, raged especially against Muslims and began a nearly systematic destruction of mosques. Not until the beginning of the 1980s did the policy soften and reverse itself, and the Muslim minorities, including the Hui, began to benefit once again from the favor of those in power. Since then, some observers have the impression that this relative clemency favors, notably among the young, a relative awareness or re-awareness and along the way a kind of religious reawakening.[11]

Let us now briefly turn to the Chinese communities of Southeast Asia, which a priori (but only a priori) seem to have nothing in common with the Hui. According to the information provided us by the Chinese sources concerning the countries of the "South Seas" (Nanyang) and the exchanges they had with the Middle Empire beginning in the Han period (from the second century B.C. to the second century A.D.), it is only after the "Mongol moment" that we truly find the existence of the first overseas Chinese colonies. At the very end of the thirteenth century, the account of the traveler Zhou Daguan, en route to Cambodia, alerts us to the presence of his compatriots established at Angkor;[12] and a bit more than a century later, during the first decades of the fifteenth century, companions of admiral Zhenghe, to whom Ming emperor Younglo had given leadership of seven large maritime expeditions (which went as far as India and the coast of Africa), describe for us the existence of similar communities at several points in Southeast Asia.[13]

From the beginning of the sixteenth century, it is the turn of the Europeans, who have begun to flow into the region, to indicate the presence of

Chinese merchants more or less everywhere. The Portuguese found them in Malaka in 1509–11, the Spanish in Manila (which, let us not forget, was a small Muslim trading post before passing to Spanish control in 1872), and when in 1596 the Dutch arrived in Banten for the first time, which was then the largest port of western Java, they reported not only that the Chinese took an active part in commerce but that they had been able to create plantations in the hinterlands that provided both pepper and sugar, the principal export products.[14] Installed since 1619 some 80 kilometers east of Banten in the little port of Jakatra (renamed Batavia for good reasons) they did not halt until they had attracted not only the junks coming from China but the Chinese population of their neighbor and rival. The conflict ended only in 1682 with the annexation of Banten by the Dutch.

In general it would be pointless from this period on to attempt to write a history and above all an economic history of Southeast Asia without taking into account the role of the communities of Chinese origin, which embodied an ideal of free enterprise, as opposed to states traditionally inclined (according to the old Confucian ideal) to the official control of commerce, which with differing results here and there came to seek protection in the trading posts that the Europeans were establishing. The importance of this apparently "objective" alliance that took place in Southeast Asia between Chinese and European merchants has long been emphasized. Competitors certainly (and how much so!) in everyday affairs, they nevertheless shared the same mercantile ideology there, where they were, the ones as much as the others threatened by the nit-picking supervision of agrarian kingdoms.

It is necessary to qualify here, taking into account regional diversity, because all the Southeast Asian Mediterranean is far from having vibrated to the same rhythms. In Insulinde, where European trading posts quickly became quite numerous, to Java and Sumatra as well as as the Moluccas and the Philippines, free Chinese merchants naturally came to find refuge in the multiple Spanish and Dutch harbors that were like so many harbingers of the great colonial systems of the nineteenth and twentieth centuries.[15] In Manila the Chinese of the Parian quarter constituted an essential stop in the abundant commerce established between Acapulco and Fujian ports. In exchange for the ceramics and silks of China, they sent on Mexican silver and also some of the most important American crops: tobacco, corn, and peanuts. To Batavia, on the other hand, Fujian Chinese exported the same ceramics, silks, and tea in exchange for sugar and pepper progressively supplemented with American crops.

This cooperation was not without its fits and starts, however, and it is precisely in these two zones of Luzon and Java that one notes the first great pogroms, that is to say the first confrontations between Chinese and Europeans: in Manila in the seventeenth century and in Batavia in 1740.[16] In Java, on the occasion of the terrible troubles that followed the pogrom and disorganized the entire island for many years, one can follow quite well the stages of a triangular game that pitted the agrarian kingdom of Mataram (central Java) against the Dutch Company on one side and the Chinese merchants on the other.

In Vietnam, where the Europeans would not take control until much later (Rigault de Genouilly only occupied Saigon in 1859), the situation remained particularly difficult for merchants wherever they were from. Nourished by a Confucian ideal all the more rigid for being imported and at the same time by a virulent anti-Chinese nationalism (probably one of the first nationalisms to have appeared in the region), Vietnamese mandarins constantly sought to reduce their southern neighbor to nothing, along with the maritime state of Champa.[17] And after the partition between Trinh and Nguyen (at the beginning of the seventeenth century), they continued in the north as in the south to restrain the initiatives of foreign merchants and to require of them the kind of concessions from which it would be impossible to escape (Phoyen, south of Hanoi; Faifo, south of Hué).[18] Although in Java, Mataram had to beat a retreat before the mercantile forces of the littoral, on the Vietnamese coast, it was always the inspectors of the centralized state who made the law. In Siam, on the other hand—the third case in this schema—Western impact always remained very limited, and in the nineteenth century, as everyone knows, the country would keep its independence, avoiding having to pass through the "colonial phase." It is worth noting, however, that in Siam the Chinese were very well integrated, perhaps even better than elsewhere—not so much because, as is sometimes said, the two communities shared a religion (i.e., Buddhism "in contrast to Islam elsewhere") but because beginning with the seventeenth century at least, the Siamese monarchy, little concerned with Confucianism, followed a very farsighted policy in commercial matters. Refraining from bullying merchants, it sought to take advantage of the profits. This transition from a system of "tribute" to a system of "profit," which has been well-analyzed by Sarasin Viraphol[19] for the seventeenth and eighteenth centuries, could not but forcefully serve the great Chinese merchants.

Another study[20] similarly shows very well how the understanding between the monarchy of Bangkok (in the person of King Chulalongkorn,

Rama V., 1870–1910) and big Chinese capital (in the family of the Khouw, who came from Fujian by way of Penang) allowed Siam to resist Anglo-Saxon ascendancy and to do so in such a way that the stanniferous districts of the peninsula of Kra (more precisely the regions of Phuket and Ranong) remained Siamese territory instead of going to rejoin the federated states that passed under British control. Followers of the *longue durée* will see in this fundamental difference between the "involution" of Vietnam and the development of Thailand, easily discernible from the seventeenth century on, one of the possible reasons for the economic gap that can be observed today between these two countries otherwise comparable in size and resources.

We will pass more rapidly over the better-known history of the nineteenth and twentieth centuries in which essentially new "Chinese minorities" are formed (in Northern Sumatra, in Cochin China, and especially in the Malaysian Peninsula) with the growth of colonial economies and the development of mines and plantations,[21] and we will come directly to the essential question, that of "integration." The majority of these Chinese have always tended in effect to assimilate with local cultures; and if not their children, then at least their grandchildren end up no longer speaking any language but that of their adopted country and thereby integrate themselves. The local societies, however, keep a certain prejudice in relation to them and have a tendency to consider them a group apart. In Vietnam they have long been known as "Minhhuong," in Indonesia and Malaysia as "peranakan," and in the Philippines as "mestizos."[22]

In the wake of World War II and independence movements, the emergence of various large and small "national bourgeoisies," often recruited in Indonesia and Malaysia in the midst of the most Islamicized urban milieu, had the effect of pushing to the periphery Chinese communities in the process of integrating. These new groups, wishing to emancipate themselves, are more and more disposed to distill what must be called a racist discourse and have a natural tendency to incriminate their principal rivals. It suffices to evoke here the new series of anti-Chinese pogroms that upset Kuala Lumpur in 1959, then Jakarta and the rest of Indonesia in 1963,[23] without mentioning numerous events, quantitatively less dramatic, which have been seen rather regularly since then.

If one now seeks to draw a parallel between the two communities briefly described, by way of a conclusion, one is surprised to note that the parallel histories in fact go back to the same roots, that is, the diverse great movements of commercial growth that took place in East Asia at least from the Tang period and often, if not always, in close relations with Islam.

The first documents that we have for the ninth and tenth centuries on the intensification of this commerce are already awash in Islamic context. The text of *Akhbar al Sin wal Hind* (851), the unique manuscript of which, found in Alep in 1673,[24] describes for us the first expeditions of the merchants of Siraf and their stops in India, Southeast Asia, and China and already names various important intermediary points along the route that took them to Canton: Barus, Srivijaya, Tioman.[25] From elsewhere we have useful testimony on "the route from Champa" that we surmise was from that period on marked by Islamic communities: two inscriptions in Arabic found in central Vietnam and probably dating from the eleventh century,[26] some Arab gold coins recently found near Trakieu (central Vietnam),[27] probably dating from the tenth century, several tombs from the Song period found southwest of the island of Hainan, in a place where we know that foreign boats coming from the south must have tried to land.[28]

But things become clearer from the beginning of the thirteenth century, the importance of which we have already seen, as much for the progress of the Hui in China as for the formation of the first Chinese overseas communities. One of the figures symbolic of this key epoch is without doubt the great Muslim merchant, Pu Shougeng, whose biography has been knowledgeably reconstituted by Kuwabara.[29] Descending from an old family of Cantonese Muslim merchants, he himself was established in Quanzhou and helped the Mongols to get a foothold in Fujian; it was very likely his kin who gave them the idea of planning the great expeditions against Southeast Asia, and notably that of 1292–93 against Java. Rich epigraphic data permit us to reconstitute quite well for the thirteenth and fourteenth centuries the cosmopolitan environment of this great port of Quanzhou (in the south of Fujian); troves of various mosques and a large number of tombstones with inscriptions in Arabic and Persian have been found there.[30] Quanzhou, which was then called Caitong (which Arabic merchants made into Zaitun), exported ceramics and silks. Marco Polo, in the thirteenth century, then Ibn Batluhah, in the following century, describes it for us as one of the great cities of the world, and our word *satin* comes from their "silk makers of Zaitun."

The period is equally crucial for Southeast Asia, because it is from this moment that the important maritime route of the northeast—the one that leaves from Fujian for Luzon, the Sulu and Moluccas islands—began bit by bit to be established and in a certain sense to double the one that follows the western coasts and that we have called the "route of the Champa."[31] The Chinese communities, as we have seen, began to multiply at that time, and it is interesting to note that various sources of the fifteenth and sixteenth centuries describe them as Islamicized. The *Xiyang fanguo zhi* (which is contemporary with the account of Ma Huan) specifies, for example, that "all the Chinese are Moslems."[32] Even though today this shocks certain rigorist temperaments from Indonesia, Malaysia, or elsewhere, who reject the idea that Islam may not always have come straight from the Middle East, it is all the more worthwhile to observe that in many places in this Southeast Asian Mediterranean a Chinese background is found as soon as one digs a bit and seeks to track the beginnings of Islam on the north coast of Java to be sure,[33] but also on Sulu and even at Brunei, on the north coast of Borneo.[34]

Let us add that for their part the Chams, who for a long time had guaranteed ties with the Muslim communities of southern China, also contributed to the phenomenon. Once their capital Vijaya (present-day Binh-dinh) had been destroyed by the Vietnamese in 1475, their networks were partially dismantled and many preferred to flee and go elsewhere (boat people *avant la lettre*), enlarging the little Muslim communities of the region. One of those was Sunan Ampel, who is said to have introduced Islam when he came and whose tomb near the oldest mosque in Surabaya, the great port of Eastern Java, is honored still.

We know, finally, that the mystic brotherhoods (*turuk* or *tarékat*) played an essential role.[35] The "brothers" who were at the same time missionaries and merchants thus wove between them a network of relations and mutual aid that permitted them to communicate between cities and largely to bypass local contingencies such as state frontiers. Thus it happens that one of these "orders," that of the Naqshbandis, founded by Baha ad-Din Nasqshband, who died and was buried at Bukhara in 1389, expanded toward the East as toward the West and spread its disciples in Turkey as well as Uzbekistan, in Xinjiang and the Malay Archipelago. It is still not easy to know exactly what direct relations there could have been between these last two regions, and the "brief history of the Naqshbandis" that Hamid Algar[36] courageously attempted to record leaves these provinces pretty much in the shadow; but it is nonetheless fascinating to see that some disciplines tied to the great Bukharian are today still found on one side and the other.

All these processes are certainly thoroughly obscure at present. On one side, the Hui have ceased—for how long a time?—to think of themselves in connection with the great Eurasian networks that nevertheless put them there and gave them their identity. As for the overseas Chinese, since the nineteenth century they have had so many reasons to "re-Sino-ize"[37] themselves that only a small number of them, a minority of a minority, still locate themselves in relation to the great current of "conversion" that carried them along and advocate the systematic and definitive Islamization of the entire community.[38]

For our part, it seems to us—but perhaps this is too optimistic—that in retracing the successive stages of this long process and historically reconstituting the great phenomenon that in fact presided over the emergence of these "minorities," we have proceeded to a certain decompartmentalization. By adequately demonstrating that they are the valuable witnesses of an important history, far from marginalizing them, we place them at the heart of the true debate.

NOTES

1. The event was notably indicated by al-Mas'udi (in the tenth century) who wrote in his *Prairies of Gold* (Paris: Société Asiatique, 1962), "The number of Moslems, Christians, Jews, and Mazdeans who perished by iron or water while fleeing the sword is estimated at 200,000" (I, 125).

2. On the importance of Central Asia in the history of Eurasia, see the recent synthesis by S. A. M. Adshead, *Central Asia in History* (London: Macmillan, 1993), and our review in *Annales, S.E.C.* (March–April 1995): 423–25.

3. In a neighborhood of the city of Kunming, the tomb of Syed Eldjell, who came from Central Asia to govern the province during the Mongol period, is still shown.

4. The etymology of the word *Hui* (or *Huihui*) is not absolutely certain. The interpretation most often proposed likens *Huihui* to *Ouigour,* and it is a fact that there was a time when the Uygurs were among the main propagators of Islam. But today the terms designate very distinct realities.

5. Traditionally, Chinese Islam follows Hanafite law; but since 1949 all citizens are subject to the same civil code, and for the Hui, like other Muslims in the PRC, multiple marriages, for example, would be out of the question.

6. With the progressive opening of China and the relative increase in trips abroad (notably pilgrimages), this statement should be nuanced.

7. Readers of English will naturally turn to the excellent work of Joseph F. Fletcher (notably "A Brief History of the Chinese Northwestern Frontier, China Proper's Northwest Frontier: Meeting Place of Four Cultures," in Mary Ellen

Alonso, ed., *China's Inner Asian Frontier* (Cambridge: Peabody Museum, 1979) or to Dru C. Gladney's recent monograph, *Muslim Chinese Ethnic Nationalism in the People's Republic* (Cambridge: Harvard East Asian Monograph, 149, 1991). Readers of French will turn first to the studies of Françoise Aubin, notably "Islam et Etat en Chine populaire," in O. Carré, ed., *L'Islam et l'Etat* (Paris: PUF, 1982), 169–88.

8. See, for example, the narrative made at the beginning of this century by the Protestant missionary Marschall Broomhall in his introduction to Chinese Islam: *Islam in China, A Neglected Problem* (published in 1910; reissued, London: Dart, 1987), chapters VIII, "The Yunnan Rebellions," and IX, "The Tungan Rebellions."

9. On the Xinjiang repression, see Chu Wen-djang, *The Moslem Rebellion in North-West China, 1862–1878, A Study of Government Minority Policy* (The Hague: Mouton, 1966). On the Yunnan repression, see the astonishing testimony of Emile Rocher, *La province chinoise du Yunnan*, 2 vols. (Paris: Ernest Leroux, 1879–1880).

10. The restoration of certain mosques and Muslim tombs of historic interests dates in effect from the 1930s.

11. A novel written by a Hui woman writer, Huo Da, and entitled in French *Le Roi du jade, Histoire d'une famille musulmane chinoise* (Beijing: Panda, 1991) cannot be too highly recommended. The story takes place in one of the old Muslim districts of Beijing and follows a Hui family through three generations. One feels at nearly every line what the identity of the community consists of, with much being said about a truly "religious" otherness (apart from some descriptions of stereotypical ceremonies such as marriages and burials). The original title was *L'enterrement musulman.*

12. Cf. P. Pelliot, *Mémoires sur les coutumes du Cambodge de Tcheou Ta-kouan* (Paris: Adrien Maisonneuve, 1951), new version followed by an unfinished commentary.

13. The large maritime expeditions of Zhenghe, nearly contemporary with the first Portuguese explorations along the coasts of Africa, have long held the attention of historians. One could begin by consulting J. V. G. Mills's translation for the Hakluyt Society of one of the richest sources we have, the report prepared by a (Muslim) companion of Zhenghe: Ma Huan, *Ying-yai Sheng-lan, The Overall Survey of the Ocean's Shores (1433)* (Cambridge: Cambridge University Press, 1970).

14. Here we turn to the special issue of the revue *Archipel* (50, 1995), devoted to Banten, where one will find studies of the economy of the sultanate as well as of an interesting and recently discovered Chinese cemetery. See also the study by Guillot, Lukman Nurhakim, and C. Salmon, "Les sucriers chinois de Kelapadua (Banten), XVII[e ·] textes et vestiges," *Archipel* (39, 1990): 139–58.

15. See here the collection of L. Bussé, *Strange Company, Chinese Settlers,*

Mestizo Women and the Dutch in VOC Batavia, VKI (Dordrecht-Riverton: Foris Publishers, 1986).

16. The best study of the "rebellion" of the Chinese in Batavia remains J. T. Vemeulen, *De Chineezen te Batavia en de troebelen van 1740* (Leyden: Ljdo, 1938). W. Remmelink's recent study *The Chinese War and the Collapse of the Javanese State, 1725–1743* (Leyden: KITLV, 1994) courageously reports the Javanese sources but unfortunately lacks a solid historical methodology.

17. See our article, "Le Campa vud du sud," BEFEO (76, 1987), 311–17.

18. Recently, in connection with the current policy of "openness," colloquiums have been held in Vietnam on the foreign districts of Phoyen and Faifo. The contributions have only confirmed, directly or indirectly, the resolutely monopolistic position of the official government.

19. See Sarasin Viraphol, *Tribute and Profit: Sino-Siamese Trade, 1652–1853* (Cambridge: Harvard University Press, 1977).

20. Cf. Jennifer W. Cushman, *Family and State: The Formation of a Sino-Thai Tin-Mining Dynasty, 1797–1932* (Southeast Asian Historical Monographs; Singapore: Oxford University Press, 1991).

21. All these recent developments are in general well set forth in the book by Victor Purcell, *The Chinese in Southeast Asia* (London: Oxford University Press, 1951, second edition, 1965), which for long served in the West as the bible regarding the overseas Chinese. The author shows his vast erudition and the work includes a good bibliography for the nineteenth century and the beginning of the twentieth, but historical perspective is not always emphasized.

22. *Minhhuong* originally meant all those who burned incense (*huong*) before the tablets of the Ming Dynasty, thus those who had fled upon the arrival in China of the Manchus. As for the word *peranakan,* it is constructed on the basis of *anak,* child, and designates those born in the host country whether the mother be indigenous or not, as opposed to those who were born in their countries of origin (*tokok*). In the Philippines, the word *metizo* in fact connotes all sorts of racial mixing but at the end of the nineteenth century was employed above all to designate culturally hispanicized Sino-Tagalog elites.

23. See our *Carrefour javanais,* vol. II (Paris: EHESS, 1990), 301–8.

24. See the introduction to the bilingual edition of J. Sauvaget, *Relation de la Chine et de l'Inde* (Paris: Les Belles Lettres, 1948).

25. Barus is on the coast of Sumatra, Sriwijaya had its center at Palembang, and Tioman is a small island to the northeast of the Malay Peninsula.

26. P. Ravisse, "Deux inscriptions coufiques du Campa," *Journal Asiatique* (2d ser.) 20:2 (October–December 1922), 247–89.

27. Oral communication from the archaeologist, I. Glover, who excavates in that region.

28. The descendants of this small community are now found in Sanya. Many

ancient steles have unfortunately disappeared during the last few years. See Chen Dasheng and C. Salmon, "Rapport préliminaire sur la découverte de tombes musulmanes dans l'ile de Hainan," *Archipel* 38 (1989): 75–106.

29. See Kuwabara Kitsuzo, "On P'u Shou-keng with a General Sketch of the Arabs in China," *Memoirs of the Research Department of the Tôyô Bunko*, vol. II (1928), 1–79; vol. VII (1935), 1–104. The last name *Pu* used by many Muslims would be an adaptation of the Arabic *Abu.*

30. Cf. Chen Dasheng and I. Kalus, *Corpus d'Inscriptions arabes et persanes en Chine Province de Fu-Jian (Quanzhou, Fuzhou, Xiamen)* (Paris: Geuthner, 1991).

31. On the establishment of this route, see R. Ptak, "The Northern Trade Route to the Spice Islands: South China Sea-Sulu Zone-North Moluccas," *Archipel* 43 (1992): 27–56.

32. Xiang Da, ed., *Xiyang Fanguo zhi* (Beijing: Xinhua shuju, 1954), 8, and, in a general way, D. Lombard and C. Salmon, "Islam et sinité," *Archipel* 30 (1985): 73–94 (translated as "Islam and Chineseness," *Indonesia* 57 (April 1994): 115–31.

33. See our *Carrefour javanais,* vol. II (Paris: EHESS, 1990), especially 44–48.

34. See, for example, Chen Dasheng, "Une pierre tombale du début du XIVe s. retrouvée à Brunei," *Archipel* 42 (1991): 47–52.

35. Regarding the importance of these *tarekat,* see G. Veinstein and A. Popovic, eds., *Les ordres mystiques dans l'Islam: cheminements et situation actuelle* (Paris: EHESS, 1986).

36. On this question, see the proceedings of the *Colloque de Sèvres* (May 1985): M. Gaborieau, A. Popovic, and T. Zarcone, eds., *Naqshbandis, cheminements et situation actuelle d'un ordre mystique musulman (Institut Français d'Etudes Anatoliennes,* Istanbul-Paris: Isis, 1990) and more particularly the studies of Hamid Algar, "A Brief History of the Naqshbandi Order," 3–44; of Françoise Aubin, "En Islam chinois: quels Naqshbandis?," 491–572; and of W. Kraus, "Some Notes on the Introduction of the Naqshbandiyya-Khalidiyya into Indonesia," 691–706.

37. A fact altogether remarkable, and one that in a certain way confirms the idea that the first Chinese emigrants had to have been Muslims, is that Chinese temples of Taoist or Buddhist inspiration founded before the nineteenth century (one could even say before 1860) are very rare in Southeast Asia. Various factors explain the "re-Sino-ization": the beginning of a female immigration (bringing a re-Sino-ization of households); the political evolution of China toward the end of the Qing; and, especially after 1911, seeking to draw emigrant communities to their cause (and to obtain financial aid from them).

38. In Indonesia, the group that advocates the conversion to Islam of people of Chinese origins has its publications and its own meetings.

Comment

Ann Laura Stoler

Denis Lombard's essay suggests a number of analytic and methodological issues in the production of minorities and more generally in the construction of social categories that we might want further to explore. First of all, he urges a move away from "anthropologically inspired" perspectives on minorities and ethnicities that stress more the "synchronic" than "diachronic" in analytic emphasis. He proposes instead a more careful historical tracing of the process of social formation itself. Second, he holds that this historical emphasis should not be on the short-term developments in minority status of particular groups but more so on the successive stages in the emergence of minorities that would rather constitute a focus on histories of the "longue durée." I comment on the second point first since this perspective motivates his subject and analysis.

Lombard's longue durée runs from the fifteenth to twentieth centuries, a sweep of some five hundred years. But in fact his span is broader still, for his appreciation of the relationship between Muslim minorities in China and Chinese minorities in Southeast Asia draws on his extensive knowledge of, and prior work on, Islamic mainland and maritime trade routes from an even earlier period.[1]

This perspective allows him to make several compelling arguments about the early entry of Islam into Asia and its expansion throughout the Malay and Indies archipelagos. Contrary to the received notion that Islam expanded into the region via the Middle East, Lombard traces a different trajectory through China and in particular through Chinese trading communities who were already identified as Islamic in the ninth and tenth centuries. That trade and Islamic expansion were linked has been argued by many others, but Lombard proposes that it was linked in ways not commonly understood. A relationship between Islamized Chinese communities and commerce is evident in Southeast Asia as well where overseas Chi-

165

nese communities on Java were already described as Islamic in the thirteenth century and more assuredly in multiple sources over the subsequent two hundred years.

The strong case is made that these two seemingly disparate communities—the Islamized Chinese in China and the overseas Chinese in Southeast Asia—when viewed in the longue durée, not only have "parallel histories," but interrelated ones, for both took shape in a similar process that joined the intensification of trade with the Islamization of communities involved in those exchanges.

Lombard's challenge to a regional historiography that has elided the early and important positioning of Islam within it is a perspective shared by others. Nancy Florida's exquisite treatment of eighteenth-century Javanese court culture argues that Dutch colonial philologists systematically excluded Islamic religious culture from its textual representations of what was "authentic," "pure," and "high" indigenous culture and quintessentially Javanese.[2] Like Florida, who makes the argument that Islam was culturally far more central to things Javanese, Denis Lombard asks us to consider a network of Islamic Chinese trading communities that were not marginal players but critical to the economic structure of Southeast and East Asia in ways that partially may account for discrepant developments within the region.

This early history of fluid movements of populations not yet identified as "minorities" contrasts sharply with the discrete and bounded social unities they have since become. Lombard makes the case that the rigidification of boundaries dividing the Chinese minority from groups around them accompanied the expansion of the Dutch colonial economy in the Indies and the development of mines and plantations throughout Southeast Asia.

But his argument goes further still. For it is not only the category of "minority" that became current in the colonial period, but a politics of violence directed at particular groups. Large-scale assaults on Chinese communities in the Philippines and on Java were not unrelated to the tensions between European trading enterprises and what they quickly recognized as financially solid and well-connected Chinese competitors.

Thinking through these long processes of minority formation invites us to ask a number of questions raised in other essays in this book but to which Lombard only briefly attends: namely, to the role that macropolities, and particularly states—be they metropolitan or colonial ones—play in the production of minorities and what stakes they have in doing so.

What political work is accomplished by designating certain populations as bounded, exclusionary, and fixed? To what extent is "minority production" a technology of rule? And if it is a technology of rule, does that mean that in the absence of minorities, expanding and/or consolidating state apparatuses would create them?

This last question is suggested by the profusion of recent work on the relationship between nationalism and racism and that on racism and the state that both converge on a similar observation: namely, that nationalisms (as Etienne Balibar, among others, notes) and modern states (as Michel Foucault underscores) not only instrumentally identify their "enemies within"' but actively produce them.[3] Whether those "interior frontiers" are politically and symbolically represented by Jews in Europe, Chinese in Southeast Asia, or "mixed bloods" in a range of colonial contexts, it is worth asking whether the designation of a group as at once a danger to the public good and in need of state intervention is not a fundamental feature in the development of the modern state's self-fashioning as protector of its citizens and as moral arbitrator. In identifying modern states as "supreme organs of moral discipline," Corrigan and Sayer, following Durkheim, prompt us to consider whether states achieve that moral stature by deciding which economic practices, and by which groups of people, constitute avarice (and which do not)—and not least whose appetites (economic, sexual, or otherwise) legitimately can be condoned or condemned as realized or potential threats to the public good.[4] The important point is that the production of minorities and the attributes assigned to them may be linked to broader processes of state formation.

Lombard's entreaty to study the longue durée is well-founded and should prompt us to consider more carefully which of its features we need to explore: for studying exchange networks and transformations in them, or who constitutes a minority and who does not, only makes sense if we understand the latter as processes of identification and containment tied to the tensions of state formation and imperial rule. It is in pushing the long- and short-term rhythms of rule up against one another that we can go beyond the production of minorities as expressions of ethnic conflict to see them as processes embedded in the taxonomic strategies of states.

Which returns me to Lombard's first point, that we need to be more "diachronic" in our approaches to minorities. Few of us would disagree that minorities are not primordial givens but the product of social and therefore historically specific constructions of social groups. But contra his claim that the making of social categories is insufficiently historical in anthropologically inspired research, I would argue the very opposite; that the "historic turn" of the last decade has rechanneled more work than ever toward the changing relations of power that prompt how subpopulations label themselves and how and when they are labeled by others. The issue that Lombard's advocacy of more historically attentive research raises then is not whether we should be doing more of it—on which we would undoubtedly agree—but what methodological, political, and theoretical problems we confront in doing so.

A new interdisciplinary generation of anthropologically minded humanists and social scientists is bringing a historical perspective to ask what counts as history at all. We are finding ourselves pushed up against disquieting issues about historiography and the politics of knowledge and what sorts of "sources" are credible to use as we tack between colonial archives and the postcolonial field. Some are asking hard questions about "collected" memories and historical narratives, about official histories and counterhistories that make up the contemporary politics of identity formation and affiliation. Not least we are finding ways of tracing the tension between fixity and fluidity in the making of those very social groupings that our own discipline participated in canonizing as discrete and bounded. If embattled groups self-consciously subscribe to some versions of the past as they make political claims and carve out their futures, and if these are accounts to which official versions of minority histories do not subscribe, then how we as historical ethnographers record and write those histories has effects that are acutely political as well. Thus called into question are both the historical "truth" of minority origins and what Michel Foucault would call the "regimes of truth" in which accounts of origin participate and on which our retelling of those accounts may also rely.

Which brings me to a final issue. How can we talk about the politics of affiliation and containment that the study of minorities demands without attending to the highly gendered dynamics of them? In passing, Lombard footnotes the emigration of women as one of many factors in the "re-Sinoization" of Southeast Asia's Chinese émigrés, but the gender and sexual politics that underwrite who will be designated as a threat to the social body and who will not may figure more prominently than his account would suggest. The contemporary tendency to look at minorities in terms of ethnicity alone should not dissuade us from looking at the micro-sites in which power relations are rehearsed and in which belonging is expressed in domestic arrangements and family formation. It is in these privatized sites, as much as in the public sphere, that we can trace the processes that allow social categories to appear fixed and fluid at the same time. Lombard's focus on the longue durée challenges us to push in promising directions: to analytic frameworks and methodologies that embrace both the macro-relations of power in which minorities are formed and to the micro-relations of power in which they are manipulated and expressed.

NOTES

1. See Denis Lombard and Jean Aubin, eds., *Marchands et hommes d'affaires asiatiques dans l'Océan Indien et la Mer de Chine 13e–20e siècles* (Paris: Editions de l'Ecole des Hautes Etudes en Sciences Sociales, 1988); and Denis Lombard, *Le Carrefour Javanais: Essai d'histoire globale,* 3 vols. (Paris: Editions de l'Ecole des Hautes Etudes en Sciences Sociales, 1990).

2. See Nancy Florida, *Writing the Past, Inscribing the Future: Prophesy in Colonial Java* (Durham: Duke University Press, 1995).

3. See Etienne Balibar, "Paradoxes of Universality," in *Anatomy of Racism,* ed. David Goldberg, (Minneapolis: University of Minnesota Press, 1990), and Foucault's 1976 Collège de France lectures on "state racism" that are unpublished but discussed in Ann Laura Stoler, *Race and the Education of Desire: Foucault's History of Sexuality and the Colonial Order of Things* (Durham: Duke University Press, 1995).

4. On state formation and moral discipline see, among others, Derek Sayer and Philip Corrigan, *The Great Arch* (London, 1985). Also see Albert O. Hirschman, *The Passions and the Interests: Political Arguments for Capitalism before Its Triumph* (Princeton: Princeton University Press, 1977) who brilliantly argues that by the seventeenth century, the state was called upon as a "civilizing medium," not to repress passions and appetites but to "harness them" (16). See my "States of Sentiment, Reasons of State: Thinking through a Colonial Oxymoron," in *Along the Archival Grain: Colonial Cultures and Their Affective States* (Princeton: Princeton University Press, forthcoming).

Cultural Interbreedings: Constituting the Majority as a Minority

Serge Gruzinski and Nathan Wachtel

From the time of the Spanish invasion, in the Andean world as in Mexico, a mere handful of conquistadors came to impose their domination upon the indigent masses. One cannot, therefore, begin by speaking of minorities nor of the marginalization of Amerindian populations, even when these decrease dramatically following the demographic catastrophe of the sixteenth century, for in spite of this they remain significantly more numerous than the Spanish. Yet it is true that the term *Indian* appears, from its origins even, as a derogatory term (see the flood of contemporary literature on savages, idolaters, and so forth) and that it is in fact applied even now in countries such as Peru and Bolivia—where the autochthonous substratum survives in many regions—to the populations least integrated into national life, who might be considered, in this sense, as "marginal." What, then, has taken place during these last five centuries?

The Indians of Mexico or the Constitution as a Minority of a Majority Population

At the time of their conquest, the Indians of Mexico City formed an agglomeration of 200,000 to 300,000 inhabitants. Against several thousand conquistadors, these Indians constituted a demographic majority throughout the sixteenth century. Even though epidemics greatly reduced their number, they were still the largest ethnic group of that city at the beginning of the seventeenth century.

Our inquiry concerns the means by which this majority was progressively transformed into a minority by the play of constraints emanating from colonial domination. To put it another way, we ask in what manner, in what stages, and in what rhythms did Occidentalization in its most diverse forms—the gaze, discourse, law, faith, work—model and phagocytize the populations that it encountered by determining their status, their margins of expression, and their modes of existence?

Minors, Neophytes, and Exempts

In the days after the Spanish Conquest, a variety of institutional and juridical measures assigned a minor status to members of the Indian population. The Indians were, in the eyes of the Church, a population of neophytes who needed special attention and a separate status. This is why the tribunal of the Inquisition did not hold any jurisdiction where the Indians were concerned. The formula of *ellos son coma niños* that the ecclesiastical chroniclers employed reveals the state of mind of the monks who felt that the Indians were placed under their tutelage and that they were to show the monks the filial obedience that children owed to their parents. At this point, the Indians were not yet a minority, properly speaking, unless a spiritual one, but rather a group treated in a special manner because they benefited from paternalistic benevolence and were regarded as needing protection as much from the abuses of the Spanish[1] as from themselves (that is, from a return to idolatry).

The Principle of the Two Republics

To speak of Indians or rather of *naturales,* as do all of the Spanish, goes back to delimiting an irremediably distinct group from that formed by the invaders. To provide it with an institutional reality, the *republica de Indios,* and a judiciary organism, the *Juzgado de Indios,* leads to differentiating it juridically from the rest of the population. The effect of this was to set apart the vanquished societies without necessarily respecting the pre-Hispanic differences by which the indigenous world was distributed among a multitude of ethnicities and states with distinct languages and origins. The Spanish domination designated and characterized an Otherness by assigning objective contours to it.

This separation, temporal and spiritual in principle, tended toward a physical separation as well. The monks even envisaged totally isolating the Indians from the Europeans, fearing the bad habits and pernicious example of the latter. By enclosing the Indian population within their network of churches and monasteries, the religious orders strove to make material a line of demarcation between conquerors and conquered. By insisting that blacks, half-castes, and those of mixed blood be chased out of indigenous communities, the monks hoped to render airtight the barrier which, it must be recalled, guaranteed their hold over the natives.

In the case of Mexico City, the distinction between the republic of the Indians and the republic of the Spanish established a physical and spatial separation between the groups. The conquerors settled in the center of Mexico-Tenochtitlan, while the conquered withdrew to the core of two parcialidades, San Juan Tenochtitlan and Santiago Tlatelolco, located in the perimeter. Provided with its own institutions, police, and resources, the Indian city offered the conquered peoples a framework within which they could preserve the remains of their heritage, maintain their own personality, or rather fashion an identity and a mode of life better adapted to the colonial context. The Indians were not yet made a minority quantitatively, nor were they systematically marginalized, but they were already placed in the periphery relative to the Hispanic center.

Interbreeding and Marginalization

The politics of the regular Church and of the Spanish Crown came to be linked to the formation of the Indians into a group provided with a particular status.[2] It was not a matter of making of them a minority but, rather, a category that could be integrated into an old regime society formed of naciones,[3] of bodies, communities, and corporations. Nevertheless, the Indians occupied a subaltern position due to their situation as conquered peoples and as former pagans.

Multiple pressures, however, stood in the way of the closing and the consolidation of the indigenous group. These pressures developed principally out of the demographic weakening due to the repeated epidemics that the indigenous population suffered. They also came from the process of interbreeding set in motion in the aftermath of the Conquest. Legitimate or illegitimate unions multiplied between Indians and Spanish. After the birth of the first half-castes, there rapidly appeared an intermediary group with a confused status, sometimes assimilated into the Spanish group, sometimes thrown back into the indigenous world. To this biological interbreeding was added the cultural interbreeding linked to the daily coexistence of Indians with Spanish. Contrary to the principle of separation, many Indians—domestics, servants, merchants—lived in the Spanish city and became accustomed to other modes of life. All this took place as if interbreeding eroded the Otherness that the prejudices and the institutions of the Spanish attempted to define.

But the effects of interbreeding were still more complex. In the city, Indianization and Hispanicization played an unequal game. The attraction exercised by the European sector prevailed and in the end largely swept away the other. This prompted the Indians and the half-castes to distance themselves from their indigenous heritage or to modify it in noticeable proportions. From the seventeenth century on, especially in the eighteenth century, the indigenous mode of life became a phenomenon if not of a minority, at least of marginalization in Mexico City. The irresistible Hispanicization of Indian elites, old nobility and recently wealthy caciques, and the mixtures of blood accentuated the process of marginalization.

The Exoticization of the Present

At the same time, the transformation of indigenous modes of life and traditions into expressions of a minority followed another path. In the sixteenth century, the role of the Indian city in Renaissance festivals is never secondary or accessory. Whether it concerns a scenic representation of the *Fall of Rhodes* (1539) or the celebration of the funeral of Charles V (1559), the Indians and the authorities of the parcialidades participated in a manner that was as extensive as it was active. Their visibility was optimal. In the following century, with the demographic decline of the Indian population, the social deterioration of its elites, and the entrenchment of Hispanic society, this intervention would take a different turn. After the flood of 1629, which affected only the indigenous population of Mexico, the Indians ceased to constitute a majority. On the contrary, they appeared thereafter as survivors of a group en route to extinction.

Throughout the seventeenth century, public and official usages of the Indian tradition developed that reduced it to exoticized forms or used it to reevaluate memories of a past abolished for good. The *villancicos* sung in Mexico, for example, put on stage Indians whose language, accent, dress, and reactions entertained the audience. The artists of Creole and peninsular Mexico in particular exploited the indigenous vein with insistence and talent. In truth it was impossible for the urban elites to ignore these Indians, who made up an integral part of their daily routines. Again it was necessary to metamorphose the Indian reality to better integrate it into the Baroque entertainment and imagination. Musicians, poets, decorators, and painters employed it as a source of flashy exoticism. They treated it as an aestheticized vision and, thus, stripped it of all displeasing or menacing harshness, purifying it of any foreign or disorienting note. This reflection of the Indian world could only be festive, the intervention of Mexicans on the stage being synonymous with joy and exhilaration:

Los Mejicanos alegres
tambien a sus usanza salen.[4]

In this expurgated form the Indian world gained its place throughout the seventeenth century in street festivals and in the most sophisticated entertainment given at the Court or in the city. It appeared in the ceremonial halls of the palace where it was unhesitatingly displayed before the gaze of viceroys and their retinue newly disembarked from the Old World. The masterpiece of Juana Ines de la Cruz, *Los Empeños de una Casa,* concludes with a *sarao* of four nations in which the Mexicans participate. While the dancers follow one another, the choir sings:

I Venid, Mejicanos,
alegres venid,
a ver en un sol
mil soles lucir.[5]

The same entertainment appears several years later in the *Comédie de saint François Borja* of Matias de Bocanegra (1612–68). The students of the Jesuit college of San Pedro and San Pablo performed it on the occasion of a visit from the viceroy, the marquis of Villena. The finale of the spectacle was assigned to graceful children in Indian costumes, who sang "tan vistosamente adornados con preciosas tilmas y trajes de lame de oro, cactles o coturnos bordados de pedreria, copiles o diademas sembradas de perlas y diamantes, quetzales de plumeria verde sobre los hombros." The actors intoned an homage to the viceroy:

Salid, mexicanos,
baila el tocotin,
que al sol de Villena
tenets en zenit.

On that occasion sixteen children danced a *tocotin* or a *mitote,* a majestic and solemn indigenous dance. The musical accompaniment strove to be faithful to Indian traditions: "A lo sonoro de los ayacatzitles dorados, que son unas curiosas calabacillas Ilenas de guijillas, que hacen un agradable sonido y al son de los instrumentos musicos, tocaba un nino cantor, acompanado de ostros en el mismo traje, en un angulo del tablado, un teponaztle, instrumento de los indios pare sus danzas, cantando el solo los compases del tocotin en aquestas coplas, repitiendo cada una la capilla, que en un retiro de celosias estaba oculta."[6]

The precision of this reconstitution betrayed an indisputable familiarity with indigenous usages, instruments, colors, pieces of clothing. The effect of exoticism that was produced was not therefore necessarily mixed with caricature or stereotype. The Creoles manifestly possessed a precise knowledge of the resources of the indigenous art, even of the Nahuatl language. Sor Juana did not hesitate to introduce Nahuatl phrases and words into her Spanish *villancicos,* even in series of couplets. An example follows:

Solo Dios Piltzintli
del Cielo bajo,
y nuestro tlatlacol
nos lo perdono.

Latin, Castilian, and the Mexican language mingle to form what this nun calls:

un tocotin mestizo
de Espanol y Mejicano.[7]

Exoticization also concerns groups other than the Indians. The peoples of African origin were also present in the Baroque festivals. In this case, the accent reconstructed by the poet provokes laughter, even as it restores for us the sonorous image of a lost world. But the miracle that the acceptance of Africano-Mexican culture would have been did not take place. The song was limited to expressing the manner in which the literate Spanish imagined the blacks who surrounded them would speak. The figure of the good Negro accompanying Christian festivities with his joviality also belonged to the repertoire of stereotypes.

The process of exoticization is linked to a cultural exploitation, in the current sense of the term, of non-European groups. This exploitation succeeded so well that it produced forms capable of being exported across the Atlantic, as was the case with the famous Indian dance, the tocotin, which arrives in Spain around 1680, perhaps even earlier.[8] This was not in any case a new phenomenon. Almost a century earlier, the vogue of African dances in Mexico, New Spain, and the Caribbean crossed the ocean to spread throughout old Europe,[9] as did the chaconne and sarabande.

The Heroization of the Past

The domestication of Indian traditions and of their patrimony operated also by the bias shown in the recovery of the indigenous past. This time, the past recovered did not conflict with a daily reality that necessarily had to be transformed. The task of inventing a past that was as glorious as it was inoffensive fell to chroniclers and historians. They were so successful in doing so that at the end of the seventeenth century the prestigious memory of Mexican sovereigns fascinated lettered Creoles and European visitors. This recovery was founded upon the first archaeological works begun at the end of the seventeenth century. In this period the Italian Gemelli Careri came to admire the sculpted stones that featured an eagle on a *nopal*, or cactus, while literate Mexicans were already speculating about the site of the temple of Huizilopochtli which some among them believed to be under the cathedral.[10] From this period the excursion to antiquities (for example, the pyramids) of Teotihuacan also became a must, requiring an indispensable extension to any stay in Mexico. Teotihuacan was to be visited in the same way one went to the Church of Guadalupe.

Gemelli Careri had the privilege of meeting the greatest connoisseur of relics of Indian civilizations, don Carlos de Siguenza y Gongora. The latter had gathered a collection of Indian codex so famous, "alhajas tan dignas de aprecio y veneracion por su antiguedad, y ser originales,"[11] that he dreamed of presenting it as a gift to the libraries of the Escurial, the Vatican, and Florence. The deciphering of the manuscripts, as well as his archaeological explorations, had given him a broad familiarity for his era and was authoritative enough to allow him to impose his vision of the past. The image that he proposed concerning the ancient Mexicans was flattering,[12] contrasting sharply with the vision of Mexicans as pagan idolaters, plunged into sin and barbarity.

But interest in the pre-Hispanic past was not merely an exercise in erudition. It satisfied more immediate designs. During this period pre-Hispanic archaeology was in tune with politics. Baroque festivals have provided us with the example of the triumphal arch conceived by don Carlos in honor of the marquis de Laguna and on which Aztec kings allegorically embodied the "political virtues." The rehabilitated vision of Indianness served a double function: It carried a message intended for the metropolis represented by the viceroy even as it served to root the memory of a young fatherland called Mexico in Indian prehistory. The Indians found themselves doubly dispossessed of their past.

The Sacralization of the Mexican Land
and of its First Inhabitants

During the same period, priests of the archbishopric of Mexico succeeded in associating the cult of the Virgin of Guadalupe with the indigenous world in an irreversible manner. The blossoming of this devotion had multiple causes, which we will examine here. It had numerous repercussions, among them, casting the Indians as guardians of a miraculous image of an exceptional nature, which allowed them to acquire a considerable influence in the Mexico valley and then throughout all of Mexico. The legend set down in the middle of the seventeenth century said the Virgin appeared to, and left her portentous mark upon, one of the members of the Indian community, Juan Diego. The Indians received in this way a certificate of Christianity and of Baroque piety: "non fecit taliter omni nationi."

The perception of the present as folklore and as exotic, the rehabilitation and exaltation of the pre-Hispanic past, and lastly divine election were inventions of the Creole elites of the seventeenth century that provided that indigenous group with an essential characteristic that remains their own today. Having become a minority, the Indians remained, in the opinion of Mexicans and in the eyes of tourists, the exotic celebrants of feathered dances, the fallen descendants of the pyramid builders, and the bearers of a superstitious and sometimes fanatical piety. However, in the seventeenth century the Indians were still a nation and not yet a discredited minority. It is not unimportant that this characterization was contemporary with a discourse that labeled three minority groups in seventeenth century society as *"secta"* and severely condemned "marranes" (maronites), "sodomites," and "idolaters" for sexual practice or religious deviance—which was not the case with Indians, quite the contrary.

The Enlightenment and Repression

The Baroque city had encouraged and even promoted a festive Indianness and an exuberant religiosity eager for marvels and miracles. Around 1800, Mexico counted 135,000 inhabitants, half of whom were Europeans. It harbored 26,500 half-castes, about 12,000 mulattoes, and another 33,000 Indians. To put it another way, the half-castes never constituted more than a strong minority; the Indians were far from having disappeared; and Europeans, or those considered as such, were indisputably the majority. The town visited by Alexandre de Humboldt was one-quarter mixed bloods, one-quarter Indians, and one-half whites. It had not therefore become a half-caste town—in that whites and Indians still represented three-quarters of its inhabitants—nor the bottomless melting pot one might imagine.

This is the context in which, in contrast to the decline begun in the sixteenth century, an important indigenous group subsisted and the policies of the agents of enlightened despotism must be interpreted. In the second half of the eighteenth century, a series of measures marked a change in course. In 1769, the Church outlawed the *nescuitiles,* representations of the Passion, and those of *Pastores y Reyes,* and it forbade the *palo del volador* and dances such as the *santiaguitos,* the *fandango del olvido de los maridos difuntos,* and the *bayle de la camisa.* There was no longer a question of the Indians offering incense to the horse of St. James (Santiago) or engaging in the frenzied dance that went with it. For the Church, the arguments were strong: the indecency of the participants, the profanation of liturgical ornaments and clothing, the mishaps, the excessive expenditures, and the grotesque aspect of the celebrations. Civil authorities would no longer put up with seeing Indians undressed in public: "La limpieza y aseo es uno de los tres principales objetos de la policia y este no solo comprehende las calles y plazas de las poblaciones, sino también las personas que las habitan cuyo traje honesto y decente influye mucho en las buenas costumbres." In truth, wearing an indigenous costume was not forbidden, but the combinations that "distorted" traditional clothing were no longer tolerated: "con andrajos u otros semejantes trapos, come suelen hacerlo a imitacion de los individuos de otras castes." Also banished were, consequently, "mantas, cabanas, frezadas, jergas o lo que llaman chispas, zarapes u otro qualquiera iron o trapo semejante." Men of the Enlightenment also intended to normalize appearances, "con la inteligencia de que siendo como es en los hombres la desnudez un indicio vehementisimo de ociosidad o de males costumbres."[13] For a population materially incapable of dressing themselves correctly, this was a signal for them to be driven back into the squalid suburbs.

In other words, in the second half of the eighteenth century, under the pressures of enlightened despotism, numerous forms of expression in the Indian town suffered all sorts of restrictions: suppression of the poorest confraternities or those without proper authorization; banning of indigenous theater; limitations imposed upon processions, on marches, and on public demonstrations of indigenous religiosity; destruction of chapels built by the Indians. This sequence of measures did not in any case concern only the indigenous world but encompassed the ensemble of popular practices, whether of half-caste, Spanish, or African origin. Projects envisioning the imposition of the Castilian language completed a mechanism under which the motivation for public order, hygiene, and decency combined to justify a progressive elimination of Indian visibility.

The Legal Death of Indians in the Town

The decrees of the Cortes of Cadiz and the decisions of the young independent state became linked to the pursuit of Enlightenment politics in their attack on even the structures of the indigenous group. In suppressing indigenous municipal institutions, the civil and ecclesiastic tribunals reserved for Indian brotherhoods and communities—*juzgado de Indios, provisorato de Indios*—the Mexican authorities undermined the foundations and effaced the prerogatives through which the Mexican Indians had maintained a collective and juridical identity and a communal existence.

Having disappeared in principle from the census, the Indians became a poverty-stricken minority; and folkloric portraits of their sordid lives appeared in the novels of the nineteenth century, such as *Los bandidos del Rio Frio of* Manuel Payno, and in the stories of travelers. The descriptions of pilgrimages to the Virgin of Guadalupe or to the Indian *chinamperos* of Xochimilco evoked a picturesque minority, drawn back into its own past, although a far less menacing one than the *léperos* of the town.

Not only did the modernization of the city create a minority out of the Indians, but the rapid expansion of industry and urbanization accelerated the proletarianization of those who had survived the colonial epoch at the same time as it drove back into the same lower-class *colonias* and the same shantytowns Indians who were without community, immigrants without roots, disconnected from all places of origin.

This rapid overview, necessarily summary and without nuance, of the fate of the Indians of Mexico City illustrates the manner in which the successive manifestations of Occidental domination—what we call Occidentalization—worked unrelentingly at transforming a defeated population first into Indians, then into a republic, and finally into a minority with a stereotyped profile before expunging them progressively from the territory of the city and the urban landscape.

Andeanization and Occidentalization

The Andean world was also, from the sixteenth century on, the theater of multiple cultural confrontations, intermixings, migrations, and interbreeding that engendered new collective identities. The processes of acculturation developed in both directions: On one side, indigenous societies subjected to the colonial system received, according to diverse modalities, Occidental contributions; and on the other, the Spanish were inevitably subjected to the influences of the American milieu (on this "inverse acculturation," which produced Creole culture, see the work of Solange Alberro on *The Spanish in Colonial Mexico*).[14] We are interested here in the phenomena of acculturation affecting indigenous societies, which themselves appear complex, variable, and even contradictory. To summarize (and simplify), one can distinguish in the Andean world two opposed types of acculturation:

First, on the one hand, principally in the framework of indigenous communities stemming from colonial "reductions," Amerindian societies absorbed a certain number of Occidental elements, integrating them into the systems of representation governed by a specifically autochthonous logic: This type of acculturation engendered what was defined precisely by the term *Indianness* and corresponded eventually to a process of Andeanization.

Second, on the other hand, the phenomena of interbreeding, at once biological and cultural, which developed principally in the urban and mining centers, gave place equally to a plurisecular social ascension, such that the boundaries between the interbred culture that resulted and Creole culture seemed at times fluid, permitting all possible intermediaries as well as slippages in both directions but from an indigenous point of view was a process of Occidentalization.

If these movements of Occidentalization and Andeanization spread in a parallel manner in distinct milieus, they nevertheless did not remain separated from one another, for these milieus continue to be linked by tight relationships, maintained by the migrating people themselves and the intermixing of populations, so much so that the processes in essence opposed each other and in fact intersected, interfered with, even influenced each other. To put it another way, these are contrary fluxes that one sees at work, in which the inverse effects nevertheless react, one upon another, to the point of mutually reinforcing each other in their antinomy: Andeanization produced an Indianness with specific characteristics that was subjected to Spanish and then Creole domination and then committed to a path of marginalization; Occidentalization led to a more or less progressive integration of the interbred classes into Creole society, more or less, for the process of Occidentalization followed neither a unilinear nor a uniform course. Between the Indian pole on the one hand and the Creole pole on the other lies the complexity of interbred identities that, contradictorily, are at the same time marked by their own traits and dissolved in the face of moving boundaries. In this unstable context, the marginalization of one appears all the more radical as the integration of the other becomes more massive and complete. It is this combined play of exclusion and assimilation that our research must attempt to bring to light, including its particular rhythms and the respective periodizations themselves, which varied according to a regional or local situation. But we know that in the end, during the course of centuries, within the same area, Occidentalization ends up prevailing over Andeanization, of which nevertheless something remains, to the extent that the residual Indians find themselves in our day, in effect, more marginalized than ever.

The question might be posed in another way: How do we make sense of the fact that Indians still remain in our own time, despite the diverse interbreedings exercised over Indianness for five centuries in a constant process of erosion? It is also appropriate to go back to the origins of colonial society and to observe that Indianness is itself the culmination of vast phenomena of interbreeding, not only with the Spanish, but also, and first of all, within the indigenous world.

At the time that they invaded the Inca Empire, the Spanish encountered several dozen ethnic groups or political formations, which little by little lost their standing as, during the colonial transformation, they dissolved individual characteristics into what has effectively become a community of Indianness. On the high Andean plateau around Lake Titicaca, the Incas had themselves imposed their dominance, one or two centuries before, over a half-dozen chieftainships or realms that still formed, at the time of the European invasion, distinct sociopolitical unities, which the Spanish designated by the term *naciones* (containing in turn diverse subdivisions). These Lupaqas, Pacajes, Carangas, Soras, and other Quillacas spoke the same language, Aymara, and shared a common universe of symbolic representations. Where among these Indians lay the limits of a sentiment of belonging to a collective entity? The lines of greatest separation might lay within the Aymara whole, among the different nations noted by colonial documentation. But the lines of separation between different social groups have a more or less strong intensity, allowing thresholds to shift at various levels according to the historical conjuncture. It is in this manner that the politics of the regrouping of the population (*reducciones*), carried out principally by viceroy Francisco de Toledo, helped to disrupt the political and socioeconomic organization of the indigenous world: The Cacique hierarchies suffered a repeated series of ruptures while affirming new autonomies. The Spanish authorities imposed in effect taxation (for the tribute and the *mita*) within the framework of the regrouped villages, which in the end formed the basic units of viceroy administration. With this progressive fragmentation, from the end of the sixteenth century to around the beginning of the seventeenth, the traditional networks of solidarity were forced to define themselves within increasingly narrow limits, passing, thus, from membership in a vast chieftainship to attachment to the indigenous community of colonial origin.

A remarkable phenomenon manifested itself in most of the regrouped villages: They were always composed of two halves, generally designated according to the categories of High and Low, which regrouped the *ayllus* of new communities. To put it another way, despite the disruptions provoked by the European invasion and by the process of dividing up the old chieftainships, the colonial communities were reconstituted everywhere on the basis of a dualistic organization. In his advice to Francisco de Toledo for the Government of Peru,[15] the auditor Juan de Matienzo officially recommended that the new villages be placed into two principal districts: hence, the recognition and application by the Spanish authorities themselves of a specifically Andean model. But the permanence of the principles of organization was from that time onward combined with profound changes regarding their exercise, for it was the same system of bipartite division and of interlockings, peculiar to Andean dualism, on which the definition of collective identities at a more local level was founded, by lowering the threshold of the largest division. Despite this reduction of under-lying territorial unity, the principles of dualistic organization nevertheless continued to inform the society globally and to assure a multiplicity of functions; it was also the same binary logic that everywhere ordered the distribution of space, the redivision of social groups, the representation of time, and finally the conception of the universe. The Andean dualistic schemes also appeared as powerful operators by means of which the indigenous world not only adapted itself to colonial domination but fur-thermore absorbed the contributions of the Occident into the interior of a system of representations that remained subject, despite reorientations and distortions, to preexisting logics.

This incorporation of foreign elements in an autochthonous unit that conserved its principles of organization accounted in particular for the most remarkable characteristics of the process of religious acculturation in the Andean world. This process did not simply amount to a series of recov-eries, reinterpretations, or translations. It is known, for example, that St. James, the knight brandishing his sword, was assimilated into Illapa, the god of lightning and of thunder, just as the superposing of Christ onto the Sun was favored by the proximity of the dates of Corpus Christi and the solstice. In practice the novelty of the process lay not in these identifica-tions in and of themselves, but in the fact that they took part in a system of classification and that the components of the syncretic combination, whether pagan or Christian, found themselves subjected to pairs of binary opposites (high-low, right-left, masculine-feminine, and so forth) of a dualistic order. In the framework of sacred topography, the saints quite logically came to occupy the upper extremity of the vertical axis, while the devils were symmetrically positioned at the lower extreme. Moreover, the original traits of Andean dualism affected, even more subtly, the Occiden-tal contributions themselves: From the time that they entered into the play of classifying categories, they were in turn susceptible to infinite divisions. In this way the Virgin disaggregated into different aspects: On the one hand she resided in the Upper World, with the saints; and on the other, she merged with Pachamama, the Earth-Mother and, in this aspect, belonged equally to the Lower World. In an analogous manner the ancient divinity for whom she was a substitute, Copacabana, the great idol of Lake Titi-caca, was on the one hand transformed into the Virgin of Copacabana, clearly celestial, but on the other, survived in the form of aquatic and infer-nal sirens.[16] In sum, despite changes, the perpetual logics in the Andean continuities were what gave order to the religious restructurings in the colonial epoch, and particularly in the seventeenth century: In the end, it was an example of the phenomenon of Andeanization.

To summarize, the model governed by a dualistic order controlled this combination of a territorial unity with pagan-Christian syncretism on which were founded the new identities born of the colonial transformations. These did not, however, follow concomitant rhythms. The conjunctures differed according to the type of phenomenon envisaged and not without some overlapping or discrepancies between contextual function and local conditions. Although the process of the fragmentation of ancient chieftainships began with the European invasion and although the indigenous communities constituting the new foundational units traced their origin generally to the reducciones ordered by the Spanish administration in the second half of the sixteenth century, the ties of solidarity that extended their networks across a large scale (regional, even interregional) often persisted up to the end of the seventeenth century and eroded only gradually. In the case of evangelization and the "extirpation of idolatries," both collided with strong forms of resistance, so much so that in an early period the two camps of belief, Christian and autochthonous, remained while giving way to reciprocal reinterpretations and not merging in a synthesis until a period that may be located approximately in the second half of the seventeenth century. The institutional expression of this pagan-Christian syncretism, namely, the system of rotation of religious offices, did not in turn seem to emerge as a regular practice until well into the eighteenth century, so that the crystallization of elements constituting the model to which Andean Indianness conformed did not take place until after the restructuring worked out over nearly two centuries.

During this time an inverse movement of Occidentalization did its work, principally in the urban milieu and in the mining centers. The history of the Indians of the cities in the Andean world during the colonial period still remains largely unknown. The case of the three principal cities of the high plateau in present-day Bolivia—Potosí, Oruro, and La Paz—will be studied by way of illustration, allowing us to enter into the details of certain colonial transformations.

Potosí, the Imperial City founded in 1545 at the foot of Cerro and well known for its fabulous silver mines, rapidly became one of the most populous cities of the Occidental world: At the beginning of the seventeenth century its population was estimated at close to 130,000 inhabitants (6,000 Spanish and 120,000 Indians). More so than in Cuzco, the old Inca capital, or Lima, the capital of the Viceroyalty, it is in Potosí that, with the flood of migrants from all parts, the intermixing of the Andean populations began, followed by the process of internal interbreeding that resulted in the dissolution of ancient ethnic identities.

The census taken in the time of Francisco de Toledo, in 1575, registered at Potosí a list of 690 taxpayers listed in the category of *yanaconas,* which is to say Indians who reside permanently in the city and who have already detached themselves from their community of origin.[17] In fact, they come from regions as far away as Cuzco (37 percent), Lake Titicaca (18 percent), Huamanga (11 percent), and some more distant still, since certain ones among them are originally from Quito, Bogotá, and even from Mexico. The census indicates that an enormous majority of the Indian yanaconas (536, or 78 percent) are *guayradores,* or miners, who use traditional Andean techniques. For nearly thirty years, in effect, from 1545 to around 1575 (when the amalgam was introduced), these Indians essentially controlled the extraction of crude ore that was later converted into silver. These Indians formed teams of workers who negotiated real contracts with the Spanish mining entrepreneurs: They procured the necessary tools for themselves and agreed to supply a fixed quantity of minerals while keeping the extracted surplus for themselves. Moreover, the Spanish had to employ the same indigenous teams to make silver from their portion of the ore. Certain sectors of the Andean world, therefore, are to be found notably engaged in the new economic networks from very early on. The other yanaconas of Potosí were essentially artisans such as tailors, cobblers, saddlers, and carpenters, who worked at crafts that the Spanish introduced. There was even a complement of forty-seven merchants whose presence appears all the more notable in the traditional economic organization in the central and southern Andes founded on the ideal of complementarity, which excluded commercial exchanges.

An anonymous description of Potosí, dating from 1603, confirms this integration into the colonial economic system in another context (after the Indians had long lost technical control over the production of silver). An enumerated table of the indigenous population indicates that 30,000 Indians worked in the mines or performed the services linked to the exploitation of mines, while 30,000 others "find themselves in this City occupied with diverse trades and activities."[18] Regarding the former, if the hardest tasks (mostly inside the mine) were carried out by the 4,780 miners forced into obligatory labor, another 10,000 free workers were required at the various stages of production. Still, this half of the population received salaries (unequal according to whether one is dealing with the mita or a voluntary engagement). The Indians occupied with other trades, which constituted the other half, appeared to be working on their own behalf. Among these, one discovers 1,000 merchants who supplied the construction timber; 2,700 who procured the wood for fuel; and, last, 10,000 Indians who transported to the city the necessary foodstuffs and fodder. The Indians in this last category were not limited to the tasks of transport: Without a doubt they also included Indians coming from communities to sell a part of their produce at Potosí and those who maintained in this way (along with the other migrants) the multiple links between the rural milieu and the urban center.

All of these Indians rubbed shoulders in Potosí, learning from one another to recognize their differences and their common condition. While it is true that the mitayos coming from the same corregimiento were attached to the same parish (the Pacajes to that of the Concepción, the Caracaras to that of San Cristóbal, and so forth), they were not the only residents, as other Indians lived there as well; nor were their neighborhoods restricted to streets and markets, for they extended in the workplace as well: The mita in effect allocated to each of its beneficiaries contingents of Indians of different origins, and inversely the mitayos of the same origin found themselves dispersed and regrouped with other Indians. There is all the more reason for free workers to have the same experience. The intermixing of the population thus affected every aspect of daily life in Potosí, leading us to conclude that it very much represented the crucible in which the gestation of a new identity took place, one in fact of interbreeding, but where at the same time permanent contact with the Spanish sector, indefinitely renewed movement of social ascent, and the opening onto vast networks reaching even to the Old World constantly sustained a strong process of Occidentalization.

Analogous phenomena occurred in a city such as Oruro, even though its silver mines were much less important than those of Potosí. It is not surprising to find that the majority of the 1,246 forasteros registered in the census of the Duke of La Palata are,[19] in 1683, employed in mining production; but one discovers that, as in Potosí, a significant part of them exercised artisanal trades (181, or 14.5 percent) or occupations linked to transportation (159, or 13 percent). Two remarkable traits, contradictory in appearance, distinguish this group of forasteros. On the one hand, more than half of them (54 percent) were born in Oruro, descendants of migrants already settled in the city; and among those who were not born there, more than a quarter (27 percent) had resided there for at least five years: The constant flux of migrations did not prevent a certain stability in that urban population. However, on the other hand, despite the long history of these migrations (of which many go back three or four generations, all the way to the time of the founding of Oruro), a very substantial majority (83 percent) of these forasteros continue to pay tribute to the caciques of their original villages. Moreover, more than half of them (54 percent) have even fulfilled their obligation of mita in Potosí "in silver" (which is to say that they paid a monetary commutation to their caciques, and one mentions only for the sake of the record the 2 percent who served in person). To put it another way, even in this urban milieu, the majority of these forasteros still conserved, at the end of the seventeenth century, ties with their communities of origin. The crucible of acculturation in Oruro extended its influence well beyond the limits of the city, through the multiple ramifications that unite the urban Indians with the more distant countryside.

The third case, La Paz, represents another example, not a mining center[20] but a commercial way station, one situated on the grand axis linking Cuzco to Potosí and which benefited as well from its proximity to the yungas, the Amazonian piedmont in which coca leaves were produced. The city of La Paz presents another peculiarity: its jurisdiction encompassed two, and later three, peripheral rural parishes organized after the model of the indigenous community (San Pedro, Santa Barbara, and San Sebastian). During the colonial period, therefore, some of the Indians of La Paz were true urbanites, while others were suburban country dwellers.[21]

If, to begin with, one examines the global evolution of the population of La Paz, to the extent that available documentation permits, one finds that the indigenous sector, taken in its ensemble, suffered long-term erosion. Our earliest information dates back to 1586, when La Paz contained 6,000 inhabitants, of which 96 percent were Indians. The first decline appears in the middle of the seventeenth century. In 1650, the population rose slightly, to 7,500 inhabitants, but among these the Indians did not represent more than 81 percent, while the category of half-castes (recorded for the first time) increased to 13 percent, and that of the Spanish only to 6 percent. A second decline appeared in 1675, when the total population had almost doubled to 12,000 inhabitants; but the Indian portion of the population had diminished to 60 percent, while the half-castes and Spanish (the two categories are confounded) made up 40 percent. Without a doubt the strong urban growth, accompanied by the swell of half-castes, meant once again great waves of migrations.[22] But then for nearly two centuries, if the population of La Paz continued to grow (above the fluctuations, which we cannot examine here in detail), on the whole a certain stability in its composition can be observed: It is, thus, that in 1854, out of some 60,000 inhabitants, 58 percent are inscribed in the category of Indians, while 42 percent are half-castes and whites (categories still confounded). It is during the second half of the nineteenth century that a new and marked decline occurs, resulting in a profound disruption of the urban landscape by the beginning of the twentieth century. The census of 1909 counted around 80,000 inhabitants, among whom one may distinguish 30 percent Indians, 32 percent half-castes, and 38 percent whites. Moreover, the evolution of the first half of the twentieth century would only continue these shifts with recompositions, thereby accentuating them. In 1942, La Paz counted more than 300,000 inhabitants, of which 23 percent are recorded as Indians, 35 percent as half-castes, and 41 percent as whites. Every bit as much as Potosí or Oruro, but according to other modalities, the city of La Paz played the role of a crucible for the process of Occidentalization.[23]

After this sketch, in broad strokes, of the global evolution of the population of La Paz, we must call attention to several particular points and examine in greater detail the distribution of categories of people in the different districts. Let us return therefore to the three rural parishes situated on the periphery. For two of these, San Sebastian and Santa Barbara, the bipartite organization seemed to disappear at the very moment of their creation following the division of the original parish, called *de las piezas* at the end of the seventeenth century. At San Pedro, on the contrary, the dualist order, with its two halves, Hanansaya and Hurinsaya, was still testified to in 1770 and did not fade in turn until after the great Indian uprising of 1781 (during which the rebel troops laid siege to La Paz for six months, spreading terror throughout Creole society). Let us clarify here that the three rural parishes were not peopled only by Indians of the community, for very early on these parishes underwent the progressive intrusion of the Spanish, who established haciendas there. These encroachments accelerated after 1781, particularly in San Sebastian and in Santa Barbara, where the category of *originarios* Indians then disappeared (although it survived in San Pedro). A second acceleration, of a different character but acting in the same direction, occurred in the second half of the nineteenth century, with urban expansion: Santa Barbara and San Sebastian saw themselves thereafter absorbed into the city itself. In fact, in 1877 the population of La Paz reached 70,000 inhabitants. This included some 6,000 more rural Indians, who concentrated in the parish of San Pedro, as a substantial majority (70 percent).[24]

When the three categories (Indian, half-caste, and white) are considered together, it is possible to see that after the same census of 1877 they can all be found, in unequal distribution, in each of the eight districts that make up the city, although San Pedro is distinguished anew by showing the most elevated percentages not only of Indians (30 percent) but also of half-castes (64 percent). Strong correspondences appear as well between the geography of the districts and the distribution of occupations: Most artisanal activity (from 70 to 90 percent of bakers, butchers, tailors, cobblers, hatters, and so forth) was concentrated in the peripheral districts. Conversely, it is remarkable that out of the entire population of La Paz, 32 percent of Indians and 36 percent of half-castes were nevertheless registered in the central districts, while 44 percent of whites were to be found also in the peripheral districts. That these last should be distinguished by characteristics more clearly Indian or half-caste is not, in the end, the least bit surprising; the essential matter is that in proportions that were, to be sure, variable, all the categories of people rubbed shoulders and intermixed in all the districts of the city.[25]

One other observation must be made on the sexual distribution within the category of half-castes, for the same census of 1877 indicates that for all of the districts of La Paz, 61 percent were women, and only 39 percent men. This strong imbalance confirms, on the one hand, the vital role that women played in the migratory movements toward the city and the processes of interbreeding. As recent work shows, it was generally migrants (or their descendants) who, from an early epoch of the colonial period, exercised the urban occupations of domestics and, above all, the activity of sellers (*regatonas*) in the market stalls.[26] But the imbalance registered by the census also indicated, on the other hand, the complex problem of identifying individuals attributed to the category of half-caste. It will be recalled here that one of the most visible criteria, and one that denoted a self-designation, for example, that of clothing, was in effect truly pertinent only for women. Half-caste men distinguished themselves little, in this view, from the Creole members of society (if not by the quality of their clothing); while half-caste women, from the sixteenth century on and throughout the colonial and later republican periods, despite the many changing fashions, wore clothing that differentiated them as much from the Spanish as from the Indians. Even today (and since around the end of the eighteenth century), in La Paz as on all the high Andean plain, the famous *pollera* (gathered and layered skirts), inherited from an ancient form of dress used by Creole women, is a quasi-emblematic sign of the *chola*.[27] Why does the latter, who does so much to distinguish herself from the Indian woman, not follow the course of Occidentalization to its end? Her daughter, especially now, doubtless does so: Did not the pollera mark a stage in the process that has continued through generations? This apparently modest costume raises the whole problem, which we may only invoke here, of the autonomy of a half-caste culture.

If the constitution of the Indians as a minority has followed, in Mexico and in the Andean world, distinct modalities and different rhythms, in the end it results in a common effacement of the collective identities created by colonial domination. During several centuries Indianization and Occidentalization have produced opposite effects, but the processes in reality have become intermingled; and it is Occidentalization that, everywhere, has finished as the victor. But this has not been entirely true, for Indians remain minorities all the same, if one is to be precise. Is this a question of last vestiges before an ineluctable and final disappearance, or will the construction of new consciousnesses of identity open other perspectives for them (as the "neo-indigenist" movements that have been developing over the course of the last few years seem to testify)? The question reaches beyond the bounds of our brief reflection here.

Yet the Mexican case as well as that of the Andean world should perhaps stimulate us to reconsider the infatuation with which we interest ourselves these days with minorities, ethnic and other; to reflect on the manner in which they spring up and construct themselves within our discourse and our imagination; finally, to scrutinize the manner in which they disappear when lucidity, usury, or the effects of fashion take our attention elsewhere. The rhetoric of alterity equally merits review in the light of a historical experience that reveals the extent to which the Creole and European intellectual elites have long been fond of a concept that embraces the most diverse strategies.

NOTES

1. "Defender estas ovejas de los lobos," in the "Carte colectiva de los franciscanos de Mexico al emperador" (17-XI-1532), published by Fray Toribio de Benavente ('Motolinia'), Memoriales (Mexico: UNAM, 1971).

2. It would be suitable in this instance to compare the case of Americans with the earlier ones of the Canary Islands and of Grenada.

3. See "Esta nacion" concerning the Indians in "Carte colectiva de los franciscanos de Mexico al emperador," 438.

4. Sor Juana Ines de la Cruz, Obras completas, t. II (Mexico, FCE), 16.

5. Ibid, t. III, 180.

6. [so ostentatiously adorned with precious ponchos and costumes of gold lamé, shoes with laces running up the calf adorned with precious stones, diadems sown with pearls and diamonds, bunches of rich, green feathers on the shoulders], *Trez piezas,* 377–79. Conceived after the model of the plays of Lope de Vega, at once edifying, humorous, and pleasant, the *Comédie de saint François Borja* tells of the conversion of a great Jesuit saint, the Duke of Gandia, grandee of Spain and viceroy of Catalonia. It is punctuated by interludes and dances such as the branle and a part of the alcancias, earthenware balls filled with flowers or ashes. Ten students of the highest nobility played a part in it that was remarked upon. [To the sound of gilded *ayacatzitles,* which are a peculiar zucchini shape, filled with pebbles, and have a pleasant sound and to the sound of musical instruments, a boy singer played, accompanied by others in the same costumes on a corner of the stage, a *teponaztle,* an Indian dance instrument, singing many stanzas to the beat of the ancient folk dance, repairing to a chapel hidden in the latticework.]

7. Sor Juana Ines de la Cruz, *Obras completas,* II: 41, 17. The "interbreeding" of cultures was so evident and so familiar that the adjective *mestizo* was itself from the common domain, to the point of being used in a villancico as popular and as burlesque as that of San Pedro Nolasco (1677).

8. Marie Cecile Benassy, 31.

9. The recovery of Indian cultures took on occasion the route of mythological allegory: In 1713, a float presented by the corporation of pulque manufacturers vaunted the virtues of pulque, the fermented juice of the agave. A Creole poet took it upon himself to invent a creational myth to attach the Mexican plant to classical mythology. Created by Hercules, born of the milk of the Goddess Juno, the pulque became that "preciosisima bebida, tenida de sus aficionados por digno brindis de la mesa de Jupiter, y aptisima pare procerizarse a deidades."

10. Giovanni Gemelli Careri, *Viaje a la Nueva Espana* (Mexico: UNAM), 123.

11. Elias Trabulse, 19.

12. Don Carlos de Siguenza y Gongora, 252: "genie arrancada de sus pueblos, por ser los mas extranos de su provincia, gente despedazada por defender su patria y hecha pedazos por su pobreza; pueblo terrible en el sufrir y despues del cual no se hallaria otro tan paciente en el padecer, gente que siempre aguarda el remedio de sus miseries y siempre se halla pisada de todos, cuya sierra padece trabajos en repetidas inundaciones."

13. [Straightforwardness and courtesy is one of the principal concerns of the police, and they know not only the streets and squares of the towns but also the people who live there, whose honest and decent dress much influences good habits.] In truth, wearing an indigenous costume was not forbidden, but the combinations that "distorted" traditional clothing were no longer tolerated: "con andrajos u otros semejantes trapos, come suelen hacerlo a imitacion de los indi-

viduos de otras castes" [those in rags and similar trappings, as if to imitate people of other castes]. Also banished were, consequently, "mantas, cabanas, frezadas, jergas o lo que llaman chispas, zarapes u otro qualquiera "iron o trapo semejante" [blankets, clothes adorned with fringe, Mexican cloths called *chispas,* sarapes, and whatever else was similar]. Men of the Enlightenment also intended to normalize appearances, "con la inteligencia de que siendo como es en los hombres la desnudez un indicio vehementisimo de ociosidad o de males costumbres" [with knowledge that human nudity is a strong indicator of laziness or bad habits], AGN (Mexico), Bando 20, no. 25.

14. Solange Alberro, *Les Espagnols dans le Mexique colonial. Histoire d'une acculturation* (Paris: Cahiers des Annales, 1992).

15. Juan de Matienzo, *Gobierno del Peru* (Paris, 1967).

16. Cf. Nathan Wachtel, *Le retour des ancêtres. Les Indiens Urns de Bolivie (XXème–XVIème siècle). Essai d'histoire regressive* (Paris, 1990), 549–58.

17. Ibid., 476–67.

18. Ibid., 478–89.

19. Ibid., 480–82.

20. Cf. Rossana Barragan, *Espacio urbano y dinamica etnica. La Paz en el siglo XIX* (La Paz, Hisbol, 1990).

21. Ibid., 85–122.

22. Ibid., 72–74.

23. Ibid., 76–82 and 75.

24. Ibid., 96–122, and 185 passim.

25. Ibid.; cf. table, 196–97.

26. Ibid., 192 and passim.

27. Cf. Rossana Barragan, "Entre pollees, nanacas y lliqllas. Los mestizos y cholas en la conformacion de la Tercera Republica," in *Tradicion y modernidad en los Andes,* Henrique Urbano, ed. (Cuzco, 1993), 43–73.

Comment

Sabine MacCormack

Serge Gruzinski and Nathan Wachtel address the question as to how we can think of Indians in Mexico and in the Andes as "minorities" from two distinct vantage points which are in part conditioned by the different histories of these two regions, while in part they arise from the particular scholarly interests that the two authors have pursued in their other writings.

Serge Gruzinski's work focuses, for the most part, on the world of the imagination, *l'imaginaire,* in colonial Mexico, on the cognitive and figurative strategies used by Europeans in order to remove the indigenous population from the center of political action and of cultural and religious experience.[1] In his essay for us, he accordingly outlines some further examples of such strategies: the physical removal of Indians from the center of Teotihuacan; their exoticization in Baroque secular and religious drama and poetry; and, during the eighteenth century, the curtailment and re-formulation of Christian ritual expression as practiced by indigenous people, a topic on which we now also have an illuminating discussion by Fernando Cervantes.[2] Each of these processes spelled out the changing economic and political desiderata of the European newcomers: Their usurpation of the most prestigious urban spaces after the initial invasion was complete; their taste for erudite and solemn display as a means of advocating the now-established political order during the seventeenth century; and later, the reformulation of Catholic piety in the light of the exigencies of the European Enlightenment. In each of these redistributions of economic, cultural, and religious resources, so Gruzinski shows, Indians were the losers, and their status as a figurative minority was accentuated.

Nathan Wachtel approaches our problem in a more anthropological and sociological fashion that at the same time highlights some differences between the Andes and Mexico. In particular, the dual organization of

Andean communities and of political authority that was prevalent before the European invasion was deliberately preserved by Spanish officials and continues to exist today. This basic fact of Andean life underlies Wachtel's discussion of the correlated concepts of Andeanization and Occidentalization. An example of Andeanization, which has obvious parallels in Mexico, is the creation of the cultural and legislative category of "Indian." This category, which has no pre-Columbian antecedents, required a non-Andean observer for its very existence. At the same time, the category, and others that arose alongside it,[3] universalizes and essentializes certain aspects of Andean life and culture as observed by outsiders in a manner that was so compelling that Andean people themselves began using these categories. In a Quechua text of the early seventeenth century, for example, the Andean author described his own people as "Indians," as though he felt that the Quechua word for people, *runa*, were insufficiently clear if used in isolation; Andeans accordingly appear in this text as "runa yndio," "Indian people."[4] Similarly, in the mid–seventeenth century, Andean shamans sometimes described themselves by the Spanish term as sorcerers, but without intending to convey the derogatory content of this term in Spanish usage of the time.[5] The point was that *idolatry* was the only available term to describe Andean religious beliefs and practices, and different Andean speakers of Spanish used it in either the received or in their own distinct and indeed anti-Christian sense. In short, Wachtel's interdependent processes of Andeanization and Occidentalization can be documented as taking place over a very broad spectrum of political and cultural life in the Andes. As Bruce Mannheim has demonstrated in his groundbreaking book *The Language of the Inka since the European Invasion,* the Quechua language itself, which was increasingly standardized by missionaries who wanted to make of it a truly "general" language of all Indians, evolved according to this same pattern.[6]

In commenting on these two overviews of the marginalization of Indians in Mexico and Peru after the Spanish invasion, I suggest that the histories of Mexico and Peru, however different they indeed are, may offer more scope for comparative research than is commonly realized.[7] With regard to the question of minorities in particular, as Gruzinski and Wachtel both point out, Indians were not, during the period being considered, minorities. Rather, the subject we are here investigating is the process whereby Indians in Mexico and Peru became second-class citizens in their own countries, how, in other words, they became minorities in a figurative sense. In addition, I comment on certain aspects of Indian self-perception in the Andes during the colonial period by way of stressing that these "minorities" were in no sense passive bystanders in their own political and cultural experience. This theme is of course not a new one in the context of Mexican and Andean studies. I only mention Miguel León Portilla's and Nathan Wachtel's influential books on the vision of the vanquished, published in 1959 and 1971 respectively, as well as Nancy Farriss's pioneering *Maya Society under Colonial Rule.*[8] Nonetheless, seeing how much scholarly interest the "exoticization" of Indians at the hands of Europeans has aroused in recent years, it may be worth observing that exoticization, both then and now, is a form of European and Western self-reflection, and that studying it cannot help us understand Indian societies in their own right. A touchstone in the interpretation of any society must always be what members of that society had to say.

The destinies of indigenous people in Mexico and Peru evolved according to patterns that were, in some respects, parallel. For example, the ever-increasing marginalization of the indigenous population from centers of political and cultural power that Serge Gruzinski discusses occurred also in the Andes. When the Inca capital of Cuzco was refounded as a "settlement peopled by Spaniards," the invaders redistributed the city's Inca palaces, thereby displacing the original inhabitants. Subsequently, considerable efforts were made in order to deconstruct the significance that the Inca city had conveyed to Andean people. Cuzco's central square, for example, was convered in sand that had been transported there from the Pacific coast. Spanish officials liked to suggest that the Incas had undertaken this project in order to keep their subjects occupied. At the same time, these officials understood quite well that the sand in the square conveyed a cosmological meaning in that it linked the sierra with the coast, and this is why, in 1559, the lawyer Juan Polo de Ondegardo as governor of Cuzco arranged for the sand to be removed and to be used in Spanish construction.[9]

From the early seventeenth century, in the Andes, as in Mexico, the marginalization of indigenous peoples took new forms. The Spanish were by this time firmly in power, which was why it was possible to recall the precolonial past, now safely neutralized and exoticized in the way that Serge Gruzinski describes, with a certain nostalgia. In the Andes, just as in Mexico, the pageants and processions that articulated the rhythms of urban life were thus graced with tableaux vivants displaying the bygone glories of the period before the Spanish arrived. During the celebrations of the beatification of Ignatius Loyola in 1610, for example, the people of

Cuzco were able to admire a splendid procession of floats carrying the twelve Inca rulers adorned in their regalia.[10] Similarly, local historians of Cuzco looked back to their city's Inca past by way of validating the political and cultural hegemony of the Creole elite,[11] much as also happened in Mexico.[12]

Imagery evoking the Inca past was popular even in the Spanish metropolis, although there, the message that the Inca empire, for all its glory, had fallen was pressed home with greater insistence. In 1649, for example, the legend about how the Incas of Cuzco had been defeated in a battle by the Spanish invaders who were assisted from on high by a miraculous appearance of the Virgin Mary was depicted on a triumphal arch in Madrid. The structure served to greet Queen Mariana on the occasion of her ceremonial entry into the Spanish capital.[13] Similarly, Calderón's play, *La aurora en Copacabana,* which was published in Madrid in 1672, recounts how an Inca prince and his consort, once they had become Christians, were content to discard their royal status and to wear the humble attire of ordinary Spaniards.[14] A similar message was spelled out in a play composed in Upper Peru for a highly educated Quechua-speaking public of Creoles and Indians: here, the hero, an Inca lord, having become wealthy thanks to engaging in a pact with the devil, ultimately finds true happiness as a humble attendant in Cuzco's parish church for Indians. César Itier has pointed out that the central message of this play concerns an appropriate understanding of free will and of the importance of correct perception.[15] But the fact remains that the play also inculcates the virtues of Christian humility in the persona of an Inca lord, not of a Creole or a Spanish hero, and the importance of humility for Indian converts dominates missionary preaching in colonial Peru. But perhaps these are not the only messages the play conveys, and further research will reveal in this and other Quechua plays an indigenous voice such as Louise Burkhart (in her recent book *Holy Wednesday*) has been able to identify in the Nahua version of the Spanish play "Beacon of Our Salvation."[16]

In short, the ceremonial rhythms of urban life in colonial Peru and Mexico resembled each other as much as did certain Spanish perceptions of the Mexican and Andean precolonial past, exoticized and fictionalized though these often were. The reason for such resemblances is to be found in the parallel processes of Hispanization that helped to bring about the increasing marginalization of Indians in both Mexico and Peru. At the same time, these resemblances point to the European antecedents on the basis of which many aspects of public life in colonial Spanish America evolved. For in Spain, as elsewhere in Europe, processions, theatrical performances, and festivals all served to validate the established order while at the same time keeping the populace in its subordinated place. Such dramatic and ceremonial displays were, in effect, methods not simply of providing entertainment, but of ordering society in hierarchies of dignity and power: undifferentiated crowds composed of members of the general populace thus stood juxtaposed with carefully delineated groups of personages whose status spoke through the positions they occupied in relation to each other, and through their gestures and attire.[17] The marginalization of Indians, and their subordination to the Spanish minority that we observe in seventeenth-century Peruvian and Mexican public rituals, was thus paralleled in Europe, even though there the duress employed to achieve the subordination of majorities to ruling elites appears to have been less pervasive, and less harsh.[18]

To study the history of Indian societies in colonial and republican Latin America amounts to confronting contradictions that are hard to reconcile. On the one hand, the extent of the demographic collapse undergone by these societies after the coming of the Europeans was so catastrophic, and the extraction of wealth by the colonial government so extreme,[19] that one is at a loss to explain the survival of these societies. On the other hand, while some cities, in particular Lima and Mexico City, were predominantly Spanish and Creole and, as Gruzinski has shown, took little cognizance of Indians except as servants and artisans, many indigenous societies did survive elsewhere. Moreover, a number of these societies were able to achieve remarkable prosperity during the colonial period.

The marginalization of Indians in colonial Peru and Mexico was thus not total, and Indians did not passively settle down to be governed by foreigners. This is why Indian strategies of survival make such a fruitful field of inquiry. Almost from the very beginning, Indians developed methods of pursuing their own ends within, or in spite of, the new system. Nathan Wachtel, like before him John Murra,[20] draws attention to the economic enterprise of Andean lords, and there are Nahua and Maya analogies. The very vocabulary used by Indians speaking their own vernacular languages shifted and changed when Spanish money entered the economy, so that these languages in themselves make up a small history of creative adaptation. The Spanish term for a small coin, *tomín,* for example, became a loan word designating "cash, money" in Nahuatl,[21] and in the Andes, Quechua still reflects the reality that money and markets were once upon a time novelties. The term *colque,* employed by colonial and contemporary

Quechua speakers to describe money, is thus the same as the term for silver, and a rich person is *colqueyok,* someone who has "silver." Furthermore, the verb *rantiy,* which originally meant "to exchange" or "to give a pledge," does duty for both "to buy" and "to sell." In colonial times, one might thus have said, "I buy by means of silver, or money," *rantini colquehuan.* For selling, on the other hand, the transaction would involve reciprocity (indicated by the verbal suffix *cu*) and be directed outward, toward a person who possesses silver, or money, so that one would say, "I sell to (toward) a person who has silver," *ranticuni colqueyokman.*[22] Such linguistic shifts do not merely highlight the impact of new Spanish ways on Indian societies, but also some of the methods whereby Indians were able to retain a degree of autonomy in adverse times. Language, as Alfredo Torero observed years ago, expresses the history of the society in which it is spoken. This is true not only in the obvious sense with respect to statements that speakers of a given language will make, but also with respect to vocabulary and morphology. It is this latter aspect that Torero had in mind. Recent work by Bruce Mannheim, César Itier, Gerald Taylor, and others reveals just how fruitful philological research can be in documenting the experience of Quechua speakers in colonial Peru.[23]

Beyond finding a place in markets and a monetary economy such as they had not known before the Spanish invasion, indigenous people throughout Spanish America were, and still are, engaged in defending and reclaiming their rights.[24] At a time when, in the sixteenth century, the Spanish Crown was organizing, governing, and mapping the newly conquered American lands, the Nahua found their own methods of describing and mapping the land in which they lived.[25] In addition, from the mid–seventeenth century, Nahua communities drew up documents, *títulos,* in their own language by way of validating rights to their land in the face of Spanish and Creole encroachment.[26] Although no such corpus of *títulos* has so far been found in Peru, there does exist at least one document that demonstrates that in the Andes likewise people were thinking of their historical origins in order to retain control of their land. The document is from Laraos, a community in the Andean foothills southeast of Lima, that had originated as a resettlement made up of several smaller villages in 1569. At the end of the sixteenth century, the colonial government undertook a series of *revisitas,* inspections of titles to land, which had the aim of transferring ownership of ostensibly vacant lands to Spaniards. It was to counteract this initiative that, in 1597, the people of Laraos arranged for the drafting of a map outlining the boundaries of their community's land.

According to the accompanying Quechua text with its Spanish translation, the boundaries between Laraos and its neighbors had been established by the Inca Tupa Yupanqui, who had personally walked along the boundary line. On August 8, 1597, the lord, *curaca,* of Laraos again walked along this boundary line with seven old men, inspecting the landmarks and boundary stones that defined the line by way of reasserting the community's claim to its land. The text was signed by the seven old men, the curaca and the Andean notary who wrote it down. Like Nahua communities in their *títulos,* so the people of Laraos were rethinking their history, and at the same time enacted it ritually in order to defend their property against the invaders and their descendants.[27]

Not all such defensive action was necessarily peaceful, and often it failed. In 1541, the Indians of New Galicia organized an armed uprising to rid themselves both of Christian missionaries and of Spanish government in order to "live happily with their ancestors, suffering no more hardship and pain." The leaders of this uprising required of their followers a very specific renunciation of all Christian ideas and rituals, and they were hoping to remove the invaders from all parts of Mexico.[28] A similar movement, known as *Taqui Onqoy,* "Song of Disease," swept through Peru in the 1560s. Here also, the aim was to expel all Spaniards, to reject Spanish food and clothing, and to prepare for the return of the old gods, even though, meanwhile, the nature and activity of these gods, as Nathan Wachtel has shown,[29] had inevitably been redefined in the light of recent experience. This indigenous project of separation from all things Spanish and Christian lived on in the Andes until the end of the seventeenth century[30] and helps us gain an insight into one aspect, at least, of what it meant to be "Indian" in early colonial Peru.

By the turn of the sixteenth to the seventeenth century, Spanish influence in the Andes had touched on and modified every aspect of daily experience. For Andean people, this inescapable fact required in response a stocktaking of who they were, an individual and collective definition of identity. It is no accident that the major Andean texts we have all date from this period. The majority of Andean people did by this time define themselves as Christian, even though, as Kenneth Mills has shown in his recent *Idolatry and its Enemies,* their Christianity invariably contained elements of thought and practice that differentiated it from the Christianity of Creoles and Spaniards. Moreover, the accommodations that Indians arrived at between their own ideas and practices, and imported Christian ones, varied, as Mills has described so well, over space and time, even within the archdiocese of Lima,[31] while in Upper Peru, the Inca past contributed its own distinctive tinge to the practice of Christianity by Andean people.[32] In Mexico likewise, Indian Christianity retained characteristics that the official church hesitated to countenance, or rejected outright.[33] In short, "Occidentalization" had and has its limits.

As Serge Gruzinski mentions, early colonial legislation tended to envision two distinct societies that existed in Spanish America, the republic of Indians and the republic of Spaniards, each governed by its own rules. The Church, likewise, issued canons regulating the lives of Indians, while other canons applied only to Spaniards.[34] This legislative distinction corresponded to a certain reality. Although Mexico and Peru were made up of distinct regional cultures, some of which retained their cultural particularity into the colonial period and beyond, the Spanish settled in the Americas with a very firm idea of who they were not: they were not Indians. The result was that, on occasion, those on whom the definition of Indianness had been imposed by force from the outside responded by insisting that they were not Spaniards. This shift in self-awareness, the necessity of declaring that one was not Spanish, was in one sense a negative effect of the invasion, an acknowledgment of the loss of power and status. But this very acknowledgment had the positive result of arriving at a new concept of identity that was now defined not only in terms of the laudable characteristics that an Indian person should espouse, but also in terms of the "Spanish" characteristics that ought to be rejected. A story to this effect that made the rounds of the Americas from the Caribbean to the Andes recounted that the Spanish invaders ate gold. In the early seventeenth century, the Andean historian Guaman Poma de Ayala applied this story to his own people's experience in describing the very first encounter between Spaniards and the Incas. As Guaman Poma understood it, the invader Pedro de Candia, one of Francisco Pizarro's treasure-hungry followers, was sent as an ambassador to the court of the great Inca ruler Guayna Capac, and a conversation took place between the Inca and his guest. Surrounded by the splendor of his court and the many golden objects that the Spanish so much desired, the Inca asked: "Is this the gold which you eat?" To which Pedro de Candia replied, "This is the gold which we eat," thus demonstrating, in his very own words, that the Spanish were, as Guaman Poma observed elsewhere, "demons and devils."[35]

While thus there were grounds why "Indians" chose to differentiate themselves from Spaniards, the legislative distinction between the two republics of Indians and Spaniards became ever more artificial because the number of persons of mixed parentage, beginning with the children born from unions between the first invading Spaniards and Indian women, grew with every generation.[36] One such individual was the historian Garcilaso de la Vega, son of the Inca royal lady Chimpu Ocllo and the captain Sebastián de la Vega. Garcilaso addressed his history not only to Indians and Spaniards, but also to Creoles and people of mixed descent like himself. In his text, he furthermore mentioned some of the African slaves who had accompanied the Spanish invaders and who arrived in Peru—as also in Mexico—in growing numbers during the sixteenth and seventeenth centuries.[37] The presence of Africans in Peru was likewise noted by Guaman Poma, who thought that they should be instructed in Christian doctrine and be kept at a certain distance from Indians.[38] Altogether, Guaman Poma, like the missionary Bartolomé de las Casas earlier, thought that the rights of Indians were best protected when Indians lived separate from newcomers, and similar ideas were expressed in Spanish legislation.[39] Such aspirations, however, were utopian: people moved around the vast territories of the Mexican and Peruvian viceroyalties relatively unhindered, and their unions gave rise to miscegenations so diverse that by the eighteenth century they seemed to defy even the most assiduous classificatory endeavors.[40]

As manifold as the mingling of races was that of cultures, life-styles, and occupations. As Nathan Wachtel observes, this "métissage culturel" contributed to the numerical and economic erosion of Andean societies.[41] "Métissage culturel" affected Andean people not only as individuals, but also as members of kin groups or ayllus and of ethnic lordships. Garcilaso and Guaman Poma, like before them several Spanish historians, noted that the Incas tended to preserve the cultural and even the political integrity of the different lordships and nations that made up their empire.[42] Polo de Ondegardo observed the same phenomenon, while at the same time grasping its practical importance. The Incas, he noted, had dealt with their subjects in groups, not as individuals. The corvée labor that the Inca state exacted from its subjects was thus distributed, not among individuals, but among ethnic groups, and would then be delegated by each group's lords, curacas, to their subordinates, who in turn delegated further, until each member of the group had been assigned his task. Polo admired the harmony and order of this procedure greatly, even though he also thought that, precisely because the Inca dealt with people in groups, through their curacas, the concept of freedom did not exist in the Andes. The Spanish, on the other hand, dealt with Andean people as named individuals, as members of distinct age groups, as residents, *origi-*

narios, or newcomers, *forasteros,* in their community, and, above all, as tribute payers.[43] Representatives of the Church, furthermore, looked to the salvation of each individual soul, or be it the control of each individual soul, in the administration of the sacraments, especially of confession. In their political and economic lives, accordingly, Andean people could and did act as individuals, and with a certain freedom, as it were. This freedom, however, was often converted into its very opposite by the burdens of tribute, forced labor, and religious coercion. Like the road to hell, so colonial legislation was paved with good intentions. But these intentions regarding the "conservation" and protection of Indians were compromised at every turn by the colonial state's primary function of extracting wealth.[44]

Yet, even here, one must not underestimate the resilience and resourcefulness of Andean people.[45] Nathan Wachtel comments on the *forasteros* who worked as miners in Oruro, while still paying their share of the tribute payments that were charged to their communities of origin, thereby contributing to the survival of these communities. On the one hand, migration did undermine the strength and integrity of Andean communities and their curacas. But on the other hand, Karen Vieira Powers has shown that in Quito at any rate, a degree of cultural cohesion has persisted until the present, despite the "the general weakening of Andean society vis-à-vis the colonizers."[46] Regional studies for other parts of the Andes, including Nathan Wachtel's own recent book on the Urus, describe this same phenomenon, in which "Occidentalization" is not the only force at work.[47]

The societies of colonial Mexico and Peru abounded in tensions and contradictions, which in turn help to understand what living within these *métissages culturels* amounted to. In the all-important religious sphere, Christianity, a religion that even in the interpretation of missionaries was predicated on human brotherhood, became in this colonial context a vehicle for defining human difference and subordination.[48] In the secular sphere, meanwhile, frequently reiterated declarations in legislation seeking the well-being of Indians were often overlooked in practice or implemented in such a way as to achieve the opposite. These contradictions were not lost on Andean people, and Guaman Poma commented on them repeatedly, the point being that the marginalization and disenfranchisement that Gruzinski and Wachtel rightly emphasize did not go unchallenged. For even though contestation and social criticism are not in themselves acts of power, they nonetheless are means of circumscribing power. Throughout his long work, Guaman Poma queried and questioned the superiority that the Spanish invaders claimed over his people, his primary argument being that the Spanish did not live by their own Christian principles. Indeed, he felt that it was, for the most part, Andean people who, in terms of both their historical experience and their conduct of life, were the true Christians.

This argument merits highlighting because aspects of it were restated, some 160 years later, in the declarations that don José Gabriel Tupac Amaru addressed to his fellow Peruvians by way of explaining why it had become necessary to throw off the "tyranny" of Europeans. What was new about Tupac Amaru's declarations was their political dimension. Guaman Poma had conducted an ethical and theological argument about Christian behavior that was incumbent on everyone, in order to challenge the marginalized "minority" status of his own people in the viceroyalty of Peru. As has been often observed, he wrote in the words of a preacher.[49] Tupac Amaru, on the other hand, wrote a language of political initiative accompanied by action. Wachtel explains the continued existence of Indian communities in the Andes in part as an outcome of their ability to restructure themselves in light of changing circumstances, and within a political arena defined from the outside by the opposing forces of Andeanization and Occidentalization. The revolt of Tupac Amaru in 1780 was one of a series of Indian uprisings during the colonial period, and it was heavily tinged by both these forces.[50] But this does not lessen its importance as an autonomous Indian political initiative. The revolt was provoked by the Bourbon administrative and financial reforms in Peru that, as Tupac Amaru viewed matters, had redefined the relationship between the dominant minority and the marginalized majority so as to include in the latter all persons except government officials recently arrived from the Peninsula. Tupac Amaru's response to this reality was to inaugurate a society for the "conservation and tranquillity of Spaniards, Creoles, mestizos, Africans and Indians," a society, that is, which included all persons for whom Peru was home. On this basis he called on his countrymen, *paisanos,* among whom he included not only Indians but all others who had been born in Peru, for their support. The manifesto describes the past as conveying a twofold legacy. First, Tupac Amaru wrote and acted as a direct descendant of the last Inca, "an Indian of the royal blood and the principal stem" for whom the Inca past was relevant not only as a historical memory, but as the fundamental antecedent on which reform had to be based.[51] Second, he addressed his countrymen in Spanish and used the political terminology that was current in his day and was of European origin. In this sense, his program was a response to 250 years of colonial experience, which informed him that the "conservation and tranquillity" of people in the Andes was only possible when the figurative minority of Indians and mestizos liberated itself from the real minority of newcomers. This real minority, in Tupac Amaru's estimation, consisted, not so much of Spaniards or Creoles, but, as he repeatedly wrote, of recently arrived "Europeans."[52] In the outcome, however, the real minority turned out to be much more substantial, in that the Creoles and Spaniards, the "countrymen" for whose support Tupac Amaru had hoped, were only too eager to oppose an Andean and Inca restoration.[53] But this alignment of the upper classes of colonial Peru with the Spanish must not diminish our appreciation of the fact that Indians were, and are, an integral part of the Peruvian people, who, as Florencia Mallon has argued so persuasively in her recent *Peasant and Nation,* have taken an active part in their nation's destiny.[54] It is in light of such active engagement in political conflict and negotiation over centuries that we should understand contemporary Indian political movements seeking participation in their countries' public life, the recuperation of expropriated lands, and national as well as international recognition of their cultures.[55]

What I hope to have contributed to our discussion is the observation that the significance of "minority" is not universal, nor is it eternal, or static. Rather, what endows the idea of minority with life and reality is the many forms of interaction that take place between minorities and majorities. On the one hand, there are the individual and collective self-perceptions by which minorities maintain themselves, and that they project to the relevant majority. And on the other hand, there is the majority's self-perception and its projection to outsiders, along with the diverse ways in which minorities can choose to process such projections. Beyond these forms of interaction, there are the realms of coercion and oppression on the one hand, and of protest, rebellion, and restoration on the other, along with the manner in which these are acted upon and processed in individual and collective memory.

NOTES

I would like to thank David Nirenberg for reading earlier drafts of this essay and for making numerous suggestions. I have done my best to implement these and very much hope that he will be satisfied.

1. See Serge Gruzinski, *Les Hommes-dieux du Mexique. Pouvoir indien et société coloniale XVIe–XVIIIe siècles* (Montreux, 1985); *La colonisation de l'imaginaire. Sociétés indigènes et occidentalisation dans le Mexique espagnol, XVIe–XVIII siècles* (Paris, 1988); Carmen Bernard and Serge Gruzinski, *De l'idolâftrie. Une archéologie des sciences religieuses* (Paris, 1988).

2. Fernando Cervantes, *The Devil in New Spain: The Impact of Diabolism in New Spain* (New Haven, 1994).

3. For example, for the term *parcialidad*, see Maria Rostworowski, "La voz parcialidad en su contexto en los siglos XVI y XVII," in her *Ensayos de historia andina. Elites, etnías, recursos* (Lima, 1993), 231–40.

4. Frank Salomon and George L. Urioste, *The Huarochirí Manuscript: A Testament of Ancient and Colonial Andean Religion* (Austin, 1991), section 1, 157, preface "runa yndio," with note ad loc.; also section 485, p. 252. See also, apart from Guaman Poma de Ayala, *Nueva crónica y buen gobierno*, John V. Murra, Rolena Adorno, and J. L. Urioste, eds. (Madrid, 1987), where the term *yndio* appears frequently; Joan de Santacruz Pachacuti Yamqui, "Relación de antigüedades deste reyno del Perú," in F. Esteve Barba, ed., *Crónicas peruanas de interés indígena* (Biblioteca de autores españoles, vol. 209, Madrid, 1968), 283, where Andean people are described as "*los yndios de aquel tiempo*" and "*los yndios del sujetos.*" Elsewhere, the author uses the term "*naturales,*" see 283; *los naturales de Tauantinsuyo,* 319 (*los españoles, y los naturales*).

5. See Sabine MacCormack, *Religion in the Andes: Vision and Imagination in Early Colonial Peru* (Princeton, 1991), 406 f.; Kenneth Mills, *Idolatry,* 253 ff.

6. Bruce Mannheim, *The Language of the Inka since the European Invasion* (Austin, 1991). By studying the changing fortunes of Quechua during the colonial period in light both of texts recorded in writing and of the history of Quechua morphology (whether written or spoken), Mannheim has demonstrated that an understanding of these matters forms an indispensable component of the history of Andean people. We can learn from Quechua philology what can be learned from nowhere else.

7. For comparative perspectives, see the essays collected in Heraclio Bonilla, ed., *El sistema colonial en la América española* (Barcelona, 1991); also, Florencia Mallon (below, note 54); James Lockhart, "La conciencia, la sociedad y la cultura. La posible relevancia de México Central para la Región Andina," in Segundo Moreno Y. and Frank Salomon, eds., *Reproducción y transformación de las sociedades andinas siglos XVI–XX,* 2 vols. (Quito, 1991), vol. 2: 509–28. For the history of art, Diane Fane, ed., *Converging Cultures: Art and Identity in Spanish America* (New York, 1996); Tom Cummins, *The Madonna and the Horse,* in Emily Umberger and Tom Cummins, eds., *Native Artists and Patrons in Colonial Latin America,* Phoebus, vol. 7: 52–83 (Arizona State University, 1995).

8. Miguel León Portilla, *Visión de los vencidos. Relaciones indígenas de la Con-

quista (Mexico City, 1959, revised and expanded, Mexico, 1989); Nathan Wachtel, *La vision des vaincus. Les indiens du Pérou devant la conquête espagnole* (Paris, 1971); Nancy M. Farriss, *Maya Society under Colonial Rule: The Collective Enterprise of Survival* (Princeton, 1984).

9. "Informe del Licenciado Juan Polo de Ondegardo al Licenciado Briviesca de Muñatones sobre la perpetuidad de las encomiendas en el Peru," *Rivista Historica* 13 (1940), 171.

10. *Relación de las fiestas que en el Cuzco se hicieron por la beatificación del . . . Padre Ignacio de Loyola . . . 1610*, edited by C. Romero in his *Los origenes del Periodismo en el Perú*, 13–21 (Lima, 1940). In 1622, the canonization of Ignatius Loyola and other saints was celebrated in Rome with imagery appropriate to that city; see Maurizio Fagiolo Dell'Arco and Silvia Carandini, *L'effimero barocco: Strutture della festa nella Rome del '600*, 2 vols., 54–57 (Rome, 1977). Here also, dignitaries participating in the celebration appeared in an ordered hierarchy, and in juxtaposition with an undifferentiated crowd of onlookers: see 55, an engraving from Paolo Guidotti, *Canonizzazione dei cinque Santi* (1622); see also 66–68, for Gian Lorenzo Bernini, *Beatificazione di Elisabetta di Portogallo* (1625). I would like to thank Irving Lavin for this reference.

11. See, for example, Vasco de Contreras y Valverde, *Relación de la ciudad del Cuzco 1649*, María del Carmen Rubio, ed. (Cuzco, 1982); Juan Morgrovejo de la Cerda, *Memorias de la Gran Ciudad del Cusco 1690*, María del Carmen Rubio, ed. (Cuzco, 1983); Diego de Esquivel y Navia, *Noticias cronologicas de la gran ciudad del Cuzco* (Lima, 1980); and David Cahill, "Popular Religion and Appropriation: The Example of Corpus Christi in Eighteenth Century Cuzco," *Latin American Research Review* 31:2 (1996), 67–110; this useful article appears to have been inspired, at least in part, by two excellent recent dissertations, which the author cites: Carolyn S. Dean, "Painted Images of Cuzco's Corpus Christi: Social Conflict and Cultural Strategy in Viceregal Peru" (Ph.D. diss., Department of the History of Art, UCLA, 1990); Carol Ann Fiedler, "Corpus Christi in Cuzco: Festival and Ethnic Identity in the Peruvian Andes" (Ph.D. diss., Department of Anthropology, Tulane University, 1985).

12. David Brading, *The First America: The Spanish Monarchy, Creole Patriots and the Liberal State, 1492–1867* (Cambridge, 1991); see also Benjamin Keen, *The Aztec Image in Western Thought* (New Brunswick, 1971); Jacques Lafaye, *Quetzalcoatl y Guadalupe. The Formation of Mexican National Consciousness* (Chicago, 1976). Tom Cummins, *We Are the Other: Peruvian Portraits of Colonial Kurakakuna*, in Kenneth J. Andrien and Rolena Adorno, eds., *Transatlantic Encounters: Europeans in the Sixteenth Century* (Berkeley, 1991), 203–31, describes how Andean lords of the early colonial period appropriated Inca royal insignia by way of asserting their domination over nonnoble Andeans, and of claiming the status of nobles alongside Spanish nobility.

208 / *The Construction of Minorities*

13. Lorenzo Ramírez de Prado, *Entrada de la Reina Nuestra Señora D. Mariana* (Madrid, 1650), cited in Juan Morgrovejo de la Cerda, *Memorias de la Gran Ciudad del Cusco 1690*, chap. 24.

14. Sabine MacCormack, "Calderón's *La aurora en Copacabana* and the Conversion of the Incas in the Light of Seventeenth Century Spanish Theology, Culture and Political Theory," *Journal of Theological Studies* 32 (1982): 448–80.

15. César Itier, "Quechua y cultura en el Cuzco del siglo XVIII," in César Itier, *Del siglo de oro al siglo de las luces. Lenguaje y sociedad en los Andes del siglo XVIII* (Cuzco, 1995), 89–111.

16. Louise M. Burkhart, *Holy Wednesday: A Nahua Drama from Early Colonial Mexico* (Philadelphia, 1996); Teodoro Meneses, *Teatro Quechua colonial* (Lima, 1983) gives Spanish versions of the six known Quechua plays; for a collection of Nahua plays with parallel texts, see Fernando Horcesitas, *El teatro Náhuatl. Épocas novohispana y moderna* (Mexico, 1974).

17. Richard Joseph Ingersoll, "The Ritual Use of Public Space in Renaissance Rome," 95–101 (diss., Architecture, University of California, Berkeley, 1985); Edward Muir, *Civic Ritual in Renaissance Venice* (Princeton, 1981), chap. 5; analogous studies for Spanish cities appear to be lacking, but see the relevant sections in A. Domínguez Ortiz and F. Aguilar Piñal, *Historia de Sevilla. El Barroco y la Illustración* (Seville, 1976), citing material from the illustrated work by Antonio de Solís S.J. (pseudonym Lorenzo Bautista de Zuñiga), *Anales eclesiasticas y seglares* (Seville, 1748). The Augustinian friar and bishop of Santiago de Chile Gaspar de Villarroel was deeply aware of the importance of ceremonial precedence that spoke in public ritual, and discussed problems of precedence arising in Lima between the Viceroy and the city's clergy, in his *Gobierno eclesiástico pacífico y unión de los dos cuchillos pontífico y regio* (Madrid, 1656–57); cf. G. Martínez Gutierrez, *Gaspar de Villarroel O.S.A. Un ilustre prelado americano. Un clásico del derecho indiano* (1587–1665), 87–89 (Valladolid, 1994). Oscar Cornblit, *Power and Violence in the Colonial City: Oruro from the Mining Renaissance to the Rebellion of Tupac Amaru (1740–1782)*, chap. 78 (Cambridge, 1995), discusses a set of ceremonial encounters in Oruro with very practical political outcomes.

18. The marginalization of Indians in Peru was noted by the Indian painter Basilio Pacheco in a picture painted for the Convent of St. Augustine in Cuzco. In this work, he adapted a European engraving depicting the funeral procession of Augustine of Hippo to the setting of Cuzco's main square. The picture shows the funeral procession moving through the square overlooked by the cathedral. At the bottom, we see the heads of a row of onlookers. Among them, Pacheco included himself, but he is looking out at the viewer of the painting, as though questioning the social order of which he is forced to be a part. See Pierre Courcelle, *Iconographie de St. Augustin* (Paris, 1965–), vol.3, plates 50 and 121, at 111; but Courcelle's identification of this painter as a follower or student of the Quiteño painter Miguel de Santiago is in error.

19. For a chilling, but far from unusual episode, see Frank Salomon, "Ancestors, Grave Robbers, and the Possible Antecedents of Cañnari Inca-ism," in Harald O. Skar and Frank Salomon, eds., *Natives and Neighbors in South America: Anthropological Essays* (Göteborg, 1987), 207–32.

20. J. V. Murra, "Aymara Lords and their European Agents at Potosí," *Nova Americana* (Torino), 1 (1978), 231–43.

21. James Lockhart, *The Nahuas after the Conquest: A Social and Cultural History of the Indians of Central Mexico, Sixteenth through Eighteenth Centuries,* 176–98, at 179 on tomín (Stanford, 1992).

22. Diego Gonzalez Holguin, *Vocabulario de la lengua general de todo el Perú,* 312, s.v. *rantini* (Lima 1608); for an exceptional collection of essays about the impact of markets and money on Andean societies, see Brooke Larson and Olivia Harris, eds., with Enrique Tandeter, *Ethnicity, Markets and Migration in the Andes: At the Crossroads of History and Anthropology* (Durham, N.C., 1995).

23. Alfredo Torero, *El Quechua y la historia social andina* (Lima, 1974); Bruce Mannheim, *The Language of the Inca* (above n. 7), and his "La cronología relativa de la lengua y literatura quechua cusqueña," *Revista andina* 8:1 (1990), 139–77; César Itier, "Les textes quechuas coloniaux: une source privilégiée pur l'histoire culturelle andine," with bibliography there cited. HREF="http://www.sigu7.jussieu.fr/hsal/hsal95.html [Sommaire HSAL95]; HREF="http://www.sigu7.jussieu.fr/hsal/">[HSAL]. I thank Bruce Mannheim for sending me a copy of this item.

24. Joanne Rappaport, "Reinvented Traditions: The Heraldry of Ethnic Militancy in the Colombian Andes," in Robert V. Dover, Katharine E. Seibold, and John H. McDowell, eds., *Andean Cosmologies through Time,* 202–28 (Bloomington, 1992).

25. Barbara E. Mundy, *The Mapping of New Spain: Indigenous Cartography and the Maps of the Relaciones Geograficas* (Chicago, 1996).

26. James Lockhart, *The Nahuas after the Conquest,* 410–18; Robert Haskett, "Visions of Municipal Glory Undimmed: Nahuatl Town Histories of Colonial Cuernavaca," *Colonial Latin American Historical Review* 1 (1992): 1–36; Stephanie G. Wood, "An Uncomfortable Fit: Nahuatl *Titulos* in a Spanish Legal Context," in Elizabeth Boone and Tom Cummins, eds., *Native Traditions* (Washington, D.C., 1998).

27. Archivo Nacional, Lima, Titulos de Comunidades 3,41C; cf. S. MacCormack, "History and Law in Sixteenth Century Peru: The Impact of European Scholarly Traditions," in S. C. Humphreys, *Cultures of Scholarship* (Ann Arbor: University of Michigan Press, 1997), 277–310 with figures 1–2. The struggle for land in the Andes continues. For a modern parallel to the events of 1597 in Laraos, see Joanne Rappaport, *Cumbe Reborn: An Andean Ethnography of History* (Chicago, 1994).

28. Robert Ricard, *The Spiritual Conquest of Mexico. An Essay on the Aposto-*

210 / The Construction of Minorities

late and the Evangelizing Methods of the Mendicant Orders in New Spain:
1523–1572 (Berkeley, 1966), 264 f.

29. Nathan Wachtel, *La vision des vaincus* (above note 8). For the documentation of this movement, see Luis Millones, ed., *El retorno de las huacas. Estudios y documentos sobre el Taki Onqoy. siglo XVI* (Lima, 1990)

30. Irene Silverblatt, *Moon Sun and Witches: Gender Ideologies and Class in Inca and Colonial Peru* (Princeton, 1987).

31. Kenneth Mills, *Idolatry and Its Enemies: Colonial Andean Religion and Extirpation, 1640–1750* (Princeton, 1997). The book is a salutary and very convincing reminder of the reality that the practice of religion (like the practice of culture) consists, primarily, of the actions and ideas of individuals. Mills thus describes, not so much which aspects of Andean religious thought and practice survived the efforts of extirpators, but what made sense to individual Andean people, why it made sense, and how this changed over time. It is in this light that one sees, furthermore, that much of the time, extirpation was not, even in the minds of the extirpators, as self-explanatory and straightforward an activity as has often been supposed. All this has very significant repercussions on how métissage culturel may usefully be studied in future, as does current work on visual expression: see Diane Fane, ed., *Converging Cultures;* Tom Cummins, *Toasts for the Inca: Andean Abstraction and Colonial Images on Inca Drinking Cups* (University of Michigan Press, forthcoming).

32. Sabine MacCormack, "From the Sun of the Incas to the Virgin of Copacabana," *Representations* 8 (1984): 30–60; Teresea Gisbert, *Iconografía y mitos indígenas en el arte* (La Paz, 1980); see also Carol Damian, *The Virgin of the Andes: Art and Ritual in Colonial Cuzco* (Miami Beach, 1995); also her "Artist and Patron in Colonial Cuzco: Workshops, Contracts and a Petition for Independence," *Colonial Latin American Historical Review* 4 (1995): 25–165.

33. William B. Taylor, *Magistrates of the Sacred: Priests and Parishioners in Eighteenth-Century Mexico* (Stanford, 1996)

34. *Concilios Limenses 1551–1772,* R. Ugarte, ed. (Lima, 1951–54).

35. Guaman Poma, *Nueva crónica y buen gobierno,* John V. Murra, Rolena Adorno, and Jorge L. Urioste, eds. (Madrid, 1987), 369. For a contemporary expression of Indian self-worth, see Olivia Harris, "Ethnic Identity and Market Relations: Indians and Mestizos in the Andes," in Brooke Larson and Olivia Harris, eds., *Ethnicity, Markets and Migration,* 351–90 at 369: "Seen from the outside, the persistence of Indian identity among peasants facilitates their exploitation by non-Indians. However, from their own perspective, there are other, far more positive reasons for their continuing classification as Indians, which have to do with their relationship with the land. While non-Indians may despise peasant culture, Indian peasants in their turn despise outsiders, who 'do not know how to work' and who live by begging from them—for this is often how they perceive the exactions of mestizos. They even feel sorry for these people who have little or no land,

who are afraid of real work, and who depend on others to produce food for them."

36. For an early example, see Maria Rostworowski de Diez Canseco, *Doña Francisca Pizarro. Una ilustre mestiza, 1534–1598* (Lima, 1989).

37. Frederick P. Bowser, *The African Slave in Colonial Peru (1524–1650)* (Stanford, 1974) is a detailed archival study.

38. Guaman Poma, *Nueva crónica,* 710, 851–52. With regard to African slaves, as so often elsewhere, Guaman Poma's social criticism was penetrating and apt: see 704 f., which recommends, with Bowser, that slaves be allowed to marry ("The African Slave," 254–67, on the obstacles to slave marriage).

39. A. Saint-Lu, *La Vera Paz: Ésprit Evangélique et Colonisation* (Paris, 1968).

40. See Ilona Katzew, *New World Order: Casta Painting and Colonial Latin America* (New York: Americas Society Art Gallery, 1996); Robert H. Jackson, "Race/Caste and the Creation and Meaning of Identity in Colonial Spanish America," *Revista de Indias* 55, no. 203 (1995), 149–73.

41. See also, for a detailed discussion of population figures, the demographic study by Karen Vieira Powers, *Andean Journeys: Migration, Ethnogenesis and the State in Colonial Quito* (Albuquerque, 1995).

42. Further on this much-discussed issue, see, e.g., Karen Spalding, *Huarochirí: An Andean Society under Inca and Spanish Rule* (Stanford, 1984); Susan Elizabeth Ramírez, *The World Upside Down: Cross-Cultural Contact and Conflict in Sixteenth-Century Peru* (Stanford, 1996).

43. Nicolás Sánchez-Albornoz, *Indios y tributos en el alto Perú* (Lima, 1978), note in particular 12–14.

44. For a ringing declaration of governmental good intentions, see Juan de Solorzano y Pereyra, *Politica Indiana,* Francisco Ramiro de Valenzuela, ed. (Biblioteca de autores españoles, vols. 252–56, Madrid, 1972), for example Book II, chap. 1, sect. 7: "Siempre procuraron, y ordenaron con grandes veras, y aprieto de palabras [the kings of Spain are the implied subject], que los Indios fuesen conservados, y mantenidos en su entera libertad y plena, y libre administración de sus bienes, como los dem ás vasallos suyos en otros Reynos"; for a critical evaluation of such statements, see Karen Spalding, "Qui,nes son los indios?," in her *De indio a campesino. Cambios en la estructura social del Perú colonial* (Lima, 1974), 147–93.

45. Jeffrey A. Cole, *The Potosí Mita, 1573–1700: Compulsory Indian Labor in the Andes* (Stanford, 1985), highlights the efficacy of passive resistance to governmental demands for Indian labor. See also Brooke Larson, *Colonialism and Agrarian Transformation in Bolivia: Cochabamba, 1550–1900* (Princeton, 1998).

46. Vieira Powers, *Andean Journeys,* 174.

47. Nathan Wachtel, *Le retour des ancêtres. Les Indiens Urus de Bolivie (XXème–XVIème siècle* (Paris, 1990).

48. A crucial component in the articulation of difference was that Andean men could not join the ranks of the clergy, nor become members of the professions. Exceptions were extremely rare.

49. Rolena Adorno, *Guaman Poma: Writing and Resistance in Colonial Peru* (Austin, 1986).

50. Scarlett O'Phelan Godoy, "L'utopie andine. Discours parallèles à la fin de l'époque coloniale," *Annales. Histoire, Sciences Sociales* 49:2 (1994): 471–95. For a well-documented overview of the revolt of Tupac Amaru, see Oscar Cornblit, *Power and Violence in the Colonial City,* chap. 9.

51. Jan Szemiñski, *La Utopia Tupamarista* (Lima, 1984), and for the earlier movement of restoration and independence of Juan Santos Atahualpa, see Alonso Zarzar, *"Apo Capac Huayna, Jesus Sacramentado."* Mito, utopia y milenarismo en el pensamiento de Juan Santos Atahualpa (Lima, 1989).

52. See Luis Durand Flórez, ed., *Colección documental del bicentenario de la revolución emancipadora de Tupac Amaru. Tomo I. Documentos varios del Archivo General de Indias* (Lima, 1980), 418–19; 425–26; 428–29; 457–58; 488–90; 520–21, for versions of Tupac Amaru's Edicto for the "conservación de los indios, españoles, mestizos, zambos y mulatos criollos y su tranquilidad." José Durand, "El influjo de Garcilaso Inca en Tupac Amaru," *Copae (Petróleos del Perú. Departamento de Relaciones Públicas),* vol. 2: 2–7 (Lima, 1971). A very useful collection of essays on Tupac Amaru was published by the Comision nacional del bicentenario de la rebelion emancipadora de Tupac Amaru, *Actas del Coloquio Internacional: "Tupac Amaru y su Tiempo"* (Lima, 1982).

53. Note the repeated calls, after Tupac Amaru and his followers had been executed, for the elimination of all things reminiscent of the Incas, or expressive of the authority and power of curacas, including the Quechua language: *Colección documental . . . Tomo II* (Lima, 1980), 198; 630–37; *Tomo V* (Lima, 1982), 611–16; 617–19.

54. Florencia E. Mallon, *Peasant and Nation: The Making of Postcolonial Mexico and Peru* (Berkeley, 1955).

55. See Edward F. Fischer and R. McKenna Brown, eds., *Maya Cultural Activism in Guatemala* (Austin, 1994); Howard Campbell, *Zapotec Renaissance: Ethnic Politics and Cultural Revivalism in Southern Mexico* (Albuquerque, 1994); Jane H. Hill and Kenneth C. Hill, *Speaking Mexicano: Dynamics of Syncretic Language in Central Mexico* (Tucson, 1986); Silvia Rivera Cusicanqui, *"Oprimidos pero no vencidos."* Luchas del campesinado aymara y qhechwa de Bolivia, 1900–1980 (La Paz, 1984, also available in English translation); Luis Miguel Glave, *Vida, símbolos y batallas. Creación y recreación de la comunidad indígena. Cusco, siglos XVI–XX* (Mexico, 1992); Peter Cole, Gabriella Hermon, and Mario Daniel Martin, eds., *Language in the Andes: University of Delaware Occasional Monographs in Latin American Studies number 4* (Newark, Del., 1994); see also Barbara Schroder, "Indians in the Halls of Academe: Rural Andean Peoples Confront Social Science," *Peasant Studies* 18:2 (1991): 97–116; several of the essays in Moreno and Salomon, eds., *Reproducción y transformación,* also bear on this issue.

Discriminating Difference: The Postcolonial Politics of Caste in India

Nicholas B. Dirks

I

On September 19, 1990, a student from Delhi University poured kerosene over his body and set himself on fire. According to some accounts, Rajeev Goswami had initially only intended to stage a mock self-immolation; as soon as he struck a match his friends were supposed to have doused him with water, waiting only for a few pictures to be snapped. The photographs and attendant press coverage would be used to draw dramatic media attention to the protests against caste reservations that had been mounting over the previous six weeks. But in the heat of emotion, in the context of an impassioned protest against a government decision that was seen as taking all future prospects of respectable employment away from young people with upper-caste backgrounds, Rajeev set his body alight without checking to see whether his friends were anywhere nearby. Photographs were taken; his burning body could be seen on the front page of every newspaper and the cover of every glossy magazine in India over the next few days. But Rajeev was by that time in the critical care ward of Safdarjang Hospital, struggling for his life with 50 percent of his body burnt. And his photograph gave way to other, similar, terrifying images. In quick succession, youths in a series of cities across northern India, from Ambala to Lucknow, followed Rajeev's example and set themselves on fire as well. Within the next month, more than 159 young people also followed suit, attempting suicide by self-immolation; 63 succeeded. Another 100 people were killed in police firings and clashes that accompanied the widespread protest.

Rajeev Goswami and his tragic train of followers engaged in these desperate acts as part of a protest by students against the government's decision to implement the recommendations of the Mandal Commission. That commission had been instituted by the Janata government shortly after it had wrested electoral power away from Indira Gandhi, ending the draconian "emergency" period of central rule between 1975 and 1977, and was charged with the task of determining "the criteria for defining the Socially and Educationally Backward Classes" and recommending "steps to be taken for the advancement of [the above-mentioned classes] of citizens so identified." It was also to "examine the desirability of otherwise making provision for the reservation of appointments or posts in favour of such backward classes of citizens which are not adequately represented in public services or posts in connection with the affairs of the Union or any States."[1] The commission was effectively being asked to carry out the letter of the Indian Constitution, which, in addition to mandating affirmative action for scheduled castes (i.e., untouchables) and tribes,[2] had empowered the president with the right to "investigate the conditions of socially and educationally backward classes within the territory of India and the difficulties under which they labour and to make recommendations as to the steps that should be taken by the Union or any State to remove such difficulties and to improve their condition."[3]

The Mandal Commission submitted its report on the last day of 1980, identifying 3,743 Other Backward Castes (OBCs) and making a series of far-reaching recommendations for the amelioration of their condition. But by 1980 the Janata government had lost power once again to Indira Gandhi, who put the report on the back burner. It was not until August 7, 1990, less than a year after the Janata Party had come back to power under the anticorruption platform and populist leadership of V. P. Singh, that the report was taken up again. On that day, Singh, the prime minister, declared that the Indian government would implement the full recommendations of the Mandal Commission. The commission had begun by assuming the constitutional mandate for reservations in the case of scheduled castes and tribes, who, reckoned to constitute 22.5 percent of the country's population, had been allocated a reservation, or quota, of 22.5 percent for government and public sector jobs. Assuming a one-to-one correlation between population and reservation for oppressed groups, the commission estimated, on the basis of its classification of castes and the 1931 census (the last census to count the population by caste), that a reservation of an additional 52 percent would be necessary. However, as the Supreme Court had earlier decided that reservations should under no condition exceed 50 percent, the commission compromised by declaring that the new reservation for OBCs should stand at 27 percent. The commission further recommended that the proposed system of reservation should be applied to all recruitment to central and state government, to private undertakings receiving financial assistance from the government, and to all government universities and affiliated colleges.

V. P. Singh's declaration was in some ways not a complete surprise; the Congress Party had never actually denounced the report, declaring its general interest in making provisions to help the educationally and socially backward, and the Janata Party had made the implementation of Mandal's recommendations part of its party platform. But the timing of the declaration was carefully chosen, for Devi Lal, an important political leader with a large backward caste constituency, had just broken with V. P. Singh and organized a huge peasant rally in New Delhi to be held on August 9. Singh managed to upstage Devi Lal, and on independence day, August 15, reiterated his commitment to Mandal in a speech delivered at the Red Fort, the impressive symbol of late Mughal rule in the heart of old Delhi. He justified his announcement by repeated references to the legacy of B. R. Ambedkar, the great leader of the Dalit (untouchable) movement (himself a Dalit) who during the nationalist movement was the figure most associated with "reserving" electoral seats and government positions for oppressed groups. Although Ambedkar broke with Gandhi in the early 1930s over the issue of separate electorates, arguing against Gandhi that the untouchable community needed both a quota for political representation and the electoral capacity to select its own leaders, he set many of the ideological terms for the establishment of reservations in independent India. Ambedkar ultimately drafted the provisions that stipulated that 22.5 percent of positions in government service and seats in government universities and colleges would be set aside by constitutional mandate for "scheduled castes and tribes," who were calculated to constitute around 15 and 7 percent of the population respectively.

II

Despite the struggle between Ambedkar and Gandhi, the legacy of Gandhi's general advocacy on behalf of "harijans" (Gandhi's term for "untouchables") and Ambedkar's political struggles worked to legitimize a major policy of affirmative action for untouchables as a constitutional guarantee in independent India. But Ambedkar's break with Gandhi had in fact been quite dramatic, and revelatory of some of the more difficult issues involved in the use of caste as a category for special protection and representation. In the Second Round Table Conference, the fruit of the major Civil Disobedience Campaign engineered by Gandhi between 1930 and 1932, plans were made for the implementation of provincial rule within India, but negotiations soon broke down over the issue of separate electorates. As background, Ambedkar felt that Gandhi and Congress had done little for untouchables, paying more attention to khadi and issues of self-reliance in the area of social reform than to the much vaunted goal of "harijan" uplift. Ambedkar had also become increasingly suspicious of Gandhi's defense of the caste system as an organic, unifying, and inclusive system that could divest itself of hierarchical ideologies; Ambedkar saw caste as part of the problem, not part of the solution, and rejected Gandhi's call for untouchables to be included within the compass of the caste system. But in the actual negotiations the most heated issue concerned the classification of the electorate. Gandhi, who was opposed to separate electorates for any group, grudgingly accepted them for Muslims, Christians, Sikhs, and Anglo-Indians but, in what was clearly his commitment to the unity of the Hindu community, drew the line when it came to untouchables. In response to the breakdown of discussions, the British prime minister, Ramsey MacDonald, announced the Communal Award on August 17, 1932, according untouchables regular votes in the general electorate and granting their demand for separate electorates in areas of their largest concentration. Gandhi responded by announcing a fast unto death. Although Congress leaders such as Nehru viewed this as a side issue unworthy of Gandhi's heroic sacrifice, many in Congress supported Gandhi, some because of their concern to protect the great Hindu base of Congress in the face of other communal interests.[4] In any event, Ambedkar was unable to withstand public pressure to defer to the force of Gandhi's fast, and in the resulting compromise, known as the Poona Pact, the electorate was maintained as joint while the numbers of seats specifically reserved for untouchables was doubled.[5]

There was general agreement about what constituted an "untouchable" caste in most parts of Madras and Bombay Presidencies and in the Central Provinces, thus making the classificatory dimension of reservation policy (as well as concerns about the separate identities of these groups) fairly straightforward. However, matters were less clear in northern and eastern India. Given this lack of clarity, the debate over classification revolved around the question of whether to identify groups on the basis of their depressed status (what could be established by their social, economic, and cultural backwardness) or in reference to the specific criteria of ritual and social exclusion. In what was perhaps the most elaborate attempt to define untouchability, J. H. Hutton, the 1931 census commissioner, and author of the influential monograph *Caste in India,* established a set of indices, including whether "the caste or class in question can be served by Brahmans . . . [and] by the barbers, water-carriers, tailors, etc., who serve the caste Hindus," "whether the caste in question pollutes a high-caste Hindu by contact or proximity," and "whether the caste or class in question is merely depressed on account of its own ignorance, illiteracy or poverty and but for that, would be subject to no social disability."[6] In other words, the question was whether to use "class" (i.e., general social and economic criteria) or "caste" (which in this case, ironically, referred to groups traditionally referred to as noncaste, or as outside the pale of caste) as the basis for classification. Interestingly enough, the position of the administrator-anthropologist Hutton was congruent with that of both Gandhi and Ambedkar; all these observers stressed the ritual exclusions shared by all untouchables, despite actual gradations of disadvantage. Although Ambedkar had always been critical of the assimilationist project of Gandhi and Congress, he broke decisively with this project in the last year of his life when he converted to Buddhism and advocated the mass conversion to Buddhism of all untouchables, in what he considered to be the final, and most decisive, rejection of the claims and hegemonic character of caste Hinduism.

If Gandhi and Ambedkar struggled throughout their lives over the definition of the caste system and the ultimate authority of Hinduism, they both agreed about the fundamentally ritual character of the social; thus Gandhi saw untouchability as a Hindu crime to be absolved by the folding of harijan communities into the main fabric of Hindu society, and Ambedkar ultimately saw religious conversion as the only way out of Hindu hierarchy. As a result, there was general agreement about the classification of scheduled castes, the newest and most neutral euphemism for untouchables, as the basis for reservations in independent India. In the delineation of the scheduled caste category, there has been no single connotative definition or principle, but selection has nevertheless proceeded primarily on the basis of ritual "untouchability," though according to Galanter this has been "combined in varying degrees with economic, occupational, educational, and . . . residential and religious tests."[7] In the final determination of scheduled castes for the constitutionally mandated reservations, Hutton's criteria and Ambedkar's general classificatory guidelines prevailed.

Although Gandhi and Ambedkar shared a fundamentally anthropological view of caste, they had very different ideas about politics. While Ambedkar was committed to the need to politicize caste, using it as the basis for organizing political constituencies and waging political battles, Gandhi was perhaps more concerned than any other major nationalist leader about the possibility that caste would become the basis for political and social conflict. Thus Gandhi felt the need to minimize caste difference and underplay caste identity, although throughout his life he was convinced that this would be best accomplished by emphasizing an ideal of caste that stressed organic unity and harmony rather than hierarchy. Gandhi used much the same definition of an ideal originary caste system as had been deployed by such earlier Hindu social reform figures as Dayananda Saraswati and Vivekenanda, defining the Sanskrit term *varnashramadharma* to mean the ideal order of things (around caste, stage of life, and the performance of duty), shorn of any hierarchy or power. Despite the serious exception taken to these political and rhetorical strategies by leaders such as Ambedkar, Gandhi saw the flip side of his nationalist struggle to be his effort to contain the growth of communalism, the growth of conflict between groups defined by the categories of caste and religion.[8] Ambedkar, on the other hand, was convinced that caste (or, rather, untouchable) identities had to be fostered in order to combat centuries of oppression by collective organization and political struggle. In a curious way, the debate between Gandhi and Ambedkar continues to rage to the present day, though the terms of debate have shifted in each successive historical moment.

While Ambedkar lost the political struggle with Gandhi in the early 1930s, by the time of India's independence, and certainly after Gandhi's death in 1948, Ambedkar's position was triumphant. As noted above, he drafted the terms by which reservations were established for scheduled castes and tribes, and despite some resentment and debate, there has been general unanimity about the importance of these constitutional provisions and guidelines. However, concerns have been expressed. Some academics within India have argued, for example, that caste reservations have "affected the morals, the administration and the society adversely"; "imped[ed] the development of secularism"; "perpetuated and accentuated the caste consciousness"; and promoted "vested interests in backwardness." [9] The noted sociologist G. S. Ghurye was always very careful to distinguish his arguments against the politicization of caste from his acceptance of the need to use extraordinary measures to combat the problem of untouchability; only in the case of scheduled castes did Ghurye approve of reservations and positive discrimination, though he disapproved of Ambedkar's attempts to politicize caste around the untouchable movement and strongly supported Gandhi's nonconfrontational and assimilationist ideals. But Ghurye was also concerned that reservations be a short-term remedy and was sharply critical of the automatic extensions granted to constitutional provisions that he felt were originally intended to be provisional.[10] And some American academics, echoing positions taken in debates over affirmative action in the United States, have endorsed concerns by many in India that reservations promote a sense of second-class citizenship and accomplishment: Lloyd and Susanne Rudolph wrote: "The price of discrimination in reverse has been a kind of blackmail in reverse; in return for access to opportunity and power the untouchable is asked to incriminate himself socially. This is not only profoundly disturbing but also an important source of alienation and rebellion,"[11] though they neglected to specify that the great locus of rebellion was among caste Hindus, not untouchables.

The subsequent history of reservation policy for scheduled castes has not always been smooth. Ironically, Ambedkar's move to encourage untouchables to convert to Buddhism created problems for the classificatory guidelines around reservations. The ritual definition of untouchability assumed that the issue of discrimination was a Hindu problem, and untouchables were categorized as Hindus (despite their exclusion from Hindu temples and their marginal, if necessary, role in Hindu ritual); when petitioned by Buddhist converts to extend reservations to them, some courts held that converts from Hinduism to religions that do not recognize caste, specifically Buddhism, led to their loss of caste identity and of their attendant eligibility for reservations.

While this problem was soon solved, the question of time limits for reservations has been more intractable. After considering the recommendations of a special committee set up to evaluate reservations,[12] the government pledged to begin dealing with the issue of descheduling, first by taking the relatively advanced caste groups off the reservation roles, then by descheduling the entire list of castes and tribes by the end of the sixth five-year plan, in 1981.[13] But the fears of Ghurye have been vindicated, at least in the sense that it has proved difficult to stop reservations once they have begun. At the same time, those who argued for the cessation of reservations on the grounds that untouchability was disappearing as a social problem and ritual evil, some suggesting that the only thing maintaining the institution has been the schedules themselves, have had to confront the fact that since the mid-1960s there has been a dramatic rise in caste violence against untouchables, particularly in rural areas. The annual report on the scheduled castes and tribes began to routinely list and measure the terrifying rise in "atrocity," which included outright murder, the causing of grievous hurt, rape, and arson, among other things.[14] In 1978 it was decided that an actual commission with much greater legislative and juridical power needed to be appointed specifically to deal with things like the reports of atrocities committed against scheduled castes and tribes. By the early 1980s, when descheduling was to have been completed, the number of atrocities was constantly on the rise, particularly in Madhya Pradesh, Uttar Pradesh, Bihar, and Rajasthan.[15] Although the causes for violence were usually said to concern land disputes, the preponderance of cases carried the full signature of caste and power; as M. J. Akbar has written: "In the autumn of 1981, Harijans were killed in several villages in Uttar Pradesh. Two of these massacres—one in Dehuli, followed by another a few days later in Sarhupur—received widespread publicity. The killers who were Thakur Rajputs, had just one message to send through murder—the untouchable Jatav cobblers had to learn their place in society and the caste hierarchy."[16] In the mid-1980s, serious antireservation riots and attacks on harijans in the city of Ahmedabad and throughout the state of Gujarat finished off the notion that untouchables were only afflicted in the countryside, or the Hindi heartland. Although there are those who would argue that reservation policy has exacerbated caste tension, no responsible observer today could claim that untouchability has disappeared. In the present climate, there seems to be little legitimate concern at present about the continuation of reservation policy for scheduled castes.

III

The widespread concern that led to the Mandal agitation was of course not about changes for scheduled castes, but rather about the extension of a similar reservation policy to other backward classes, and that, too, well after the drafting of the original constitutional provisions empowering the president to appoint a committee and take measures to better the conditions of the socially and educationally backward. The president in fact had appointed such a committee well before the Janata government recruited Mandal to this task; in 1953 Kaka Kalelkar was asked to head the Backward Classes Commission to investigate the possibility of establishing reservations for OBCs. The first task was to determine how to identify the backward classes. Whereas there had been widespread agreement about the classification of the Scheduled Castes and Tribes before independence, there had been no such consensus or precedent at all, at least at the central level, for the backward classes. The constitutional mandate had used the term *class* rather than *caste,* concealing what were already massive differences about the role of caste in postindependent India, not to mention the difficulties experienced by the British in colonial days over the use of caste for any all-India enumeration and classification. Nehru was particularly reluctant to acknowledge the role of caste in India's new social policy, but at the same time he was especially concerned to break the hold of the past on vast sections of the population: "We want to put an end to . . . all those infinite divisions that have grown up in our social life. . . . we may call them by any name you like, the caste system or religious divisions, etc."[17] Part of the difficulty later confronted by the commission in finding adequate data to draw up their lists of backward groups was due to the fact that the British, to allay what they saw as the hyperpoliticization of caste through the census, had ceased using caste categories after 1931; but part of the difficulty was also that Sardar Patel, home minister until 1950, had rejected caste tabulation as a device because he did not want to confirm British characterizations of India as caste-ridden. But the embarrassment had contradictory effects, as in the case of the eminent anthropologist N. K. Bose who saw the specific purpose of the Backward Classes Commission as being to lessen the hold of caste: "It is . . . the desire and will of the Indian nation to do away with the hierarchy of caste and of its consequent social discrimination, and prepare the ground for full social equality."[18] Like Ambedkar, Bose argued for the use of pollution and exclusion indices in assigning backward-class status. Ambedkar himself clarified his wording in the constitutional mandate when he observed that "what are called backward classes are . . . nothing else but a collection of certain castes."[19] If there was major concern about linking backwardness and caste, there was at the same time a consensus among many of independent India's founding fathers that the backwardness of India was itself in large part about the continued hold of caste; colonial shame, as well as colonial discourse, was writ large upon the initial social ventures of the new Indian state.

Although the category of backwardness was both vague and unprecedented at the central level, certain states had developed clear ideas of the
salience of the category well before independence, most significantly in
conjunction with the development of anti-Brahman movements in
Mysore, Maharashtra, and Madras. The term *backward classes* first
acquired a formal significance in the Princely State of Mysore, where in
1918 the government appointed a commission to consider the problem of
disproportionate Brahman participation in public service. In 1921 preferential recruitment of "backward communities" was instituted; all communities aside from Brahmans were classified as backward. Reservations for
backward communities were instituted in Bombay after 1925, when a government resolution defined *backward classes* as all except for "Brahmins,
Prabhus, Marwaris, Parsis, Banias, and Christians." But perhaps the most
important precedent in the prehistory of the backward-class movement
was established in Madras Presidency, where the non-Brahman Justice
Party was formed in 1916 specifically around a platform of addressing the
preponderance of Brahmans in colleges, universities, and government service.[20] The early development of the anti-Brahman movement, which
spawned long-lasting political changes around caste politics throughout
the Indian subcontinent, took place in the context of the first major British
reforms, specifically the Montagu-Chelmsford Reforms that opened up
Indian participation in municipal and local councils after 1918. The Justice Party, which was labeled antinationalist because of its rejection of
Congress's calls for noncooperation, played an important role in setting
the terms for local electoral reforms and successfully contested the 1920
elections in Madras. Through a combination of legislative and political
means, the Justice Party managed to put sufficient pressure on the British
government to have them issue what became known as the first and second
communal GOs (government orders) in 1921 and 1922 respectively. The
first GO encouraged affirmative action in a general sense in order to distribute government appointments among various castes and communities,
and to prepare caste-wise tables documenting the caste constituencies of
government servants. The second GO expanded and formalized the provisions of the first, extending the provenance of affirmative action not only
for new appointments but for all government employees, as well as to matters of promotion for employees already in service. The ultimate aim of the
communal legislation was to remedy a situation in which Brahmans—who
constituted only 3 percent of the population—held almost all government
jobs, by increasing non-Brahman participation to over 50 percent. These

procedures were codified through a roster system that operated until 1947 and then provided the precedent for strong backward-class legislation around reservations in Tamil Nadu after independence.

The anti-Brahman movement provided an organizational impetus for the development of legislative interventions to address issues of social justice and access to power for so-called backward communities; it certainly had dramatic effects on Brahman hegemony in colonial administration and postcolonial politics. However, the originary relationship between anti-Brahman movements and caste-based affirmative action also raises issues about the instrumental appropriation and political entailments of the backward-classes category. The Justice Party hardly represented a fringe group of lower-caste groups wedged uneasily between untouchables and dominant castes, whether Brahman or non-Brahman; the classificatory breadth of the backward category in Mysore, Maharashtra, and Madras, no matter how dominant Brahmans had become in the previous hundred and fifty years of British rule, also suggests the tenuousness of the rhetoric behind much backward-class legislation. The history of the Justice Party provided ample evidence of the relationship between reservation politics and complicity with British colonial rule.

The connection between anti-Brahman movements and backward-class mobilization also helps explain, for example, why the eminent sociologist G. S. Ghurye was so adamantly opposed to the use of caste for reservations. Ghurye, a Maharashtrian Brahman and a staunch nationalist, was skeptical from the start about the rhetoric of the Maharaja of Kolhapur, who spearheaded the Maharashtrian non-Brahman movement and was given to requesting "the protection and guidance of the British government until the evil of caste-system becomes ineffective" in connection with the early implementations of home rule.[21] Ghurye acknowledged Brahman dominance in administrative positions, but noted that the initial complaints of non-Brahman activists had been addressed by non-Brahman political mobilization alone: "An analysis of the membership of the various local bodies in the presidencies of Bombay and Madras clearly proves that the non-Brahmans know their rights and are generally keen to conduct a strong campaign against any measure which they feel unjust to them."[22] Ghurye argued very strongly against the policy of reservations, which he viewed as "opposed to the accepted criteria of nationality and the guiding principles of social justice."[23] Ghurye accepted that the non-Brahmans might have legitimate grievances and exist as a single class in structural terms, in relation to social matters, "because the attitude of the Brahmins as regards food and social intercourse, and religious instruction and ministration towards them, has been uniform."[24] But he strongly opposed the notion that legislative sanctions or reserved posts would address this issue: "Whatever liberalizing of the Brahmin attitude in this respect has taken place during the last forty years is mainly due to education and social reform campaign and not to the very recent reserved or communal representation."[25] Indeed, Ghurye argued that the "restriction on the numbers of the able members of the Brahmin and the allied castes, imposed by this resolution of the government, penalizes some able persons simply because they happen to belong to particular castes," at the same time clearly abandoning "the accepted standard of qualifications and efficiency."[26] Ghurye not only believed that reserved representation was not necessary, but that it is harmful "in so far as it tends to perpetuate the distinction based on birth," something he felt was both counterproductive and antinational: "To harp on the caste differences and to allow special representation is to set at naught the fundamental condition for the rise of community feeling."[27] Given the collaboration between the non-Brahman movement and the British, Ghurye's argument was not altogether far-fetched, even if his own sense of caste identity, and more general commitment to a Gandhian injunction for national unity and Brahmanic trusteeship, doubtless generated no small measure of his concern.

Ghurye was not the first to argue against the policy of reservations and the effects of politicizing caste, but he was one of the first Western-educated anthropologists to play a major role in the debate. Further, Ghurye was also one of the first to argue that the politicization of caste was not merely a natural outgrowth of the traditional institution but a conscious design of British colonial policy. The principal colonial lesson of the great rebellion of 1857, according to Ghurye, was that the "safety of the British domination in India was very closely connected with keeping the Indian people divided on the lines of caste."[28] Ghurye quoted James Kerr, the principal of the Hindu College of Calcutta, as having written that the spirit of caste "is opposed to national union"[29] and argued more generally that a policy of divide-and-rule on caste grounds influenced the policy and conduct of many British officials. He further suggested that the British were so receptive to the arguments on the part of leaders of the non-Brahman movement in favor of reservations and caste quotas precisely because, "as a logical development of the attitude of the Government [reservations] nursed, rather than ignored, the spirit of caste."[30] And so, when writing against the non-Brahman movement in his own Bombay Presidency,

Ghurye used an anticolonial argument to support his concern that national life, due to the rise of caste enmity and conflict, could "be reduced to an absurdity."[31]

But his agenda was mixed; he concluded his chapter on the effects of British rule on caste by noting: "Even the apex of the ancient scheme, the priesthood of the Brahmin, which has been the great bond of social solidarity in this finely divided society, is being loosened by caste after caste. At about the end of the British rule in India, caste-society presented the spectacle of self-centred groups more or less in conflict with one another."[32] His arguments against colonial policies of divide and rule, eloquent and persuasive though they were, stood side by side with his nostalgia for an age in which the otherworldly prestige of the Brahman could be acknowledged for its innocent capacity to hold Indian society together.

The intellectual and ideological background of backward-class legislation was thus complicated by its connection to non-Brahman movements that had not always established secure nationalist credentials, even when critiques of this movement emerged directly out of positions of caste privilege. As we have seen, objections to this legislation ranged from concerns that the economic conditions of backwardness were being obscured on the one hand to the kinds of concerns raised by Ghurye on the other. But there was still strong political pressure to do something about the condition of the backward classes, from figures such as Ambedkar who played significant roles in the drafting of social policy, from the redistributional ideology of the new socialist state, as well as from the effects of developing forms of electoral democracy. Nevertheless, the provisional decision to use caste groupings as the basis for assembling a roster of disadvantaged communities invoked the colonial contradictions inhabiting any refiguration of caste classifications in postindependent India. When the Backward Classes Commission released its report after two years of work, it presented a list of 2,399 backward groups[33] and recommended various measures for their advancement. The commission was deluged, both before and after the release of its report, by communities claiming to be backward; the commission was also seriously hampered by the lack of good data reflecting all the caste groupings across the subcontinent and their social and economic standing. The problems encountered by earlier generations of British census officials (in particular the noted figure H. H. Risley who was concerned to develop a comprehensive ethnological survey of the entire subcontinent in his anthropological inquiries around the turn of the century) were experienced all over again. Caste turned out to be a very dodgy category; there was tremendous variation across India in the size, extent, and autonomy of classificatory rubrics around caste, and despite the best efforts of British officials and ethnographers, caste was still only one of many foci of social identity. Further, many caste groups were by no means uniform in their social and economic standing. And since the political consequences of classification had by now far exceeded those occasioning many of the political battles over census designations in earlier decades (which had been so severe that the British stopped using caste data after 1931), the commission found itself in the thick of political contestation.

IV

The chairman of the commission himself virtually repudiated the report, concluding at the end of his deliberations that "it would have been better if we could determine the criteria of backwardness on principles other than caste."[34] Nehru was also unhappy with the commission's criteria: "the Commission had to find objective tests and criteria by which such classifications were to be made; they had to find indisputable yardsticks by which social and educational backwardness could be measured. The report . . . has not been unanimous on this point; in fact, it reveals considerable divergence."[35] As the decade wore on, these reservations found increasing consensus. When the report was submitted to Parliament in 1956, it carried with it the negative evaluation of the minister of home affairs, who thought that the emphasis on caste demonstrated "the dangers of separatism;"[36] the minister added that the caste system was undeniably "the greatest hindrance in the way of our progress toward an egalitarian society, and the recognition of specified castes as backward may serve to maintain and perpetuate the existing distinctions on the basis of caste."[37] Indeed, the minister requested each state government to undertake ad hoc surveys to determine the numbers of backward classes at the same time affording them all possible consideration in local government schemes. In the meanwhile there was growing criticism from academics and public intellectuals about the reliance on caste; significant here was the presidential address by M. N. Srinivas to the anthropology section of the Indian Science Congress in 1957, in which he suggested that it was time to give serious thought to evolving "'neutral' indices of backwardness. . . The criteria of literacy, landownership and income in cash or grain should be able to subsume all cases of backwardness."[38] As a consequence of growing negative opinion, and the negative reception accorded the commission report, it was not actually taken up by Parliament until 1965, by which time there seemed even greater antipathy to the use of caste categories to alleviate the social distress of backward communities; between the early 1950s and early 1960s the tide seemed to have turned entirely. When the report was presented in parliamentary discussion, the central government's spokesman reiterated his opposition to communal criteria, arguing that they "were contrary to the Constitution, would perpetuate caste, and would create in the recipients both vested interests and a sense of helplessness."[39] The report was dropped, despite some agitation from various backward-classes organizations, and individual states were advised to use economic criteria in their own redistributional and reservation policies.[40]

It may therefore appear odd that the very issue that seemed to have died so convincing a death would have been resurrected more than a decade after what seemed the final chapter in the debate. Indeed, the Mandal Commission was convened by Morarji Desai, a staunch Gandhian who would hardly have been ideologically in favor of politicizing caste per se. But the 1977 election manifesto of the Janata Party, drafted under the influence of populist rhetoric harkening back to Jayaprakash Narayan's challenge to Congress and Indira Gandhi, promised the establishment of an independent and autonomous civil rights commission "competent to ensure that the minorities, scheduled castes and tribes, and other backward classes do not suffer from discrimination or inequality."[41] The manifesto specifically pledged that it would work to "reserve between 25 and 33 per cent of all appointments to Government service for the backward classes, as recommended by the Kelkar [sic] Commission."[42] Desai accordingly appointed a five-member commission in December 1978 under the chairmanship of B. P. Mandal, an MP from Bihar, with a charge that was largely the same as that which had been used for the 1953–55 commission. But by the time the report was ready, Janata had lost its mandate and Indira Gandhi was ready to come back to power. The Mandal report was set aside, and though vague references were made to it by different parties, usually positive, it awaited the return of Janata rule. But even when a Janata victory brought V. P. Singh into power in the autumn of 1989, along with a platform commitment to the implementation of the Mandal report, the actual decision to institute Mandal in August 1990 took most observers by surprise.

I have already rehearsed the reaction to Mandal, the fact that scores of young people attempted suicide to protest what they felt as the loss of any chance at all to secure government employment, the most prestigious and secure form of general employment in India. The protest turned out to be the undoing of V. P. Singh; within a matter of months he was forced out of office after a vote of no confidence in Parliament, and although the Janata Party held onto power a bit longer, Mandal appeared to sink Janata as well. At the same time, many have argued that the furor over Mandal fed into BJP attempts to gain increased legitimacy and popularity during this time. If Mandal was one of the two big political issues of this period, Mandir (temple) was the other, namely, the BJP call to replace the Babur Mosque (Babri Masjid) in Ayodhya with a temple to Lord Rama. The agitation over Mandal was certainly behind the development of a new political rhetoric by the BJP, which stressed that Hinduism was a much better focus for social identity than caste; from 1990 onward the BJP, and many other forces on the right, have not tired of stressing the way in which emphasis on caste identity works against the spirit of national unity, in language reminiscent of that mobilized around reservation politics by commentators such as G. S. Ghurye in the context of the nationalist movement, and in ways specifically calculated to take advantage of public reaction against Mandal. The debate over Mandal brought together strange allies and arguments, complicating the politics of position and renewing the centrality of caste in public debate. Once again, as had been the case in the debates over reservations in the first years of Indian independence, academics took a variety of positions, and technical anthropological arguments both developed national prominence and revealed at least some of their political entailments. But the arguments were different now and revealed as well the myriad complexities circulating around the status of caste in a political climate vastly changed from that of the more optimistic 1950s, when secular and socialist dreams were widely shared and little contested.

V

The mainstream English-language press was predominantly negative in its initial reaction to and treatment of V. P. Singh's decision to implement the recommendations of the Mandal Commission, sometimes aggressively so. Inderjit Badhwar began the cover story in *India Today,* India's leading fortnightly news magazine (which is published in English as well as in a number of regional languages), by writing that "as events unfolded during the fortnight it became clear that what Singh was trying to reap was a harvest of shame. He had been reduced, like all power-hungry politicians before him, to a vote-hungry power broker shamelessly using the two elements that have ever bloodied and divided this nation—religion and caste."[43] Using extraordinarily strong language, Badhwar characterized the antireservation protests as completely spontaneous and suggested that the "Government would even back a caste war for narrow partisan gains."[44] *Frontline,* the news magazine run by the *The Hindu* newspaper group but reflecting the Marxist intellectual commitments of its editor, was much more supportive of Mandal, but in a long feature article by Anand Sahay noted that the really radical recommendations of Mandal, that advocated serious land reform and economic redistribution, were naturally left completely aside in the Mandal wars. Sahay quotes Mandal with approval as having noted that "reservations in government employment and educational institutions, as also all possible financial assistance, will remain mere palliatives unless the problem of backwardness is tackled at its root."[45] The *Economic and Political Weekly,* a serious intellectual journal with solid left credentials, published a number of exchanges on Mandal, but reflected general agreement about the importance of reservations for backward groups. But for the most part, *India Today* set the tone of elite public debate. K. Balagopal, in a review of some of this debate, complained that: "There is perhaps no issue on which we are such hypocrites as caste. Nor any other which brings out all that is worst in us with such shameful ease. The moment V. P. Singh announces the decision to implement the Mandal Commission's recommendation of reservations for the backward castes, an avalanche of obscenity hits the country. It carries before it the Press, the universities, and opinion-makers of all kinds."[46] Balagopal was unapologetic in his defence of Mandal, noting that "so long as caste remains one of the determinants of property and power, so long as it is used by the rich and the powerful as a means of maintaining and strengthening their domination, it remains the moral right and indeed the political duty of the poor and the deprived to use their caste identity in the struggle for their liberation."[47]

Rajni Kothari, one of India's leading political scientists and editor of the influential book *Caste in Indian Politics,* wrote an assessment of the reservation debate in relation to his earlier theoretical arguments about the politicization of caste.[48] Kothari had earlier argued that "casteism in politics is no more and no less than politicisation of caste," a process that he felt played an important role in the facilitation of democracy and the growth of social awareness. Kothari held that Mandal would continue this process in useful ways. He wrote that "caste formations are at once aggregative and dis-aggregative, emphasizing the secular dimension of a plural society. Caste, indeed, is the great secularizer in a society being pulled apart by convoluted religions bent upon tearing apart the social fabric." Indeed, Kothari noted that caste was an indigenous institution that was playing a modern democratic role, "something that social anthropologists should have noticed long back, but given their class background, they have been unable to."[49] Kothari continued to see evidence of the formation of class configurations out of "dispersed and fragmented caste identities," but in ways that reflected regional differences and specific political movements. He further argued that the work of the Mandal Commission was built on the recognition of the salience of these movements, not on any attempt to exacerbate the pernicious influence of caste: "It is the backlash from the upper and 'foreward' castes against the upsurge that is casteist, not the upsurge itself." Finally, Kothari was adamant about the secularizing function of caste in contemporary India: caste is a "bulwark against religious fundamentalism and its fascist overtones. It is caste playing a secular historical role that we are witness to in the growth of social mobility that the Mandal Commission and its various antecedents have given rise to." This was perhaps the strongest argument made in defense of Mandal by a leading, mainstream academic figure.

Kothari's article occasioned a strong letter from three other prominent Indian social scientists, M. N. Srinivas, A. M. Shah, and B. S. Baviskar.[50] While they took care to praise his earlier scholarly work, they disputed his claim that when castes grouped themselves together for political purposes they lost the quality of being castes. They then argued that the political process not only failed to erase divisions within caste/class groupings but provided new opportunities for exploitation and the enrichment of elites, a process they claimed would be further enhanced by Mandal. They concluded their letter by noting that "the ploy of caste-based reservations, encouraging caste-based politicisation, is not the solution to these problems. For all we know, this will benefit only the rich and the influential in all the castes and leave the poor and weak where they are. All in all, in his passion for creating a political order of his choice, Dr. Kothari has ignored the ground realities of the social order. We hope he is not one of those intellectuals who place the state before the social order"—a rather ominously phrased hope, that. For these authors, the politicization of caste would have negative consequences, though they stressed the lack of fit between caste and class rather than the pernicious character of caste itself.

Other authors responded to the Mandal debate by suggesting various ways in which caste would be hardened and rendered even more divisive a force within the Indian nation. In another letter to the *Times* responding to Kothari, one Dr. Harendra Mehta noted that "the menace of the Mandal recommendations is that it would further the imperial designs of the British by the caste based reservations of public posts."[51] The eminent sociologists Veena Das[52] and André Beteille have also noted that reservations effectively reproduced colonial policies of divide and rule; the leading economic historian Dharma Kumar has specifically argued that the colonial construction of castes as essentializing identities that work to displace notions of civil society from the political to the religious (and then perversely back again) provides the unfortunate precedent for the architects of reservation policy.[53] All these scholars echo the eloquent critique of colonialism by G. S. Ghurye, which of course prefaced his own critique of reservation policy. The affiliation of postcolonial reservation policy with colonial attempts to play the caste card to antinationalist ends has become almost an accepted litany, betraying some of the fundamental contradictions in Indian nationalist ideology.[54] Ashok Guha wrote that, "in its tenure, the V. P. Singh government's most conspicuous success has been the restoration and solidification of the caste barriers that time and change have been slowly eroding. In the process it has accomplished the permanent division of the Indian polity—an achievement that eluded the British in their efforts to divide and rule India on the basis of caste and religion."[55] Indeed, I have found that my own scholarly position on the colonial transformations of caste has become far more popular now that it (or arguments similar to those I have made) can be used to document the pernicious effects legislative (or juridical) reifications of caste might have in the postcolonial period; much to my surprise, work that was motivated by a particular critique of colonial history has been aligned with and used to support serious critiques of Mandal.[56] In the case of the Mandal debate, the politics of position have had the effect of making the position of politics particularly contradictory, critiques from the left and the right mixing promiscuously in ways that permit charges of retrograde politics and casteism from virtually all sides.

Ashok Guha argued strongly that the effect of Mandal would be to further harden caste identities and conflicts. He wrote that, "The defenders of reservations argue that Mandal did not invent the caste system, that caste is a fact of life. . . . The charge against them is only of fortifying it by rewarding membership in certain castes. But this is no less serious a charge. . . . Reservations then are sociologically archaic and politically divisive."[57] Dharma Kumar has suggested that the frequent use by Mandal defenders of the long experience of caste reservations in southern India and the fact that they have not been correlated with disproportionately high levels of communal or caste violence missed some fundamental points, in particular the fact that in the south it was very largely the small minority of Brahmans who were affected by reservations, most of whom have migrated either to the private sector or outside of southern India; Kumar notes that the threatened groups in northern India tend to be more extensive, more tied to rural landholding, more likely to engage in violence and political reaction. Kumar is correct in her explanation for why Mandal has occasioned the protest it has in the North, though her argument if anything might be used to justify reservations rather than argue against them. Kumar further notes that caste consciousness in India has been on the increase; she directly correlates this with political mobilization around reservations.[58]

André Beteille, whose writings on caste inequality have set the standard in Indian sociology,[59] has also addressed the issue of the relevance of the history of reservations in southern India for the debate on the pros and cons of Mandal. Beteille also noted the colonial character of reservation policy: "The circumstances under which caste quotas were imposed in south India in the high noon of colonial rule were totally different from the ones under which they are being sought to be instituted today after more than 40 years of national independence. . . . It will not do to erase from our collective memory the fact that caste quotas, like communal electorates, were inventions of colonial times."[60] Beteille goes on to detail the southern experiment, like Kumar noting the very different circumstances of the non-Brahman movement from the movements on behalf of backward castes in the North (once again, not owning up to the extent to which this seems further to justify the use of reservations in the north). He further notes that the southern experiment is not the raging success it was held up to be; he argues that caste quotas in southern universities have worked against intellectual excellence,[61] and that the question of relative efficiency can hardly be answered in the context of the vastly different administrative histories of north and south ("All that we can say perhaps is that there are many ways to ruin the administration, and not just through caste quotas"). Beteille notes that the only clear lesson of the southern experience is the irremoveability of caste quotas once implemented; though always justified as provisional measures, they develop political constituencies and dependencies that simply do not let them disappear. Beteille concludes his editorial article with the extraordinary claim that "what has sustained the movement [against Mandal] and given it its peculiar intensity is not any kind of political organisation, but a certain sense of moral outrage. It is this sense of moral outrage and not any political force that has unsettled every political party. It is true that the British policy of pitting caste against caste, and community against community in the name of justice and fair play, aroused widespread resentment and hostility, but it did not create the kind of response that has now come to the surface. Perhaps Indians of an earlier generation could never feel towards their alien rulers the sense of outrage that their descendants now feel towards the leaders they have themselves freely chosen." Quite apart from the curious suggestion that outrage in the context of democratic rule can far exceed that of, or directed toward, a colonial situation, Beteille here clearly shares the sense of outrage that reservation policy, a policy that he sees as irrevocably tied to colonial rule, special interests, and undemocratic outcomes, has been restored by responsible government forty years after independence. A group of social scientists from the Madras Institute for Development Studies, which was exempted from Beteille's critique of southern Indian institutions of higher education (though on the grounds that caste quotas were not there enforced), replied in the pages of the same newspaper: "It is not self generated 'moral outrage' but callous anti-reservationist bystanders who have egged on the Sati-like 'self-immolations.'"[62] Neither side in this argument could actually begin to explain the enormity of political suicide, but each sought to appropriate irrational sacrifice to the rationalizations of their political position.

Not all contestants in the Mandal debate were quite so partisan. Veena Das, though elsewhere arguing vociferously against Mandal, came out in favor of an American style of affirmative action over and against the use of quotas.[63] Ashis Nandy was far more ambivalent than usual; while sympathizing with the protesting students, and wishing that some political party would show the moral courage to come out against the Mandal Commission, he said that he was "close to being a supporter of the Mandal commission . . . because I think caste does play a role and irrespective of your educational and economic status certain things are not available to you."[64] Upendra Baxi, vice-chancellor of Delhi University, spoke eloquently about how both the protest and the debate tended to miss the basic issues, some concerning the need to begin reservations far lower down in the system if they were to do any good, others having to do with the necessity to recognize the technical nature of the judicial and legislative process.[65] P. Radhakrishnan, a social scientist at the Madras Institute of Development Studies who has done extensive research on the history of reservation policy, wrote that, "while the decision to implement the Mandal report itself is of an extreme nature, the reactions to it have also been so. . . . Since the Constitution has provisions for reservations for the OBCs, it is the government of India which has to be blamed for its failure to implement these provisions for about four decades now and having allowed the state governments to politicise the matter."[66] Radhakrishnan was one of many who expressed support for the idea of reservations but argued the need for much better criteria and classificatory guidelines in the establishment and implementation of genuine social reform.

VI

Despite much muddiness in the general debate, what did become clear was the extreme ambivalence surrounding caste, and the accompanying crisis in the left when matters of caste were involved. Aditya Nigam argued, against the spirit of much debate: "A left position need not necessarily be identified either by its crusading ardour against merit and efficiency or by its messianic zeal for reservations. What it certainly needs to recognise, in no uncertain terms, is that merit and efficiency are largely socially determined and therefore, any consideration on merit alone works inherently against the underprivileged."[67] This moderate position seemed extremely welcome given the extraordinarily polarized character of the debate. But the sorest spot in the debate, again, had to do with the position of caste itself. Shiv Visvanathan put the matter well:[68]

For years a whole generation of sociologists talked of caste as a fundamental reality. We talked of the vitality of the caste system and how it adapted to industry and the city. We boasted about the modernity of tradition. M.N. Srinivas made his reputation with concepts such as sanskritisation and westernisation. His epigoni added to it in innumerable ways writing about caste associations and caste rituals. The literature of this generation provided the framework of many reports and many of these luminaries served as consultants to commissions on reservation. . . . Instead of condemning [caste] as a parochial structure, they spent hours portraying it as a protean system quite at home in office and the city. They celebrated the grammar of purity and pollution, heralding the sheer geometry behind it. This was the world that the doyens of the era, Srinivas, Shah, Karve, Dumont, M.S.A. Rao, gave us. . . . Marxists attacked such a view but only succeeded in reducing it to a caricature. Now suddenly caste has become threatening, stifling, even worse than communalism. It is no longer protean; it is Procrustus, terribly constricting, absolutely threatening to a way of life. . . . Caste is now casteism and everyone has reservations about it.

Visvanathan sees the ambivalence around caste as reflective of a whole series of contradictions at the core of the lives of Indian intellectuals, beginning within the university, but permeating the abstractness of intellectual engagements with social and political realities. In making this argument, he has nicely characterized the contradictions around caste itself, the way the anthropologization of the Indian social imaginary has run aground against the specter of caste politics. While others have argued that the Indian elite always felt a certain civilizational embarrassment about caste, Visvanathan asserts that caste became a marker of a certain kind of identity, simultaneously belonging to the private sphere and affiliating the most modern (and Western) of spirits with the domesticating comfort of tradition. Thus the appeal of Srinivas et al., whose notions of Westernization, Sanskritization, and compartmentalization[69]—the latter meaning the capacity to situate caste solely within the domestic sphere, the home, frequently as a matter of fashion and family—became the happy pieties of the secular elite; thus the establishment of a certain anthropological orthodoxy that resolutely resisted serious engagement with history and politics.

When analyzing the changing character of caste in contemporary India, G. S. Ghurye noted that the interdependence of caste groups was being replaced by caste solidarity, what he also called "caste-patriotism."[70] Ghurye lamented that "conflict of claims and oppositions has thus replaced the old harmony of demand and acceptance," noting later in his argument that caste-solidarity has now "taken the place of village-community."[71] Ghurye also commented that the modern phenomenon of marriage among different subcastes was further contributing to the growth of this phenomenon of caste patriotism, anticipating other arguments about the increasing ethnicization of caste. M. N. Srinivas wrote in a similar vein: "In general it may be confidently said that the last hundred years has seen a great increase in caste solidarity, and the concomitant decrease of a sense of interdependence between different castes living in a region."[72]

Srinivas was less directly critical of caste solidarity than Ghurye, though he shared Ghurye's concern about the rise of conflict between caste groups and the politicization of caste in relation to the non-Brahman movements of Madras and Mysore. Edmund Leach formally theorized what both Ghurye and Srinivas were addressing when he wrote that the caste system was changing fundamentally when it shifted from interdependence to competition; for Leach, invoking Durkheim, this meant that the caste system was dying, at least as the traditional system it had always been.[73] In their general sympathy for Brahmanic views and their nostalgia for the harmony of the past, both Ghurye and Srinivas agreed with Leach, though they stressed the way in which caste was not so much dying as being reborn, if now in increasingly sinister ways. Louis Dumont, whose theories of caste have been so enormously influential, and who argued that the religious elements of caste encompassed the political and economic, has noted that Ghurye and Srinivas were both characterizing a process he names as "substantialization."[74] Dumont, despite his overt Brahmanical perspective on caste and the conservatism of his general theoretical views, actually welcomed these changes: "Anti-Brahman schemings, although they have a demagogic and somewhat violent side, are a positive aspect in the struggle against caste."[75] But again, Dumont sees this as the effective death of the real caste system, a system that was free from political strife and struggle, that he, along with Ghurye, Srinivas, and Leach, among others, idealized as fundamental to Indian tradition and culture.

Whether caste is dying, or being reborn as a monster, the political entailments of these theoretical positions have been clearly revealed in the debates over the years about reservation policies and the politics of caste more generally. Whereas the debates over caste in anthropology outside of India have raged free of an immediate political terrain (though with all sorts of implications for the instantiation and naturalization of Orientalist perceptions about the character of tradition and modernity in India), the debates within India have taken place not only in academic corridors (which themselves have not been so autonomous after all—as Visvanathan noted, not only did anthropologists play important roles in the making of policy, they set the questions about Indian society that all Indian civil servants and academics had to answer on standard competitive examinations) but in public debates over the nature of history, the character of society, the changing meanings and relations of tradition and modernity, the responsibilities and the risks of redistributional policy decisions that would use the category of caste. If caste has been taken as the inevitable

and indomitable category to define minorities in need of positive discrimination, it is perhaps equally inevitable that many have reacted to these
measures by decrying not just the politicization of caste but the tacit
acknowledgment that caste, interdependent or competitive or both, seems
destined to stay on as fundamental in India's social and political life.

Despite the colonial ethnologist H. H. Risley's failure to establish his
views about the fundamentally racial character of caste,[76] caste has
become like race in its contradictory positionality: caste is seen on the one
hand as the fundamental determinant of privilege in a society that is still
bound by histories of prejudice and exploitation, and on the other as the
only natural way to make social distinctions, even granting the extent to
which economic markers would be generally accepted as the most scientific way to consider the problem of redistribution. This is neither to suggest that caste is a natural category nor even that it is seen by most social
scientists as one. Ironically, in a modern world where the economic is
increasingly naturalized as the fundamental condition not just of the
human but of the condition of freedom (relating to individuals, markets,
entrepreneurial capital, multi- or transnational utopias, and so forth), the
natural distinctions of the social, around notions such as race and caste,
have become deeply inscribed as the signs of the modern, the necessary
exceptions that prove the truth of the rule. Caste, like race, is used to
obscure the salience of class divisions, even as it is one of the most recognized (and, regrettably, predictable) markers of class position.

In the case of India, the history of colonialism plays a fundamental role
in the elaboration and naturalization of the contradictions around caste. If
there is a general consensus that caste is a retrograde force, there is also
widespread acceptance of the social fact that caste is the natural focus of
political mobilization and economic redistribution, as well as the somewhat illicit marker of cultural identity and traditional pleasure.[77] If it is the
case that an uncanny alliance has now developed between critiques of
colonial history and denunciations of reservation policy, in what is surely
a curious disavowal of the way caste is still the most conspicuous marker
of social privilege in India even as it is genuinely hardened by reservation
policy now as it was by colonial classificational regimes earlier, it must be
recognized that the power of colonial history was precisely to complicate
the politics of modernity in colonial places. Colonialism worked to affili-
ate progress and reason with domination and humiliation, to demonstrate
that the modern was always an argument for British rule rather than
Indian independence, to naturalize the contradictory necessity that tradi-

tion would raise its head time after time (however modern tradition always is) to announce both the perils of the modern and the contradictory allure of the old. If it is no longer easy for a critic such as myself to excoriate the colonial construction of Indian society without worrying that I will play into anti-Mandal forces (or worse, BJP Hindu fundamentalist ones), it may be because I have necessarily affiliated myself with the rationalizing conceits of demystificatory critique, assuming that one can fight reason only with reason, that one can dispense the power of a certain kind of history only with a powerful account of the same kind of history.[78] For reasons I have adumbrated in this paper, the contradictions of caste may stay with India for a very long time, outliving both colonial critiques and various forms of substantialization and politicization. Caste may indeed be the most telling reminder of the postcolonial character of India's contemporary predicament, the chilling sign that India's relationship to history and tradition will continue to be necessarily mediated by the colonial past.

Because of the continuing power and claim of colonial history, and because of the steady salience of caste for determining and reflecting social (and economic) position, it is likely that most political debates about issues concerning social distribution will continue to invoke caste as the principal classificatory category for social action. While it is clear that caste will be seen by many as a retrograde substitute for class politics, it is also clear that caste politics will continue to be the ground for powerful social movements in India. Ironically, a social institution that calls such persistent attention to issues of differential privilege and access to wealth will also continue to have contradictory effects. Class-based political movements will necessarily be linked to caste-based movements, in part benefiting "forward" groups in "backward" castes. And left politics will inevitably focus more powerfully on the majoritarian "Hindu" community than on "minorities" who figure disproportionately in any objective classification of "underprivileged" communities in India. If caste is the historical sediment of inequality in Indian society, it is also the sociological precipitate of processes that have worked to naturalize the position of the Hindu majority. Caste-based politics obviously work against the extreme claims and interests of the Hindu right, but neither provide an unambiguous basis for social and economic redistribution nor militate sufficiently against the current communal crisis in India. Nevertheless, caste may be the only successful terrain on which noncommunal and socially progressive politics might be built in the present political climate. The contradictions of colonial history seem destined to stay with independent India for a long time to come.

Although it could be argued that the most appropriate example of a minority in the case of India would be the Muslim community, my present research concerns caste rather than religious communities. While this paper began as a consideration of the construction of untouchability in contemporary India, it became, for a variety of reasons, a general consideration of the role of caste more generally in marking "minority" groups for the purpose of redistributional policies in the form of positive discrimination. I am grateful to my research assistant and graduate student, Parna Sengupta, for locating many of the materials used in this paper.

1. Quoted in Hiranmay Karlekar, *In the Mirror of Mandal: Social Justice, Caste, Class and the Individual* (Delhi: Ajanta Publications, 1992), 4.

2. In this paper I will not consider the case of scheduled "tribes," the development of a national policy toward "tribals," and the peculiar history of the relationship of the category of tribe to that of caste. Suffice it to say that I need to write an entirely separate essay on this issue. However, it can be noted here first that the tribal population of India was estimated at between 5 and 7 percent of the population and was judged to be very unevenly distributed, with preponderant populations in states such as Orissa and Madhya Pradesh. Second, there has been very little controversy about the provisions for scheduled tribes, in part because actual implementation has stressed protective and developmental schemes rather than actual reservations. The anthropological dimensions of the debate over how to classify tribals is in fact extremely interesting, ranging from Verrier Elwin and Furer-Haimendorf's insistence on completely separate sociological identities to Ghurye's belief that tribals were particularly "imperfectly integrated classes of Hindu society." See G. S. Ghurye, *Caste and Race in India* (Bombay: Popular Prakashan, 1968), 19. The former view prevailed, in part because of Elwin's role in drafting tribal policy under Nehru. Finally, the general policy of government toward scheduled castes was assimilationist, whereas the policy toward tribals was in part to preserve their separate integrity. For a summary of some of these issues, see Marc Galanter, *Competing Equalities: Law and the Backward Classes in India* (Berkeley: University of California Press, 1984), 147–53.

3. Clause 340, quoted in Agrawal and Aggarwal, *Educational and Social Uplift of Backward Classes: At What Cost and How?* (New Delhi: Concept Publishing Company, 1991), 18.

4. Galanter, *Competing Equalities,* 31.

5. Despite the sense on the part of some that Gandhi had acted against the best interests of untouchables, and on the part of others that Ambedkar had worked against the best interests of nationalism, the Poona Pact did raise concern about untouchables to a new height. Whereas some Congress leaders had worked to advocate specific rights of untouchables, particularly concerning issues such as temple entry, Congress now dedicated itself to the cause of removing untouchabil-

ity. A conference of Hindu leaders, convened in Bombay on September 25, 1932, to ratify the Poona Pact, unanimously adopted the following resolution: "This Conference resolves henceforth, amongst Hindus no one shall be regarded as an untouchable by reason of his birth, and that those who have been so regarded hitherto will have the same right as other Hindus in regard to the use of public wells, public schools, public roads and all other public institutions. . . . It is further agreed that it shall be the duty of all Hindu leaders to secure, by every legitimate and peaceful means, an early removal of all social disabilities now imposed by custom upon the so-called untouchable classes, including the bar in respect of admission to temples" (Galanter, *Competing Equalities*, 33).

6. J. H. Hutton, *Caste in India: Its Nature, Function, and Origins* (Bombay: Oxford University Press, 1961), 194.

7. Galanter, *Competing Equalities*, 134; he goes on to note: "The resulting list, then, designates all of those groups who in the view of Parliament require the special protections provided by the Constitution: it defines who may stand for reserved seats and enjoy benefits and reservations for the Scheduled Castes. But it does not necessarily include every person or group that might be considered "untouchables" by any conceivable definition. It omits some groups which historically suffered disabilities (e.g., Ezhuvas) or which would be untouchables in terms of the 1931 census tests. And it excludes non-Hindus (other than Sikhs) who would clearly seem to be untouchables within the judicial test of 'origin in a group considered beyond the pale of the caste system'" (134). Galanter also surveys the change over time in the list, finding it remarkably constant, and consistently bound to an idea the caste should play the primary role in designating the scheduled castes.

8. *Community* in recent Indian usage has come increasingly to stand for a section of the population differentiated by religion or caste or both; e.g., Muslim, Hindu; Brahman, non-Brahman; caste Hindu, untouchable. *Communalism*, or *communalist*, refers to persons or ideologies that stress community for political purposes, or in the context of social/religious antagonism.

9. For full quotations and citations, see Galanter, *Competing Equalities*, 73–74.

10. Ghurye, *Caste and Race in India*, 292.

11. Lloyd and Susanne Rudolph, *The Modernity of Tradition: Political Development in India* (Chicago: University of Chicago Press, 1967), 150.

12. The Lokur Committee.

13. See Rudolph and Rudolph, *The Modernity of Tradition*, 149, n. 49.

14. The Commission for Scheduled Castes and Scheduled Tribes was established in 1978.

15. See Report of the Commission for Scheduled Castes and Scheduled Tribes, 1982–83.

16. M. J. Akbar, *Riot after Riot* (New Delhi: Penguin Books, 1988), 45.

17. Galanter, *Competing Equalities,* 166.

18. N. K. Bose, *Culture and Society in India* (Bombay: Asia Publishing House, 1967), 188 (reprint of "Who are the Backward Classes?" *Man in India* vol. 34).

19. Galanter, *Competing Equalities,* 166.

20. Eugene Irschick, *Politics and Social Conflict in South India: The Non-Brahman Movement and Tamil Separatism, 1916–1929* (Berkeley: University of California Press, 1969), 218–74; 368–72.

21. Ghurye, *Caste and Race in India,* 287–88.

22. Ibid., 288.

23. Ibid., 289.

24. Ibid.

25. Ibid., 290.

26. Ibid., 283; he went even further to suggest, "Perhaps, in the name of justice and efficiency, the time has come when the interests of the Brahmins have to be protected against the majority party" (291), though ultimately he dismissed this idea as well because of his argument that special representation was unnecessary and harmful.

27. Ibid., 290.

28. Ibid., 285.

29. Ibid.

30. Ibid., 283.

31. Ibid., 291.

32. Ibid., 303.

33. This reckoning constituted a population of 116 million, about 32 percent of the total population of India. This figure did not include women as a separate group, although the Commission recommended that all women in India made up what was in effect a backward class (Galanter, *Competing Equalities,* 169).

34. Galanter, *Competing Equalities,* 172.

35. Quoted in *Frontline,* September 1–14, 1990.

36. Galanter, *Competing Equalities,* 173.

37. Ibid.

38. Quoted in Galanter, *Competing Equalities,* 175.

39. Quoted in Galanter, *Competing Equalities,* 178.

40. Marc Galanter, whose splendid book provides much of the information used in the preliminary pages of this paper, makes the point that as a result of the dropping of the report, the major story of preferential discrimination in favor of backward groups has been played out in the courts, both at the Center and in the states. The bulk of his massive study concerns this legal history.

41. Galanter, *Competing Equalities,* 186.

42. Ibid., 186–87.

43. *India Today,* September 15, 1990, 34.

44. Ibid., 35.

45. *Frontline,* September 15–28, 1990, 27.

46. *Economic and Political Weekly,* October 6, 1990, 2231.

47. Ibid., 2234.

48. Rajni Kothari, *Caste in Indian Politics,* 1970; "Caste and Politics: The Great Secular Upsurge," Op ed piece, *The Times of India,* September 28, 1990.

49. This had also been argued by the political scientists Lloyd and Susanne Rudolph, in *The Modernity of Tradition.*

50. M. N. Srinivas, A. M. Shah, and B. S. Baviskar, "Kothari's Illusion of Secular Upsurge," Letter to Editor, *The Times of India,* October 17, 1990.

51. *The Times of India,* November 13, 1990. Mehta is not only a BJP sympathizer but argues in this same piece that it was the threat of Islam that in this case produced the modern hereditary forms of caste. I obviously don't want to suggest that these views go along necessarily with the critique of colonialism, but the fact that they can go together is not insignificant as well.

52. Personal communication, and see interview in *India Today,* May 31, 1991.

53. This in a paper, "From Paternalism to Populism: The History of Affirmative Action in India," delivered to the Center for South and Southeast Asian Studies, the University of Michigan, October 1991.

54. By this I refer to the fact that arguments made against the British, and in the context of British colonial rule, are frequently used uncritically in the postcolonial period, when despite the continued salience of national unity as a concern, issues of social justice and redistribution must be addressed in new and less defensive ways.

55. Ashok Guha, "Reservations in Myth and Reality," *Economic and Political Weekly,* December 15, 1990.

56. Veena Das told me in a private communication that she has cited my work; Dharma Kumar cited my work in the paper she delivered at the University of Michigan noted above. While not all arguments against Mandal can be automatically designated as unprogressive, there is little doubt that the primary political instincts behind colonial critiques and Mandal critiques would appear to most observers as fundamentally different, if not completely opposed.

57. Guha, "Reservations in Myth and Reality," 2718.

58. Dharma Kumar, "The Affirmative Action Debate in India," *Asian Survey,* 1992, 290–302.

59. See Beteille, *Caste, Class, and Power: Changing Patterns of Stratification in a Tanjore Village* (Berkeley: University of California Press, 1985); *Castes: Old and New, Essays in Social Structure and Social Stratification* (Bombay: 1969); *Society and Politics in India: Essays in a Comparative Perspective* (New Delhi: Oxford University Press, 1992).

60. André Beteille, "Caste and Reservations: Lessons of South Indian Experience," *The Hindu,* October 20, 1990. It is important to note that these invocations of colonialism come on the part of scholars who have until very recently either

ignored or seemed completely unpersuaded by arguments about the importance of writing colonial history into sociological theory.

61. A point made even more strongly by Dharma Kumar, "The Affirmative Action Debate in India," 290–302.

62. Op Ed article, *The Hindu,* October 27, 1990.

63. *India Today,* Special Forum, "Caste vs. Class," May 31, 1991.

64. Interview with Ashis Nandy, *Frontline,* October 13–26, 1990.

65. Interview with Upendra Baxi, *Frontline,* October 13–26, 1990.

66. P. Radhakrishnan, "OBCs and Central Commissions," *Seminar,* vol. 375, November 1990.

67. Aditya Nigam, "Mandal Commission and the Left," *Economic and Political Weekly,* December 1–8, 1990.

68. Shiv Visvanathan, "Mandal's Mandala," *Seminar,* vol. 375, November 1990.

69. This concept was initially that of Milton Singer, *When a Great Tradition Modernizes* (New York: Praeger, 1972).

70. Ghurye, *Caste and Race in India,* 300.

71. Ibid., 301.

72. *Report of the Seminar on Casteism and Removal of Untouchability,* 1955, 136. For Srinivas's general views, see *Caste in Modern India and Other Essays* (London: Asia Publishing House, 1962) and *Social Change in Modern India* (Berkeley: University of California Press, 1966).

73. Edmund Leach, ed., *Aspects of Caste in South India, Ceylon, and Northwest Pakistan* (Cambridge: Cambridge University Press, 1960), 6–7.

74. Louis Dumont, *Homo Hierarchicus: The Caste System and Its Implications* (Chicago: University of Chicago Press, 1990), 222.

75. Ibid., 222.

76. See Dirks, "Castes of Mind," *Representations* (winter 1992).

77. I argue elsewhere that caste, in some ways like the domestic domain as identified by Partha Chatterjee, has taken on the symbolic role of a traditional space used by many, particularly in upper caste groups, to take shelter from the contradictions of colonial history. See Chatterjee's argument in *A Nation and Its Fragments* (Princeton: Princeton University Press, 1994).

78. See Dirks, *The Hollow Crown: Ethnohistory of an Indian Kingdom* (Ann Arbor: University of Michigan Press, 1993); "Castes of Mind"; "Recasting Tamil India," in C. J. Fuller, ed., *Caste in India Today* (New Delhi: Oxford University Press, 1996).

Making Minorities: The Politics of National Boundaries in the Soviet Experience

Ron Suny

Soviet peoples, for the most part, did not consider themselves "minorities," as they were often labeled in the West, but peoples, even nations, living in their historic homelands. Like other claims about the Soviet nationalities, this seemingly transparent statement of "fact," in fact, covered (and perhaps covered up) much more opaque aspects of the formation of "nations" within the body of the Russian Empire and the Soviet Union. First, in most cases what might be recognized as nations were formed only quite recently and in a paradoxical relationship with the intentions and practices of the Soviet government. Second, while it was true that these nations were most often majorities in their constituted "homelands," the homelands themselves were more a product of Soviet policy than of the internal cultural and social construction of the indigenous peoples (the "natives"), referred to in Sovietological terminology as the "titular nationalities." But, third, even the majorities of non-Russian republics and regions lived within relations of power between the national peripheries and the Russian core or metropole of the Soviet empire (a deliberately chosen formulation) as minorities (*natsmeny* in Soviet jargon) in the larger context of a political system in which boundaries between administrative units were more formal than substantive. Finally, minorities existed in yet another sense, as either diaspora populations of nations consolidated elsewhere in the union (e.g., Armenians in Russia), or as people without any designated homeland within the Union of Soviet Socialist Republics (e.g., Soviet Greeks), or as small peoples that had no other homeland except that within a Soviet homeland of a larger people (e.g., the Gagauz in Moldavia). By the end of the Soviet period, people living apart from their homeland or with no homeland at all numbered about seventy-three million. Minorities existed as a result of complex historical experiences and the discursive understandings and internal and external representations that constructed them as minorities. More specifically, minorities were created in the process of nation-making. The constitution of national communities affiliated with state apparatuses constituted other communities as minorities.

The very attention given to "national minorities" has ebbed and flowed in the changing historical conditions of the last two hundred years. It is striking how the problems of national minorities, already recognized in the discourses of the "principle of nationality" and "national self-determination" in the late nineteenth and early twentieth centuries, rose to public and intellectual attention in the interwar years. Exacerbated by the Versailles settlement and the confrontation with the impossibility of creating the desired utopia of "each nation its own state, each state its own nation," the problem of national minorities became the subject of dozens of monographs and political analyses and the object of concern by the League of Nations.[1] While the *Encyclopedia of the Social Sciences* in the 1930s recognized the immediacy of the problem of "Minorities, National" with a separate article, its successor, the *International Encyclopedia of the Social Sciences,* in 1968 subsumed nationality in a more general sociological treatment of "Minorities" that included religious, linguistic, racial, and other subjugated groups. The earlier article, by Max Hildebert Boehm, began by defining a national minority as "a distinct ethnic group with an individual national and cultural character living in a state which is dominated by another nationality and which is viewed by the latter as the particular expression of its own individuality."[2] The minorities referred to are always in "a defensive position" and do not include ruling or privileged minorities. Though Boehm elaborates the objective criteria that lead to the sense of minority oppression, he notes its connection to the development of modern nationalism and the context of a politics of popular sovereignty and majority rule. The later article, by Arnold M. Rose, heightens the subjective perceptions that lead to the construction of minorities, which, however distinguished from the majority objectively, are constituted when they "think of themselves as a differentiated group and are thought of by the others as a differentiated group with negative connotations." Minorities are furthermore "relatively lacking in power and hence are subjected to certain exclusions, discriminations, and other differential treatment."[3] As a reading of these two articles, separated by thirty years, illustrates, the trajectory of scholarly thinking on minority problems has moved toward an acceptance of the discursive construction of minority, an appreciation of the incompleteness of the ethnic construction of nations and the presence of "imperial elements," and a recognition of the heightened danger to vulnerable ethnic minorities in the nationalizing states of the twentieth century.[4]

By now the idea of nationality and "race" as social and cultural constructions has been widely accepted in social science and historical scholarship. What remains to be specified are the ways in which these identifications are conceived and perceived. Though in conventional usages its definitions range from citizenship to ethnicity, I propose to consider nationality as the modern, secular form of identity based on a notion of shared "ethnic culture" (itself constituted, changing, and contested) of a community that has acquired a degree of coherence and consciousness that enables its members to be mobilized for collective political goals. Nationalities exist within the modern (from the late eighteenth century) discourse of the nation that cohered around the notion of bounded territorial sovereignties in which the "people," however constituted (civilly or ethnically), provide legitimacy to the political order. In this discursive universe, nationality (and the nation, which may be imagined in nonethnic terms) is seen as an ancient, even primordial community based on common descent, the most natural division of the human species with a durable, continuous historical existence, and a shared destiny. Conceived of as a basis for political autonomy or independence, with claims to a specific territory constituted or imagined as the people's original "national" homeland, nationality is both a real historical position, in the sense that a given group of people share certain communalities (which may include language, culture, geographic space, historical experience) and a discursive formation that achieves its greatest coherence with self-consciousness.

National identity involves the passive identification with this imagined community called the nationality or nation, while nationalism is the more robust discourse or movement that holds the nation to be the primary and highest location of loyalty and identity, even as it is itself imagining and constructing that nation. As a doctrine nationalism holds that humanity is divided into nations, that political power lies within the collectivity of the nation, and that the nation is only fully realized in sovereign states.[5] In many cases modern nationalities and nations evolved from premodern ethnoreligious communities, or what Anthony D. Smith has called "ethnics." Since I have said it better elsewhere, allow me the pretension of quoting myself:

> Though ethnic and nationality might be distinguished in any number of ways—size, attachment to territory, secular versus religious identity, "soft" versus "hard" boundaries—the most fundamental difference is not some "objective" characteristic internal to the group, but rather the discursive universe in which it operates and realizes itself. A modern nationality, with all its familiar qualities and political claims—popular sovereignty, ethnicity as a basis for political independence, and a claim on a particular piece of real estate—are only possible within the modern (roughly post–American revolution) discourse of nationalism. Whatever Greeks in the classical period, or Armenians in the fifth century, were, they could not be nations in the same sense as they would be in the age of nationalism.[6]

In modern times the project of the nation has been to make the political and national unit congruent, to bind the state and nationality into a single community, and further to "nationalize" the state (make its population, language, and culture as homogeneous as possible) and "statify" the nation (empower the nation politically through dominance of the political apparatus). The project of the nation is to create a nation-state, something like those model states of western Europe (Portugal, Spain, France, and Britain) that have appeared to nationalists to be political communities based on a single, primordial ethnicity. In fact, these idealized types of nation-states themselves fail to fit the expectations and aspirations of nationalists, and most nations have been seen by some scholars of nationalism as small empires. In his study of "internal colonialism," Michael Hechter argues that even in Britain, one of the earliest national states, an English core historically dominated and exploited a Welsh, Scot, and Irish periphery through a cultural division of labor that over time contributed to the further development of distinctive ethnic identifications on the periphery. Internal imperialism here had the effect of creating national minorities through a culturally stratified division of labor that gave advantages and disadvantages to people based on ethnicity. What look to be relatively homogeneous nations today were the hard-won result of efforts at statebuilding and internal national integration and consolidation that homogenized certain social and cultural differences. But it is only after the fact that one can determine whether state-building with national integration or empire-building with inequitable relations between core and periphery has occurred. If the core has been successful in integrating the population of its expanding territory into accepting the legitimacy of the central authority, then state-building has occurred, but if the population rejects or resists that authority, then the center has only succeeded in creating an empire.[7] Empires might be seen as failed or incomplete nations. Since very few nations are fully homogeneous and multinational states are often dominated by a single nationality with other nationalities in subordinate relationships, the metaphor of empire applies much more widely than its conventional usage.

While they appear in the homogenizing, essentializing discourse of nationalism to be stable, even permanent political and cultural constructions, nations, I would argue, are far more fragile and changing. Threatened both by transnational developments, like migration, communication revolutions, and the globalization of labor and capital, as well as by subnational fragmentations, like regionalism, nations need constantly to be reinforced, their internal distinctions ameliorated or erased, their members disciplined and socialized into national subjects, and their boundaries and definitions policed.

In contrast to many of the historians of nationalities who celebrate the antique roots of their nations and the moments of past glory that mark a progressive liberation from colonialism, in my own work I have tried to explain the ways in which relatively inchoate ethnicities became consolidated into more coherent and conscious nationalities in the late imperial and Soviet periods.[8] My own narrative has stressed the relative weakness of identity with the nation in the grand sense among the peoples of the Russian Empire and the Soviet Union in the early decades of this century, the limits of national consciousness largely within an urban intelligentsia, and the fragility of nationalism as a mobilizing force—except in the case of a handful of nationalities during the Russian civil war. In the late Russian Empire, national appeals were almost always combined with populist and socialist rhetoric, and the loyalties and identification of the largely peasant populations were far more often with localities or supranational religious communities than with the national community proposed by a fraction of the intelligentsia. All nationalist movements in the Russian Empire, except the Polish, argued in favor of autonomy within a liberated Russia rather than full sovereignty and independence. This may have been a prudent tactical choice—witness the risky dealings of Georgian Social Democrats, like Noe Zhordania, with German agents promoting Georgian independence during the world war—but in most cases independence was either a desperate choice made in the face of few alternatives or was actually foisted on the peoples of the empire by foreign powers. This said, however, the years of civil war (1918–21) witnessed the appearance of independent states along the Russian periphery, some of which were formally recognized and physically supported by the Great Powers of Western and Central Europe, as well as the Ottoman Empire, the United States, and Japan. The appeals of the nationalist intelligentsia, many of whom led the fledgling states in the years of Bolshevik weakness and Soviet conquest, gained a resonance before the war's end. The boundaries of the nationally conscious community expanded rapidly as populations were mobilized in life and death struggles over their loyalty to class or nation. Using the terms of Miroslav Hroch, nationalism jumped from stages A and B, where it was largely located in a patriotic intelligentsia, to stage C, where a newly mobilized town and country gave it nearly irresistible power.[9] By 1920 Lenin's government was prepared to compromise with the evident power of nationalism, either by recognizing the independence of states that their armies and allies could not incorporate into the new Soviet republics or by coopting nationalists into their own project of building a multinational federation.

The Soviet leadership conceived of the USSR as a nonnational state, and no notion of a Soviet nationality (analogous to the Yugoslav nationality under Tito) was allowed to develop. When internal passports were reinstituted in 1932, a Soviet citizen could not declare Soviet nationality on his or her passport but choose only from the officially sanctioned list of nationalities (Uzbek, for instance, but not Sart). That choice was constrained by the nationality of one's parents, and only in the case of mixed parentage could a descendant choose one or the other. Nationality, then, was related to descent, to ancestry, within the limits of the official Soviet inscription of existing nationalities. Ironically for a state that saw itself as overcoming nationalism and eventually fusing the peoples of the world into a single internationalist community, Soviet nationality policy reinforced national identification with substate nationalities, not with the all-Soviet "people," and gave nationality a powerful salience in social and political life. Nationality was hardened, fixed, in many cases unalterable, certainly not the "cultural construction" or perceptual identity of poststructural or postmodern theorists. It had to do with biology and belonging to a community of descent, not with choice or a community of consent.

Lenin had been determined to combat Russian chauvinism and had sought to create institutions and practices that would prevent the reemergence of a Russian-dominated state. Thus, the Soviet Union was designed to be neither an empire, in which one people dominates and exploits others in an inequitable arrangement, nor a nation-state, in which the state is identified with and works to include others into a single nationality. Furthermore, Lenin rejected the most radical Marxist thinking on the nationality question, that of Rosa Luxemburg, Iurii Piatakov, and Nikolai Bukharin, which proposed that no recognition at all be given to nationality and that class alone be promoted as a relevant social category. Lenin was adamant in his support for national self-determination (to the point of secession!) and was convinced that ethnic separatism and nationalism were caused by inequitable treatment of non-Russians, cultural repression, and imperialist exploitation. Only a tolerant policy toward non-Russians, he argued, would draw them into the new, egalitarian federation.

The Soviet program of integration of non-Russian peoples into a single multinational state was at one and the same time a grand vision of a non-imperialist, internationalist state and a deeply contradictory, and ultimately imperial, project. Unlike the empire it replaced, the Soviet Union was committed to respect the diversity of the peoples of the federation and to give them forms of political institutionalization and cultural rights that they had never enjoyed. But as an official form of identity, like class and gender, nationality carried with it privileges and unintended burdens and disadvantages. The official category of nationality gave Soviet citizens an identification with units of government below that of the Union itself, with their republics or autonomous districts. As Rogers Brubaker points out, "the thoroughgoing state-sponsored codification and institutionalization of nationhood and nationality [was accomplished] exclusively on a substate rather than a statewide level."[10] This unusual notion of formally recognizing nationality at a substate level was carried out with great effort and cost through the 1920s and into the early 1930s until, beginning in 1931–32, Stalin's government began a rapid retreat from the full institutionalization of national representation.

The vision proposed in the initial arrangements that formed Lenin's plan for the USSR was of a multinational federation in which all peoples were given equal rights and opportunities and a positive model was provided for peoples outside the Union to encourage them to join. Based in their ideological commitments to internationalism and anti-imperialism, their conviction that international socialist revolution was on the horizon, and their realistic acceptance of the multinationality of the Eurasian continent that they ruled, the Leninists' policy of state-building was at the same time an elaborate and costly exercise in the building, not of a single nation, but literally of dozens of nations. Not only would there be no dominant majority nationality, but by creating territorial enclaves for nationalities down to the village level there would not even be many national minorities. Each compact group of people would have its own unit in which to live and work.[11]

Nationality for the Soviet government was an objective characteristic of the human personality conditioned by historical experience, linguistic and ethnic culture, and—in Stalin's formulation—by location in a specific territory.[12] Each citizen had a nationality that was passed on from parents to children, but the full rights and privileges that accrued to nationality were available only in specific national territories belonging to that nationality. An Armenian might be represented by Armenian officials, educated in Armenian, and have available Armenian radio only in Armenia or in Armenian territories in other republics, but would not have such privileges automatically available elsewhere.[13] Nationality was borne by persons and by territorial units, but territories were most often multinational, and people did not always live in their national territories. The principles of personal ethnocultural nationality connected to descent and national territory connected to a numerically dominant nationality pulled in opposite directions that are caught in the dual usage of the word *nation* in English. On the one hand, *nation* is that collectivity of people, regardless of where they live, who conceive of themselves as a shared community of common origin and destiny. On the other hand, *nation* is used to mean state, a territorially bounded polity that may or may not be congruent with a single ethnic community. Seldom do the boundaries of the nation, in the first sense, and the state (or nation in the second sense) coincide. National diasporas and national minorities are testimony to the bad fit between nations and nation-states. In our own times the nationalizing state attempts to bring those two ideas of the nation together, to homogenize the state and repatriate the diaspora, but that particular utopian solution often requires the bloodiest of methods—ethnic cleansing and genocide.

The Soviet state was not immediately faced with the problems inherent in these contradictory ideas of the nation (they would have to be faced by the successor states of the USSR). Within the Union both could coexist. The state determined which rights were available and where, and independent associations or lobbies of nationalities were not permitted. Though migration, urbanization, and industrialization were expected to move peoples toward a more universal, nonethnic culture, in the 1920s the government did not promote assimilation into a common Soviet or Russian culture and, in many ways, worked against assimilation to allay the fears of non-Russians.[14] The government's initial solution to multinationality was to multiply national territories and to shift boundaries between them to approximate as closely as possible the existing ethnic lines. As they created national units and drew ethnic lines, Soviet officials defined ethnicity, sharpening the distinctions between certain groups, like Bashkirs and Tatars, and eliminating other distinctions, even consolidating new nations, as with the various groups that were amalgamated into the Uzbek people.

Making Uzbekistan

The story of the Uzbek people illustrates a number of dimensions of Soviet nation-making and the production of minorities. The Central Asian steppe and deserts were populated by Turkic- and Mongol-speaking tribes whose identities were both imposed from outside and generated within. *Uzbek* was a name first used by foreigners and applied to Tatar tribesmen following Ghlyath ad-Din Muhammad Uzbek (Ozbeg) Khan, a fourteenth-century descendant of Genghis Khan. In Persian sources of that time Ozbeklyan (Uzbeks) referred to these Tatar troops on the Volga, with their capital at Saray, and had nothing to do with the people who eventually would bear the name *Uzbek*.[15] Between the 1360s and 1380s the eastern Qipchaq Plains were known as the Uzbek region. Still further removed, the name Uzbek was applied to Turkic-Mongol tribes roaming in Siberia near the Tobol River. Siberian tribes, the subjects of Abul Khayr Khan, were united into an Uzbek confederation between 1428 and 1468. After the Timurids wrote of the Uzbeks as uncouth, the term *Uzbek* fell out of use, by the sixteenth century, and was replaced by *Turklar* and *Tajiklär* for nomads and *Sart* for urban dwellers and settled peoples. Only distant foreigners, like the Safavid historians, continued to refer to *Uzbeks*.[16]

By the early twentieth century the eponym *Ozbek* (*Uzbek* in Russian) was no longer widely used. The Russians referred to the settled peoples as *Sarts* and the nomads as *Kyrgyz* (present-day Kazaks; today's Kyrgyz were then known as *Karakyrgyz*) and Turkmen. Throughout Central Asia the term *Sart* had a pejorative sense, especially when used by nomads like the Kazaks.[17] The linguist Evgenii D. Polivanov (1891–1938) noted that

Russian settlers in Central Asia spoke of the local people as Sart, Sartishka, or *zver* (beast).[18] No single homogenizing term existed for the nomads and settlers who together would become the Uzbeks after 1924. Soviet ethnographers who studied the region concluded in 1925 that "Uzbeks could not conceive of the same sort of unified and distinct ethnic group for themselves as the [nonurban] Kazaks, Kirgiz, or Turkmens." Uzbek cultural-linguistic boundaries were "extremely diffuse," and those called *Uzbeks* by some and *Sarts* by the Kazaks "had nowhere created a particular ethnic identification for themselves."[19]

The larger Central Asian region was known to the Russians as Turkestan—not by the regional names later established by the Soviets (Uzbekistan, Turkmenistan, Kyrgyzstan, and Tajikistan)—and the first Soviet administration in the region was the short-lived Turkestan Autonomous Government (Qoqan Autonomy) (December 1917–March 1918). The Muslim modernizers, known as *Jadids,* spoke of a single millet (community) making up Turkestan, and one newspaper noted that the *khälq* (ethnicity) in the region was 98 percent Muslim. A generalized Turkestani or Muslim identity remained predominant on the official level when the Soviets created the Autonomous Turkestan Republic on April 30, 1918.

But as the central Soviet government moved toward a federal system based on ethnocultural territories, rather than on larger regional units, boundaries between nationalities, both geographic and cultural, had to be drawn. In January 1920, the Turkestan Commission, appointed by Lenin, decided

> to acknowledge as necessary the administrative regrouping of Turkestan according to the ethnographic and economic circumstances of the territory. Also required is to outline the following groupings: Turkmens (of Transcaspia), Uzbek-Tajiks (Samarkand, Farghana and part of Sir Darya Oblast'), Kirgiz [that is, Kazaks] (part of Sir Darya Oblast', Amu Darya Otdel and Semirechenskaia Oblast').[20]

Turkestan was to be divided among a number of constituent peoples, while the emirates of Bukhara and Khwarazm with related peoples were to remain semi-independent states. Nevertheless, as Edward Allworth writes,

> For several more years Turkistan spelled place, territory, history, statehood, and people. The designations Kazak, Turkmen, Uzbek, and the

like seemed to refer to literature, languages, and subordinate ethnicity and remained disconnected from government, nation, and politics. Some spoke of *Turkistanlilär* (Turkistanians) as a single community (millet) made up largely of Turki. . . . As late as 1920 or 1922 uncertainty persisted concerning the designation *Uzbek* in general communication. . . . Indifference to Uzbek as a heading showed itself in both the Turkic and the Slavic written languages in Central Asia at least until 1925.[21]

The making of new republics in Central Asia was a process at one and the same time of ethnic consolidation of subnational groups (tribes, settled populations, etc.) into larger nationalities and the breakup of certain regional, religious, and even tribal unities. The potential unity of the diverse cultural and linguistic affiliations of Central Asia was broken up by new borders, though the supposition that the Bolsheviks splintered Central Asia in a deliberately Machiavellian move to prevent future Muslim unity requires more evidence than has been available to those scholars who have put forth such a claim. Ethnographers were employed as experts in ethnic definition, but political opportunism, lobbying by locals, and historic administrative divisions all played roles in the eventual boundaries between peoples and territories.

Whatever the motivations of Lenin and Stalin, the new "nations" being created were as problematic as the Turkestani or Muslim community being fragmented. In 1924 the Turkestani Communist leader Fayzullah Khoja complained that "existing political borders of the republics of Central Asia (Turkestan, Bukhara, etc.) are artificial. These borders unjustly tear apart each of the tribes [*elät*] that lives in those republics," and he spoke of an "artificially contrived hostility between the ethnic groups [*khälqlär*] of Central Asia."[22] But the tearing apart was accompanied by amalgamation. What had been tribal and local affiliations were combined into new nationalities. As the Fifth Bukharan Congress of Soviets admitted on September 20, 1924,

Although the majority of the population's makeup of Central Asian *oblasts* historically, in fact, belongs to the Turkic nationality, in the course of its history the population split into tribes distinguished by way of life, daily existence, and economic situation. Constant clashes, wars, and antagonism compel us to regard these tribes as separate, independent nationalities . . . [The congress] finds it imperative to put the life and destiny of all nationalities in their own hands [and] for this reason to create an Uzbek republic.[23]

As nomads and settled peoples were combined into a new nationality, the term *Sart* that had distinguished settler from nomad disappeared altogether, and all were now categorized as *Uzbek*.

The ethnic segmentation of the region was not accomplished without opposition. Late in 1923 delegates from Farghana to the Twelfth Congress of Soviets of the Turkestan ASSR called for creation of an autonomous Farghana because the region was ethnically heterogeneous. But after the congress (January 1–8, 1924), the Central Asian Bureau resolved that the local regions should follow the decisions of the Eighth, Tenth, and Twelfth Congresses of the Communist Party for "divided-up" [*äjrätish*] nationality territories.[24] Only in February did the Central Committee of the Bukharan Communist Party declare that it was time for Central Asia to be divided along ethnic lines, and Fayzulla Khoja proposed the establishment of an ethnic Uzbekistan. Fearful of the consequences of partitioning their country along ethnic lines, the Communists of Khwarazm also protested, but in vain. On April 28, 1924, the Central Asian Bureau of the Communist Party declared its support for dividing Central Asia along "ethnic" lines, choosing some ethnic distinctions to be more salient than others.[25]

The borders of the new republics were set by state authorities and did not correspond to the boundaries of the states that had existed in the region. The Emirate of Bukhara was divided among Uzbekistan, Turkmenistan, and Tajikistan, while the Khiva Khanate was parceled out to Uzbekistan, the Karakalpak autonomous region within Uzbekistan, Turkmenistan, and Kazakhstan, and parts of the Kokand Khanate were found in Uzbekistan, Tajikistan, Kyrgyzstan, and Kazakhstan. The very drawing of borders left minorities on each side, though many people re-identified themselves with the titular nationality of the republic in which they found themselves. Since ethnicity was contested rather than clear, and populations were mixed, conflicts developed over the disposition of major cities. In August–September 1924 there was a conflict over which republic would have Tashkent. Kazakhs had controlled Tashkent during the mid–eighteenth century, and in the early 1920s Kazakhs lived around Tashkent, though not as much within the city where Sarts dominated. Tashkent went to the new Uzbek republic. The Tajik-dominated cities of Bukhara and Samarkand also went to Uzbekistan, creating an urban Tajik minority within the Uzbek state. Similarly, large numbers of people who became Uzbeks (that is, Turkic-speakers rather than Tajik Persian-speakers) ended up in the Tajik Autonomous Soviet Socialist Republic, formed by the end of 1924 within the RSFSR (Russian republic). On May 11, 1925, the Twelfth All-Russian Congress of Soviets formally approved the breakup of Turkestan. As Allworth points out,

> The Russians never held a plebiscite among the population of Central Asia and called no popular referendum to select the group name most desired by the Taranchis or the Sarts for the 1920s. The authorities arbitrarily selected dead or dying medieval designations and conferred them on the people of the region by political decree.[26]

Now that states had been formed, nations had to be created to fill them. A people without a common history had to be given one. The tribes within the borders of Uzbekistan were reconstituted as a nation, while distinctions were drawn between this new people and those of neighboring republics. In the fall of 1926 a new Uzbek latinized alphabet was introduced, ending the usage of Arabic script that linked present to past and was intelligible to all literate Islamic peoples of Central Asia. Soviet authorities developed an Uzbek language based on the Tashkent dialect of Qipchaq-Uzbek, which pronounced certain consonants differently from other dialects. In 1935 four letters marking vowel sounds were eliminated, thus differentiating Uzbek from other Turkic languages.[27]

From the 1920s the Soviet policy of "nativization" or "rooting" (*korenizatsiia*)—called *yerlilashdirish* (localization, indigenization) or *milliylashdirish* (nationalization) in Uzbekistan—promoted local ethnic and linguistic culture and the development of native cadres in the government and party. By March 1, 1928, Uzbek personnel in the apparatus had reached 23.5 percent. Though *korenizatsiia* was envisioned as an anticolonialist program, it was largely carried out by a party heavily populated by Russians and Russian speakers. One Communist leader from Samarkand wrote: "Uzbekification goes on among us in such a way that Uzbeks and coachmen-Uzbeks sit at the head of institutions; one rides, the other drives, and Russians direct the work. Is this really Uzbekification? Isn't this colonialism on the Russian side?"[28]

Cultural nativization meant both cultural recovery and innovation. The Timurid statesman and Herat poet Mir-Ali Shir Nawaiy (1441–1501), the author of *Sadd-i Iskandariy* (Alexander's Wall), was appropriated as part of the Turkic (and more specifically Uzbek) legacy. Official Soviet historiography in the 1930s categorized Timur as an Uzbek, playing down his Mongol heritage. But the limits on permissible "nationalism" were strictly policed. In 1936–37 officials criticized the interest in the Chaghatay literary past as nationalism. A theory of ethnogenesis developed around 1940 that emphasized that the Uzbek people existed before its name. An ancient people living in a distinct territory with an unbroken line of language development was conceived as the basis for the modern nation. After Stalin's death, the oral epic *Alpamish,* which earlier had been condemned as too Muslim, was reclaimed as part of the Uzbek heritage.

By the last decades of the Soviet period a number of prominent Western writers on Soviet nationalities argued that Soviet nation-formation among Muslims had largely been a failure and predicted that a common *Homo Islamicus* would unite Muslims against *Homo Soveticus.*[29] But with the loosening of central Soviet authority under Gorbachev, the power of republic and national allegiances was demonstrated with a bloody ferocity in Osh (Kyrgyzstan), where Kyrgyz and Uzbeks fought one another over land, and in the Uzbek part of the Ferghana Valley, where Uzbeks and others turned on the immigrant Meskhetian Turks, who had been exiled from their native Georgia to Central Asia by Stalin. Less violent frictions divided Uzbeks and Tajiks. According to the official Soviet census of 1989, the city of Samarkand was populated by 100,000 Tajiks and 140,000 Uzbeks, though any visitor was far more likely to hear Tajik on the streets than Uzbek. In 1988 Tajiks in both Samarkand and Bukhara demonstrated to have these cities annexed to the Tajik Soviet Republic, imitating the actions of the Armenians of Nagorno-Karabakh in Azerbaijan.[30] In general, the predicted unity of Muslims proved much more ephemeral than the ethnic and republic identifications that had been consolidated during the Soviet period. And at the same time the Central Asians, far more than the non-Russians in the Baltic or Transcaucasian republics, acquiesced in their subordinate status in the modernizing program of the Soviet empire. There was little extralegal dissidence in the Muslim republics, and in the last years of the USSR and the first post-Soviet years the sounds of conflict between Russians and Muslims were considerably more muted than between peoples who had traditionally been Muslims.

The story of nation-making in Soviet Central Asia was one in which subnational identities were lost as populations were blended into a larger, designated "nation," and in which supranational identities, such as Islam or Turkestan, were eroded as a result of the interventionist, antireligious, and territorializing policies of the Soviet state. Through the extension of mass education, people acquired literacy in one of the major literary languages identified with the republic-level nationality. The salience of the new national identification was reflected in high intermarriage rates among the subnational ethnicities that made up the new nation but very low rates between different national (and non–Central Asian) populations.[31] Among Uzbeks the subnational groups, such as Kipchaks or Kuramas, were in a variety of ways pressured to identify themselves as Uzbek, though subnational identification and consciousness did not disappear. In the post-Soviet period there has been a revival in many areas of regional, clan, and subnational ethnic identification, though the newly independent, nationalizing states may prove to be even more assimilationist toward such peoples than the Soviet regime was. Boundaries have produced minorities throughout the region, like the Tajiks and Kyrgyz in Uzbekistan or the Uzbeks in Tajikistan, and among the legacies of Soviet colonialism has been the migration and exiling of European and Far Eastern populations to Central Asia. In Soviet times the Russians, Ukrainians, Armenians, and Jews of Tashkent shared a collective identity as *Evropeitsy* (Europeans), and though many left around the time of the dissolution of the USSR, the city remains a cosmopolitan capital.

Nation Making on the Volga and the Formation of the USSR

For Soviet nation-makers the problem of minorities was intractable, connected as it was with the very process of nation formation. In the Volga region, where powerful anti-Soviet movements contested Soviet power from the first days after the October coup, Soviet leaders experimented with a number of state-building projects to win over the non-Russian peoples of the region.[32] But what satisfied one people, the Tatars of Kazan, was anathema to most of their kindred people, the Bashkirs. And smaller peoples, like the Chuvash and Mari, feared becoming impotent minorities within ethnically defined states dominated by the more urbanized and advanced Tatars. Tatars and Bashkirs basically speak the same language with some minor dialectical differences, but their sense of separate identity stems from the more settled nature of the Tatars and the nomadic, pastoral life of the Bashkirs, particularly in the more easterly regions. Paradoxically the Bashkirs were more consistent in their ethnic identification. The word *Bashkir* dates from at least the tenth century. From the sixteenth century Bashkirs were a somewhat privileged estate in the Russian Empire, and for almost seventy years (1798–1863) they were constituted as the Bashkir Host, tsarist defenders of the eastern frontier. With the loss of their privileged status in the late nineteenth century, Bashkirs were threatened by advancing Russian settlement, encroachment on their grazing lands, and assimilation (in the more westerly regions) into a Turco-Tatar community.

Tatars, on the other hand, were more divided in their sense of ethnic identity. Many of their intellectual leaders preferred an identification with the general Muslim community, others with a Tatar-Bashkir people, still others with either a Tatar, Bulgar, or Turco-Tatar "nation." Because of their close association with Bolsheviks in Kazan and their own leftist activists, like Mir-Said Sultan-Galiev, the Tatars convinced Lenin and Stalin to support a Tatar-Bashkir Republic in 1918. But the bulk of the Bashkir activists, rather than be subsumed in a common polity which they feared would be dominated by Tatars, turned toward the Whites and open combat with the Red Army. The Tatar-Bashkir Republic never had more than a formal existence, however, and was opposed from a number of directions. Internationalist socialists were against any concession to the principle of nationality, while the smaller peoples of the Volga—the Chuvash, Mari, and Baptized Tatars—rejected the Muslim hegemony of the Tatars in the republic. When the leadership of the Bashkir autonomy movement defected back to the Bolsheviks early in 1919, Moscow dropped the idea of a Tatar-Bashkir republic and supported an autonomous Soviet Bashkortostan. Eventually a number of the smaller ethnic groups of the Volga and Ural region were also given their own autonomous districts or republics, but the progressive dividing of the region, as much as possible along ethnic lines, could not overcome the complex mixing of ethnicities in the region that made it impossible to preclude minorities and diasporas within the autonomous territories. Again, many Western scholars have insisted that the overriding Soviet motivation in its nationality policy was "divide and conquer," but Daniel Schafer in his close study of the Tatars and Bashkirs concludes that "the declaration of a Tatar-Bashkir republic and then a separate Bashkir republic was indeed a policy of *divide et impera,* but the enemy that Lenin and Stalin sought to divide was not a Turkic nation-in-formation (be it Turko-Tatar or Tatar-Bashkir), but the anti-Bolshevik movement."[33]

Ideology and opportunism, improvisation and invention, rather than a master plan or sinister antinational motives, appear to have been the ingredients that led to the multinational mosaic of autonomies in the Soviet Union. The Soviet state and its nationality policy was never simply the product of a top-down, center-initiated, ideologically generated, imposed solution to the problem of maintaining a multinational empire. The non-Russian peripheries generated their own solutions, some rejected, others accepted by Moscow. "Facts" were created politically and militarily far from Moscow that the Soviet leadership found expedient to accept. Much of what became the Soviet Union was forged in state weakness rather than strength. But in the context of fragmented and conflicting identities, the Soviet state was able to intervene forcefully into the very making of new nations.

At the very end of 1922 four Soviet republics—the RSFSR, Ukraine, Belorussia, and Transcaucasia—joined to form the Union of Soviet Socialist Republics. The process of state- and nation-building had, in many senses, only begun. Within these larger republics a number of autonomous republics and districts based on nationality were formed. They either represented a distinct nationality living in its own designated homeland, like the Abkhaz in Georgia or the Bashkirs in the RSFSR; or a separated diaspora population, like the Armenians in Nagorno-Karabakh in Azerbaijan or the southern Osetians in Georgia; or a distinct religious minority, like the Ajars (Muslim Georgians) in southern Georgia. At a lower level, national soviets were formed for smaller populations, as in Ukraine for Germans, Jews, and Poles. By 1930, at the height of the movement to create national territorial soviets, there were 127 national districts in the RSFSR, 27 in Ukraine, and 18 in Transcaucasia, not to mention the 4,264 national village soviets in the RSFSR, the 1,085 in Ukraine, and the 67 in Belorussia.[34] Though at one level, and in some republics, Soviet nationality policy had the effect of homogenizing smaller ethnicities into larger "nationalities," elsewhere, and at different times, Moscow was called upon to protect minority ethnic populations and mediate potential conflict. Making nations also made minorities. Within and among the nations that the Soviets created were minority populations that depended on the long reach of the imperial state for protection against the nationalizing agendas of the larger nationalities.

By the time Stalin consolidated his autocratic dictatorship in the early 1930s, the Soviet Union had a pyramid of nationality institutions in which tens of millions of people lived in formalized homelands. Though all real sovereignty was lost to those nationalities, the processes of nativization and cultural and cadre development continued. What had been largely peasant nations, like Ukraine and Belorussia, turned with the forced industrialization of the 1930s and the consequent urbanization into socially differentiated nations with their own working classes and intelligentsias. Ethnicities and ethnoreligious communities increasingly became self-conscious nationalities and nations with the potential to be mobilized for national political goals. When the hypercentralized power of the Stalin years was diffused to a limited degree among the union republics in the 1960s and 1970s, a number of minorities petitioned to Moscow for support against the local national Communist elite. When the Soviet system withered from within and the central government abdicated its will to rule its own empire at the end of the 1980s, the nations-in-making moved quickly to take over the state apparatuses left them by the Soviet system and declare themselves nation-states ready to play in the international arena. In many cases the ethnic minorities and diaspora populations that now found themselves outside the empire and at the mercy of new nationalizing states looked toward Moscow for assistance. The Abkhaz and Osetians, the Karabakh Armenians, and the Slavic peoples and Turkic Gagauz of Moldova all sought outside support against the new national governments of their home republics. The tragic result of the formation of nations in the USSR was violent and bloody confrontation in the late-Soviet and post-Soviet period between majority and minority populations over the definition of the nation, its cultural and linguistic content, and its boundaries.

NOTES

1. See the short bibliography attached to Max Hildebert Boehm, "Minorities, National," *Encyclopedia of the Social Sciences,* Edwin R. A. Seligman, ed., vol. X: 518–25 (New York: Macmillan, 1933, 1937); and C. A. Macartney, *National States and National Minorities* (London: Oxford University Press, 1934).

2. Ibid., 518.

3. Arnold M. Rose, "Minorities," *International Encyclopedia of the Social Sciences,* David Sills, ed., vol. X: 365–71, at 365 (New York: Macmillan and The Free Press, 1968).

4. For an elaboration of the imperial nature of modern nation-states, see Michael Hechter, *Internal Colonialism: The Celtic Fringe in British National Development, 1536–1966* (Berkeley: University of California Press, 1975). On nationalizing states, see Rogers Brubaker, "Nationhood and the National Question in the Soviet Union and Post-Soviet Eurasia: An Institutionalist Account," *Theory and Society* 20 (1) (February 1994): 47–78; Dominique Arel, "Ukraine: The Temptation of the Nationalizing State," paper prepared for the AAASS, November 17–20, 1994.

5. Here I am following the definition given by Anthony D. Smith, *Theories of Nationalism*, 2d ed. (London: Duckworth, 1983), 21.

6. Ronald Grigor Suny, *The Revenge of the Past: Nationalism, Revolution, and the Collapse of the Soviet Union* (Stanford: Stanford University Press, 1993), 13.

7. Michael Hechter, *Internal Colonialism: The Celtic Fringe in British National Development, 1536–1966* (Berkeley: University of California Press, 1975), 60–64.

8. This is the central argument of Suny, *The Revenge of the Past*.

9. Miroslav Hroch, *Social Preconditions of National Revival in Europe*, Ben Fowkes, trans. (Cambridge: Cambridge University Press, 1985).

10. Brubaker, "Nationhood and the National Question in the Soviet Union," 50. Few states have engaged in the practice of formally institutionalizing nationality at the substate level. Brubaker mentions the Hungarian half of the Habsburg Empire after 1867, where Hungarian speakers were constituted as a nation but other peoples in Hungary were forced to identify with the Hungarian nation. One might add the example of present-day Ethiopia, where a government of a minority people has instituted a policy of formal recognition and institutionalization of substate nationalities.

11. "No other state," writes Brubaker, "has gone so far in sponsoring, codifying, institutionalizing, even (in some cases) inventing nationhood and nationality on the sub-state level, while at the same time doing nothing to institutionalize them on the level of the state as a whole" (ibid., 52).

12. Stalin's enormously influential definition of nation was generated in a prorevolutionary pamphlet (1913) commissioned by Lenin as an answer to the Austro-Marxist idea of "extraterritorial national cultural autonomy." He wrote: "A nation is an historically constituted, stable community of people, which emerged on the basis of a common language, territory, economic life, and psychological make-up manifested in a common culture" (I. V. Stalin, "Marksizm I national'nyi vopros," in *Sochinenlia*, 11 (Moscow: Gosizpolit, 1951), 296.

13. There were exceptions to this rule in the 1920s and after, e.g., Armenian schools and theaters in Moscow, Baku, and Tbilisi, where there were no formally constituted Armenian national territories.

14. This point is made strongly by Terry Martin in his dissertation, "An Affirmative Action Empire: Ethnicity and the Soviet State, 1923–1938" (Ph.D. diss. in history, University of Chicago, 1996).

15. The discussion of the ethnogenesis of the Uzbeks comes largely from Edward A. Allworth, *The Modern Uzbeks: From the Fourteenth Century to the Present* (Stanford: Hoover Institution Press, 1990).

16. Ibid., 43.

17. Martha Brill Olcott, *The Kazakhs* (Stanford: Hoover Institution Press, 1987), 18.

18. Allworth, *The Modern Uzbeks*, 178.

19. Ibid., 179, 181.

21. Ibid., 184–85, 191.

22. Ibid., 195.

23. Ibid., 201.

24. Ibid., 199.

25. Moscow briefly conceded to keep the Khwarazmian republic as the only heterogeneous state in Central Asia, but in July the Executive Bureau of the Khwarazm Communist Party reversed itself and called its earlier decision mistaken. The Central Committee in Moscow declared that the republic should be divided ethnically.

26. Ibid., 206.

27. Ibid., 237–38.

28. Ibid., 220.

29. See particularly chapter 8, "Homo Islamicus in Soviet Society," in Helene Carriere d'Encausse, *Decline of an Empire: The Soviet Socialist Republics in Revolt,* Martin Sokolinsky and Henry A. La Farge, trans. (New York: Newsweek, 1979), 250–65; and the critique of this thesis by Michael Rywkin, *Moscow's Muslim Challenge, Soviet Central Asia* (Armonk, N.Y., 1982), 105–7.

30. Dilip Hiro, *Marx and Muhammad: The Changing Face of Central Asia* (London: HarperCollins, 1994), 173–74.

31. Robert Kaiser, "Nations and Homelands in Soviet Central Asia" and "Social Mobilization in Soviet Central Asia," in Robert Lewis, ed., *Geographic Perspectives on Soviet Central Asia* (London: Routledge, 1992), 251–312.

32. This section on the Tatars and Bashkirs in the revolution and civil war is based on the work of Daniel Evan Schafer, "Building Nations and Building States: The Tatar-Bashkir Question in Revolutionary Russia, 1917–1920" (Ph.D. diss. in history, University of Michigan, 1995).

33. Ibid., 348.

34. Martin, "An Affirmative Action Empire," chap. 4, 54.

Comment

Marc Ferro

Ron Suny's analysis concerns two essential aspects of the minority problem in the Union of Soviet Socialist Republics. In the first place, it constitutes a sharpening of the theories on these issues developed in political science by considering the schema Soviet theoreticians had constructed; it thus completes the cycle begun long ago by Boersner.[1] In the second place, Suny applies this apparatus to a case study that he completely commands, that of Central Asia and the Caucasus in the 1920s, examining in detail the example of Uzbekistan.[2]

We would like to supplement this contribution, on one hand, by establishing a diagnosis of the situation of these populations at the time of perestroika and, on the other, by observing the effects of the leaders' policies, such as they were perceived from below, an approach that R. Karklins recently advanced.[3]

To begin with, one notes that locally the policy of de-Russification carried out since the 1920s, resulted in certain Muslim republics in the process of a sort of self-government by their indigenous population. Even in Kazakhstan, where in 1986 Russians made up close to two-fifths of the total population, out of 300 leaders, more than half were of Kazakh origin.[4] What is more, responding to a survey that asked, "if the citizens had the feeling that during recent decades past the natives' power had grown," 67 percent of Kazakhs responded "yes," while 57 percent of Balts responded "no," that it had decreased.

In these conditions, it is astonishing that Gorbachev could have been surprised that the Baku militia failed to stop the massacre of Armenians; more than 50 percent of the militia's soldiers were of Azerbaijani origin. They replied to him that "Azeris were certainly not going to fire upon Azeris in order to protect Armenians." It is not at all surprising, on the contrary, that the dismissal of a highly placed official, such as the First

265

Secretary of the Party, could have set off the riots of Alma-Ata, not because he was hostile to perestroika but because a Russian was being substituted for a Kazakh. Similarly, it was not the transfer of authority from Armenians, victims of the Azerbaijanis, to Dushanbe in Tajikistan that was considered an affront, but the fact that they could be given priority housing, by decision from Moscow, while there were thousands of homeless in the region.

There was also a tendency of the republics, each in its own way, to achieve a de facto autonomy, asking furthermore that its population become homogeneous. Here one grasps the fundamental difference from Algeria which, from an indigenous point of view, had no autonomy at all: neither the prefects, the mayors, the judges, nor the police commissioners were Arab in 1954. But the difference stops with regard to Chechnya, maintained in the Russian Federation by a juridical fiction which resembles that of Algeria, "those three French departments."

Second, one notes that although the republics of Central Asia had governed themselves before independence, in their daily life at least, this did not necessarily mean that they had separatist wishes. Unlike Morocco or Tunisia in the 1950s, these Muslim republics did not all necessarily have in view the project of an irreversible rupture, the stages of which would be arranged with Moscow. On the contrary, in Central Asia, there was a sort of *inverse separatism,* in the sense that the republics' leaders tried to influence the central authorities of the former USSR. For example, Pavlov, the finance minister—one of the participants in the coup d'état against Gorbachev—had direct ties with the Uzbek state apparatus and its mafia; he was suspicious of any modification of the statutes of the republics. Conversely, and in this context, it is hardly surprising that, just before the conflict between Yeltsin and Gorbachev, the majority of these same republic leaders were on the side of Gorbachev, who wanted to preserve the union, and against Yeltsin, because along with the proclamation of Russia's sovereignty there was included a process that would lead to the separation of each republic, and that would ruin the advantages that these republics received from the center. It is not surprising that in these conditions, their political machines took the side of the putschists.

Third, one notes that the changes Gorbachev wanted—perestroika, perceived in Russia as an opening toward liberty—were in the Muslim republics perceived as a danger for the future of traditional social relations that communism had in some way perpetuated—the president of the Soviet was often a former khan, tribal links remained, and so forth.[5] Furthermore, all of Islam was alarmed that while it called for the opening of mosques, the central power was openly flirting with the Orthodox Church. Each demand from an Islamic country was seen as the sign of a possible allegiance to the Iranian ayatollahs, a behavior that led to a veritable Islamic political movement the likes of which had not been seen since the 1920s and the variants of which reinforced the identity of each republic vis-à-vis its neighbor: from the Shiite integralism that dominated Tajikistan to Azerbaijan's more secular Islam. This phenomenon of identity reinforcement, linked to the requirements for the survival of the governmental apparatus in each republic, played against both the reunification of "Turkistan" and the absorption of this Islamic group by its neighbors, Turkey, Iran, or Pakistan. It should be added that the tempo of the Islamic Revolution, in Iran or elsewhere, and of the crisis of the Soviet republics did not coincide, which undoubtedly prevented a drift of Soviet Islam toward these countries that shared ethnic identity.

Another observation: The republics on the southern rim found themselves in a situation that was both post- and precolonial. Postcolonial, as Alain Blum has shown, in the sense that the departure of the Russians preceded, and by a lot, both perestroika and independence; that, except for the case of Chechnya, would otherwise have been labeled a successful decolonization, since young Russians working abroad (in lieu of military service) were appealed to.[6] It was only in Kazakhstan, where Russians maintained positions of responsibility, that conflicts of a colonial sort continued. Precolonial, where ethnic conflicts that predated Russian conquest reappeared between Georgians and Abkhazians, for example, and certainly between Turks and Armenians. In other circumstances, Russians found themselves arbiters, as if centripetal and centrifugal forces were canceling each other out, according to time and place.

Above all, the observations made with regard to the Muslim or Caucasian republics take on a specific significance if the latter are compared to the non-Muslim populations of Siberia. At the Siberian Congress of Krasnioarsk, held in 1992, one delegate pointed out that the goal of the meeting was to put pressure on Moscow; another, that it was not a question of separating from Russia but rather a warning about the separatism of the republics of Tuva, Yakutsk, and Buryatiya, all in the heart of the Federal Republic of Russia, and so forth. The Evenki explained that they looked to move from territorial to national autonomy, but in a Russian, not Siberian, framework. This last point suggests that in formulating demands an ethnic element was not necessarily a key factor and that there was not necessarily an ulterior separatism among all the non-Russian peoples either, although the Baltic peoples were absolute and single-minded on separation, which was favored by the majority of Ukrainians, Armenians, and other Christian populations. But when the Tatar republics, in the heart of the Russian Federation, claimed their sovereignty, it was to control their own resources: and in Siberia, the same demand came simultaneously from Russians, Yakuts, and Buryats. It was this that was at the origin of the Chechen war, even if it ultimately became anti-Russian.

Thus falling back on identity, the birth or rebirth of a nation, linked most often to ethnic, ethnolinguistic, or even religious considerations, can be associated just as well with more political considerations, combined or not with these other factors. Autonomy can intersect all these elements, without necessarily leading to the nation-state, a formation after all that can at some times be permanent, sometimes transitory.

NOTES

1. D. Boersner, *The Bolsheviks and the National and Colonial Question* (Geneva, 1957).

2. R. G. Suny, *The Baku Commune,1917–1918* (Princeton, 1972), 414.

3. R. Karklins, *Ethnic Relations in the USSR, the Perspective from Below in the USSR* (Boston, 1986).

4. *Biobibliografia Obscestvovedou Kazaxstana* (Alma Ata, 1986).

5. C. Humphrey, *Karl Marx Collective: Economy, Society, and Religion in a Siberian Collective Farm* (Cambridge, 1983), 524.

6. A. Naitre Blum, *Vivre et Mourir en URSS, 1977–1991* (Paris, 1994). See also G. Charachidzé, "L'Empire et Babel, les minorités dans la perestroika," *Le Genre-Humain, Face aux drapeaux* (October 1989).

Essentialisms of Aboriginality: Blood/Race, History, and the State in Australia

Aram A. Yengoyan

The minority debate in Australia regarding the status of Aboriginal Australians within the national polity brings forth a number of issues that are far from resolution. Within the contemporary context, this debate invokes a vast range of historical, cultural, and economic forces as well as political ones, which not only make the issues all the more complex, but also project the more distant and recent past into the present with more force than they originally possessed. My aim is to draw together, through different perspectives, the various threads that the minority debate takes on. The playing-out of history and initial cultural contact in the present invokes a lively and vitriolic debate, especially in contemporary land rights issues that now embroil virtually all of Australian society.

First, it goes without saying that Aboriginals and the idea of Aboriginality are such that they do not and will not define themselves as a minority. The fact that the Aboriginal societies have inhabited Australia for nearly 40,000 years means that they were the first and sole occupants of Australia and that the land is theirs, a circumstance interrupted by Captain James Cook in only 1788 at which time the forces of British colonialism and imperialism dispossessed the Aboriginals of that which is truly their own.

Second, the history of black-white contact is replete with numerous accounts of population and cultural carnage that persisted throughout the nineteenth century and in some remote areas until the 1930s (Elder 1988). While most Aboriginal cultures still occupy their traditional lands, it is especially in those areas where they have been dispossessed through mas-

269

sacres, population decline due to disease, and forced relocation that Aboriginal peoples feel they must confront the state (national and local) as a means of reacquiring the heritage the past endowed to them.

Last is the issue of the symbolic value of land. For Aboriginal cultures, land is the source of all being and existence. Virtually all facets of the religious pantheon from ritual to myth to cultural ontology are explicable only through an understanding of the role that land and place play in establishing the spiritual force as it emanates throughout local cultures and provides emotional sustenance. The return to ancestral lands and tracks is vital for all Aboriginal peoples, for it is the land-place and the tracks that unite living groups with their ancestors and their past deeds. From the Euro-Australian perspective, space/place/land itself means little if anything, for the issue to white Australians is not land per se but the production and the commoditization of production. Captain Cook took the Australian land mass on behalf of the British Empire, but it was mainly because of what land promises economically, namely, production, which is so central to the European vision of conquest. Even to this day, our tax laws on land reflect this difference: unutilized lands are normally taxed much less than land under production.

The history of European and Aboriginal contact has been written in many ways, but there is also a strong sense of silence on the issue. Until the 1950s, most scholars writing the history of Australia were silent on the role of Aboriginal populations. In part this silence was related to the notion that the Aboriginal past would die out, and by the 1930s, it was assumed that assimilation policies toward Aboriginal peoples meant that these cultures and peoples were in radical decline and would eventually pass away. However, this did not occur. Furthermore, historians left the Aboriginal discussion to anthropologists who still saw Aboriginal cultures through the faulty concept of "the ethnographic present," which stressed a timeless, unchanging perspective of Aboriginals, effectively divorcing them from history and cultural transformations. By the 1950s and 1960s, anthropologists finally moved toward a historical perspective, especially as it was invoked through the illuminating writings of C. D. Rowley (1970, 1971a, 1971b, 1986).

The silence is now vocal. Not only have historians and anthropologists turned to Aboriginal history, but Aboriginal writers themselves are writing local histories as well as collecting oral histories and biographical case histories and shedding light on local variants of contact.

The Roots of Primitivism in History

The European expansion and colonization throughout the world after 1500 brought forth a whole set of new experiences and interpretations that signaled that the Western world was approaching the pinnacle of evolutionary growth. If Hegel felt that the modern nation-state of his day was the culmination of political and social development, it is not by accident that such an interpretation created, perpetuated, and verified what Western exploration had encountered by 1750 or even earlier. A few historical encounters, such as China, might prove equal to the Western accomplishments, but overall, most historical moments in the exploration and expansion indicated that many of the encountered "others" were only marginally human and some of the "others" might not be human at all. This historical trajectory not only enhanced the West, but it also created a vast spectrum of potentially unbridgeable differences.

One of the dominant issues in the depiction of Aboriginals in the early contact period is the extent to which Europeans thought of the Australian Aboriginal as falling within the realm of humanity. In the dichotomy of nature/culture, it was evident to early pre-Cook navigators that these ancient inhabitants of continental Australia were either an extension of nature or somewhere in between nature and culture. Vignettes from early maps, mostly before Cook but also in some cases after Cook, portray the Aboriginal in two ways. One is a depiction of a thick tropical or temperate forest which has trees, vines, ferns, and a range of animals including kangaroos, wallabies, emus, and dingoes. Embedded within this "thick" natural conception are individual natives forming a portrait that all men and beasts are part of nature. Another theme semi-isolates humans from "thick" nature but adds tails on Aboriginals, thus forming a composite that while Aboriginals are really not nature they are also not like our Western sense of cultured humanity. These vignettes dominate our conceptions, especially when they portray the Tasmanians.

Throughout the nineteenth century, the Aboriginal is portrayed as fully human although as the lowest and most base conception of humanity. This form of primitiveness is manifest in their limited technological development, the absence of any form of government, the lack of agriculture, and in the total picture of social life as a gross extension of nature. Here, the totalizing image is that Aboriginal social life is geared only toward survival. Again, nature sets the parameters of this survival, and the Aboriginals cannot go beyond the natural limits of their environment (see Donaldson and Donaldson 1985 for a more complete account of this cultural description).

The primitivism of the Aboriginal gains a greater contrast when early voyagers and explorers portrayed the Polynesians as being almost like the early Greek states. Polynesians are dressed in togas and wear olive branches as headgear, which are the early markings of a civil society. In this contrast, it is clear that the idea of government is essential in bringing forth the contrast between British notions of the state of nature manifested by Aboriginals as opposed to the state-like systems of rule by law expressed in Polynesia (Smith 1985).

By the nineteenth century, this primitivism was also endowed with special attributes that the early explorers felt to be critical in the exploration of the interior of Australia. Carter (1992) notes that European explorers in central Australia seldom used photography, although it was well known by the nineteenth century, both in Australia and elsewhere. These explorers attributed special visual keenness to Aboriginal trackers, namely, the ability to operate in the desert with a highly developed sense of mnemonics which functioned as mapping and tracking devices in a way that could not be captured through photography. All of these special attributes were primarily an extension of desert and environmental adaptations that made the Aboriginal unique.

In another way, the British encounter with Aboriginals in Australia is unique. Historically, British common law declared Australia *terra nullius*. While the continent was inhabited by indigenous societies, the British presence operated on the presupposition that the land was empty, even though in many areas local peoples actively resisted British military ventures and colonial expansion. The declaration of *terra nullius* also meant that the land was not conquered but simply settled. One of the most drastic results of this policy was that treaties were never made with Aborigines, consequently the land interests of whites were never reconciled with indigenous claims regarding land use and land tenure (Tonkinson 1990:216).

Within the British empire and its resulting colonial structure, the declaration of *terra nullius* in Australia was unique. It never was experienced in any other British colonial context.

Thus, the British colonization of New Zealand and the conflict between the British and Maoris resulted in the defense of Maori lands by warriors in a series of pitched battles culminating in the Treaty of Waitangi (1840), which acknowledged the existence of the Maoris as owners of the land (Rowley 1970:15). In Australia, no treaties were ever signed, thus land was annexed by the British government as Crown lands. Furthermore, all land remained Crown land since "native" claims were nonexistent. In New Zealand, the Treaty of Waitangi was eventually violated by the Crown in the following decades, but it provided the foundation on which contemporary Maori populations could make a valid and at at times effective claim for restoring their rights to their land.

History: Race and Blood

Contemporary writers on race and the foundations of racism toward aboriginal peoples are divided regarding their interpretations. One interpretation is that race as a biological issue is an expression of structured class inequality and an ideology justifying the colonial situation. In such explanations, racial ideology must be assumed to be a dependent variable, since it would vary according to how local class relations articulate whites, full-blooded Aboriginals, and those whose ancestry would be labeled as "half-caste." Cowlishaw (1986, 1987, 1988) argues that race and the ensuing racism is primarily created from differential class relations, but over time, the ideology of inequality embeds and reveals itself in a racial ideology. Through a sociological and anthropological analysis of a rural New South Wales town, Cowlishaw contends that race per se is not an essentialism. What is missing in this analysis, however, is the extent to which skin color is linked to personal and group identity. Color, like gender, cannot be turned on and off, and thus its existence is all the more embedding and embracing in comparison to certain cultural and behavioral traits that might be individually variable or at least not as binding on the individual as color and gender.

Other writers on the subject place more emphasis on how skin color and race might underlie social class and patterns of inequality. In an excellent summary on the issue of race, blood and aboriginal identity, Tonkinson (1990:207) notes, "Skin color is not irrelevant for Aborigines, although they do not accord it the same prominence as whites do. As noted in the foregoing discussion of local identity, Aborigines apply color labels but do not attribute any necessary behavioral concomitants to color, though there are individual exceptions." However, Trigger's (1989) analysis is more open to the idea that skin color and black ancestry have a greater impact on the attribution of psychological, cultural, and class factors as they relate to the formation of ideological divisions of superiority and inferiority.

Throughout these varied opinions, a few generalizations can be made. One is that European ideas on race, racial differences, and the allocation of socioeconomic attributes have had an impact on aboriginal peoples' thoughts on these issues. This does not mean that precontact Aboriginal groups had no social cleavages or ideas of difference. Such forms of difference existed, but the underlying logic that created a sense of difference was culturally specific. More important, all the writers note that the use of the category "blood" is central to understanding how difference is created and what it includes. The use of terms like *white-fella, black-fella, yella-fella* is based on the idea that they differ in blood, and consequently peoples of different blood have different physical features, different habits and thought, and they interact differently with one another. But blood is not simply a matter of exclusion or a matter of drawing boundaries between individuals and groups. Blood itself is what holds and binds individuals who share a common biological, cultural, and social experience. Thus matters of inheritance, be it biological or social, combine all the attributes that form a collective expression as a binding tie in which groups are constituted and that define how they relate to others who are different.

In the historical context, race is the great dividing issue. Although the Aboriginal population was and is a very small fraction of the total population (now less than 2 percent), the racial gap of White and Black, or what the Aboriginals call *white-fella/black-fella,* is a divide that cannot be breached. On top of this biological dichotomy, cultural and social attributes are added to make the contrast all the more apparent, even glaring. Racial difference, then, becomes the idiom that captures and magnifies all other differences.

By the late nineteenth and early twentieth centuries, however, this dichotomy was further twisted by Christian missionaries and later welfare policies. Full-blooded Aboriginals were converted to Christianity, especially in those areas where the local cultures were greatly decimated. Thus, throughout Victoria, New South Wales, and parts of South Australia and Queensland, local missions were the only institutions that embraced Aboriginal peoples. While some actual conversion occurred, it is evident that these people were dying off, and the task was to "smooth the dying pillow."

If race created the great divide, blood ties and links created a middle arena in which the civilizing force of Euro-Australian life might bring benefits. The working assumption was that if an individual Aboriginal had some fraction of "white" blood he/she might be saved and directed toward the benefits of Western civilization. Unions and marriages between blacks and whites fostered "half-caste" offspring, and any fraction of white blood then became the key ingredient for personal enhancement. Thus, blood becomes the barometer for cultural salvation or semisalvation. This attitude was translated into the arena of missionization, welfare institutions, adoption, homes for parentless children, and so on. Up until the 1950s, children were removed from mixed unions or marriages and sent to welfare and other social institutions in various parts of southeast and eastern Australia, mostly in urban areas or large towns. Even if parents were residing together as a family, the removal of children served as a means of redirecting infants to a different social climate by which they could be "saved." But the potential to "save" a child depended directly on the fraction of white blood in one's veins. Blood became the essentialism through which all the benefits of white society as well as the enhancement of personal progress would unfold.

Aboriginal Self-Consciousness: The Importance of Blood

Throughout the history of White Australia, the history of Aboriginal people has been one of cultural trauma and degradation that reached a pinnacle by the 1930s. However, in the past thirty years, a growing sense of self-awareness combined with the regeneration of their own cultural and historical destiny has gradually assumed new and creative proportions.

The various threads, which created a common yet unique experience, come from a broad range of historical and contemporary events, from a common shared experience, and from an evolving sense of identity that has its roots in urban areas as well as more tribal contexts of the interior. In the precontact period, Aboriginal peoples were loosely understood within a "tribal" context where a tribe was primarily a language or a dialect group. At least two or three generations of anthropologists enhanced this kind of "tribal" thinking in the literature by providing tribes with discrete boundaries, and by stressing internal social and cultural differences, thus creating a reality of small groups/societies which fit well within the social anthropological dogma of tribal structures. At the same time, certain features of Aboriginal cultures were understood as pan-Australian with regional differences. Some of these differences were produced by external influences such as the Macassan contacts with Arnhem Land, the Melanesian intrusion into northern Queensland, and the dominant changes brought forth by colonial Australian regimes and missionary activity in the southeast part of the continent.

The discourses and voices on the creation, maintenance, and reproduction of the ideas on Aboriginality come from various quarters of Aboriginal society and from the academics who have written on the subject. A national consciousness on Aboriginality started in the 1930s through the efforts of William Cooper who was the Honorary Secretary of the Australian Aborigines' League. Up to the 1930s and even beyond, each of the states created laws restricting Aboriginal involvement in the labor pool, partly by dividing the "half-castes" from tribal peoples, but also by limiting any form of social and spatial mobility (Bourke 1994:40). The logic of these restrictions was always expressed under the rubric of protectionism of the Aboriginal population but in reality left them isolated, divided, and without any mechanisms for a national voice regarding their plight and their future. The first national census that enumerated the Aboriginal population was as late as 1966–67; it was conducted by the Commonwealth government long after it was recognized that policy and practice toward Aboriginal groups could no longer be left solely at the state level.

Since the 1960s, the debate on Aboriginality has increased with no closure, and the literature is not only voluminous but also highly variable in regard to how the subject is approached (see Allen 1988; Attwood 1989; Beckett 1988a, 1988b; Bourke, Bourke, and Edwards 1994; Cassidy 1988; Hollinsworth 1992; Keeffe 1988; Keen 1988; Peterson 1989; Rowley 1986; Tatz 1979). Most writers on the Aboriginality theme stress a common set of features that constitute what it means to be an Aboriginal. The centrality of a common heritage that goes back to about 40,000 years ago is critical as a historical claim. At the same time, this historical dimension also has a biological component. Aboriginality is something that is in one's blood as well as in one's behavior. As Keeffe (1988:68–69) notes, citing an interview, Aboriginals have only one blood gene because they have always been in Australia by themselves. This is contrasted to Europeans and Asians who have three or four blood genes due to historical mixture. Biological distinctiveness makes Aboriginals different but also creates a canopy that embraces various local populations which administrators and anthropologists have claimed are not Aboriginal. The best case for this process is Tasmania. Anthropologists and archaeologists have claimed that the "Tasmanians are extinct," but when these views were aired on the national and international media, Tasmanians who were part-Tasmanians took quick offense by claiming that they are all Aboriginals. The old policy of fragmentation by blood and culture no longer holds, and thus the category Aboriginal has reshaped the dubious distinctions that were carried over from the nineteenth century. If blood means something that is inherited, its social and cultural ramifications are also far-reaching. Identity is based on a commonality of spiritualism with the land and a strong moral and ethical commitment to the value of caring and sharing, which becomes the basis of consensus decision making. The idea of giving is vital to all Aboriginal social networks, be it urban, rural, or tribal. In this context, giving is a classic example of what Marcel Mauss (1954) meant by *totales prestations* in which the exchange is initiated by the giver who perceives a need on the part of a potential receiver. This commitment to giving, sharing, and caring embraces goods, services, child care, and a whole range of needs, most of which are normally unspoken.

If these features are the essentialisms of being Aboriginal, the movement within Australia has also projected itself into the contemporary context by the creation of cultural symbols as meaningful emblems of Aboriginality. Keeffe (1988:71) notes that the colors of the Aboriginal flag are black for their race, yellow for the sun that sustains all life, and red for the blood that has been shed by past generations. The flag itself is not only an emblem but also an expression of resistance, as is the Aboriginal tent embassy in Canberra. Furthermore, Aboriginal consciousness was not limited to political actions and resistance within Australia. An Aboriginal passport was issued in 1988 and while the federal government rejected it, it was used by a delegation of Aboriginals as entrance to Libya (Tonkinson 1990:217). However, it could not be used on their return to Australia. Disputes over Uluru (Ayers Rock) in central Australia are also pivotal since Uluru as a sacred site has been converted to a national park by the Commonwealth government in conjunction with the Northern Territory Administration. Tourists come from various parts of the world, but the local Pitjantjathara who own Uluru can no longer camp next to it. Many of these symbols that emerge from primordial ties of speech, blood, and custom are in a state of contestation with national, state, and local aims.

The Essentialism of Land as Heritage

Of all the cultural, economic, and political issues that are debated and contested within the context of Aboriginality, the most volatile issue is the land rights movement. For Aboriginals, land is the spiritual and symbolic basis of existence, with the ideas of being and emotional sustenance as expressed from birth through death all fused with the land. In these traditional societies, land (along with what is below its surface) is the critical referent to which all myth and cosmology are expressed as a living ongoing existence. Even in urban contexts, Aboriginal societies and their members commonly possess a strong feeling and affinity of what land they belong to. Given a kinship framework in which both paternal and maternal ties are vital to express existence, it is evident that these ties to land can range over vast territories. Even if individuals have never experienced the land, they are fully aware of historical and mythic connections through oral histories. Over the past two decades throughout the continent, Aboriginal peoples have petitioned to get traditionally held lands returned to them. The land rights issue started with the Gurindji in Arnhem Land in 1966. What was a local matter gradually evolved into a national concern, and it is far from being resolved. The land rights movement has had some limited success; Aboriginals have taken possession of their lands in certain localities in central Australia, in the western desert, and also in Arnhem Land. However, one of the major arguments raised by Anglo-Australians regarding this shift in ownership questions what the Aboriginals are doing with land, namely how it is, or is not, utilized for production and commoditization. Throughout the Northern Territory, the major enduring complaint by Anglo-Australians is that nothing is being produced. Once again, land is simply a matter of use value. For Aboriginals, space/place/land per se is what life is all about, for it is only the land and locality that can provide emotional sustenance, an essential factor not realized in the production from the land.

The land rights movement coupled with demands for the return of traditional lands and sacred sites has become a partial impediment to the extent that capital ventures are now cautious in regard to large-scale investment that might be curtailed by local-level Aboriginal protest. Aboriginality has had a critical and dynamic role in redirecting national aims toward particular groups and problems that would have been all the more vulnerable if pan-national Aboriginal organizations and movements were absent.

Aboriginals and the State

Any understanding of Aboriginality in the past and present within the Australian context requires a detailed analysis of the role of the nation-state. The policies of the nation-state, in this case the Australian state, have had critical and long-reaching effects on Aborigines and Aboriginality. Beckett (1988b:3) notes that the situation of Aboriginals within the history of Australia has consistently been a problem, and the solution must come from the state. But one can go further by arguing that the state itself is the problem, and the solution must come from rethinking the role of the state.

By creating bureaucracies that deal with Aboriginal problems and concerns such as poverty, malnutrition, and high death rates, the state has created and fostered the perpetuation of a state of dependency that becomes enduring with no end. The creation of the welfare state which has reduced many Aboriginal peoples to wards of the state has had dire and negative consequences that have recycled back upon themselves. This welfare state is the logical growth of a form of internal colonialism that has isolated Aboriginal peoples from one another and buttressed the barriers between black and white. If the White Australia policy was a matter of national defense in relationship to what was conceived of as an external threat, the creation of the White Australia policy also had an impact on Australia's first inhabitants. Not only did Aboriginals become wards of the state under this policy, but it promulgated and enhanced all of the attitudes of racism and ethnocentrism which have firm foundations throughout all of Australian history.

Aboriginals live in Australia as a state, but they are outside of Australia as a nation. As Beckett (1988b:6–12) notes, the fact that citizenship has always been denied to them not only made them wards, but it also created the Aboriginal with no rights and no privileges in the context of civil society. While they could not be deported, it was felt that they would go the way of all "extinct races." By the 1950s and 1960s, however, when it was clear that they were not going into extinction, the role of national and state policies took on more of a policing nature. Given the fact that Aboriginal peoples could not be proletarianized as a labor force, the state charged itself with the responsibility to guarantee that local Aboriginal communities would not be a hindrance to capitalistic ventures in the form of mining and oil exploration.

Aboriginality as an Essentialistic Ideology

Many writers on Aboriginality claim that it is an ideology, and like most ideologies it has the role of persistence and also resistance (Keeffe 1988:67–80). But all ideologies, if they are to have a lasting impact, must resonate with certain cultural values and symbols that are meaningful and productive to the individuals and groups who adhere to any such movement. Ideologies are a reasoned set of notions concerning the path of politics. In one sense this is a kind of culture, since over historical time and even in the short run, ideologies, like culture, are a product of shared thought. However, the major difference between culture and ideology is that while culture is a set of conscious and unconscious givens or ontological axioms unquestioned by participants, ideologies are willfully developed paths of explanation that, in theory, are consciously developed through reasoned and rational action. It is the ideological domain that emerges through group or class interests as a means of contesting state power structures. The created ideologies, as rational and willful as they might be, are not created out of a vacuum. Symbols of ideas, meanings, and actions—the ideological structuring of any interest group, part of the class structure, or group defined by race and blood—are always mediated by cultural forms and expressions that are part of the historical-cultural basis of small societies.

In stating that Aboriginality is an ideology or expression of an ideology, it must be stressed that this ideology is not simply one of a misplaced or false consciousness. Aboriginality as an essentialism rests and resonates on certain cultural features that have a vital meaning for Aboriginal societies and their participants, but as an ideology Aboriginality is also part of a political process. The cultural foundations of being Aboriginal, whether rural or urban, are based on ideas of land, the right to self-determination, and a strong commitment to foster what it means to be an Aboriginal. Again, it is the idea of blood that combines the past (be it cultural, biological, or linguistic) into the present as a means of expressing and displaying the idea that the assimilation policies of the 1930s and 1940s are no longer viable and that Aboriginal peoples must no longer be pawns and wards of state bureaucratic structures that control their destiny. Politically, the move toward self-determination is expressed in the desire for land, an education system that is bicultural as well as bilingual, and an interest in political participation at various levels of government with a dominant concern to resurrect what is culturally vital as an emergent reality.

Yet, some social scientists maintain that this position is a falsehood. Von Sturmer emphatically argues that "'Aboriginality' is a fiction which takes on meaning only in terms of white ethnocentrism . . . This identity can be nothing more than an expression of faith. It represents an ideological position far removed from the concrete situations from which it is presumed to have drawn its substance" (1973:16–17). In response to this statement, Eleanor Bourke states that "To some Aboriginal people, this would parallel a claim that European Jewish identity is a result of its reaction to Nazi Germany" (1994:45).

Furthermore, the illusion that Aboriginals possess little or no power persists among social scientists. Writing in the early 1980s, Howard states that "Aborigines lack both the ideological and economic bases of power in contemporary Australian society; for the most part, they control neither things nor ideas" (1982:1). However, within the past ten years it is apparent that Aboriginal ideology has been skillfully crafted on a cultural foundation that has clear and vocal meaning for both blacks and whites in Australia. During the summer of 1993 and 1994, the mention of the word *Marbo* (the court case that entitled Aboriginals to land) brought forth the fright, tension, and racial antagonism that are always close to the surface. Australian newspapers ran vicious cartoons on how disruptive the *Marbo* act had become, and a resolution of this issue is far from sight.

Minority Status

It is clear that Aboriginals do not define themselves as a minority nor do they desire to be placed in that category by others. Though they are a minute fraction of the total Australian population, Aboriginals feel that their constitution is based on their own cultural parameters, which cannot be usurped by the dominant society. These persisting cultural features are reflected in many ways. For instance, conversion to Christianity has always been a moot issue, and the history of Christian missionary activity indicates that such conversions are highly problematic. Furthermore, the role that Aboriginals have played in the Australian wage economy is also marginalized by the fact that they have few cultural or social underpinnings that support and enhance a proletarian-type wage economy.

Nevertheless, White Australia continues to define Aboriginals as a minority based on the idea that they are few in number, have little or no power, and normally do not partake in national political and cultural life. But now there is a highly vocal cadre who will not retreat to the bush or to urban ghettos. Aboriginal claims on traditional land holdings will continue as the first step in correcting a historical disgrace. What the future holds is hard to say, but it is clear that the forces of Aboriginality are such that the younger generations realize that there is no backing down from their challenge to the national hegemony. To the dominant white society,

Aboriginals will always be a minority that will be difficult to incorporate and/or assimilate into white Australian society. Again the fundamental barrier is race and blood.

In 1988, the Australian government held a series of celebrations and enactments to commemorate the 200-year anniversary of Cook's "discovery" of Australia. Aboriginal protests occurred throughout many parts of the country, claiming that the start of White Australia in 1788 was the beginning of the demise of Black Australia. Although the national media attempted to minimize the demonstrations and highly vocal rallies, Aboriginality as a form of minority persistence and resistance conveyed to the world community that there is another type of Australian in Australia. The parallels between the 1988 protests in Australia and those of the 500-year anniversary of Columbus in the New World are striking. But the fact remains that Australia as one country contested by basically one minority proved to be a powerful example that helped focus the issues and debate in regard to equality under the law as well as directly attack state hegemony.

The great curtain of silence over British colonialism and imperialism in Australia has been partly lifted, and the invisible minority is no longer invisible. A historical legacy intertwined with racism and ethnocentrism persists, but small cracks are appearing in the reality and mirror of state hegemony toward its only minority.

Discussion

Throughout the various writings on the Australian Aboriginal, both by whites as well as Aboriginal writers, one notices that portraits of Aboriginal culture(s) stress a particularistic quality as opposed to any expression of universalism or universalistic thinking. This aspect of particularism is rooted in blood and tradition, in the way that life is connected to space/place/land. In many ways the dilemma of particularism is that on one side the cultural existence of local societies is viable and creative as an emergent reality. On the other side is the concern for transforming socio-cultural existence to meet challenges as they emerge from the national polity, be it new policies or practices in and through which Aboriginal peoples must respond. The political activism and the focus on land rights by Aboriginal leaders, either regional or national, have taken on a universalistic mode of argumentation. Most Aboriginal leaders or spokespersons realize that the claims they argue for also exist in other parts of the world under national regimes that are more politically repressive than those in Australia.

This universalistic depiction at the national and global level has had an impact on Australian policy toward its only indigenous minority. Yet, the depiction of what Aboriginals are cannot be framed only by what white Australia thinks they should be. Whereas other minorities (south Europeans, Asians) entered Australia and soon became "hyphenated Australians," the hyphen model will not work for Aboriginals. In part, this is due to policies regarding race, racial differences, and the inheritance from the White Australia policy of the late nineteenth century. The other side of the issue is that Aboriginals are the original inhabitants and thus an expression of inclusion is made (correctly) on the assumption that inclusion can only mean a loss of identity and blood. Cultural and historical narratives of their past simply cannot be negotiated away in a national polity based on one language, one flag, and one race.

The perceptions of Anglo Australians toward Aboriginals is difficult to determine, especially if the question is one of a national guilt and shame that whites have toward blacks. The colonial experience has been a succession of carnage and tragedy, and probably most Anglos feel a sense of shame about the past that must be rectified. Over the past thirty years, the federal and state governments have responded to this historical shame by increasing expenditures on Aboriginal needs and causes, be it for health, education, or assistance in reacquiring land, and to a limited extent for greater political involvement on the national level.

However, since the *Marbo* decisions, the various debates and the resulting fear have hardened the ill-feeling and hatred that whites have toward blacks. Now the white narrative is such that blacks are characterized as lazy, wasteful, and never satisfied with what "we" have done for them. This plus the fear that "all the land" will go back to the Blacks has sent negative shock waves from Canberra to the deepest reaches of the interior desert and pastoral lands. Of course, this portrait varies throughout Australia, for in most cases religious and academic interests have supported and still continue to support Aboriginal claims and needs.

And last is the issue of essentialism, anti-essentialism and anti-anti-essentialism. My interpretation of the importance of race (or blood), land, and the spirituality that Aboriginal peoples endow to place and space has been framed in a highly essentialistic perspective. What is critical in this analysis is to describe and express the evolving concept of Aboriginality as based on a series of cultural features that are not only real in and of themselves but that also elicit the major foundations that provide the cultural basis of Aboriginality as an ideology and as part of a highly visible political culture.

Blood, based on transmitted biological and cultural factors, is a pivotal and essential factor in what constitutes Aboriginality, and thus it cannot be dissolved into something else. This idea is difficult to express to Western audiences, for numerous reasons. One is that the writings on race and how race is constructed have stopped over the past thirty years. Within anthropology, the common thinking takes various directions. One is that if we do not talk or write about race, the problem will evaporate. Another is that race is no longer a scientific concept, thus it should be dropped. A third is the denial that anyone accepts or acts in terms of race or racial categories, thus race is a non-issue. Apart from the science of the above, it is also clear that many or most societies throughout the world think and act in terms or categories that are grounded in race. In many cases, it is part of primordial sentiments along with other feelings that are the cultural and social bases of group identity. This is not only a local concern but also affects how societies project themselves within the national and international polity. Essentialisms and primordial sentiments, which have been noted by anthropologists, have also been critical to the development of many contemporary nation-states, and they must and should be accepted as realities that cannot be dissolved away or reinterpreted within academic and intellectual debates. Over thirty years ago, Geertz (1963) dealt with the comparative problem of how primordial sentiments are expressed in a variety of structures and institutions and how "New States" and civil polities must accommodate or incorporate such essentialism. What has been learned now is that the problem of local-level sentiment is still an issue for "Old States."

Our general concern is to signify the existence of these local-level essentialisms as realities and identities that cement and bind societies to their past and probably their future. For anthropologists, it is ethnography that attempts to establish what these essentialisms are and how they operate to provide emotional sustenance to actors. But above all, ethnographic descriptions must be understood and accepted as an approximation or even a portrait of an emerging and evolving reality, a reality that cannot be dissolved in the trafficking of theory and theorists. Recently, Sahlins (1993) was even more explicit on this point:

No good ethnography is self-contained. Implicitly or explicitly ethnography is an act of comparison. By virtue of comparison ethnographic description becomes objective. Not in the naive positivist sense of an unmediated perception—just the opposite: it becomes a universal understanding to the extent it brings to bear on the perception of any society the conceptions of all the others. Some Cultural Studies types seem to think that anthropology is nothing but ethnography. Better the other way around: ethnography is anthropology, or it is nothing.

If one reads with a sense of openness the anti-essentialism tracts throughout the social sciences and the humanities, be they in theory, critical theory, cultural studies, forms of comparison, and all approaches to description, it is clear that the attack is on the idea of essence(s). Furthermore, we must always be cautious and intellectually vigilant by realizing that traveling theories travel at the expense of other traditions whose voices and sounds are muted. But as Said (1983:226–47) and the various authors in the volume edited by Clifford and Dhareshwar (1989) critically emphasize, the movement of theory, intellectual trends, and scholarly fads to other contexts without a hiatus or even a change in venue can only be understood as traveling theory combined with and supported by Western intellectual imperialism. Local essence(s), local and cultural essentialisms, and primordialism in all its expressions become grist for heavy global theories that in the long run rewrite the local into the global.

Anti-essentialism as a framework that challenges our own theories and modes of interpretation is one thing, however, one of the dangers of taking this position to its logical end is to argue that nothing exists—there is no there, there. The backlash to anti-essentialism ranging from studies in feminism to structural and poststructuralist accounts of African-American literary theory is superbly set forth in Diana Fuss's *Essentially Speaking.* Yet, on both sides of the argument between essentialism and anti-essentialism, we must be on guard against all forms of intellectual terrorism that always operate against the voiceless and the unsaid, such as Australian Aborigines.

REFERENCES

Allen, Harry. 1988. "History Matters—A Commentary on Divergent Interpretations of Australian History." *Australian Aboriginal Studies* 2:79–89.
Attwood, Bain. 1989. *The Making of Aborigines.* Sydney: Allen and Unwin.
Beckett, Jeremy R., ed. 1988a. *Past and Present: The Construction of Aboriginality.* Canberra: Aboriginal Studies Press.
———. 1988b. "Aboriginality, Citizenship and Nation State." In *Aborigines and the State in Australia,* special issue. *Social Analysis* 24:3–18.

Bourke, Colin, Eleanor Bourke, and Bill Edwards, eds. 1994. *Aboriginal Australia: An Introductory Reader in Aboriginal Studies.* St. Lucia: University of Queensland Press.

Bourke, Eleanor. 1994. "Australia's First People: Identity and Population." In *Aboriginal Studies,* ed. Colin Bourke, Eleanor Bourke, and Bill Edwards, 35–48. St Lucia: University of Queensland Press.

Carter, Paul. 1992. *Living in a New Country: History, Travelling and Language.* London: Faber and Faber.

Cassidy, Julie. 1988. "The Significance of the Classification of a Colonial Acquisition: The Conquered/Settled Distinction." *Australian Aboriginal Studies* 1:2–17.

Clifford, James, and Vivek Dhareshwar, eds. 1989. *Traveling Theories, Traveling Theorists.* Inscriptions, Group for the Critical Study of Colonial Discourse and The Center for Cultural Studies. Santa Cruz: University of California Press.

Cowlishaw, Gillian. 1986. "Race for Exclusion." *Australian and New Zealand Journal of Sociology* 22:3–24.

———. 1987. "Colour, Culture and the Aboriginalists." *Man* 22:221–37.

———. 1988. *Black, White or Brindle: Race in Rural Australia.* Cambridge: Cambridge University Press.

Donaldson, Ian, and Tamsin Donaldson, ed. 1985. *Seeing the First Australians.* Sydney: George Allen and Unwin.

Elder, Bruce. 1988. *Blood on the Wattle: Massacres and Maltreatment of Australian Aborigines since 1788.* Frenchs Forest, N.S.W.: Child and Associates.

Fuss, Diana. 1989. *Essentially Speaking: Feminism, Nature and Difference.* New York: Routledge.

Geertz, Clifford. 1963. "The Integrative Revolution: Primordial Sentiments and Civil Politics in the New States." In *Old Societies and New States: The Quest for Modernity in Asia and Africa.* New York: Free Press.

Hollinsworth, David. 1992. "Discourses on Aboriginality and the Politics of Identity in Urban Australia." *Oceania* 63:137–55.

Howard, Michael C. 1982. "Introduction." In *Aboriginal Power in Australian Society,* ed. Michael C. Howard, 1–13. St. Lucia: University of Brisbane Press.

Keeffe, Kevin. 1988. "Aboriginality: Resistance and Persistence." *Australian Aboriginal Studies* 1:67–81.

Keen, Ian, ed. 1988. *Being Black: Aboriginal Cultures in 'Settled' Australia.* Canberra: Aboriginal Studies Press.

Mauss, Marcel. 1954. *The Gift.* Glencoe: Free Press.

Peterson, Nicolas. 1989. "A Colonial Image: Penetrating the Reality of the Message." *Australian Aboriginal Studies* 2:59–62.

Rowley, C. D. 1970. *The Destruction of Aboriginal Society.* National University Press.

————. 1971a. *Outcasts in White Australia.* Canberra: Australian University Press.

————. 1971b. *The Remote Aborigines.* Canberra: Australian National University Press.

————. 1986. *Recovery: The Politics of Aboriginal Reform.* Ringwood, Vic.: Penguin Books.

Sahlins, Marshall. 1993. *Waiting for Foucault.* Cambridge: Prickly Pear Press.

Said, Edward W. 1983. "Traveling Theory." In *The World, the Text and the Critic.* Cambridge: Harvard University Press.

Smith, Bernard. 1985. *European Vision and the South Pacific,* 2d ed. New Haven: Yale University Press.

Tatz, Colin. 1979. *Race Politics in Australia: Aborigines, Politics and Law.* Arrnidale: University of New England Publishing Unit.

Tonkinson, Myrna Ewart. 1990. "Is It in the Blood? Australian Aboriginal Identity." In *Cultural Identity and Ethnicity in the Pacific,* Jocelyn Linnekin and Lin Payer, eds. Honolulu: University of Hawaii Press.

Trigger, David S. 1989. "Racial Ideologies in Australia's Gulf Country." In *Ethnic and Racial Studies* 12:209–32.

von Sturmer, J. 1973. "Changing Aboriginal Identity in Cape York." In *Aboriginal Identity in Contemporary Australian Society,* ed. Donald Tugby. Milton, Qld.: Jacaranda Press.

Comment

Alban Bensa

In commenting on the interesting article by Aram A. Yengoyan (the passages from his essay are cited in italics), I tried to consider the situation of black or white Australia—on which I am not a specialist—with regard to global transformations that currently affect the Pacific region. The remarks that follow have been developed based on references to research on Aboriginals, the rise of native nationalisms in the Pacific (in particular the independence movement of the Kanaks of New Caledonia), and the history of the anthropology of Oceania.

It goes without saying that Aboriginals and the idea of Aboriginality are such that they do not and will not define themselves as a minority.

Out of a total population of 16 million inhabitants, Australia has no more than 160,000 Aboriginals, or barely 1 percent. With respect to other colonies of Pacific peoples, Australia presents the smallest proportion of natives: the Maoris constitute 15 percent of the population of New Zealand, the Kanaks 43 percent of New Caledonia, native Fijians comprise 45 percent of that country's population, where Fijians of Indian origin are slightly more numerous. In these places where Europeans settled by the thousands, even millions, attracting in their wake other populations from Asia, Indonesia, then all the continents, the Oceanians have progressively been made a minority on their own soil. However, it is striking to note that these colonized, despoiled, and often decimated people have maintained themselves on an ideological and political level. They have not stopped challenging the majority communities in terms of law, morality, and culture.

Around the 1970s, the flowering of independence movements was accompanied by emphasis on an inclusive "tradition," above and beyond often very important local differences, as a way of life and thought specific to the first occupants of the Pacific. The emerging nationalisms then develop a pan-Oceanic ideology that likes to present itself as distinct from Western values. This perspective seeks to highlight a cultural basis, even an art of living, which would be common to all the native societies of the Pacific. The evocation of these sources paints the portrait of an Oceanic civilization that rises above and beyond all particularisms and would itself bear a philosophical and ecological message. The ideology of the Pacific Way, which allowed certain leaders to advance the idea of a precolonial, egalitarian Oceania free from conflicts, was part of an attempt at cultural promotion indispensable to any fight for liberation. The circulation of people and ideas throughout Oceania contributed to the creation of a shared base of political and cultural claims. Among the officials of the insular Pacific states formerly under Anglo-Saxon tutelage, rare are those who have not attended the university centers in Guam, Suva, or Auckland, or Mossman's famous Australian School for Pacific Administration in Sydney. Management training, initiation into international politics, and the establishment of multiple contacts among individuals from every corner of the Pacific contributed considerably to the formation of an Oceanic elite (cf. Wittersheim and Bensa 1977).

Clearly, the theme of "The Pacific Way of Life" could not take on the allure of a veritable political program in Australia inasmuch as the Aboriginals have no hope of forming an independent state. Nonetheless, "Aboriginality," conceived as the quintessence of an irreducibly distinctive quality, could have the aim of requiring Australian authorities to recognize fundamental rights. In Australia and in the other colonies of settlement in the Pacific, the expression of malaise experienced by those who felt themselves dispossessed of their former sovereignty associated a specific discourse about the earth and artistic creation with the exaltation of their identity. But when, as in New Caledonia, the prospect of real political independence is not utopian, one sees this through the foundations of culture or the evocation of a mystical link to the soil alongside a more direct discourse, less troubled by cultural postulates. There, as elsewhere, identity claims are a specific form of political ideology, emphasized or slighted according to relations of power.

The arguments supporting the image of a firm cultural identity borrow much from ethnological writings. The anthropology of Australian Aboriginals, and anthropology in general, is always ready to underscore local particularities. Thus have the boundaries of "tribes," cultural or linguistic areas, or microdifferences categorized in museums reinforced regionalist doctrines. We know that this privileging of ethnic groups was often in step with the circumscription of native peoples orchestrated by colonial administrations. Additionally, anthropology favored the reduction of the national to the local (the "coutumes" of France, the "folklore" of Central Europe, the "tribal practices" of Papua New Guinea, and so forth), thus sparing reflection about the construction of national unity by means of the state.

The French people are not merely the sum of their diverse regional practices, just as the Aboriginals cannot be reduced to the total of all the practices and beliefs ethnologists have described them as having. For the cultural concept of "the people" we need to substitute a political reevaluation of the very notion. Without going further, let us say that "the people" constitute themselves from the moment when they think of themselves as the locus of the exercise of a power that they can assume themselves or delegate to others. It is thus imprecise, as Claude Lévi-Strauss proposed in his day (1983), to create binary oppositions—between customs and the law, between usages, regions, or traditions and centralized public power— without inquiring about the interactions and the diverse and reciprocal mediations that produce these entities. In the case of Australia, for example, the multitude of "tribes" listed and opposed to one another by anthropological classification should be considered within the framework of their global difference from the white colonizers. It is in reference to this process of discrimination that the idea of a people is elaborated. As Jean-Marie Tjibaou points out (1996:121–22), a people "is a nation born from the fight against colonization, from adversity. It is a collective reaction, a reality that organizes itself."

The working assumption was that if an individual Aboriginal had some fraction of "white" blood, he/she might be saved and directed toward the benefits of Western civilization.

The construction of Aboriginality is as much a result of Aboriginals as of Australians of European origin. It cannot be reduced to an endogenous development of Aboriginal culture that, after many setbacks, would nonetheless experience a renewal uniquely stimulated by its own dynamic. This phenomenon of the expansion of an identity is only comprehensible in light of the history of relations between those who were defined, in whatever different ways, as Aboriginals and state power exercised for more than two centuries by whites. The interaction between natives and colonials has, over more than two centuries now, endlessly redrawn the contours of Aboriginality among whites, influenced first of all by racist ideologies about the theory of degeneration, which tended to assimilate Aboriginals with convicts, then by the most clear-cut segregation, passing along the concept of "whitening," according to which the Aboriginals could disappear after five generations of forced marriages with whites. This sociobiological concept was deliberately put in practice in specialized institutions where children of mixed unions were assembled and required to procreate with persons whose skin was whiter than theirs. This policy, undoubtedly inspired by bovine animal husbandry, created little by little a population of *déracinés*. As J. R. Beckett has explained (1998:198), "assuming the legal authority of the parent, without transmitting 'blood', the state turned its wards into orphans, cut off from their Aboriginal kin without acquiring European kin."

So far as we know, the assimilation associated with this particular form of "ethnic cleansing" by way of racial mixing was not put into effect in other colonies of settlement in the Pacific. What I have called "a racism of annihilation" prevailed in New Caledonia (A. Bensa 1995:108 ff). Europeans, aside from their active contribution to native depopulation (wars, massacres, divisions, destruction of thriving cultures), long sustained the idea that the Kanaks were physically going to disappear upon contact with the white race. It was thus futile to think about their assimilation or about the progressive emergence of an eventual category of people of mixed race. Today, in that archipelago of the South Pacific, the Caledonian population on the whole seems not to take into account either skin color or "blood ties." Belonging to the Kanak world or the European world is based upon cultural criteria. Children raised in a Melanesian milieu are considered Kanaks, while those who grew up in white households, even if also the product of mixed marriages, are considered Europeans. Thus, it is not unusual to find very light-skinned people who call themselves Kanaks, and blacks who tell you they are "whites." Historically, this singular conception led to the absorption by the Kanak universe of almost 10,000 Europeans liberated from the penal colony at the end of the nineteenth century. As Isabelle Merle has discovered and shown (1995), these former convicts left no descendants in white society, to the point of not appearing in the censuses of Europeans. Their children, products of unions with Melanesian women, were always fully Kanaks, even if, today, their origin is still remembered.

The Australian state, wanting to institute a rupture between biological and cultural heritage among people having one or several Aboriginal ancestors, indirectly contributed to the return to Aboriginality for those who believed themselves to have been dispossessed of it. It was above all the "half-castes" who in effect forcefully developed the reconstruction of Aboriginality. That quest was nourished by a personal identity crisis leading to identification with the supposed archetypes of ancient Aboriginal culture. In this regard, the works and teachings of anthropology played a catalytic role, made all the more effective in that the dominant problematic of the ethnology of Aboriginal societies had remained atemporal, as Aram Yengoyan rightly points out. The emphasis that anthropologists placed on religious thought, "kinship structures," and the hunter economy provided all the victims of Australian colonial politics—Christianized Aboriginals, as well as those disaffiliated and/or employed on ranches or in the cities—with a language of cultural and moral resistance. Everywhere in the world, "classic" ethnology, as functionalism or structuralism defined it, constitutes an inexhaustible reservoir of traditions, which is to say, of decontextualized antidotes to present ills.

If these features are the essentialisms of being Aboriginal, the movement within Australia has also projected itself into the contemporary context by the creation of cultural symbols as meaningful emblems of Aboriginality.

Beginning in the 1970s, the reactivation of the past took a distinctive turn among Aboriginals with the rise of acrylic painting on canvas (Myers 1991). This pictorial technique, introduced into the Australian desert by whites, ended the long period of abandonment of artistic activities following the colonial trauma. New Aboriginal painters quickly invented an original style that permitted all native peoples a global identification in an aesthetic form. Dot painting and the treatment of themes explicit to the "Dreaming Time" and to the natural environment defined a neotraditional universe. This creation, to which several thousand Aboriginals today devote themselves, is a pure reinvention of traditions, or rather, the reconstruction of a "modern tradition" that enjoyed a striking success both in Australia and worldwide. It is significant that one of the best-selling works in Australia presenting this art in its unity and its diversity is entitled "Aboriginality" (Isaacs 1992). In these works, Europeans found the mysteries of an Aboriginality purified of the miasmas of colonization and modernization. They even wanted these paintings, on sale in an ever thicker network of galleries, to be commented upon by Aboriginals in the ethnologico-religious style: *The Dream of the Honey Ants, The Dream of Kadaitcha Told to Children,* and so on. (cf. Glowczewski 1991). Thus was born an Aboriginal art that certain critics already classify as "classic" (Caruana 1993) and that many associate purely and simply with the pre-colonial world. The success of this construction with its undeniable artistic richness has not prevented other Aboriginals, most often "half-castes," from putting forth works of a different type. With what is called "urban art," the apparent homogeneity of the first modern Aboriginal pictorial style (dot painting, inspired by the desert) was turned on its head. The artists, without denying the strong sense of identity associated with these pioneering works, often become very conventional and explicitly put forward the political issue (their suffering due to their rootlessness) and the influence of modern Western art (cf. Bensa 1996).

It is at the moment when contemporary Aboriginal painting had invaded the fashionable aesthetics of the entire country (building decoration, clothing motifs, and so forth) that, for the first time since the beginnings of colonialism, the Aboriginals obtained, in court, the right to have some lands returned. Is not the *Marbo* case of 1992 a concrete expression of the utterly new legitimation that the Aboriginals were able to acquire through their cultural battle?

Reference to "the earth" is common among the Kanaks, the Maoris, and the Aboriginals. The notion of "earth" was largely overinterpreted, as if it were a question for all who claimed it, of a sort of ethnic emblem destined to display difference and thus to support demands. The discourse on the sacredness of the soil, to which ethnologists were often quite happy to give their blessing, is one of the most well-trod vulgates of pan-Oceanic ideology that developed through land claims by advocates of autonomy and independence. Aboriginals and their supporters thereby contrast nonutilitarian conceptions of the soil to the productivist and mercantile European outlook.

The link that united Oceanians with their space would thus be of a mystical order, which gives it a quality both ineluctable and mysterious. "People belong to the earth" was a favorite saying often attributed to Oceanian natives, and the phrase enjoyed an extraordinary success among most European journalists. It lent credence to the idea that the existence of indigenous societies is largely dominated by religiosity and ritual. It is important, it seems to me, to resituate this pronouncement within the construction across Oceania of a native ideology contesting the European powers. The right to recover one's lands is expressed in an exotic turn that implies, for those willing to give way to it, that land claims should obey not so much the demands of justice as the metaphysical necessity of recovering a part of one's personal identity. The "sacred" earth is thus inseparable from "Kanak totemism" or Aboriginal "Dreaming Time," another politicocultural variant on the theme of the incommensurable difference between the Oceanian way of life and that of others. Rather than simply say that they claim their lands because they belong to them, the Oceanians are constrained, where they are in the minority, to equip themselves with a supplement of soul in order to impose their claim on their adversaries.

Culture is a battle, not only for the Aboriginals, but also for a not-negligible fraction of the populations of large, industrialized countries. Does not the opposition, largely constructed by anthropology, between the economically useful and the culturally necessary, between practical reason and cultural reason, also lie at the heart of the contemporary problematic underlying the crisis of work and the productivist representations that were formerly associated with it? It is thus not accidental that a fringe of the Western middle classes in the United States and Australia, strongly affected by job insecurity and conflicting indicators of identity, recognize themselves in the antiutilitarian discourse of Indians and Aboriginals. Affirming the primacy of the symbolic comes back to finding a way out of the condition of emptiness into which one is plunged when one sees the socioprofessional category or social segment to which one belongs progressively on the way to extinction: Aboriginals, hippies, Indians, and, to some extent, even anthropologists all the more easily have recourse to "everything is symbolic" when they belong to a social universe placed in difficulty by economic and bureaucratic pragmatism. Thus they engaged in developing a discourse of mystic character about fallen nobilities. In the relative success of Aboriginals in modern Australian cultural combat, it is possible to see the effect of an ideological alliance between these dominated natives and those in the white Australian world who also feel themselves dominated and marginalized. The worldwide fashion of ethnicity, identity, and authenticity is perhaps not so much the result of the success of minorities in imposing themselves as of the slippage of entire sections of the industrial world into material precariousness and self-doubt. Hence, contrary to the affirmations of culturalism, Aboriginals are not recognized as different because in essence they are or would be but because, elsewhere on the planet, more and more people feel as though they, too, have become different in a process of marginalization due to this crisis. In this perspective, the Aboriginals, far from representing a hypothetical past, are perhaps the very image of our future:

Furthermore, historians left the Aboriginal discussion to anthropologists who still saw Aboriginal cultures through the faulty concept of "the ethnographic present," which stressed a timeless, unchanging perspective of Aboriginals, effectively divorcing them from history and cultural transformations.

New constructions of Aboriginality are redrawing the contours of the purported difference between Europeans and those who neither think like nor want to be "like whites." But it appears that anthropologists still evince some difficulty in envisioning today's Aboriginal reality, strongly marked by urbanization (90 percent of the Aboriginal population), appropriation of the most modern forms of art, techniques of communication, and so forth. As Nicholas Thomas vividly demonstrates (1994), Aboriginal culture belongs to that of colonialism. It is thus necessary to engage in a considerable effort at denial of the actual conditions of contemporary Aboriginal existence in order to continue to celebrate eternal Aboriginality: "This celebration of Aboriginality is thus limited to the traditional, and presents contemporary Aboriginal life through works of art that can be construed as traditional by a primarily American readership unfamiliar with the postwar history of Aboriginal painting" (Thomas 1994:177–78). This work of the learned invention of tradition has found in the writings of archaeologist Robert Lawlor (1991) one of its most extreme forms, since this author wants to show that Aboriginals are vestiges of an epoch before the Stone Age (the Wood Age). They are said to have persisted in this existence by placing themselves under the authority of the Dreaming Time, which would have put them on guard against the evils of all modernization. Many Europeans also see in Aboriginals the incarnation of a naturalist metaphysics attached to the preservation of the environment and of human relations. This idealized image of the primitive is, in its ecological version, the new avatar of the "society against the State" of which Pierre Clastres (1974) has made himself the herald in France.

The Aboriginals, for their part, do not necessarily understand things in the same way. Some of them turn away in derision, defining their own Aboriginality, as Nicholas Thomas clearly explains (1994:191), "through the experience of assimilation and its rejection, as something that can be recovered through self-identification, rather than a quantity that 'authentic' Aborigines possess more of than others."

Integration in the recent past (colonization, social and political problems) within the construction of Aboriginal identity goes against the received notion according to which "culture" constitutes a stable and coherent totality. Thus, the relationships that Aboriginals maintain with their seemingly strongest emblems and symbols undoubtedly deserve to be rethought. In that respect, connections to the earth as they are expressed today are valuable as an example. As Jeremy Beckett has well shown, reference to the soil can function as an appeal to the past in order to support very contemporary interests. Aboriginals, outside the claims of each currently recognized community, have brought earth to the level of collective reference, which connects widely separated groups: Isn't being Aboriginal ultimately to belong to the group of those who can assert land rights by reference to being native, without the power that Europeans have to refer to some written right of property? It is the same with purely religious considerations, which today, in the discourse of numerous displaced Aboriginals, have a tendency to be homogenized into a pieced-together assemblage related to Aboriginality in general (cf. Isacs 1991).

Aboriginals live in Australia as a state, but they are outside of Australia as a nation.

If Aboriginals can appear as exterior to the Australian nation, even though they have been citizens of that country since 1969, it is because, in the end, in the eyes of the majority, they constitute nothing more than an ethnic group. Aboriginality presents, however, some of the traits of a nationalist ideology, but this is expressed in a very unstable demographic context, which considerably limits its import. It is nevertheless remarkable that so small a part of the population has come to concern so large a part of the administration without truly threatening the sovereignty and institutions of Australia. It is not the same when demographic conditions make it possible to imagine that the natives will not always be a minority, as is the case in New Caledonia.

If the Kanaks can imagine giving themselves a constitution, they must then rethink their relationship to their own culture, which must be able to support a national ambition for self-government. That emerges from profound transformations in the image that the Kanaks offer of their "traditions" and their relationship to them. In order for the culture to become national and to support the emergence of a state, it must undertake considerable work on itself: attenuating regional and linguistic differences, searching for inclusive symbols, and putting into place cultural policies addressed to the entire country. The policy of the current Agency for the Development of Kanak Culture, as seen in the opening of a Kanak Cultural Center in Noumea, is certainly heading in this direction. It is interesting to note that the Aboriginals are also trying to imagine cultural centers; but their nationalism, unable to embody a state, can only be a regionalism. The pan-Aboriginal ideology at present developing has only been able to take a truly national turn at the level of artistic expression. In effect, one sees Aboriginal paintings and references to Aboriginality occupying a larger and larger place in the image Australia wants to give of itself. As with the origins of European nations, the specialists in tradition (anthropologists, archaeologists, art historians, and so forth) find themselves mobilized, whether they want to be or not, by this vast enterprise of promoting Aboriginality. Unwittingly, anthropology will, in this regard at least, have played, perhaps more in Australia than elsewhere, a decisive role.

REFERENCES

Bensa, Alban. 1995. *Chroniques Kanak: l'ethnologie en marche.* Paris: Peoples authochtones et développement.
Beckett, Jeremy R., ed. 1988. *Past and Present: The Construction of Aboriginality.* Canberra: Australian Institute of Aboriginal Studies, Aboriginal Studies Press.
Bensa, Elise. 1996. *La peintre aborigène contemporaine: construction d'une identité.* Université René Descartes. Manuscript (mémoire de maîtrise), Paris.
Caruana, Wally. 1993. "L'univers de l'art." *L'art des Aborigènes d'Australie.* Paris: Thames and Hudson.
Clastres, Pierre. 1974. *La société contre l'Etat.* Paris: Editions de Minuit.
Glowczewski, Barbara. 1991. *Yapa, peintres Aborigènes de Balgo et de Lajananu.* Paris: Baudoin Labon.
Isaacs, Jenifer. 1991. *Australian Dreaming: 40.000 Years of Aboriginal History.* Sydney: Ure Smith Press (1st ed., 1980).
———. 1992. *Aboriginality, Contemporary Original Paintings and Prints.* Ste. Lucia: University of Queensland Press.
Keen, Ian, ed. 1994. *Being Black: Aboriginal Cultures in "Settled" Australia.* Canberra: Australian Institute of Aboriginal Studies, Aboriginal Studies Press.
Lawlor, Robert. 1991. *Voices of the First Day: Awakening in the Aboriginal Dreaming.* Vermont: Inner Traditions International.

Lévi-Strauss, Claude. 1983. "Réflexion sur les libertés." In *Le regard éloigné.* Paris: Plon.

Merle, Isabelle. 1995. *Expériences coloniales. Nouvelle-Calédonie (1853–1920).* Paris: Belin.

Myers, Fred. 1991. "Representing Culture: The Production of Discourse(s) for Aboriginal Acrylic Paintings." *Culture Anthropology* 6, no. 1: 26–62.

Thomas, Nicholas. 1989. *Out of Time: History and Evolution in Anthropological Discourse.* Cambridge: Cambridge University Press, Cambridge Studies in Social Anthropology, no. 67.

———. 1994. *Colonialism's Culture: Anthropology, Travel and Government.* Cambridge: Polity Press.

Tjibaou, Jean-Marie. 1996. *La présence kanak,* ed. Alban Bensa and Éric Wittersheim. Paris: Éditions Odile Jacob.

Wittersheim, Eric, and Alban Bensa. 1997. "Nationalisme et interdépendence: la pensée politique de Jean-Marie Tjibaou." *Tiers-Monde* 39.

Between Stigmatization and Mobilization: AIDS in French Society

Claudine Herzlich

A minority may be conceived of in purely statistical terms. However, that designation most often implies the idea of a group perceived as different by the larger group in which it lives. This group is the object of practices of segregation, of discriminatory, even aggressive, treatment on the part of the majority. A minority can be isolated, the victim of spontaneous or ritualized violence. The majority social order affirms its own existence through the rejection of the minority; but a true minority only exists if it is conscious of itself, if it recognizes itself as a specific group: a collective identity is implied. This collective identity may develop from feelings of inferiority and the internalization of stigmatization but it can also embody a positive otherness.

The establishment of a minority is most often based on national, religious, ethnic, or even cultural differences. Can such a definition apply to an illness like AIDS? Sociologists working on illness have all had as a first goal thinking of it as an intrinsically social condition and thus to show how the organic effects of the disease give way to a particular social status, that of an "ill person." However, the status of sick person cannot, as such, be compared to that of being a member of a minority. First, as Talcott Parsons argues, the ill, as a whole, rarely form a distinct group, separate from the healthy. "The sick are tied up, not with other deviants to form a 'sub-culture' of the sick, but each with a group of non-sick, his personal circle and, above all, physicians. The sick thus . . . are deprived of the possibility of forming a solidary collectivity."[1] Next, even if Erving Goffman refers to the ill and physically handicapped, to their visible signs, as in danger of stigmatization; all sick people are not necessarily stigmatized.[2] In today's societies, sickness, provided it has been identified by a doctor, constitutes a legitimate status.

299

Historically, however, illness has often provoked fear and rejection. The violence of these reactions is linked to the importance of the threat that the illness represents, to its ability to fracture the social order and to the danger that each person perceives for himself in the illness of the other. The fear of contagion is the most common reason. It is therefore epidemic diseases, transmissible diseases for which one can observe rapid diffusion and often dramatic results, that provoke fear and rejection. These sicknesses are also linked to the attribution of responsibility: the sick people, in this case, are considered as responsible and guilty.

Nonetheless, the frequency of the reactions of fear, avoidance, or even rejection does not imply that, in all cases, the sick people form a "minority" in the sense of being lastingly set apart or subject to discriminatory treatment as a specific group. The contrast with plague and leprosy is enlightening: The return of the plague in Europe in the fourteenth century provoked intense fears and alarming rejection of the ill. In the eyes of all, it was a manifestation of the wrath of God, a scourge striking a sinful humanity. But this scourge was undifferentiated, it did not imply the specific guilt of some but overwhelmingly punished all people. The reactions of rejection as well as measures of public health established material barriers between the ill and the healthy (buffer zones, lazarets, quarantines) that, brutal as they seem, were thus above all pragmatic. They attempted to protect society from danger but did not claim to distinguish the groups whose relation to the illness carried a specific meaning. They isolated physically but did not stigmatize socially. Moreover, the plague nearly always killed like lightning: no group of plague victims had the time to form a group. One cannot, in this case, use the notion of minority.

Leprosy, on the other hand, did not appear as a blind scourge. Its victims were often considered personally guilty. The idea of danger rests in the notion of taint. Certainly, though the leper was impure, he was also, in medieval hagiography, the prototype of the miraculously cured: leprosy could be a sign of election. In both cases, the sick do not therefore live in undifferentiated anonymity. Add to this the fact that this illness, endemic to Europe for centuries, is a sickness of long duration: the mutilations that it engenders bit by bit give time to identify the ill, to perceive their difference. Medieval society thus felt the need to develop a sophisticated ritual of exclusion and created, in isolating them, communities of lepers. In the large leper colonies, where the ill lived for months and sometimes years, the life of the sick was not limited to the internalization of rejection and stigmatization; one finds there forms of sociability and of solidarity. This formed, writes Françoise Bériac, a "society of the excluded."[3] According to current categories, lepers do seem to have constituted a "minority."

Can we have recourse to the same idea to discuss syphilis and tuberculosis at the end of the nineteenth century?[4] Both are understood as "social illnesses": they are not just matters of a single, physical body; they concern the social body, certain elements of which more than others appear gangrenous. The discourse is stigmatizing above all with regard to syphilitics, "rotted" ones, whose personal responsibility seems heavy. At the end of the nineteenth century, the obsession with degeneracy, the physical decadence of the population, and the eugenics project explicitly made the syphilitic its target. Practice toward the tubercular was more segregationist, however, at least if they belonged to the lower classes. As long as tuberculosis was merely consumption, a romantic illness affecting, according to conceptions of the times, the rich and women, sensitive and exceptionally talented beings, the ill person was condemned but neither rejected nor stigmatized, much less banished to a group apart: Even if the illness was seen as the expression of a profound truth about the consumptive, it did not make him guilty. The discovery at the end of the nineteenth century of the popular character of the illness as well as evidence of its bacterial origin changed the relationship to the sick: tuberculosis revealed the moral deficiencies that afflicted the proletariat. Society therefore had to defend itself against moral deficiency just as it had to protect the healthy from the danger of encountering carriers of the bacilli. Inquisitive and authoritarian, the antituberculosis fight gathered the ill together, isolated and restricted them. In sanitariums for the populace, the sick were cut off from their professional activities and separated from their families, surviving as a group apart. There were revolts among the tubercular.

Nowadays, the mastery of infectious pathologies has temporarily made us forget the reality of collective illness as well as the danger that it can pose; representations of sick people and their status have been transformed. A person suffering from a chronic illness is often the only one to know he is afflicted; disease perceived as an individual state neither concerns those around him nor the social order. He thus cannot constitute himself as part of the "minority" of sick people because, as Parsons noted, they do not make themselves part of any collective reality.[5] The appearance of AIDS in the beginning of the 1980s, however, clouded this shift, mistakenly believed to be definitive, from the collective epidemics of the past to the chronic individual diseases of today.

AIDS and Discrimination against Minorities

In the framework of the development of the AIDS epidemic at the beginning of the 1980s, it is generally forgotten that just before its appearance, a stigmatizing discourse associating death and sex, fault and punishment circulated about another ailment, genital herpes.[6] No one had, however, imagined considering people afflicted with herpes as members of a "minority." They appeared simply as ill individuals.

On the other hand, as soon as the first cases were pinpointed in France as well as in the United States, in 1981, the "mysterious illness" was associated with specific, often stigmatized, groups.[7] The emphasis was placed first on male homosexuals: until July 1983, prior to the appearance of the term *AIDS,* all terms used in the French press to name the disease referred to homosexuality.[8] But as early as 1982, it was known that this disease also affected hemophiliacs, intravenous drug users, and Haitians. The criteria for negative judgments placed on these categories of the afflicted persons varied. In the case of homosexuals, the group most affected, disfavor was based on minority sexual practices but without social depreciation: homosexuals belonged to all social classes. In the case of drug addicts, on the contrary, the condemned behavior was usually accompanied by social marginality.

The disease, however, created the danger of a double stigma, and the notion of "groups at risk" could seem the epidemiological translation of unfavorable social connotations that contributed toward a hardening; it juxtaposed the troubling term of *risk* to the reality, self-contained, of *groups.* On this basis, a moral discussion developed attributing to the sick, above and beyond responsibility for their own condition, responsibility for the return of an epidemic threatening the entire society. A discourse of fault and accusation dominated communications about AIDS. In 1985 panic was unleashed by the discovery, by means of the first screening tests of HIV-positive individuals, of "healthy carriers" capable of transmitting the disease without anyone being aware. Fear of a generalized spread of the evil elicited attempts at discrimination.

At the same time, the first collective initiatives emerging from homosexual milieus—in particular from highly cultured members of the middle classes, sometimes occupying prestigious professions—began to be structured with a double aim, that of aid to the ill and of a fight against discrimination toward "groups at risk."[9] On the other hand, public powers were slower to react; in France they would not really intervene (by the announcement of Prime Minister Laurent Fabius to the National Assembly, June 20, 1985, of the decision to screen voluntary blood donations) until there was manifest danger of extending the disease to a population beyond the "groups at risk." In the United States, in 1985, at the time of the first international conference on AIDS in Atlanta, Secretary of Health Heckler gave proof of the same indifference: "We must conquer AIDS . . . before it affects the heterosexual population and threatens the health of our general population," she declared. Other organized bodies—political parties, unions, the churches—also remained silent for quite a long time.[10]

In the first period, reactions to AIDS clearly showed the possibility of a conjunction between bodily affliction and social stigma. They fit the mold of traditional responses to epidemics and conformed to the logic of discriminatory attitudes toward minorities. Belonging to groups with socially devalued behaviors, suspected of being responsible for their condition, the first to be ill seemed on the way to becoming the focal point of all the temptations toward discrimination. For this reason, in many cases, members of these discredited groups at first refused all association with the disease and even tried to deny its existence. At first, homosexuals wanted to see only fantasies without objective basis, pure manifestations of homophobia, in the information on AIDS. In France, until 1985, the French Association of Hemophiliacs considered the HIV contamination of blood products as only a minor risk.[11] In Quebec, the Haitian community mobilized itself to obtain "its official withdrawal from the classification of groups at risk."[12] In the United States, the black community long refused to consider the disease as a problem that concerned it.[13] In all these cases, during several months or years, the fear of a double stigma, social stigmatization of the disease redoubling that to which each of the groups concerned was subject, overcame the recognition of a threat to health.

Toward a "Liberal Management" of the Epidemic

In the course of the second half of the 1980s, however, while the disease had clearly entered into public consciousness,[14] this configuration was progressively transformed. In the media, a desire to master emotional outbursts replaced evocations of fear and accounts of panic, and, among all participants, attitudes of nondiscrimination, nonsegregation, and solidarity prevailed little by little over temptations of rejection. One can find an indication of this in the transformation of the vocabulary used. Labels such as the *homosexual syndrome* or the *gay plague* were dropped in 1983–84, while use of the term *AIDS* became general; then came awareness of the negative connotations of "a group at risk." On the other hand, usage spread of the phrase *people affected* (*personne concernée*) to designate both those infected (HIV-positive or symptomatic) and those close to them. This reflected the desire to avoid all discrimination by preserving an opaqueness as to the health of individuals, taking note of the confidentiality due with regard to private life. Finally, the term *contagious disease* to designate AIDS progressively gave way to *transmissible disease*. It was a question of dissociating this disease from the epidemics of the past and, by abandoning the traditional vocabulary of contagion, of de-dramatizing the disease and warding off fear of simple contact with those who were ill.[15]

Observers of the development of AIDS also agree in judging the first responses to have been inadequate at the level of health payment[16] and the efficacy of medical treatments but acknowledge that on the other hand the disease has been given "liberal management" on the judicial plane,[17] avoiding coercive errors. Between 1984 and 1987,[18] the temptation of repressive legislative measures was seen in several European countries and the United States. In May 1988, in contrast, the World Medical Association, attached to the World Health Organization (WHO), recommended that governments avoid all discriminatory action with regard to people symptomatic or carrying the HIV virus; in the course of 1989, European institutions did the same. In France a law promulgated in July 1990 reinforced these antidiscriminatory measures with regard to health and, in spite of recurrent pressures, no authoritarian measure for tracking or screening tests has been adopted.[19] Globally, a cruel conflict between concern for public health and individual freedom has therefore not resulted. Moreover, in response to a survey conducted in the French homosexual press at the end of the 1980s, many readers thought that, even if they were individually confronted with rejection in their daily lives, AIDS would provide the occasion for better acceptance and normalization of the fact of being homosexual[20] rather than reinforce the stigma. In the United States, some legal experts believed that the lack of discrimination toward those afflicted had a basis in the civil rights movement of recent decades, the values of which many public health experts shared; they wrote that the present epidemic could, for its part, serve to reinforce these rights: "AIDS may itself transform and refine ideas about individual rights."[21]

On their side, campaigns of information and for prevention (the first national public campaign in France dates from 1987) quickly focused on the development of solidarity among those infected and at the same time on raising awareness of the danger and promoting the voluntary adoption of behavior to lessen risk. It is thus necessary to modify the view put forth by some historians at the onset of the illness that although AIDS by its characteristics and means of contagion constituted a disease of a very different kind from classical epidemics, it was nevertheless close to them in the similarity of individual and group reactions to it.[22] This was true early on, but progressively developed societies have instead turned their backs on the coercive solutions of the past: A model of consensual intervention had held sway over the repressive means by which the danger of epidemics had traditionally been controlled. On the political level, since 1986 and 1987, when the *Front National* took a position insisting on the obligatory screening of "populations at risk" and asking for the creation of "sidatoriums" (AIDS sanitariums), AIDS has not constituted an occasion for conflict by French political parties but on the contrary has been the object of quite broad agreement.[23]

The French Confront AIDS

The various results of surveys show that public opinion has followed this evolution and has gradually adopted attitudes with regard to infected persons in which tolerance and compassion tend to predominate. For the last several years, the World Health Organization has stimulated the implementation, in nearly fifty countries, of a series of standardized quantitative surveys called KABP,[24] designed to test the impact of informational campaigns and to permit evaluation of the perception of the disease in the population as a whole. In France, the first survey of this type was conducted on a sample of the population of the Ile-de-France in 1987;[25] it was repeated, on a national scale, in 1990, 1992, and 1994.[26] In the 1987 survey, almost everyone (93.7 percent) of those interviewed considered the AIDS patient as having "need of sympathy and solidarity" (the percentage is 96.6 percent for a cancer patient), and 95.9 percent declared that he "has a right to the best medical treatment possible." The legitimacy of the patient's status is thus clear; on the other hand, the feeling of danger is strong. In 40.7 percent of the cases, respondents considered the AIDS patient to be "dangerous to others" and in 20.2 percent of the responses as "responsible for what happens to him" (such responses are quite rare with regard to a cancer patient). One of the aims of the survey is to distinguish two types of extreme attitudes: one, founded on free consent and individual accountability, attached to liberal management of the disease and one favoring the repressive management of AIDS.[27] Between the two poles, the authors describe an array of intermediary positions; they are thus not wrong to ask, "Tolerance or exclusion: the razor's edge?"

Furthermore, as soon as they became aware of the gravity of the illness, the interested groups have themselves also been tempted by coercive attitudes. In the first survey of French homosexuals conducted by M. Pollak in 1985, two-thirds of those questioned (64.5 percent) wanted an obligatory screening of the whole population; 11 percent considered it legitimate to isolate those who were symptomatic with the disease, and 9 percent those who were HIV-positive. Two years later, a shift appears: no more than 17.3 percent want screening, and calls for isolation have practically disappeared.[28]

Among the general population, the national surveys of 1990 and 1992 show a distinct evolution at the same time as the general level of information is better and the appreciation of the risks becomes more realistic, an attitude of nondiscrimination with regard to relations with those afflicted becomes established bit by bit: In 1990, only 7 percent of those questioned said that they were willing to work with a person with HIV, 9 percent to continue seeing the person socially, and 16 percent would refuse to eat at the person's home. By 1992, these results had improved, particularly among the categories of people who had previously been less tolerant, such as those with a level of education below the *bac* [the degree on leaving college preparatory secondary school].[29] The desire for coercive measures in order to manage the disease (isolating AIDS patients or administering a screening test without consent, for example) also has a tendency to decline. Finally, although the "scandal of contaminated blood" exploded in France precisely at this time, and its effect on hemophiliacs became known, respondents refused to contrast "good" people, involuntary victims, from the others.[30]

These results of quantitative surveys were confirmed elsewhere by a qualitative investigation conducted in 1992 through in-depth interviews, thus allowing great freedom of expression to those questioned.[31] The majority of them adhered in their discussions to the values of solidarity and tolerance, which seemed henceforth to dominate the perception and relations with the victims of the disease. But furthermore, they exercise a form of social hypervigilance, tending to show that henceforth these attitudes have the value of norms by which those interviewed feel authorized to vigorously denounce breaches and missteps. This normative surveillance produces some unexpected effects. Invited to express their understanding of the origins of the disease, those interviewed did not hesitate to question the statistical relationship, incontestable in itself, between homosexual practices or intravenous drug use and the occurrence of the disease. Spontaneously transforming themselves into sociologists of the labeling process, they choose to see there the result of discriminatory attitudes. "It has all been put on their backs instead of telling things as they really are," an eighteen-year-old unemployed worker says with regard to drug addicts, in one example. A forty-three-year-old journalist expresses the same idea: "I think that they have tried to make [them] carry the blame because they are black, or homosexuals because they are homosexuals and from that the entire world has supposedly been contaminated. Drug addicts, too, because of course drug addicts are nasty. . . . I think that they want to discredit some groups."

AIDS: A Test of Tolerance and Justice?

In these interviews, AIDS appeared as a proving ground for principles of equality, justice and solidarity in a society confronted with multiple cleavages and conflicts. In transforming epidemiological information into rumors that express a desire to harm discredited groups, those interviewed showed first of all their desire to react to these cleavages and to oppose what they perceive as a desire to manipulate a naive general population. They also revealed that AIDS had become a problem with multiple connotations and meanings, going beyond the framework of health and the individual cases of those infected, permitting each of them to express belief in a set of fundamental values and to measure the values of others.

This evolution in the management of the disease and in the attitudes toward it was not a foregone conclusion and should perhaps be considered a historical first. In societies rife with social conflicts and prey to multiple anxieties, awareness of frailties or new dangers usually reinforces a tendency to discriminate against "minorities." The progressive extension of this disease could thus easily have led to the segregation of the ill under the guise of protecting the healthy and not, as has actually been the case, to a greater solidarity toward those struck by a disease that has come to be seen as a universal plague.

The decisive factor has certainly been the effective action of the first associations in the fight against the disease. Composed mainly of homosexuals in 1984–85, these associations were immediately confronted by a dilemma: how to alert the most vulnerable and make them aware of the danger, without risking increased condemnation by doing so? Their efforts at informing and persuading were therefore inscribed within a strategy aimed beyond the specific categories of those first infected, in order to make AIDS a cause that concerned the whole society: AIDS, these associations repeated, could "touch everyone."[32] This perspective was quickly relayed by the professionals who, at the same time, were seeing the spread of the disease among new categories of the population, in particular heterosexuals. It was indispensable that AIDS clearly become "everyone's affair" and no longer only the concern of minorities, so that preventive action could take root. This strategy drew force from the consensus uniting all the participants; in France it was solidly based on a foundation of universality anchored in all social groups. It was as representatives of a "general cause" and not as representatives of special interest groups that the associations were able to make themselves heard in France.

Promotion of the values of solidarity and equity could equally build on attachment to individual rights and human dignity, important in a period of surging large-scale ideologies promising collective well-being. However, another factor was determinant: in our societies, illness has a role of legitimation. The sick have rights, in part annulling traditional cleavages and habitual hierarchies—and in addition, the moral exigency for compassion toward them is particularly strong. It is because this was a matter of ill people that a quite good climate of tolerance was established in France with regard to drug addicts, prostitutes, and above all homosexuals. The behavior of these groups with regard to their disease, as patients, has additionally been a determinant factor. In modern societies, we admire the ill, no longer when they serenely accept their pain and death but when they show themselves "responsible" toward their illness, capable of fighting against it or surmounting it. Among the different groups concerned, homosexuals are the objects of the most favorable judgments[33] in large part because they appeared in the second half of the 1980s exemplary in their means of adaptation to risk and their reactions to the disease.

Finally, informational campaigns allowing us to better understand the nature of the illness have reduced the fear: With time, the message that the AIDS virus is, in fact, fragile and difficult to transmit has gotten through. Evaluation of its risks, which became more realistic, also encouraged tolerance and solidarity.

Daily Life of Those with AIDS: The Limits of Tolerance

Through AIDS, French society sometimes seemed to want to give itself proof of its capacity to repair fractures and recompose social ties. However, these things are not simple: All the authors agree that the norms of tolerance remain fragile. Quantitative surveys show that various "points of fixation" of fear persist and engender, like a return of the repressed, an ambivalent attachment to the possibility of authoritarian measures. The best example of this is the attitude toward screening tests: If, between 1990 and 1992, one notes a stronger rejection of applying these tests in a coercive environment (in prisons, for example), opposition somewhat diminished to the idea of a general screening of the entire population.[34] Here the limits of the effects of information are measured: Experts' arguments about the ineffectiveness for public health of this step had only weak impact.

It is necessary therefore to be wary of too quickly seeing the comforting example of the adoption of a democratic consensus based on the facts, reason, and solidarity. This has its limits and ambiguities. The qualitative research already cited illustrates well the possibility of an unexpected return of the irrational and of the persistence of the old reflex of seeking scapegoats: The very people who refuse to connect homosexuality or drug addiction to AIDS are ready, on the other hand, to believe in rumors attributing the origin of the disease to the malevolent intentions of depraved scientists or perverse governments. The designation of guilty parties for an inexplicable evil reappears here, rerouted to other targets than the groups habitually discredited, and an almost too-perfect societal vigilance gives way to fantasy.

Above all, the belief in some norms of tolerance does not prevent the sick, at an individual level, from throwing themselves into situations where condemnation and discrimination revive. These involve numerous aspects of their life. One of the most serious problems in France is undoubtedly that of the screening test done without the knowledge of the patient in different professional, penitential, or hospital contexts. We hardly have systematic data on the frequency of these practices, which are against the law and therefore hidden; but no one, among the various observers of the disease, denies its occurrence in certain cases. It can be noted, paradoxically, that it is the least stigmatized group, that of hemophiliacs, sometimes considered as "innocent victims," that has systematically been the object of such testing in the middle of the 1980s. The use of tests by certain insurance companies to refuse insurance to those who are HIV-positive, in a context juridically ambiguous, is also an occasion for intense conflicts with organizations involved in the fight against the disease.[35]

Of a more everyday nature, relationships with colleagues, family, and friends are also at issue. Currently, we do not have, for France, any reliable global data concerning the repercussions of the disease on the work situation. In annual surveys of homosexuals, eight out of ten respondents share the opinion that "AIDS provokes reflexes of fear in one's social circle."[36] Studies conducted in several countries[37] of AIDS patients or HIV-positive people, most frequently homosexuals, show that stigmatization and rejection may target the disease—expressed by the tactics employed to avoid physical contact—or homosexuality of which the social circle of those infected was often unaware. They report many disapproving judgments expressed toward them and frequently mention instances of isolation in the workplace and the rupture of relationships with parents, brothers and sisters, and friends. Certainly, it is sometimes difficult in these statements to separate actual stigmatization from that which has been anticipated or feared.[38] In addition, in numerous cases, the sick person receives important support from their social circle. Nevertheless, the difficulties reported in all the research for those who reveal their condition to others can be considered significant.

Those who are HIV-positive but asymptomatic experience this problem as much as those with symptoms: Breaking the silence about their condition is always felt as problematic, and the "secret" is only shared under conditions perceived as intimate and confidential. This maintenance of silence can have as its intention continuing to live as normally as possible or protecting those near from the anxiety unleashed by announcement of the disease. Nevertheless, it is clear that it reflects above all the fear that disclosure will bring about ostracism and expulsion. Furthermore it is striking that HIV-positive homosexuals sometimes think it is in their interest to keep silent about their condition even within the homosexual community.[39] In addition, the desire to keep the secret concerns hemophiliacs contaminated by blood products as it much as it does homosexuals and drug addicts. Fear of possible stigmatization extends even to hemophiliacs who have escaped contamination: thinking that they have perceived signs of suspicion, some of them begin to hide their hemophilia.[40]

Several lessons may be drawn from these analyses: First, the appearance, in the course of the 1980s, of a new epidemic disease has not, at least in the developed countries and in France in particular, contributed to the production of a "new minority." It has even, to a certain extent, introduced a standard of acceptance of discredited groups. But, on the one hand, the standard of tolerance goes against other very powerful logics, like the economic logic of the insurance companies. On the other hand, modern societies lack models of comportment for facing misfortune. Normative orientations on the collective level do not mean that each person, individually and in the variety of everyday situations, is capable of confronting fear, of controlling his fantasies, and, even more fundamentally, knowing how to enter into a relationship with another perceived as different. Mastering these different situations implies emotional capacities, behaviors, and thought processes that not everyone possesses to the same degree and which depend, at least in part, on constraints and resources connected to each person's position within the social structure.

In the second place, though AIDS has not been the cause of the production of new minorities, it does carry with it the mark of customary social inequalities and of the most traditional forms of domination, which intersect with the problem of discrimination against certain groups. Neither countries, nor races, nor social groups, nor the sexes are equal with regard to AIDS. We know that today the epidemic is spreading more quickly in third world countries than in developed countries and that it clearly brings to light the importance of the inequalities between North and South. In these societies, the socially most fragile groups are also subjected to the most brutal discrimination. The Yokohama Conference during the summer of 1994 brought to light the situation of women in African and Asian countries, where they are the most dominated to begin with, who are isolated and rejected because of their infection.[41]

In developed societies, social and ethnic factors equally interfere with the development of the epidemic—one knows that in the United States the black community has become the principal victim of the disease—but, in addition, social position strongly influences a person's ability to deal with the disease. The less-favored social categories absorb the information from prevention campaigns less well; mastery of the system of care and their relations with their doctors are more difficult. Today, in France, the characteristic effects of the disease tend to interact with the insecurity to which it gives rise. One study, conducted among patients sheltered by the association Apparts,[42] clearly illustrates how, for fragile populations such as drug users, foreigners (in irregular situations or not), and holders of uncertain jobs, the onset of illness most often means loss of employment, disruption of ties to family and friends, lack of social protection and difficulties in access to care. Rather than the sudden appearance of new minorities, one sees former, familiar relationships reappear between marginality and illness.

Social position contributes also to forming the image of those affected and, consequently, accentuates or lessens the risks of stigmatization. Their standing helps to legitimize or discredit their actions, their claims, and their complaints. From this point of view, it is clear that the old nineteenth-century problematic of "social ills" can reappear, associated with drug addicts. On the other hand, the first group afflicted, that of male homosexuals, most often members of the middle classes and highly educated, had at their disposal the greatest assets and enjoyed the most legitimacy for effectively mobilizing against the disease and developing collective responses through the creation of organizations to fight against AIDS. Their specific role must also examined.

The Evolution of Associations for the Fight against the Disease

It has often been emphasized that, in all developed societies, the group phenomenon represents the most original aspect of the history of AIDS and stressed that this had a central role in dealing with this ailment.[43] How can one analyze the development of these associations in the perspective of reflection on "minorities"? They played a role in the transformations of identity that AIDS implies, as do all grave illnesses. More specifically, they acted to control the menace of stigma weighing on those infected, and they fought all attempts at discrimination. Could we consider then that they constitute an example of an "active minority,"[44] defined as a cohesive group characterized by a positive self-awareness, a will to influence the majority, and an innovative cultural and social role?

Although strongly affected by the disease from the beginning, France was rather slow to react, among European countries or compared to the United States.[45] The first organizations, founded on close personal proximity to the illness (that is, on the fact of knowing oneself to be ill or infected or being close to a sick person) did not attract more than a few dozen members. They remained few in number from 1983 to 1987. From that date on, in contrast, one witnessed a proliferation without precedent: Ten to twenty organizations were founded each year. In multiplying, these associations became extremely diverse; among them it is difficult to identify a predominant model. They remained separated, however, essentially as a function of the type of contamination. Even today, in the group movement as a whole, male homosexuals are still always overrepresented and their organizations are the most active. On the other hand, drug addicts are rare in the principal associations, even if AIDS has been the occasion for the emergence of their first forms of collective organization. Hemophiliacs and those who have undergone multiple transfusions, for their part, have organized themselves into particular associations.

At the same time, while certain associations have stayed "general," others devote themselves more specifically to a type of intervention (to information and prevention, to contacts with research in the context of perfection of treatments, to social programs to cover the costs of caring for the sick, to care at home, to emotional or juridical support) or again they have specialized in the care of a certain population: the problems of women or children, for example. They have been innovative on a number of fronts: in the doctor-patient relationship, by the creation of new structures in the health system and of original proposals for the support of the ill. Nonetheless, they have their weaknesses: in particular, the illness and death of many of their members inevitably introduces a discontinuity in action.

The manner in which these associations have managed problems of collective identity in France and have reacted to the threats of stigmatization is not univocal, and it has evolved. In 1981, the first persons interested in AIDS were the doctors confronted, in the hospital setting, with the first sick patients. Certain homosexuals mobilized soon afterward and tried to create the first networks of mutual aid. Various authors who have studied the French organizations fighting AIDS agree in underscoring that, in contrast to the situation in other countries, the militancy of the French homosexuals was in decline at the beginning of the 1980s. The mobilization that occurred is thus less a restructuring around a previous militancy than a new structuring around the disease, newly constituting its objectives and its means of action.[46]

The creation of the first associations (Aides and Vaincre le Sida in 1983 and 1984) parallels the beginning of a collective awareness. Composed mostly of volunteers, but including among them numerous doctors and health professionals, they began to act following a complex strategy. In addition to efforts to inform and the first attempts to develop preventive action, the organizations strove to develop an emotional support system for those infected. For the HIV-positive, in particular, the association became a place for an apprenticeship in living with HIV and for restoring a positive self-image. The sociability that developed in these organizations is based therefore both on homosexuality and proximity to the illness. From another point of view, however, the French organizations, especially Aides, tend to minimize (in the public image that they present of themselves) the relative size of their homosexual component. They challenged the idea of a "gay cancer," that is to say the association between AIDS and homosexuality, and combated all the stigmatizing metaphors. At the same time, in the double goal of contributing to the effort at prevention and avoiding stigmatization, they placed themselves in the universalistic ideology of French society and are making AIDS a "general cause" by developing the slogan that has transformed the image of the illness: "AIDS can touch everyone."

Several years later, while organizations multiply and diversify, attitudes are polarizing, some cleavages appear, and ruptures occur. While some, distancing themselves from a homosexual identity, initiate a strong movement of professionalization and develop the ambition of becoming part of professional networks of social action and of the health-care system,[47] others value above all the person who is HIV-positive or symptomatic, to the extent of representing him as a "social reformer."[48] Toward 1990, a new generation of more radical associations formed explicitly around the homosexual reality came into being. The model for this is the American organization Act Up. They challenge the strategy of "universalization of the cause" used by the first associations and prefer to develop a strategy of rupture, attacking political power and declaring it responsible for the development of the disease.

An Active Minority Role?

What assessment can one make of the actions of these groups? Up to what point and in what sense can one consider them as "active minorities"? The development of their activity shows that they cannot be considered as a unified whole. The organizations seem rather more like a diversified cloud whose history is marked by rapid development, a shifting of constantly redefined stakes, and the birth of conflicts leading to ruptures and regroupings.

Furthermore, by the diversity of problems that it poses, AIDS demands the intervention of multiple actors. At the current stage, the epidemic encounters the problems of the functioning of health systems as well as those of sexuality, individual rights, the organization of medical research, familial structures, and so forth. Around public provision for those

afflicted, the defense of their rights, the development of large-scale thera-
peutic techniques, and the perfection of campaigns of prevention, fresh
networks are constituted that are the site for the intermingling of diverse
experiences, competencies, and itineraries in all developed countries.
Group members, doctors and health workers, social workers, media professionals, researchers, and administrative officials interact, knotting
alliances and negotiating compromises around partly common and partly
divergent goals. Thanks to the exceptional attention it has drawn, AIDS
has also been the occasion, for various groups and individuals, to advance
their own objectives, to find ways of acting and acquiring the legitimacy to
do it. In this perspective, it is hardly possible to consider people infected
with AIDS and their associations as a self-contained minority. The most
adequate notion for taking into account this diversified ensemble is perhaps the deliberately fluid one proposed by interactionist sociologists, of a
"social world": a fluid social space, a "cultural area which is delimited neither by territory nor by formal belonging"[49] but by the existence of
debates, negotiations, alliances, and conflicts around a common problem.

Associations constitute, however, the point of crystallization for this
social world and are carriers of its capacity for innovation. The efficacy
that they have demonstrated in the establishment of original plans for the
support of the ill is one of the essential sources of their legitimacy, of positive judgments that are attached to militant members, as well as of the
financial, media, and political support that they receive. It is necessary to
emphasize that, paradoxically, this effectiveness is largely founded on a
competence usually little understood: experience of the illness. It is their
experience or their proximity to the disease that transforms the volunteer
members into "experts" of a new type, to whom the political partnerships
directed by the public authorities in France, since 1989, have accorded a
growing legitimacy.[50]

In such a context, unexpected itineraries start up:[51] On the basis of their
intimate experience, militants behave within associations like social workers or psychologists. They become health educators or experts to public
agencies. And even people or groups usually strongly discredited can
attain, as the result of double personal experience "outside the norms"
(one linked to the illness and one given by membership in "hard to reach"
populations), an unprecedented social function and unusual prestige. It is
thus that in the United States, in research on the attitudes of drug addicts
faced with AIDS, former drug addicts are hired as "ethnographers"[52] or
that prostitutes from third world countries present at the international

convention in Yokohama in 1994 are considered as "agents of prevention."[53] Positions usually considered as deviant are legitimated as a function of the capacity of the people who occupy them to respond to the threat that AIDS constitutes.

One can thus conclude that associations have not only succeeded in swaying representations of AIDS and erasing the conception of an illness only concerning discredited groups. They have managed furthermore to weaken the double stigma weighing on these groups. In France, above all in the case of homosexuals but also to a lesser degree for drug addicts, the valorization of which the groups are the object encompasses not only those infected but holds for the entire category and brings renewed reflection on their status and their rights.[54] It is thus largely thanks to groups that help those with AIDS that they have not been treated as "minorities," unleashing avoidance and discrimination. On the other hand, these groups' capacity for influence, their impact as a factor of social change above and beyond the single problem of AIDS, and, in a sense, their role as an "active minority" have been indubitable.

Because this article was conceived in 1995, it represents the way in which one could think of AIDS in France during the first half of the decade. Since then, social scientists are agreed that the status given AIDS in Western societies during the first fifteen years of its development must be understood in terms of "AIDS exceptionalism," in large part thanks to the efforts of active minorities. That, in essence, is the analysis developed in this chapter. But AIDS is a rapidly evolving phenomenon, and this analysis already has a historical quality. In more recent years, two important changes have intervened. First, awareness has grown of the rapid development of the pandemic on a global level. At that scale, the problem is not posed in terms of relations between majority and minority but of relations between the rich and developed countries of the north and the countries of the south. Furthermore, the arrival in 1996 of new treatments, which are efficacious even if they do not cure, has broadly changed the fate of those afflicted and of their social situation. AIDS thus no longer resembles a chronic disease but a general condition. Today, therefore, one speaks of a "normalization" of AIDS. Paradoxically, however, numerous concerned militants and some researchers in the social sciences fear that the disease will lead not to more authoritative policy but to a revival of stigmatizing of the sort traditionally associated with minorities. The future will reveal if this danger is real: The social and cultural history of AIDS is neither set nor sealed.

NOTES

1. T. Parsons, "Social Structure and Dynamic Process: The Case of Modern Medical Practice," *The Social System* (New York: Free Press of Glencoe, 1951), 477.

2. E. Goffman, *Stigma* (New York: Prentice-Hall, 1963).

3. F. Bériac, *Histoire des lépreux au Moyen-Age: une société d'exclus* (Paris: Imago, 1988).

4. In particular, see C. Quetel, *Le mal de Naples. Histoire de la syphilis* (Paris: Seghers, 1986); P. Guillaume, *Du désespoir au salut: les tuberculeux aux 19ème et 20ème siècles* (Paris: Aubier, 1986).

5. On this point, C. Herzlich and J. Pierret, *Illness and Self in Society* (Baltimore: Johns Hopkins University Press, 1987).

6. See C. Herzlich and J. Pierret, "Une maladie dans l'espace publique, le sida dans 6 quotidiens français," *Annales, Economies, Sociétés, Civilisations* (1988), n. 5, 1109–34. In March 1983, whereas fewer than ten articles had been dedicated to AIDS in the principal national daily newspapers in France, the paper *Libération* had published a series of articles concerning sexually transmitted diseases in which the "herpes psychosis" held a larger place than what was then called the "gay cancer." All the themes that would soon be associated with AIDS were evoked with regard to the herpes "epidemic" raging in the United States.

7. It is, however, difficult in France to use the term *community* with regard to them.

8. Herzlich and Pierret, "Une maladie." Still today, the disease continues to be perceived as a homosexual one even though it affects, throughout the world, more heterosexuals than homosexuals. In reality, we know that worldwide, there are actually several AIDS epidemics with different characteristics, in particular the mode of contamination. Here, we refer primarily to the French situation. In the spirit of a Franco-American comparison, the essential difference resides in the fact that in France, the disease is not associated with an ethnic group, while in the United States, the black community has been particularly touched.

9. As early as the spring of 1983, the French press reported the mobilization of American gays fighting against the illness. These people created the "Gay Men's Health Crisis" in New York in January 1982. See C. Perrow and M. F. Guillen, *The AIDS Disaster* (New Haven: Yale University Press, 1990). In France, the group "Vaincre Le Sida" was created in August 1983 and the group AIDES in December 1994. On this second group, see E. Hirsch, *Aides Solidaires,* (Paris: Editions du Cerf, 1991).

10. See the collection by P. Farve, *Sida et politique* (Paris: l'Harmattan, 1992).

11. See D. Carricaburu, "L'association française des hémophiles face au danger de contamination par le virus du sida: stratégie de normalisation de la maladie at définition collective du risque?" *Science Sociales et Santé* 9, no. 3–4 (1993): 55–81.

12. M. Perreault, "MTS et sida: construction sociale d'une épidémie mondiale," in F. Dumont, S. Langlois, and Y. Martin, *Traité des problèmes sociaux* (Institut Québecois de Recherche sur la Culture, 1994), 202.

13. See H. L. Dalton, "AIDS in Blackface," *Daedalus* 118, no. 3 (1989): 205–27.

14. For an analysis of the role of the press in the process of the emergence of a problem into public and political space, see Herzlich and Pierret, "Une maladie"; also Favre et al., *Sida et politique;* and E. Conan, "Le sida dans l'espace public," *Esprit* (April 1988): 64–68.

15. See G. Fabre, "La notion de contagion au regard du sida, ou comment interfèrent logiques sociales et catégories médicales," *Sciences Sociales et Santé* 11 (1993): 5–32.

16. In France, financially, care of the sick is wholly covered by Social Security after 1987.

17. M. Pollak, "Les gais et le sida," *Gai Pied Hebdo,* November 29, 1990.

18. See M. Pollak, *Les homosexuels et le sida, sociologie d'une épidémie* (Paris: A.M. Métaillé, 1988), 155–59.

19. It is necessary to note, however, that insurance companies are exempt from certain of these legal obligations. On this point, please consult the work coordinated by P. Lascoumes, C. Divernet, and O. Talpaert, *L'accès des séropositifs à l'assurance: hypocrasie ou incurie?* (Paris: Aides Fédération Nationale, 1993).

20. Pollak, "Les gais et le sida," argues that 41 percent of respondents to the study are of that opinion; only 3 percent think that "because of AIDS, homosexuals will go back in the closet."

21. T. B. Stoddard and W. Rieman, "AIDS and the Rights of the Individual: Toward a More Sophisticated Understanding of Discrimination," *The Milbank Quarterly,* special edition: *A Disease of Society: Cultural Responses to AIDS* 68, no. 1 (1990).

22. See, for example, P. Bourdelais, "Contagions d'hier et d'aujourd'hui," *Science Sociales et Santé* 7 (February 1989): 12–17.

23. See Favre, *Sida et politique.*

24. "Knowledge, Attitudes, Beliefs, and Practices." These studies focus on information and beliefs concerning the disease, eventual changes in behavior, and attitudes toward the symptomatic and HIV-positive. This type of study has important limits, nonetheless its essential value lies in the possibilities of the comparisons it authorizes: comparisons between different countries on the one side, but also of temporal change.

25. See M. Pollak, W. Dab, and J. P. Moatti, "Système de réaction au sida et action préventative," *Science Sociales et Santé* 7, no. 1 (1989): 111–35.

26. J. P. Moatti, W. Dab, M. Pollak, et al., "Les attitudes et comportements des français face au sida," *La Recherche* 21 (July–August 1990): 888–96; and J. P.

Moatti, W. Dab, and M. Pollak, "Les français et le sida. . . . Les comportements évoluent," *La Recherche* 23 (October 1992), 1202–11.

27. The classic sociodemographic factors generally take into account this difference: compared to the "repressives," the "liberals" are younger, more concentrated in intellectual parts of the middle class. But this contrast is also rooted in more personal attitudes (notably, a feeling of security based on the capacity to adapt individually to risk) and, finally, in ideological or general ethical positions, such as positions on the death penalty, abortion, or religious practice.

28. See M. Pollak and M. A. Schiltz, *Six années d'enquête sur les homo- et bisexuels masculins face au sida: livre des données* (Paris: G.S.P.M., March 1991), 64.

29. In 1992, 49 percent, versus 39 percent two years earlier, have a maximum "score of tolerance."

30. Two-thirds of the people questioned opposed treating drug addicts as delinquents and considered homosexuals to be "people like any others."

31. The interviews were conducted with 60 people of differing age, sex, sociocultural level, profession, geographic origin, and family situation. See G. Paicheler and A. Quemin, "Une intolérance diffuse: rumeurs sur les origines du sida," *Science Sociales et Santé* 12, no. 4 (December 1994): 41–72.

32. See M. Pollak, "Histoire d'une cause," in *Autrement,* special edition *L'homme contaminé,* no. 130 (1991): 24–39.

33. One could note, for example, that the wish to establish obligatory screening tests was less strong with regard to them than with regard to drug addicts and prostitutes; see Moatti et al., "Les attitudes, et comportements."

34. It went from 45 to 39 percent.

35. On this point, see P. Lascoumes, "VIH, exclusions et luttes contre les discriminations. Une épidémie révélatrice d'orientations nouvelles dans la construction et la gestion des risques," *Cahiers de recherche sociologique* 22 (1994): 61–75.

36. Pollak and Schiltz, *Six années d'enquête,* 69. This proportion is remarkably stable over time.

37. For France, see D. Carricaburu and J. Pierret, "From Biographical Disruption to Biographical Reinforcement: The Case of HIV-Positive Men," *Sociology of Health and Illness* 17, no. 1, 65–88; for the United States, see R. Weitz, "Living with the Stigma of AIDS," *Qualitative Sociology,* 13, no. 1 (1990): 23–38; for Brazil, see L. Laurindo Da Silva, "The Evolution of AIDS: Illness and the Polarization of Values," *Journal of Homosexuality* 24, no. 3 (1993): 293–305.

38. A recent study conducted in Scotland showed that the stigma anticipated was greater than the stigma felt by those afflicted and stronger than the enacted stigma; the study also showed that members of the general population questioned had rather favorable attitudes with regard to AIDS sufferers but attributed stigmatizing attitudes to others. See G. Green, "Attitudes towards People with HIV:

Are They as Stigmatizing as People with HIV Perceive Them to Be?" *Social Science and Medicine* 41, no. 4 (1995): 557–68.

39. See M. R. Kowalewski, "Double Stigma and Boundary Maintenance: How Gay Men Deal with AIDS," *Journal of Contemporary Ethnography* 17, no. 2 (1988): 211–28. Kowalewski shows how the phenomenon of double stigmatization can play out within the gay community.

40. Carricaburu and Pierret, "Biographical Disruption."

41. See J. Pierret, "L'épidémie au féminin," *Le Journal du sida,* special edition (*Yokohama,* fall 1994), 60–61.

42. Apparts is an organization for helping AIDS victims, which dedicates itself in particular to sheltering homeless and poverty-stricken patients. See S. Rossman, "Des appartements thérapeutiques pour les malades du sida. Typologie et devenir des résidents," *L'Évolution Psychiatrique* 59, no. 3 (1994): 1–13. The study shows, however, that marginal persons, AIDS victims, can be, because of their illness, the object of solidarity unusual in this segment of the population.

43. The constitution of groups around an illness largely predates the development of AIDS. In France, the oldest date from the beginning of the century. However, the mobilization around AIDS is unprecedented.

44. See S. Moscovici, *Psychologie des minorités actives* (Paris: PUF, 1971).

45. In Finland, for example, the first associative actions date from 1982 and precede the appearance of the first case of AIDS.

46. For France, Pollak, "Histoire d'une case"; P. Adam, "Experience intime et action collective," *Informations sociales* 32 (1993): 79–83, and "Médecins et associatifs dans la lutte contre le sida: vers une redistribution des compétences," *Panoramiques* 2, no. 17 (1994): 105–11. For the United States, see S. C. Oulette Kosaba, "AIDS and Volunteer Associations: Perspectives on Social and Individual Change, *Milbank Quarterly* 68 (suppl. 2, 1990): 280–94; and M. T. Wright, "Volunteering in AIDS Programs: A Synthesis of Current Theory and Practice," English language version of "Die Herausforderung, sich zu bekennen. Ehrenamtliche Mitarbeiter in US-amerikanishen AIDS-Hilfe-Organisationen," *Deutsche-AIDS-Hilfe* (1994).

47. With, in certain cases, substantial budgets, recruitment of employees, hierarchical organization of functions, and so forth. For an example of this kind, see S. Rosman, "Entre engagement militant et efficacité professionnelle: naissance et développement d'une association d'aide aux malades du sida," *Sciences Sociales et Santé* 12, no. 2 (1994): 113–40.

48. D. Defert, "Le malade réformateur social," *Gai-Pied Hebdo,* June 29, 1989, 58–61.

49. A. Strauss, "A Social World Perspective," in N. Denzin, *Symbolic Interaction,* I (Greenwich, Conn.: JAI Press, 1992), 119–28.

50. The year 1989 witnessed the creation of the ANRS (Agence Nationale de

Recherche sur le Sida), the AFLS (Agence Française de Lutte contre le Sida), and the Conseil National du Sida. However, the ANRS disbanded in 1993.

51. For an analysis of the variety of "careers" at the heart of the social world of AIDS, see C. Wiener, "Arenas and Careers: The Complex Interweaving of Personal and Organizational Destiny," in D. R. Maines, ed., *Social Organization and Social Process: Essays in Honor of Anselm Strauus* (Aldine–de Gruyter, 1991), 175–88.

52. See C. Wiener, "Arenas and Careers."

53. See A. Gianni, "Sexualité et prévention. Le parti-pris des idéologues," *Le Journal du sida,* special edition (*Yokohama,* fall 1994), 76–79.

54. It is thus that the problem of recognizing homosexual couples has come to be posed. Even though it is the object of much greater reticence, the problem of the status of the drug addict is also posed in new terms.

Comment

Kim Lane Scheppele

This essay raises the question of whether AIDS victims can constitute a minority group, and I think this might be a good occasion to ask what it is that we might mean by a minority group, how one might constitute oneself as a minority group. And I think that is what Claudine Herzlich gives us, a kind of handbook for how not to become a minority group in describing the strategies that AIDS victims have used. As she points out, AIDS victims were initially a stigmatized group, which is often the beginning of a kind of minority status. But they mobilized through a series of very interesting associational forms to deny their minority group status and to try to universalize their claims and through this process, I think, have convinced her that AIDS victims are not a minority group at least in part because you cannot constitute minority group status around a disease. Disease, she says, is in some ways a legitimating reason for being in a certain kind of disadvantaged social position and so is not so easily the site of this kind of stigmatization. But of course, in the case of AIDS, there was exactly that kind of stigmatization made at the beginning, because what was being focused on were not the symptoms but the pathways through which people actually got the disease. And this makes it a more challenging kind of case.

I would like to try to generalize from some of the things that Herzlich mentions, to ask why it is that some groups become minorities and some do not. Now I think in most of the examples in this volume we see an element both of the construction by outsiders of a group as a potential minority group and of a self-identification by insiders. Without both those processes working at the same time, it is very difficult to constitute a group as a minority group. In the case of AIDS, the group denies its status as a minority and tries to make itself more like an interest group. I think that there may be five different dimensions or criteria that we use for analyzing what constitutes minority group status, and I have named these, rather arbitrarily: insularity, narrativity, modality, inevitability, and juridicality. The idea of insularity refers to the fact that there has to be some way of identifying where the boundaries of a group are. It is extremely difficult to label a minority group, I think, unless there is some sense of a clear boundary, which makes the conversion stories Lucette Valensi discusses very interesting because obviously there the boundaries were more or less permeable. AIDS victims, as Herzlich demonstrates, try to deny exactly this; one of the strategies they used for generalizing their claims was to say anyone can get AIDS, even though people knew from fairly early on that there were certain pathways that made some people much more likely than others to get AIDS. By making it a general risk, suggesting that anyone could fall into our category, they denied the boundaries. I think that is one of the strategies for avoiding the status of a minority group. Another point about insularity is that one of the characteristics of ethnic and religious minorities is that if you are in the category, the chances are that your family is, too, along with many of your friends. So when you mobilize your networks, you are often mobilizing people who are situated in society in much the same way that you are. This goes to the issue of assimilation and whether the extent to which groups are really walled off varies historically. But in the case of AIDS, if someone has the disease, that does not mean their family has it, and it certainly does not mean their friends have it. One of the strategies of mobilization was to bring families and friends to act as advocates for AIDS victims, thereby again decreasing the sense of the boundary between the group and the larger society. It is hard to tell exactly where the boundaries were.

A second criterion is narrativity. Minority groups come with stories, and this is the point of mobilizing history. I think this shows in Ron Suny's essay. When you are going to construct an ethnic status or an ethnic group status, the question is what do you construct it out of. There are many possible ways of doing that, but one element in this kind of construction is a lineage story, about where the group came from, where in history this kind of people was produced. Now the narratives that get told around AIDS are quite strikingly different from those in this book about both religious groups and ethnic groups. The AIDS narratives are narratives of how individuals come to acquire AIDS. You get it through homosexual practices, through having a mother who had it, through drug use, through blood transfusions, and so forth. The stories are stories about how individuals get this status, not stories of a people, and so the potential for narrating this identity as a group identity is really quite different. Does being constituted as a minority group require having a collectivist narrative about how this group came about? One way of denying status as a minority group may lie in these individual narrations.

A third factor is what I call modality, which may be the wrong term. I mean to imply that if we think about a group, we are often not thinking of a whole group but, rather, the modal individual in that group, its typical member. We need to ask why it is that minorities are always constituted as groups. In part, I think, this has to do with the project of collective narration. A group is obviously going to be constituted of a number of individuals who will have many dissimilarities as well as many similarities, and one of the ways of establishing a kind of common group identity is to have a modal group member or someone who stands as representative. This, I think, is where a lot of group stereotypes come from, from the assumption that a certain modal group member is actually like all the others. And one of the ways in which minority groups may be able to alter their minority group status is by changing the popular conception of who the modal group member is. I think this was a strategy quite strikingly used in the AIDS case. Initially it was thought to be the "gay plague," as Herzlich mentioned, and so the modal member of the category was thought to be a gay man. As the disease progressed and as activist networks got formed, the idea of who the modal group member was became much more diverse, and it became impossible to say that all AIDS victims were gay men. It became impossible to say that all AIDS victims were guilty of some kind of blameworthy behavior, which is the importance of the cases of hemophiliacs and babies born to drug-addicted mothers. The category of "innocent victim" gained great prominence, which confused the category and made it very difficult to establish the modal member of the group. Without that, I think it is quite hard to constitute an identity as a minority group. I was surprised that Herzlich did not make more of the enormous crisis in France around the hemophiliac case, where the Ministry of Health, at least arguably, had some role in not preventing the distribution of tainted blood products to hemophiliacs. I wonder whether that did not have some impact. It must have generated some public consciousness that not all of the people who got AIDS got it through some kind of personally blameworthy behavior and may account for the increased toleration that we see toward the whole category, even if people do not distinguish ultimately between those who got AIDS in one way and those who got AIDS in another.

The fourth characteristic I wanted to discuss is inevitability, and here I was very struck by Claudine Herzlich's description of risk groups. The idea of a risk group is, I think, really quite fascinating, especially in its relation to minority group status. In his work on the rise of statistical thinking, Ian Hacking has alerted us to how it permeates modern society in all kinds of ways. We now in fact think quite frequently about people in terms of the probability that they will have certain characteristics and certain kinds of trajectories in their lives. But I think that statistical thinking has not yet carried over into the formation of minority groups. In the case of AIDS, people are more or less likely to become victims of AIDS depending on what sort of risk group they are in, and the discussion of AIDS often revolves around the discussion of the categories of people likely to contract AIDS: homosexual men, drug users, and so forth. With respect to minority group identities, however, we usually do not think in terms of the characteristics that may probabilistically place people into the group. It is very difficult to imagine a minority group status growing out of the probability that your parents might be Latvian, for example. You either are or you are not. In some sense group membership is inevitable. If you possess the critical characteristic, you are definitely in the group, and it is not that if you possess that characteristic, you *may* be in the group, which, I think, is the relationship between the social categories and being a victim of AIDS. I am less confident about this than about my other dimensions or criteria, but I think it is quite interesting that, despite the pervasiveness of statistical thinking, you do not belong to a minority group by dint of having a probability of possessing the relevant characteristic.

Finally, I would like to consider something that I call juridicality for lack of a better word, and that is partly because my own specialty is law and thinking about rights. The essays in this volume illustrate different kinds of arguments that minorities may make about legal claims and legal status. Broadly speaking, the claims that groups make divide into two types. One is the sort of claim that says, because we have this minority group status, because we have this special identity, we have claims to special kinds of rights. This is a kind of separatist strategy, the idea being that there might be group or individual rights that you exercise by virtue of being a member of a group, membership in which provides a special kind of claim that someone without membership in that group cannot make. On the other hand, there are universalistic claims that everyone has a right to, for example, equal human dignity, equal right to health care, equal right to privacy. As a group, AIDS victims clearly adopted the second approach. They did not say we have a special set of claims that makes us different, but made universalistic claims. And I think that in some ways undermined the possibility of their being thought of as a distinctive minority group.

That leads back to the point I made at the beginning. The constitution of a minority group is in some ways the intersection of two different kinds of processes. One is the identification by outsiders of a group as a minority group and the other is the self-identification of insiders. Their legal claims can work in opposed ways; a kind of legal status can be imposed by a dominant society that is hostile to a minority group as well as by a tolerant society that is trying to provide a space for minority groups. And the fact that a minority group may claim special legal status does not make it so. I think it is worthwhile looking at the kinds of claims that groups make and at the responses of law in these particular settings.

So I would ask whether there are certain kinds of groups that lend themselves better to being identified as minorities, certain kinds of bases for group formation, I suppose, that lend themselves better to being identified as minorities, and other bases of group identification that run into a whole series of problems with conceptions of what we take a minority group to be. And so I think that the chances of successfully claiming minority group status may be improved if you are in a group that has some kind of social or biological insularity, has a collectivist narrative about where the group came from, is identified with a modal group member more or less maximally different from the mainstream, and has minimized internal differences within the group and maximized the difference between the group and those outside it. And minority group status is more likely if membership in the group is not optional but follows inevitably from possession of a specific characteristic, if the juridical claims in some ways reinscribe the differences, and if universalist claims are not used to make this group like all others.

Contributors

Alban Bensa is Directeur d'Études at the École des Hautes Études en Sciences Sociales. His publications include *Chronique KanaK: L'ethnologie en marche,* with A. Goromido (Paris, 1995); "The Political Order and Corporal Coercion in Kanak Societies of the Past," *Oceania* 68 (1997); and, with E. Wittersheim, "Nationalism and Interdependence: the Political thought of J.-M. Tjibaou," *The Contemporary Pacific* (Honolulu, 1998).

David D. Bien is Professor of History, Emeritus, at the University of Michigan. His publications include "Religious Persecution in the French Enlightenment," *Church History* 30 (1961); "Catholic Magistrates and Protestant Marriage in the French Enlightenment," *French Historical Studies* 11 (1962); "Offices, Corps, and a System of State Credit: The Uses of Privilege under the Ancien Régime," in *The Political Culture of the Old Regime,* vol. 1, *The French Revolution and the Creation of Modern Political Culture,* Keith Michael Baker, ed. (Oxford, 1987) and "Old Regime Origins of Democratic Liberty," *The French Idea of Freedom,* Dale Van Kley, ed. (Stanford, 1994).

André Burguière is Directeur d'Études at the École des Hautes Études en Sciences Sociales. His publications include *A History of the Family* (with C. Klapisch-Zuber, M. Segalen, and F. Zonabend), 2 vols. (Cambridge, 1996); *Histoire de la France* (with Jacques Revel), 4 vols. (Paris, 1989–94); and *Paysages et Paysans* (Paris, 1991).

Juan R. I. Cole is Professor of Middle Eastern and South Asian History at the University of Michigan and editor of the *International Journal of Middle East Studies.* His publications include *Colonialism and Revolution in the Middle East* (Princeton, 1993) and *Modernity and the Millennium* (New York, 1998).

327

Nicholas B. Dirks is Chair of the Department of Anthropology at Columbia University. His publications include *The Hollow Crown: Ethnohistory of an Indian Kingdom* (Ann Arbor, 1993); *In Near Ruins: Cultural Theory at the End of the Century* (Minneapolis, 1998); and "Reading Culture: Anthropology and the Textualization of India," in *Culture/Contexture,* E. V. Daniel and J. Peck, eds. (Berkeley, 1996).

Todd M. Endelman is William Haber Professor of Modern Jewish History at the University of Michigan. He is the editor of *Comparing Jewish Societies,* an earlier volume in the *CSSH* book series (Ann Arbor, 1997); his other publications include *Jewish Apostasy in the Modern World* (New York, 1987) and *The Jews of Modern Britain, 1656–2000* (Berkeley, 2000).

Marc Ferro is Directeur d'Études Émerite at the École des Hautes Études en Sciences Sociales. His publications include *October 1917: A Social History of the Russian Revolution* (London, 1980); *Colonization: A Global History* (London, 1997); and *The Use and Abuse of History* (London, 1981).

Sylvie-Anne Goldberg is Maître de Conférences at the École des Hautes Études en Sciences Sociales. Her publications include *Dictionnaire Encyclopédique du Judaédique due Judaïsme: esquisse de l'histoire du peuple juif* (Paris, 1993); *Crossing the Jabbok: Illness and Death in Ashkenazi Judaism in Sixteenth-Century Prague* (Berkeley, 1996); and *La Clepsydre: contes et décomptes du temps juif* (Paris, 2000).

Raymond Grew is Professor of History, Emeritus, at the University of Michigan and former editor of *Comparative Studies in Society and History* and editor of the *CSSH* book series. His publications include *School, State, and Society: The Growth of Elementary Schooling in Nineteenth-Century France—A Quantitative Analysis,* with Patrick J. Harrigan (Ann Arbor, 1991); "Finding Social Capital: The French Revolution in Italy," *Journal of Interdisciplinary History* 29 (1999); and "Food and Global History," in *Food and Global History,* Raymond Grew, ed., (Boulder, 1999).

Serge Gruzinski is Directeur d'Études at the École des Hautes Études en Sciences Sociales. His publications include *The Conquest of Mexico* (Cambridge, 1990); *Painting the Conquest* (New York, 1992); and *The Image of War* (Durham, 2000).

Jean Heffer is Directeur d'Études at the École des Hautes Études en Sciences Sociales. His publications include *Les Etats Unis et le Pacifique: histoire d'une frontière* (Paris, 1995); with C. Fohlen and F. Weil, *Canada at Estats-Unis depuis 1770* (Paris, 1997); and with P. Ndiaye and F. Weil, *La démocratie américaine au XXe siècle* (Paris, 2000).

Claudine Herzlich is Directeur d'Études at the École des Hautes Études en Sciences Sociales. Her publications include *Health and Illness: A Social-Psychological Analysis* (London, 1993); *Illness and Self in Society* (Baltimore, 1989); and *Cinquante ans d'exercice de la médicine en Ranee: carrièeres et pratiques des medécins français* (Paris, 1993).

Christiane Klapisch-Zuber is Directeur d'Études at the École des Hautes Études en Sciences Sociales. Her publications include, with David Herlihy, *Tuscans and Their Families: A Study of the Florentine Cadasto of 1427* (New Haven, 1985); *Women, Family and Ritual in Renaissance Italy* (Chicago, 1985); and she is the editor *of History of Women in the West*, vol. 2, *The Middle Ages: Silent Voices* (Cambridge, Mass., 1995).

Earl Lewis is Professor of History and of Afro-American Studies and Dean of the Horace H. Rackham School of Graduate Studies at the University of Michigan. His publications include *African-Americans in the Industrial Age: A Documentary History* (Boston, 1996); *In Their Own Interests: Race, Class, and Power in Twentieth-Century Norfolk, Virginia* (Berkeley, 1991); and "Connecting Memory: Self and Power of Place in African-American Urban History," *Journal of Urban History* 21 (1995).

Denis Lombard was Directeur d'Études at the École des Hautes Études en Sciences Sociales from 1938 until his death in 1998. His publications include *Le Sustanat d'Atjeh au temps d'Iskandar Muda (1607–1636)* (Paris, 1967); *Le carrefour javanais: essai d'histoire globale* (Paris, 1990); and, with J. Aubin, *Asian Merchants and Businessmen in the Indian Ocean and the China Sea* (New Delhi, 2000).

Sabine MacCormack is the Walgreen Professor for the Study of Human Understanding, Professor of Classical Studies, and Professor of History at the University of Michigan. Her publications include *Religion in the Andes: Vision and Imagination in Early Colonial Peru* (Princeton, 1991);

Art and Ceremony in Late Antiquity (Berkeley, 1990); and *Shadows of Poetry: Vergil in the Mind of Augustine* (New York, 2000).

Jacques Revel is Directeur d'Études and Président of the École des Hautes Études en Sciences Sociales. His publications include, with A. Burguière, *Histoire de la France,* 4 vols. (Paris, 1989–94); *Jeux d'echelles: La microanalyse de l'expérience* (Paris, 1996); and, with L. Hunt, *Histories: French Conceptions of the Past* (Paris, 1996).

Kim Lane Scheppele is Professor of Law and Sociology at the University of Pennsylvania and served as co-director of the Program on "Gender and Culture at Central European University in Budapest. Her publications include *Legal Secrets: Equality and Efficiency in the Common Law* (Chicago, 1988), and she is preparing a book on the development of constitutionalism in Hungary since 1989.

Ann Laura Stoler is Professor of Anthropology, History, and Women's Studies at the University of Michigan. Her publications include *Race and the Education of Desire: Foucault's History of Sexuality and the Colonial Order of Things* (Durham, 1995); *Tensions of Empire: Colonial Cultures in a Bourgeois World* (Berkeley, 1997, coedited with F. Cooper); and "Racial Histories and Their Regimes of Truth," in *Political Power and Social Theory* (1997).

Ronald Grigor Suny is Professor of Political Science at the University of Chicago and formerly held the Alex Manoogian Chair in Modern Armenian History at the University of Michigan. His publications include *The Making of the Georgian Nation* (Bloomington, 1994); *Looking Toward Ararat: Armenia in Modern History* (Bloomington, 1993); *The Revenge of the Past: Nationalism, Revolution, and the Collapse of the Soviet Union* (Stanford, 1993); and *The Soviet Experiment: Russia, the USSR, and the Successor States* (Oxford, 1998).

Lucette Valensi is Directeur d'Études at the École des Hautes Études en Sciences Sociales. Her publications include *Venice and the Sublime Porte: The Birth of a Despot* (Ithaca, 1993); *Jewish Memories,* with N. Wachtel (Berkeley, 1991); and, with A. L. Udovitch, *The Last Arab Jews: The Communities of Jerba (Tunisia)* (Princeton, 1984).

Nathan Wachtel is Directeur d'Études at the École des Hautes Études en Sciences Sociales. His publications include *The Vision of the Vanquished: The Spanish Conquest of Peru Through Indian Eyes, 1530–1570* (New York, 1977); *Jewish Memories,* with L. Valensi (Berkeley, 1991), and *Gods and Vampires: Return to Chipaya* (Chicago, 1994).

Aram A. Yengoyan is Professor of Anthropology at the University of California, Davis. His publications include "Religion, Morality, and Prophetic Traditions: Conversion among the Pitjantjatjara of Central Australia," *Conversion to Christianity: Historical And Comparative Perspectives,* Robert W. Hemer, ed. (Berkeley, 1993); "Origin, Hierarchy and Egalitarianism among the Mandaya of Southeast Mindanao, Philippines," *Origins, Ancestry and Alliance: Explorations in Austronesian Ethnography,* James J. Fox and Clifford Sather, eds. (Canberra, 1996); and "No Exit: Aboriginal Australians and the Historicizing of Interpretation and Theory," *American Anthropologist* 100 (1998).

Index

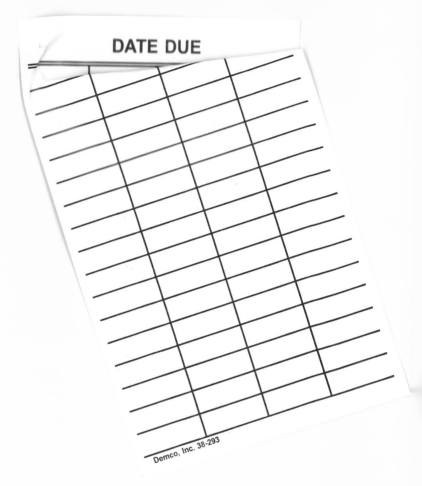

DATE DUE

Demco, Inc. 38-293